Equity Valuation and Analysis with *eVal*

Third Edition

Russell Lundholm
University of British Columbia

Richard Sloan
University of California, Berkeley

McGraw-Hill Irwin

EQUITY VALUATION AND ANALYSIS WITH EVAL, THIRD EDITION

Published by McGraw-Hill, a business unit of The McGraw-Hill Companies, Inc., 1221 Avenue of the Americas, New York, NY 10020. Copyright © 2013 by The McGraw-Hill Companies, Inc. All rights reserved. Printed in the United States of America. Previous editions © 2007 and 2006. No part of this publication may be reproduced or distributed in any form or by any means, or stored in a database or retrieval system, without the prior written consent of The McGraw-Hill Companies, Inc., including, but not limited to, in any network or other electronic storage or transmission, or broadcast for distance learning.

Some ancillaries, including electronic and print components, may not be available to customers outside the United States.

This book is printed on acid-free paper.

2 3 4 5 6 7 8 9 0 DOC/DOC 1 0 9 8 7 6 5 4 3

ISBN 978-0-07-352689-8
MHID 0-07-352689-4

Senior Vice President, Products & Markets: *Kurt L. Strand*
Vice President, General Manager: *Brent Gordon*
Vice President, Content Production & Technology Services: *Kimberly Meriwether David*
Editorial Director: *Tim Vertovec*
Executive Brand Manager: *James Heine*
Managing Development Editor: *Gail Korosa*
Marketing Manager: *Dean Karampelas*
Director, Content Production: *Terri Schiesl*
Project Manager: *Erin Melloy*
Buyer: *Sandy Ludovissy*
Cover Designer: *Studio Montage, St. Louis, MO*
Cover Image: *Comstock Images/Jupiter Images/RF*
Media Project Manager: *Prashanthi Nadipalli*
Typeface: *10/12 Times New Roman*
Compositor: *MPS Limited*
Printer: *RR Donnelley*

All credits appearing on page or at the end of the book are considered to be an extension of the copyright page.

Library of Congress Cataloging-in-Publication Data

Lundholm, Russell James.
   Equity valuation and analysis with eVal / Russell Lundholm, Richard Sloan.—3rd ed.
      p. cm.
   ISBN 978-0-07-352689-8 (alk. paper)
1. Corporations—Valuation. 2. Business enterprises—Valuation. 3. Stock price forecasting.
4. Investment analysis. 5. eVal (Electronic resource) I. Sloan, Richard G. II. Title.
   HG4028.V3L796 2013
   332.63'221028553—dc23

                                                                2012033282

The Internet addresses listed in the text were accurate at the time of publication. The inclusion of a website does not indicate an endorsement by the authors or McGraw-Hill, and McGraw-Hill does not guarantee the accuracy of the information presented at these sites.

www.mhhe.com

About the Authors

Russell Lundholm

Russell Lundholm is the Alumni Professor of Accounting at the University of British Columbia Sauder School of Business. He holds a PhD in Business Administration and a Masters of Science in Statistics from the University of Iowa. He has also taught at the University of Michigan from 1993 to 2010, and at Stanford University from 1987 to 1993. Professor Lundholm's research has been published in the *Review of Accounting Studies*, the *Journal of Accounting Research*, *The Accounting Review*, *Contemporary Accounting Review*, the *Journal of Finance*, the *Review of Financial Studies*, *Econometrica*, and the *Journal of Political Economy*. His principal teaching specialty is financial statement analysis, with a particular emphasis on financial forecasting and equity valuation. His work has been covered extensively in the popular press, including *Forbes*, the *New York Times*, the *Wall Street Journal* and *Fortune*. He regularly speaks to organizations in the industry about forecasting and valuation techniques.

Richard G. Sloan

Richard G. Sloan is the L. H. Penney Professor of Accounting at UC Berkeley's Haas School of Business. From 2006 to 2009, Professor Sloan served as a managing director in equity research at Barclays Global Investors. He has also held faculty positions at the University of Michigan's Ross School of Business and the University of Pennsylvania's Wharton School. Professor Sloan's research focuses on the role of accounting information in investment decisions and is published in leading accounting, finance, and economics journals. He is widely recognized and has received numerous awards for his research on earnings quality. He is also the current Managing Editor of the *Review of Accounting Studies*. Professor Sloan holds a PhD from the University of Rochester and a BCom from the University of Western Australia.

Brief Contents

Contents

Chapter 6
Cash Flow Analysis 142

Chapter 7
Structured Forecasting 166

Chapter 8
Forecasting Details 185

Preface

We wrote this book because we saw a void between the abstract theoretical treatment of equity valuation and the practical problem of valuing an actual company using real-world data. We give serious treatment to the underlying theory of financial analysis and valuation, but our main goal is to be able to arrive at a pragmatic answer to the all-important question, "what is this company really worth?" To answer this question, we adopt a very different approach from other textbooks. The key differences can be summarized as follows:

1. Our focus is on generating good financial statement forecasts.
2. We provide detailed practical guidance on how to obtain and analyze relevant real-world data.
3. We demystify the mechanics of equity valuation.

Our overriding theme is that good forecasts of the future financial statements are the key input to a good valuation. Most other aspects of the valuation process are mechanical and can be programmed into a computer. In fact, this text is supplied with *eVal*, a fancy Excel spreadsheet that takes care of these mechanical tasks. As with many other textbooks, we discuss topics like business strategy analysis, accounting analysis, financial ratio analysis, and so forth. However, we always do so with a clear view to how these analyses help us to generate better financial statement forecasts.

We also provide plenty of advice on where to go to obtain the most relevant raw data. Armed with such a rich source of data, we are able to provide you with plenty of practical examples and limitless opportunities for you to practice doing your own analyses.

A final goal of this book is to demystify the valuation process. In the past, we have seen students become lost in a sea of valuation formulas and inconsistent spreadsheet models. For example, students get confused as to whether they should use a DDM, DCF, or RIM valuation formula and whether they need to use the CAPM, APT, or MFM to compute their WACC. They become obsessed with learning acronyms and formulas but flounder when asked to provide a plausible valuation for an actual company. Using *eVal*, we demonstrate that these different formulas are easily reconciled and refocus students on developing the best set of financial forecasts to plug into these formulas. This reinforces our main point that the key to good valuations is good forecasts.

THE *eVal* SPREADSHEET

We created this spreadsheet because we realized that students were spending way too much time building and debugging their valuation spreadsheets and, consequently, way too little time thinking about the forecasts that they put into their spreadsheets. The tail was definitely wagging the dog. They also couldn't talk to one another because each student tackled the spreadsheet problem differently—it could take hours just to figure out why Jill's value estimate differed from Jack's value estimate. By building one "mother-of-all spreadsheet valuation models" and making it completely transparent and completely general, we turned our students' attention back to the real problem at hand, which is forecasting the future financial statements. Thus, *eVal* was born. As we used the early version of the program with students, we discovered that we could use *eVal* to organize the entire historical analysis, forecasting, and valuation process. All the pieces of the puzzle could finally be kept in one place. We found that once we had familiarized students with *eVal,* we could effectively teach complex valuation cases that would previously have been overwhelming.

The *eVal* spreadsheet helps in doing valuation and it helps in *learning* valuation. There are many software products and web services today that take a few forecast inputs from you and then spit out a valuation, as if by magic, but how they arrived at the result is hidden in a black box. In contrast, this book and the *eVal* spreadsheet that accompanies it are designed to be completely transparent at every stage of the valuation process. The software displays the valuation implications of your forecasts in both discounted cash flow models and residual income models, and it shows exactly how the flows of value from these models are linked to your financial statement forecasts.

HOW DOES ALL THIS HELP YOU?

The theory of financial analysis and valuation is more compelling when linked to real-world examples. The abstract theory of financial statements, ratios, and valuation formulas can be covered in a few boring lectures. What makes this topic exciting is seeing how an organized approach to studying a real company leaves you so much better informed about the firm's future. Is Apple really worth more than any other public company in the world? The answer is probably yes, once you understand its free cash flow generating ability. Lululemon Athletica is scorching a new trail in the sports apparel market with growth rates and valuation multiples that leave competitors like Gap in the dust. Is it really the superstar stock that Wall Street analysts and bankers claim it to be? A careful analysis suggests that, unless we all start wearing yoga pants to work, its strategy is unsustainable and it is not such a superstar after all. Royal Caribbean Cruises wants to build six more cruise ships in the next three years, but can they generate enough cash from the existing ships to pay for the new ones? A careful study of their cash flows shows that they will almost certainly be borrowing lots of money to buy these boats. Financial statements, accounting rules, financial ratios, and valuation models are all pretty dull beasts on their own, but if we can use them to answer questions such as these, we can really bring them to life. By blending the theory of equity analysis with practical application, we feel that students learn both more effectively.

Throughout the text, we use the retail department store chain Kohl's as an illustrative example. It is also the default company in *eVal,* so you can readily see how the theory translates into real forecasts and valuation implications. The back of the book contains a series of cases for classroom illustrations and student assignments. Most of the cases require students to analyze real-world companies. These cases are an integral part of the learning experience. We find that students only really begin to understand the material when they try to apply it to real-world cases. The final section of each chapter identifies which cases and questions are relevant to the material covered in that chapter. Many of these cases are revisited in adjacent chapters. One chapter will address business strategy analysis; the next will address accounting analysis, and so on. We recommend that you pick a subset of the cases and follow them throughout the book. It is hard to do a meaningful job of evaluating a firm's financial ratios if you haven't first analyzed its strategy and accounting policies. This is why we put the cases at the end of the book instead of trying to allocate entire cases to specific chapters. Several of the cases are tailored directly to the *eVal* spreadsheet, and financial data for these cases are included in the spreadsheet.

CASES AND WEBSITE

A challenge in writing cases on real-world companies is the determination of the information to include along with each case. Traditionally, case writers have preselected the most relevant information for inclusion in the case. This approach has two disadvantages. First, the case writer is robbing the student of the opportunity to learn one of the most important skills in equity analysis: identifying the relevant information. Second, to the extent that the case writer omits relevant information, the richness of the case is compromised. We adopt a new approach to this problem by posting a broader set of information on our dedicated website (http://www.lundholmandsloan.com). Each case contains links out to its own set of information, and the student must take responsibility for identifying the relevant information. For example, we may provide a 100-page 10-K along with the case, and the student must be able to navigate the 10-K and extract the relevant information. We think that the ability to extract relevant information is one of the most important skills of a real-world equity analyst, and our cases provide students with the opportunity to develop this skill.

One of the real world problems that students will encounter if they are studying a company outside our list of cases is how to get financial data into *eVal*. Our website provides another spreadsheet, titled "datamaker.xls" that takes inputs from various financial data sources and translates them into a block of data that can be cut-and-pasted into *eVal*. This step might require some customization by the user, as the formats used by data providers are constantly changing. In the not-too-distant future, the XBRL data provided by the SEC should be able to link directly to *eVal,* so check back at the website periodically for updates. Also, the latest copy of *eVal* can always be found there, so if you mess yours up, come here to grab another copy. Finally, we also have a series of PowerPoint slides and associated instructional materials for the text and cases. If you are an instructor, contact your McGraw-Hill representative to obtain these materials.

CHANGES FOR THE THIRD EDITION

The third edition of the book retains the basic structure of the second edition. The biggest change is with the *eVal* software and associated data. Previous versions included highly customized software along with standardized financial data. Many instructors commented that this made the valuation process too much of a black box. Students didn't necessarily appreciate what was going on in the software, they couldn't customize the software, and they took the supplied standardized data at face value. Moreover, we ran into numerous issues with software compatibility and data updates. The new version of the software is a very transparent series of related Excel spreadsheets that can be easily customized by the user. We have also dropped the standardized data in favor of letting the user obtain data from original sources. As described in the previous section, our website provides a spreadsheet titled "datamaker.xls" to facilitate this process. But we believe that there is no substitute for obtaining financial data directly from firms' financial statements. As discussed above, you can find the latest software and user tips at www.lundholmandsloan.com.

While the number and titles of the chapters remain the same, we have significantly updated the text, incorporated recent developments, added seven new cases, and ironed out a few wrinkles from the second edition. Throughout the book, we have updated the running example of Kohl's. The financial crisis provided a very significant economic shock to the world economy, and we show how this affected Kohl's and its competitors in different ways. New ratios and new cash flows at Kohl's required new interpretations in Chapters 5 and 6, and a new economic landscape required new forecasts in Chapters 7 and 8.

We have also made a number of significant additions to the chapters. Chapter 2 contains a significantly revised and updated set of links and associated descriptions for sources of information. We have also enhanced the section on "Manual Input of Data," using Kohl's as a working example. Chapter 3 contains an additional section titled "Understanding Kohl's

Business," where we illustrate the application of the material covered earlier in the chapter. Chapter 4 has been updated to reflect recent changes in accounting standards. We have also added a new section on Applying Accounting Analysis to Kohl's to illustrate the application of the material covered earlier in the chapter. Chapter 5 now includes more discussion of how to treat large cash balances (are they operating or are they financing?), and Chapter 8 introduces a new empirical method of estimating a firm's economies of scale. Because Chapter 9 relies on financial statistics such as industry beta's and recent risk-free rates to estimate the cost of capital, the data used in this chapter has changed significantly, although the basic models introduced here remain the same. Chapter 10 on Valuation has changed very little, but we did find a nifty option value calculator online that we refer the reader to when valuating contingent claims. Finally, we updated the statistics on valuation ratios in Chapter 11. Given the financial crisis, these graphs give students a lot to talk about.

We have also added several new cases at the end of the book. They are as follows:

Apple and the iFad

This case covers the amazing comeback story of Apple. Students get to analyze Apple's strategy, including its consumer-centric focus and unique integration of proprietary hardware and software. Apple's excessive deferral of revenue on the iPhone provides a nice issue for accounting analysis. Finally, students get to see how Apple's amazing ability to generate free cash flows justifies its lofty valuation.

The Gabelli Utility Trust

A gap in existing cases was that students couldn't really begin discussing valuation until they got past Chapter 10. This case provides a simple valuation case that can be covered as earlier as Chapter 1. Gabelli Utility Trust is a closed-end fund holding a portfolio of publicly traded utility stocks. As such, its intrinsic value can be easily determined by summing up the market values of its holdings. Or can it? Curiously, the price of this stock has traded at around a 40 percent premium to its net asset value for many years. Even Mr. Gabelli himself can't figure out why. This case illustrates how even simple financial statement analysis can identify a mispriced security and challenges students to confront potential market inefficiencies.

The Restaurant Industry in 2011

This is an updated version of an old favorite that was becoming outdated. Chipotle Mexican Grill replaces Panera Bread as the new rising star.

Building *eVal*

This case walks the student through the construction of the entire *eVal* spreadsheet (with considerable hand-holding). It is a mix of an Excel skills exercise and a self-guided test. The goal is to remove *eVal* from the "black box," enabling students to fully understand the links between financial statements, ratios, forecasting assumptions and valuations.

Hogs and Chestnuts: Who Profits When the Chinese Eat?

This is a comprehensive analysis, forecasting, and valuation case based on two food producers in China. The first part of the case develops a value estimate for a hog processer, and presents staggering statistics on pork consumption in China. The second part of the case centers on American Lorian, a chestnut producer who became a public company in the United States through a process known as a "reverse merger."

Creating Your Own Standardized Data

This is a short exercise that helps the student identify sources of publicly available data, and then raises issues that arise when free-form data must be standardized into a specific list of accounts.

The 80-Minute Forecast

This is a fun in-class case exercise. The class is divided into teams, and each team forecasts a very specific input for a company. As the clock ticks down, each group must hurry to report their answer so the professor can enter it into a premade spreadsheet. The inputs are for a quarterly EPS forecast and it works for almost any company, so can be used to study a company that is currently in the news.

ACKNOWLEDGMENTS

Before getting down to business, we would like to thank everyone who has helped us in the preparation of all three editions. Patricia Dechow and Kai Petainen have been involved throughout and have provided valuable and timely feedback. We also would like to thank the following people for excellent suggestions on how to improve the text: Noel Addy, Mississippi State University; Ervin Black, Brigham Young University; Michael Butak, Boise State University; Mike Calegari, Santa Clara University; Ted Christensen, Brigham Young University; Bryan Church, Georgia Institute of Technology; Paul Hribar, Cornell University; Amy Hutton, Boston College; Bruce Johnson, University of Iowa; Joshua Livnat, New York University; Sarah McVay, University of Washington; Steve Monahan, INSEAD; Panos Patatoukas, University of California, Berkeley; Michael Sandretto, University of Illinois; Akhtar Siddique, Georgetown University; Richard Simonds, Michigan State University; Vic Stanton, University of California at Berkeley; Sarah Tasker, University of California, Berkeley; Damir Tokic, University of Houston; Peter Wysocki, University of Miami; and Ray Sturn, University of Central Florida. We would also like to thank Editorial Director, Tim Vertovec; Marketing Manager, Dean Karampelas; Managing Development Editor, Gail Korosa; Project Manager, Erin Melloy; Media Project Manager, Prashanthi Nadipalli; Proofreader, Julie Grady; and Project Manager, Vivek Khandelwal. Finally, we'd like to thank our significant others, friends, students, colleagues, families, pets, and everyone else who had to put up with us while we worked on this project.

Text

CHAPTER ONE

Introduction

1.1 GETTING STARTED

On a typical business day, over $250 billion worth of shares are traded on major global equity markets. Most of the shares traded represent equity interests in the business activities of corporations. The prices at which these trades take place determine both the fortunes of the traders and the allocation of much of the global economy's scarce capital resources. Our objective in this book is to provide a framework for determining the fair value of these equity interests. If we are successful, you will not only be in a position to make a good living, but will also be making the global economy more efficient.

This book and the associated *eVal* software provide you with a systematic framework for valuing equity securities. There are many books written on the topic. Our approach is unique in that we seek to provide the best possible marriage between theory and practice. We provide a framework that is both theoretically rigorous and readily amenable to practical implementation. The *eVal* software is a flexible tool for the analysis and valuation of equity securities. It will provide you with hands-on experience in building financial models and estimating the value of equity securities. The use of spreadsheet-based financial modeling software is ubiquitous in practice. However, such software can be a dangerous weapon in the hands of an inexperienced user. Our aim is to provide you with a firm grounding in valuation theory and a good understanding of the techniques that have evolved to facilitate practical application of the theory. The end result is that you either confidently produce a sound valuation for an equity security, or you clearly identify why you are unable to do so.

Valuing equity securities necessarily involves uncertainty. We give plenty of guidance on what constitutes a reasonable forecast in an uncertain world. We also point out many sources of data that are available to aid you in constructing your forecasts. We are living in the middle of an information explosion. The Internet puts an ever-increasing array of financial data at our fingertips. In the spirit of practical advice, we will suggest places to find the best, juiciest tidbits of information and how to incorporate them into your analysis. All this work will reduce the uncertainty in your forecasts, but plenty will still remain. No one knows exactly how the future will unfold; uncertainty is the nature of the beast.

This introductory chapter outlines our equity analysis and valuation framework. We begin with an overview of the nature of business activities. Next, we provide a brief discussion of equity valuation theory. We then explain the critical importance of financial statements in the practical application of equity valuation theory. Finally, we outline the steps in our systematic approach to valuation and show you how *eVal* guides you through these steps. Throughout the book, we use Kohl's as a working example. In case you haven't heard of this company, Kohl's is a department store chain featuring clothing items and housewares. This chapter provides a road map for the entire equity valuation process, and we will refer back to this road map frequently as we walk you through each of the intermediate steps.

1.2   OVERVIEW OF BUSINESS ACTIVITIES

Equity securities represent ownership claims in the business activities of profit-seeking entities. The valuation of an equity security must therefore begin with a thorough analysis of the entity's underlying business activities. Business activities can be divided into three broad categories to facilitate analysis: *operating activities, investing activities,* and *financing activities.* Each category is described below.

Operating Activities

Businesses typically generate profit for their owners by providing customers with goods and services in return for cash or other consideration. As long as the consideration received exceeds the costs incurred in providing the goods and services, profit is generated. *Operating activities* are those that are directly related to the provision of goods and services to customers. For example, in a restaurant business, the purchase, preparation, and serving of food to customers are all examples of operating activities. Washing the dishes and cleaning the restrooms are also operating activities, since these are part of the package of services that a restaurant provides to its customers. The operating activities are the primary means through which the owners of the business hope to make a profit.

Investing Activities

Nearly all businesses must make investments in productive capacity before they can begin to provide goods and services to their customers. For example, a restaurant business requires a restaurant building, furniture, and cooking equipment. Purchases and sales of resources that provide productive capacity are referred to as *investing activities.* We define investing activities with respect to the nature of the goods and services that the firm is in the business of providing. If the firm is in the business of retailing cooking equipment, then the purchase of an oven is an operating activity. However, if the firm is in the business of providing restaurant meals, then the purchase of an oven is an investing activity, because it provides the productive capacity required to provide meals.

Why bother to distinguish between operating activities and investing activities? Investing activities involve resource commitments that are expected to provide benefits over long periods of time. Investments take place in anticipation of future operating activities and the profits from operating activities must be sufficient to provide a competitive return on investment for the investments to have been worthwhile. Because the resources acquired in investing activities provide benefits for long periods of time, it can take a long time to find out how profitable these investments have been. In addition, the investing activities that a company makes today may be used to support future operating activities that differ from the current operating activities (e.g., a new line of business). It is therefore useful to separate our analysis of the performance of a business's current operating activities from its investments in productive capacity to support future operating activities. In the long run, however, operating and investing activities are closely linked. Operating activities are made possible by past investing activities, and the profits from operating activities should be evaluated in relation to the cost of the investing activities that made them possible.

Financing Activities

In order to acquire the resources necessary to engage in operating and investing activities, businesses require financing. The owners of the business provide the initial financing in the hope that the business will provide them with a competitive return on their investment. In a corporation, these owners are the holders of the common equity securities. If a business is financed solely by its equity holders, and immediately distributes the net cash flows generated by its operating and investing activities back to its equity holders, its *financing activities* consist of these simple cash flows between the equity holders and the business. In practice, however, there are many other sources of financing. For example, a business can issue debt, preferred stock, and warrants, to name just a few alternatives. In addition, a business need not immediately distribute all the cash generated by its operating and investing activities. Instead, the business may choose to invest this cash in financial assets, such as bank accounts, treasury bonds or financial securities issued by other businesses. Financing activities incorporate all such transactions.

Financing activities are distinct from operating and investing activities. A firm can finance a given set of operating and investing activities many different ways without affecting the nature of the operating and investing activities. But this does not mean that the firm cannot add value through financing activities. Financing activities create the opportunity for the owners of the business to leverage the return from their operating and investing activities, to minimize taxes and transactions costs, and to exploit inefficiencies in capital markets. Investment bankers and corporate lawyers specialize in advising businesses on their financing activities, and the large fees that they charge speak to the potential value that can be created.

1.3 OVERVIEW OF EQUITY VALUATION THEORY

The basic theory of equity valuation is straightforward and well established. Equity securities are financial instruments, and, as such, their value is equal to net present value of the future cash distributions that they are expected to generate. These cash distributions traditionally have taken the form of cash dividend payments, and so the value of equity often is expressed as the net present value of the expected future dividend payments, as shown in the following equation:

$$\text{Value}_0 = \sum_{t=1}^{\infty} \frac{\text{Cash Dividend}_t}{(1 + r)^t}$$

where

Value_0 = value of equity at time 0

Cash Dividend_t = expected amount of cash dividends to be paid in period t

r = discount rate

This valuation model is widely known as the dividend-discounting model. However, dividends are not the only way that cash can be distributed to equity holders. Stock repurchases have become increasingly popular. While dividends represent routine cash payments made on a pro rata basis to all equity holders, stock repurchases involve the business buying back its own stock from specific equity holders. Nevertheless, both transactions involve distributing cash from the business to its equity holders. Another consideration in the valuation of equity securities is that companies often seek new cash infusions through the issuance of additional equity securities. These equity issuances can be thought of as negative cash distributions that should be netted against the positive cash distributions associated with dividends and stock repurchases in order to determine the net cash distributions to equity holders. So the dividend-discounting model is more precisely expressed as

$$\text{Value}_0 = \sum_{t=1}^{\infty} \frac{\text{Cash Dividend}_t + \text{Stock Repurchases}_t - \text{Equity Issuances}_t}{(1 + r)^t}$$

where

Cash Dividend_t = expected amount of cash dividends to be paid in period t

$\text{Stock Repurchases}_t$ = expected amount of cash to be paid out via stock repurchases in period t

$\text{Equity Issuances}_t$ = expected amount of cash to be raised via equity issuances in period t

Throughout the remainder of the text, we will avoid this mouthful and simply refer to the numerator as "distributions to equity holders."

What determines the amount and timing of distributions to equity holders? Since equity holders are the owners of the business, they have the residual claim on the net cash flows available from a business's operating, investing, and non-equity financing activities. In practice, distributions to equity holders are made at the discretion of management, based on a variety of factors. The major factors are:

- How much cash did the business's operating activities generate?
- How much cash was used for investing activities in order to maintain or expand the scale and scope of the business's operating activities?
- How much cash is required to make scheduled payments to providers of non-equity capital, such as interest and principal payments on loans?
- How much cash should be retained in the business in the form of financial assets to provide for future cash flow needs?

In the long run, the cash flows generated by a business's operating activities are the key driver of distributions to equity holders. However, the other factors listed above can make the amount and timing of a business's operating cash flows very different from the amount and timing of the distributions to its equity holders.

In summary, while the basic theory of equity valuation is quite straightforward, the devil is in forecasting the future distributions to equity holders. There are many different equity valuation formulas floating around academia and practice. These formulas implicitly use different variables to forecast future distributions to equity holders. For example, practitioners are fond of substituting variables like earnings, "EBITDA," and "NOPAT" for cash distributions. These substitutions can be justifiable if done in a way that maintains consistency with the underlying dividend-discounting model. However, practitioners all too often throw caution to the wind and come up with formulas that require heroic assumptions to reconcile with sound valuation theory.

1.4 THE ROLE OF FINANCIAL STATEMENTS

The financial statements are the primary device for bridging the gap between theory and practice in equity valuation. Some finance texts criticize financial statements and their underlying accounting principles on the basis that they do an imperfect job at measuring value. However, these criticisms represent a basic misunderstanding of the role of financial statements in equity valuation. Financial statements are not designed to directly estimate equity value, and accounting book values rarely match market values. Instead, the role of the financial statements is to provide a detailed description of the financial consequences of a firm's historical business activities. In other words, the financial statements summarize the past operating, investing, and financing activities of a firm, and show how these activities affect the past, present, and expected future cash flows. The purpose of the financial statements is not to directly forecast the future cash flows.

Given that the financial statements do not directly forecast how future business activities will affect future cash flows, what is their role in equity valuation? Their role is twofold:

1. They provide the language for translating forecasts of future business activities into forecasts of cash flows.
2. By describing the cash flow implications of past business activities, they provide a good starting point for determining the cash flow implications of future business activities.

The first role of the financial statements in valuation is to provide a language for describing how a firm's future business activities will affect its future cash flows. We cannot forecast cash flows in a vacuum. The role of the financial statements is to identify and categorize the activities of a firm that have cash flow implications. A set of financial statements tells us how the various operating, investing, and financing activities of a firm combine to produce cash flows. In order to forecast a firm's future cash flows, we first need a set of financial statements that capture the various intended operating, investing, and financing activities of the firm. We can then begin the process of forecasting the cash flow implications of these activities. For instance, by forecasting sales and accounts receivable, we can derive a forecast of the cash collections from customers. By constructing a complete set of forecasted financial statements, we can systematically derive the cash distributions to equity holders.

The second role of the financial statements is to provide historical data on the cash flow implications of a firm's past business activities that may prove useful in forecasting its future cash flows. Many firms engage in similar business activities for multiple periods. Over time, these business activities are subject to change. Nevertheless, these changes are rarely so drastic as to make the results of past business activities completely irrelevant to the prediction of the future. Thus, the most common forecasting procedure is to start with the past financial statements and then modify those statements based on changes that are anticipated to occur in the future. The effectiveness of this procedure varies widely. For firms in mature industries with established products and stable customer demand, past results can be a very good predictor of future results and the past financial statements will be very relevant in estimating firm value. In contrast, for start-up firms in emerging industries with evolving products and growing customer demand, past results can be a poor predictor of future results. Past results also will be a poor predictor of future results for firms making significant acquisitions or changes to their business activities. But we have to start somewhere, and the past is usually the best place to start when forecasting the future.

1.5 THREE STEPS OF EQUITY VALUATION

The discussion thus far indicates that the equity valuation process can be broken down into three distinct steps, which are illustrated in Figure 1.1. *Understanding the past* is the first step. This analysis must go beyond simply looking at the firm's past financial results. You need to understand the firm's financial results in the context of the industry and economy in which the firm operates, and you need to look for clues about planned changes in future business activities. The second step involves using our analysis of the past in *forecasting the future.* This step is structured around forecasting the future financial statements, from which we will derive our estimates of future cash distributions to equity holders. The third step comprises *valuation.* In this step, we convert our estimates of future cash distributions into a single estimate of firm value. The *eVal* software provided with this book will guide you through each of these steps. In this section, we give an overview of the three steps and introduce you to *eVal.*

Understanding the Past

The first step involves examining relevant information about the business. This step begins with the systematic collection of pertinent information, which we refer to in Figure 1.1 as *information collection.* If the equity security is publicly traded on a major exchange in the United States, then the usual starting point for information collection is the firm's financial filings with the Securities and Exchange Commission (SEC). However, there are a myriad

FIGURE 1.1 **The Three Steps of Equity Valuation**

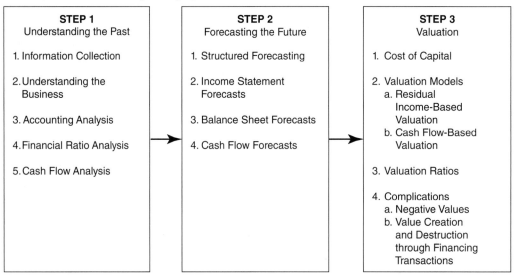

STEP 1 Understanding the Past	STEP 2 Forecasting the Future	STEP 3 Valuation
1. Information Collection	1. Structured Forecasting	1. Cost of Capital
2. Understanding the Business	2. Income Statement Forecasts	2. Valuation Models a. Residual Income-Based Valuation b. Cash Flow-Based Valuation
3. Accounting Analysis	3. Balance Sheet Forecasts	3. Valuation Ratios
4. Financial Ratio Analysis	4. Cash Flow Forecasts	4. Complications a. Negative Values b. Value Creation and Destruction through Financing Transactions
5. Cash Flow Analysis		

of other information sources that should be investigated, ranging from company press releases to industry and macroeconomic data. Today, much of this information is available via the touch of a screen. We provide a more detailed discussion of the most important information sources in Chapter 2.

Once the pertinent information has been gathered, we begin the process of analyzing this information. We need to *understand the business.* This process is primarily qualitative in nature and is aimed at developing a detailed understanding of the business activities in which the firm is engaged. What does the business make, how is it made, and who buys it? Who are the main competitors, what are the industry characteristics, and how is the industry related to the general economy? We also want to identify the elements of a firm's business strategy that are expected to make it more successful than its competitors. Just as investors strive to find securities that will provide abnormally high investment returns, company managers strive to find real investment opportunities that will provide abnormally high profits. Competition among managers limits the availability of such investment opportunities. Your business analysis should leave you with a clear understanding of the firm's business plan, and some opinions about whether this plan represents a viable strategy for generating abnormally high profits. We cover the basics of business analysis in Chapter 3.

Armed with a thorough understanding of the business, we can start to scrutinize the historical financial statements. This step is called *accounting analysis.* The objective here is to develop a thorough understanding of how the economic consequences of the firm's business activities are reflected in the financial statements. The financial statements report on the periodic financial position and operating performance of a business. Over long periods of time (i.e., many years), the cash flows from a firm's operating and investing activities become known with perfect certainty, and so the economic consequences are easy to measure. But over short periods of time (i.e., a quarter or a year), the periodic cash flows can have little relation to the long-run economic consequences. This problem arises because a firm's operating and investing cycles often span many years. Firms often produce and hold inventory over several months, invest in assets that will provide benefits over several years and reward employees with retirement benefits that will be paid after several decades. As a result, the net cash flows to a firm over short periods of time provide a very noisy signal of the long-run cash flow consequences of a firm's activities.

This is where accrual accounting comes to our aid. The primary objective of accrual accounting is to provide a better indication of the long-run cash consequences of a firm's business activities. For instance, investing in a productive asset is not merely a cash outflow; the accrual accounting system tracks the store of future benefits that this investment represents by recording an asset on the balance sheet. But, while the accrual accounting process undoubtedly creates useful information, it is also fraught with distortions. Some distortions are a direct consequence of following generally accepted accounting rules, while others may be intentionally created through managerial manipulation of the rules. Accounting analysis is concerned with understanding a firm's accrual accounting choices and their implications for the interpretation of the associated financial statements. Accounting analysis will help you understand the key strengths and weaknesses of a firm's financial statements, identify where management may have attempted to mislead you, and help you draw informed conclusions about the economic consequences of the firm's past business activities. Accounting analysis is the subject of Chapter 4.

Once you have a solid understanding of a firm's financial statements, you are set to use the financial statements to evaluate the financial performance of the firm. Chapter 5 develops a systematic *financial ratio analysis* framework to facilitate this task. This analysis shows us how the components of a firm's financial statements interact to produce overall financial performance. What margin does the firm earn on its sales? How much investment is required to generate the sales? How aggressively does the firm use debt financing? This analysis enables us to quickly identify the key drivers of financial performance and spot any irregularities. When combined with accounting analysis, financial ratio analysis provides the basis for evaluating the economic consequences of a firm's past business activities and the success of its business strategy.

Ratio analysis focuses almost exclusively on a firm's accrual accounting statements—the income statement and the balance sheet. However, in order to remain solvent, fund new business opportunities, and ultimately make cash flow distributions, a firm also must carefully manage its cash. A firm's cash flows are detailed in its statement of cash flows, and the analysis of this information is the topic of Chapter 6. *Cash flow analysis* is concerned with understanding the cash flows from a firm's operating, investing, and financing activities. A sound business strategy should anticipate the cash flows associated with each activity and make sure that they articulate. Also, firm value is ultimately dependent on the distribution of cash flows to equity holders. Unfortunately, some firms choose to invest surplus cash flows in wasteful ways rather than making timely distributions to equity holders. These and other related issues are explained in Chapter 6.

Forecasting the Future

Once you understand the past, you are ready to forecast the future. The tasks involved in this step are summarized in the second box of Figure 1.1. Our goal in this step is to forecast the future financial statements. Recall from our earlier discussion that the financial statements represent the language for converting forecasts of future business activities into forecasts of future cash flows. In Chapter 7 we introduce *structured forecasting*—the systematic way that we go about developing forecasts. Rather than attempting to directly forecast the amount for each line item of the financial statements, we frame the forecasting problem using the same types of ratios that you will study in Chapter 5. You express your forecasts about the firm's operating, investing, and financing activities by developing forecasts of these ratios, and then derive the implied values for the underlying financial statement line items.

Chapter 7 also discusses earnings-per-share (EPS) forecasts. EPS forecasts are the most popular way of summarizing expectations of financial performance for equity holders. On the surface, the computation of EPS might sound pretty simple—take the forecasted earnings and divide it by the number of shares. But what number of shares should you use? Your forecast of the future number of shares depends on both your forecast of the amount of new equity that is expected to be issued/repurchased between now and the forecast date and the stock prices at which the issuances/repurchases are expected to occur. While our pro forma financial statements will provide us with dollar forecasts of issuances and repurchases, they do not provide us with forecasts of future issuance and repurchase prices. Thus, per-share analysis turns out to be quite a complex topic involving some thorny issues.

The *eVal* software requires a number of specific forecasting assumptions. In Chapter 8 we give you advice concerning *detailed forecast construction.* The process begins with the very first line on the income statement, the "Sales" forecast. Most firms have business models that center around providing goods and services to customers in return for sales revenue. For these firms, the sales forecast is the single most important forecast; it represents the starting point for most other forecasts. For example, most of the remaining lines in the income statement capture the costs that are incurred in the firm's operating activities, and many of these costs depend on the level of business activity, as summarized by the sales forecast. But the costs also depend on the efficiency with which the business is run and the prices at which the inputs for the business (such as materials and labor) are purchased, so forecasting these costs is not as simple as taking a fixed percentage of sales.

Income statement forecasts concern operating activities. Balance sheet forecasts concern the impact of the operating, investing, and financing activities on the resources and obligations of a firm. The forecasting of the balance sheet can be divided into two distinct tasks. First, we must forecast the resources and obligations necessary to sustain the forecasted operating activities from our income statement. Operating activities typically require investments in working capital (e.g., inventory) and long-term capital (e.g., property, plant, and equipment) and can also result in obligations (e.g., accounts payable and pension benefits for employees). The forecasted amount of operating resources and obligations depends on both the forecasted level of operating activity and the efficiency with which the firm is forecasted to conduct its operations. The second distinct task is to forecast the resources and obligations associated with the firm's financing activities. Most firms hold some financial resources (e.g., cash and marketable securities) and use some non-equity financing (e.g., debt and preferred stock). The forecasting of the individual financial resources and obligations on the balance sheet involves determining the amount and mix of financing that is used to support the firm's operating and investing activities.

The next task is to create cash flow forecasts. As discussed earlier, the financial statements provide the language we use to describe the economic consequences of business activities. Ultimately, these economic consequences are represented by cash flows and the statement of cash flows reports these cash consequences. Contained within the cash flow forecasts are implied forecasts of the net cash distributions to equity holders, the key inputs for equity valuation, so this is a critical step. Fortunately, cash flow forecasting is quite straightforward. As you may recall from your introductory accounting classes, we can derive a statement of cash flows from an income statement, along with the associated beginning and ending balance sheets. So, we simply use our income statements and balance sheet forecasts to construct our cash flow forecasts. In fact, the *eVal* software handles this step for us.

The forecasted financial statements are often referred to as "pro forma" financial statements ("pro forma" is Latin for "a matter of form"). The last step is to apply the same ratio analysis and cash flow analysis that we discussed in Chapter 5 to the pro forma financial statements. This final step provides a reality check on the plausibility of our forecasts. For example, we may find that our forecasting assumptions imply a level of profitability for a firm that far exceeds the historical industry average. Such performance may be justified through some unique feature of the firm's business strategy. But in the absence of a compelling justification, we should revise the forecasting assumptions to bring profitability back to plausible levels. Similarly, our pro forma cash flow analysis may reveal that our forecasting assumptions imply that a firm must raise substantial additional capital. If the firm has no plans to raise new capital, or would have difficulty accessing capital markets on the forecasted terms, we should revise our forecasting assumptions accordingly.

Valuation

With your forecasts of the future fundamentals under your belt, you are ready for step three: valuation. The tasks involved in this step are summarized in the third box of Figure 1.1. First you need to decide on the necessary valuation parameters. The most important of these is the "discount rate," or *cost of capital,* which enters the denominator of our equity valuation model. Unfortunately, there is much disagreement concerning the selection of an appropriate cost of capital. In Chapter 9, we discuss popular techniques for estimating the cost of capital and provide some broad guidelines for handling this issue.

A second issue in constructing the valuation models is whether we choose to discount the cash distributions directly to equity holders using the cost of equity capital, or whether we discount cash flows to all providers of capital (i.e., common equity plus preferred stock and debt) using a weighted average cost of capital, and then subtract the value of the non-equity capital to derive equity value. Again, *eVal* does the valuation both ways, both give the same answer, and the choice between the two approaches is largely a matter of taste. Chapter 10 provides a detailed explanation of the valuation gymnastics involved in these alternative *valuation models.*

The remaining steps are the equity valuation computations themselves. The good news here is that *eVal* does all of the work for you. *eVal* provides computations using both a *residual income valuation model* (RIM) and a *discounted free cash flow model* (DCF). Why do we need two valuations? Well, we don't, since it turns out that both of these valuations will give you exactly the same answer. These are simply two different algebraic formulations of our basic valuation theory. Regardless of the formula used, it is your forecast of the future financial statements, along with your valuation parameters, that ultimately determine equity value. The only issue here is whether you would like to look at computations based on earnings or cash flows. By providing you with both sets of computations, you will be able to effectively communicate your equity valuation work to fans of either model.

Financial analysts often communicate their beliefs about the value of a firm in terms of *valuation ratios.* Some of these are quite straightforward, such as the price-to-earnings ratio, defined as the market price divided by EPS. Others are much more complex, like the PEG ratio (don't ask). In Chapter 11 we discuss some of these ratios, what they represent, and how they can be used to screen for potentially underpriced or overpriced stocks. These ratios are commonly used heuristics, but they are just that, they are no substitute for a comprehensive valuation analysis.

The final step in the equity valuation process is to consider some *complications.* If you are lucky, none of these complications will apply to your valuation. Unfortunately, one or more of these monsters often rear their ugly heads. We mention them here briefly only to alert you to their existence. Chapter 12 provides more detailed coverage.

The first complication concerns negative equity values. Real world stock prices cannot be negative, but models can be constructed in *eVal* that generate negative equity values. If you find yourself with a negative equity valuation, then you should read Chapter 12. A second and related complication concerns the abandonment option. If you come up with a positive equity valuation, but your sensitivity analysis reveals that negative valuations are also reasonably likely, then you need to consider the abandonment option.

A third complication arises when we introduce the possibility that a firm may create or destroy value through transactions in its own mispriced securities. For example, if a firm's stock is overpriced relative to its intrinsic value, it can create value for its existing equity holders by issuing additional shares of the overpriced stock. Thus, not only do we have to correctly determine the intrinsic value of a firm's operating and investing activities, but we also have to forecast how much additional value will be created or destroyed through the firm's financing activities.

A final and related complication concerns contingent equity claims. Contingent equity claims provide holders with the option, but not the obligation, to purchase shares of common stock for a prespecified exercise price. Firms issue contingent claims on their equity for a variety of reasons. For example, firms can raise capital by issuing warrants, firms can reduce the interest rate paid on debt by issuing convertible debt, and firms can compensate employees using employee stock options. Because the holders of contingent claims

FIGURE 1.2
eVal Start-Up Screen

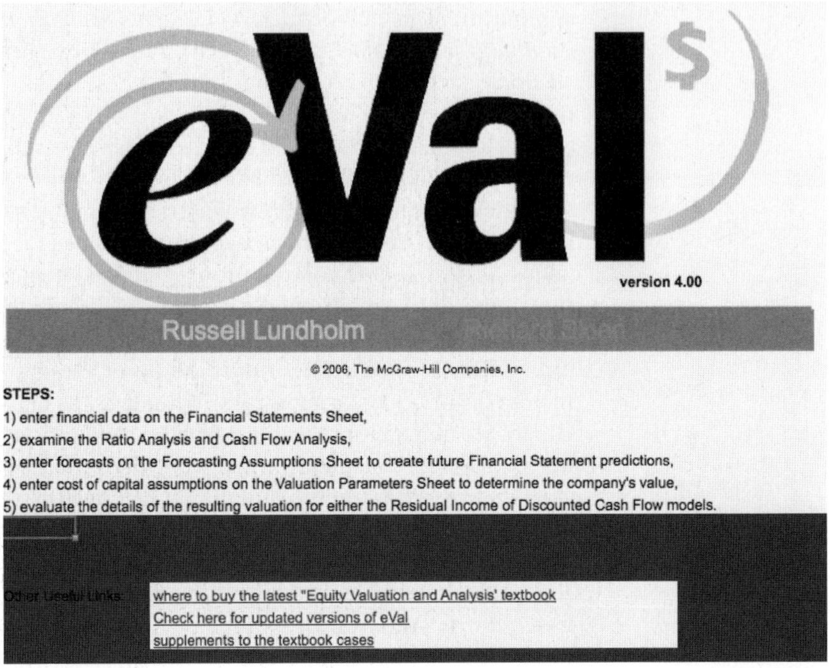

only have to exercise their claims when it is profitable to do so, the claims themselves will have value as long as there is some probability of a profitable future exercise. These claims can therefore result in new equity securities being issued for consideration less than fair value.

We are now at an ideal point to introduce *eVal*, our Excel-based financial modeling software. If you haven't already done so, go to www.lundholmandsloan.com and click on the *eVal* link to get the latest copy for the program and other related material. Each time you start a new model in *eVal*, the introductory window, which is shown in Figure 1.2, will greet you. The *eVal* software is really just a connected series of worksheets that you can access by clicking on the tabs at the bottom of the screen (or on any of the hyperlinks scattered through the program). To build a model, you simply work through the worksheets by clicking through the tabs at the bottom of the window.

1.6 THE ROLE OF *eVAL*

The worksheets in *eVal* are organized around the same three steps that are outlined in Figure 1.1. While we have sequenced the worksheets from left to right so as to systematically walk you through these steps, you are free to

FIGURE 1.3   How the *eVal* Software Facilitates the Equity Valuation Process

STEP 1 Understanding the Past	STEP 2 Forecasting the Future	STEP 3 Valuation
What You Do: • Obtain and analyze financial and non-financial information on the business • Enter historical financial statement information into *eVal* using standardized format **What *eVal* Does:** • Provides basic consistency checks on the historical data • Performs systematic ratio analysis on historical data • Performs systematic cash flow analysis on historical data **Associated Worksheets in *eVal*:** • Financial Statements • Ratio Analysis • Cash Flow Analysis • Credit Analysis	**What You Do:** • Modify *eVal*'s default forecasting assumptions based on the insights from your analysis in STEP 1 **What *eVal* Does:** • Provides a forecasting template listing all required forecasting assumptions • Provides historic values and suggests 'naïve' default values for all forecasting assumptions • Prepares pro forma financial statements from the forecasting assumptions • Performs ratio and cash flow analysis on pro forma financial statements **Associated Worksheets in *eVal*:** • Forecasting Assumptions • Ratio Analysis • Cash Flow Analysis	**What You Do:** • Enter cost of equity capital and other valuation parameters **What *eVal* Does:** • Performs residual income valuation to both common equity holders and all capital providers • Performs discounted cash flow valuation to both common equity holders and all capital providers • Maintains internal consistency between valuation models • Provides EPS forecast schedule • Provides model summary and sensitivity analysis **Associated Worksheets in *eVal*:** Valuation Parameters Residual Income Valuations DCF Valuations EPS Forecaster Model Summary

skip between them as you wish while you build your model. Figure 1.3 summarizes what you do, how *eVal* helps, and the associated *eVal* worksheets for each of these three steps.

The first box in Figure 1.3 summarizes how *eVal* assists you in step one, *understanding the past. eVal* provides a standardized template in which you can enter the firm's historical financial statement data. It also provides some basic consistency checks on your data, such as checking that the balance sheet does in fact balance. Next, *eVal* performs systematic financial ratio analysis and cash flow analysis on the firm's historical financial statements. The second box in Figure 1.3 summarizes how *eVal* helps you in step two, *forecasting the future. eVal* provides a comprehensive forecasting template, along with default forecasting assumptions that are reasonable for the average firm in the average industry in the average year. However, you should avoid relying heavily on these defaults. We are not licensed soothsayers; our defaults are simply based on the naïve extrapolation of past data. You should use your detailed information analysis from step one to provide more accurate forecasting assumptions. Once you have updated the assumptions, *eVal* will prepare the pro forma financial statements implied by these assumptions and will perform a detailed financial ratio analysis and cash flow analysis on the pro forma financial statements.

The third box in Figure 1.3 summarizes how *eVal* helps you in step three, *valuation.* You have already done most of the hard work in steps one and two, leaving *eVal* to do most of the work in step three. Your final remaining task is to enter basic valuation parameters, such as the cost of capital, into *eVal.* Next, *eVal* provides detailed valuation calculations using both the residual income (RIM) and discounted free cash flow (DCF) valuation models. You can use the formulas in the valuation spreadsheets to trace all of the amounts entering the valuation calculations back to the pro forma financial statements prepared in step two. *eVal* also ensures that the valuations obtained using the RIM and DCF models are identical. While this feature is simply a reflection of the consistent application of valuation theory, it is important from a practical perspective. One of our strongest motivations for creating *eVal* was the hundreds of hours that we spent trying to reconcile inconsistent valuation models. *eVal* also provides a detailed analysis of the earnings-per-share (EPS) implications of your pro forma financial forecasts, which helps you to benchmark your forecasts with those of Wall Street analysts. EPS is the most closely tracked summary measure of firm performance and EPS surprises are a big catalyst for stock price changes. If your EPS forecasts are more accurate than the consensus forecasts of Wall Street analysts, the differences between your forecasts and the consensus should provide the basis for identifying price revisions. Finally, *eVal* provides a summary of your valuation model.

eVal is not password protected. You are free to customize it however you like. For instance, you might want to add more descriptive names for the line items on the financial statements sheet in order to tailor your model to a specific company. Or you might want to add a sheet that does more detailed segment analysis that culminates in your sales growth forecast. However, we strongly caution you against changing any of the formulas or calculations. This model has been road-tested by thousands of previous students and practitioners—it has no bugs. We can't make the same promise once you start changing things.

1.7 CLOSING COMMENTS

In this chapter, we provided you with an overview of the theory of equity valuation and introduced a framework for its practical application. We also highlighted the role played by the *eVal* software in helping you to implement this framework. If you have a reasonable background in accounting and finance, this overview is probably enough to get you up and running with *eVal*. However, the "garbage-in, garbage out" maxim rules the day. Software like *eVal* cannot protect you from your own bad forecasting assumptions. In the 11 chapters that follow, our main purpose is to provide you guidance in selecting the most informed valuation inputs.

We close each chapter with a list of relevant cases, links, and references. All cases may be found at the back of the book and supporting resources may be found at www.lundholmandsloan.com. Links give you the URLs for relevant resources on the Internet. These URLs can change; an updated list is maintained at www.lundholandsloan.com, so check there if you hit a dead link. References give the full reference for works cited in the chapter that provide an in-depth analysis of specific topics covered in the chapter.

1.8   CASES, LINKS, AND REFERENCES

Cases

- The Gabelli Utility Trust

Links

- Lundholm and Sloan website: www.lundholmandsloan.com

Information Collection

2.1 INTRODUCTION

The heart of a good valuation is a good forecast, and a forecast is only as good as the information that is used to support it. So the more relevant information you collect, the more accurate your forecasts will be. You may be thinking that information collection is time consuming and costly, and that our "more is better" advice ignores this aspect of the trade-off. But our advice comes from years of experience watching students and practitioners underinvest in information collection. The chapters that follow talk in more detail about how to interpret information. This chapter focuses on describing the most important sources of information and explains how to enter historical financial statement data into *eVal*. By focusing your information collection efforts where they yield the best insights and using tools such as *eVal* to organize your data collection and analysis, you will maximize the payoff from information collection.

We begin by identifying the key sources of company-specific data. For public companies whose securities trade on exchanges in the United States, filings with the Securities and Exchange Commission (SEC) are the most important source of company-specific information. We identify the most important filings and describe their contents. We then discuss other data sources, such as company websites, company press releases, news stories, and analysts' reports. Next, we identify and briefly discuss industry and macroeconomic information. Finally, we explain the process for inputting historical financial statement data into *eVal*.

Throughout this chapter, we will give you links to sources of information on the Internet. We simply name the site in the text and, at the end of the chapter, give you the URL that gets you to the site. Please remember that these sources are continually being revised and some of the links provided may be dead or stale. We maintain an updated version of these links on our website www.lundholmandsloan.com.

2.2 COMPANY INFORMATION

You should spend most of your time collecting company-specific information. Over half of the variation in a typical stock's price is company-specific and unrelated to market or industry information. This analysis will typically start with the mandatory financial reports and then extend to discretionary company disclosures (e.g., press releases) and information provided by third parties (e.g., sell-side analyst reports).

SEC Filings

Public companies issuing securities in the United States are required to file a number of detailed financial reports with the Security and Exchange Commission (SEC), which in turn makes these reports available to the public. These SEC filings represent the most important source of company-specific information and provide the natural starting point for the collection of company data. A summary of the most important SEC filings is provided in Figure 2.1. A more detailed description of SEC forms is available on the SEC's website.

FIGURE 2.1   **Guide to Common SEC Filings**

Filing	Description
Form 10-K	This is the annual report filed by most companies. It provides a comprehensive overview of the company's business (see Figure 2.2 for details). Depending on company size, it must be filed within 60 days of the close of the fiscal year.
Form 10-Q	This is the quarterly financial report filed by most companies. It includes unaudited financial statements and provides a continuing view of the company's financial position during the year. Depending on company size, it must be filed within 35 days of the close of the quarter.
Form 8-K	This is the "current report" that is used to report the occurrence of any material events or corporate changes that are of importance to investors and have not been previously reported.
Proxy Statement (Form DEF 14A)	The proxy statement provides official notification to designated classes of shareholders of matters to be brought to a vote at a shareholders' meeting.
Form 13F	This is the quarterly report filed by institutional investors managing over $100 million. It lists the name and amount of each security held at the end of each quarter.
Schedule 13D	This filing is required by 5 percent (or more) equity owners within 10 days of the acquisition event.
Schedule 13E	These are filings required by persons engaging in "going private" transactions in the company's stock or by companies engaging in tender offers for their own securities.
Schedule 13G	This is similar to Schedule 13D but is only available in special cases where control of the issuer is not compromised.
Schedule 14D	These are filings required pursuant to a tender offer.
Form 3, Form 4, and Form 5	These are statements of ownership filings required by directors, officers, and 10 percent owners. Form 3 is the initial ownership filing, Form 4 is for changes in ownership, and Form 5 is a special annual filing.
Registration Statements (Forms S-1 and S-3)	These are filings that are used to register securities before they are offered to investors. The most common registration filings are Forms S-1 and S-3.
Prospectus (Rule 424)	This document is made available to investors in a security offering. It comes in varieties 424A, 424B1, 424B2, 424B3, 424B4, 424B5, 424B6, and 424B7.

Listed first in Figure 2.1 is the annual Form 10-K, usually the most relevant SEC filing for our purposes. Domestic publicly traded companies are required to file this form within 60 to 90 days of their fiscal year end, depending on their size. If you were going to read only one document about the company before starting your valuation, this would be the one. This can be quite a lengthy document, but it follows a standardized format and familiarizing yourself with this format will improve your ability to efficiently process the contents.

The basic format of a 10-K is summarized in Figure 2.2. The first item, the description of the business, provides a detailed discussion of the company's business activities. Companies are required to provide a long list of

FIGURE 2.2   Items of Disclosure Contained in Form 10-K

Item	Description
Cover Page	Lists company name, fiscal year end, state of incorporation, each class of publicly traded securities, and other information.
Item 1—Business	Identifies principal products and services of the company, principal markets and methods of distribution, and other key attributes and risks of the business.
Item 2—Properties	Location and character of key properties.
Item 3—Legal Proceedings	Brief description of material pending legal proceedings.
Item 4—Submission of Matters to Vote	Information relating to the convening of a meeting of shareholders, whether annual or special, and the matters voted upon.
Item 5—Market for Common Stock	Principal market in which common stock is traded; high and low quarterly stock prices for the last two years; number of stockholders; dividends paid during the last two years; future dividend plans.
Item 6—Selected Financial Data	Five-year summary of selected financial data, including net sales and operating revenue, income from continuing operations, total assets, and long-term obligations.
Item 7—Management's Discussion and Analysis	Discussion of results of operations, liquidity, capital resources, off-balance-sheet arrangements, and contractual obligations. Discussion should include trends, significant events and uncertainties, causes of material changes, effects of inflation and changing prices, and critical accounting policies.
Item 7A—Disclosures about Market Risk	Provides qualitative and quantitative disclosures about market risk (e.g., interest rate, exchange rate, and commodity price risk). Requirements apply to financial instruments and commodity instruments.
Item 8—Financial Statements and Supplementary Data	Two-year audited balance sheets, three-year audited statements of income and three-year audited statements of cash flows, along with supporting notes and schedules.
Item 9—Changes in and Disagreements with Accountants	Description of any changes in and disagreements with independent auditors on any matter of accounting principles or practices, financial statement disclosure, or auditing scope of procedure.
Item 9A—Controls and Procedures	Opinion of top management and auditors regarding the effectiveness of the company's internal controls and procedures over financial reporting.

information on things such as the principal products sold, sources and availability of raw materials, key patents, trademarks and licenses, seasonalities, key customers, competitive conditions, government regulations, and risk factors associated with the business. The SEC designed this item to be a thorough and objective overview of a company's business activities, and is a great starting point for getting to know a company.

The next three items in the 10-K provide information about other aspects of the company that the SEC decided were worth singling out. Item 2 requires a description of the property of the company, Item 3 requires a description of any material pending legal proceedings against the company, and Item 4 requires a description of any matters submitted during the fourth quarter to a vote of security holders. You should scan this information for anything important, but there isn't usually too much here. Item 5 requires summary information concerning recent stock price and dividend activity, and Item 6 provides summary financial data for the last five years. You can obtain the information in Items 5 and 6 in more detail from other sources, but since it provides a convenient summary, you may want to scan through it.

Item 7 contains management's discussion and analysis of the firm's financial condition, results of operations, off-balance-sheet arrangements, contractual obligations, and critical accounting policies. Referred to as the MD&A, this is a must read. The discussion and analysis of financial condition requires management to identify any factors that might cause the company's liquidity to change. It also requires a description of the company's material capital expenditure commitments, the purpose of such commitments, and the anticipated sources of funding for the commitments. Finally, the company is required to discuss any pending changes in the company's capital structure. The discussion and analysis of results of operations requires management to walk the reader through the line items in the company's income statement, identifying any unusual or nonrecurring items and explaining any significant changes during the last two years. The discussions concerning off-balance-sheet arrangements, contractual obligations, and critical accounting policies are relatively recent additions in response to the accounting scandals at Enron and WorldCom. These discussions can be useful for identifying potential problem areas in the company's financial reports. But if a company is really "cooking the books," it is unlikely to tell you exactly how it is doing it right here. Lastly, because much of the material in the MD&A is forward-looking, it normally finishes with a long list of all the risk factors that add uncertainty to these forecasts. As you can see, the management discussion and analysis requires management to divulge a wealth of information that is useful in forecasting. Moreover, the company's auditor is required to review the information in the MD&A. So read the MD&A carefully and completely.

Following the MD&A is Item 7A, requiring disclosures about the company's exposure to certain market risks, such as interest rate risk and currency risk. This item provides useful information for financial services companies and other companies holding large amounts of financial instruments or engaging in significant hedging activities. Next is the all-important Item 8. Item 8 contains the company's financial statements and supplementary data. This item includes annual balance sheets for the last two years and annual income statements and statements of cash flows for the past three years. This section must also include a detailed description of significant accounting policies, detailed supporting notes and schedules, and the external auditor's opinion on the financial statements. The analysis of these financial statements is one of our most important tasks, and is the subject of Chapters 4, 5, and 6.

Item 9 contains information about changes in and disagreements with the independent auditors on accounting practices and financial disclosures. If the company's auditor either resigned or had a major accounting disagreement with management in the past two years, you will find out here. Most of the time you will find nothing in this section, but you should always check it out just to be sure. It usually takes a serious disagreement for the company and auditors to get to the point of hanging out their dirty laundry in Item 9. A relatively recent addition to Form 10-K is Item 9A. This item was added by the Sarbanes-Oxley Act and basically requires the senior management and auditors to attest to the effectiveness of the company's controls over its financial reporting system.

To summarize, the 10-K is the most important SEC filing and your starting point for analyzing a company. The most important parts of the 10-K are the description of business in Item 1, the MD&A in Item 7, and the financial statements in Item 8. The main drawback of the 10-K is that it is only made available once a year. Our main interest in the other SEC filings in Figure 2.1 is to gain access to more timely information.

The second filing listed in Figure 2.1 is the Form 10-Q filing. This is the quarterly version of Form 10-K. It must be filed within 45 days of the end of the quarter, for each of the first three quarters of the fiscal year (the annual 10-K filing handles the fourth quarter). These filings are not as detailed as the 10-K and do not give you the description of the business and much of the other information that comes with the 10-K. But, obviously, they are more current. They typically contain a summary version of the MD&A and abbreviated, unaudited financial statements. You should plan on reviewing all 10-Qs filed since the most recently available 10-K. You also should make sure that you are familiar with the information in the most recent 10-K before attempting to read the intervening 10-Qs, since the 10-K provides the necessary background to understand the information in the 10-Q.

The third filing listed in Figure 2.1 is the Form 8-K filing. This filing is used to report significant current events on a timely basis. Examples of events that warrant an 8-K filing include a change in control of a company, the acquisition or disposition of a significant portion of the company's business operations, bankruptcy, change in auditors, and the resignation of key directors or officers. Most companies also announce their quarterly earnings via newswires significantly in advance of filing their 10-Ks and 10-Qs and they are required to file the text of these announcements on an 8-K. These earnings announcements provide timely updates on financial performance, but you should remember that they are voluntary disclosures by management that are only loosely regulated and often emphasize non-GAAP definitions of earnings that are made up by management to make performance look better. The 8-K filing must generally be made within four days of the event being reported.

There are lots of other forms that a firm must file with the SEC; the most common ones fill out the remainder of Figure 2.1. Most of these other filings aren't as relevant for our purposes as the 10-K, 10-Q, and 8-K, but here are a few of the more interesting ones. Whenever shareholders are required to vote on something (which is usually at least once a year), the firm must file a proxy statement. This statement also gives the lowdown on management compensation. So if you think management is skimming too much off the top, this is the place to see just how much they are taking. There are a few different filings related to proxy statements, but the most common one is filed under the designation DEF 14A. Also, insider trades (i.e., trades by management in the company's stock) are reported on Forms 3, 4, and 5. Note that these forms are filed directly by the managers themselves, rather than under the name of the company. Finally, if a company issues new securities, it will typically file a Form S-3 to register the securities and a Form 424B3 for the final prospectus.

All of the above filings can be accessed directly from the EDGAR database on the SEC's website. It can sometimes be a challenge to find the exact filing that you are looking for. Companies frequently file one form and then later file an amendment to the form (appending a "/A" to the form name). They also incorporate information in a required filing by referencing another filing. But be persistent, especially when seeking the 10-K and 10-Q. They should be out there somewhere.

Company Website

You can learn much about a company's business by surfing its website. Most companies have a dedicated investor relations section of their website providing financial information about the company. In fact, the development of the Internet and the passage of Regulation FD (Fair Disclosure) by the SEC have proved to be a boon to small investors. Regulation FD was introduced by the SEC in 2000 and basically prohibits companies from selectively disclosing nonpublic information to a few individuals, such as portfolio managers or Wall Street analysts. In order to comply, most companies immediately put any information that they have disclosed to other investors onto their website.

One "must read" in the company website is the press release section. Company press releases often provide more timely information than periodic SEC filings. However, you also should remember that any financial information in these press releases is not subject to the same standards as the company's financial statements on Forms 10-K and 10-Q. Good examples are press releases related to quarterly earnings announcements. These press releases are made days or even weeks ahead of the corresponding 10-Q filing. However, companies often make up their own pro forma measures of earnings in their press releases and typically emphasize good information and downplay bad information. So always read these press releases with a grain of salt. Another document that you will often find on the website is the annual report to shareholders. Be careful not to confuse the firm's annual report with its official 10-K filing. There are fewer required disclosures in the annual report than in the 10-K and, for many companies, the annual report is little more than a marketing document. You will see lots of fancy graphs and images of happy employees and customers all designed to convince you that the company is financially healthy, very profitable, an exemplary corporate citizen, and especially kind to animals and small children.

If you check out the company's website shortly after an earnings announcement, you will frequently find an audio file that replays the conference call that management had with analysts to discuss the most recent quarter's results and perhaps also a transcript of the call. These can be a rich source of information, but can be short-lived; some companies remove them from the website after a week or two. After listening to a few of these, you will notice that they tend to be shortsighted and long-winded. Most analysts are primarily interested in forecasting the next quarter's results, and most CEOs are counseled to refrain from expressing opinions about the future.

Financial Press

The company isn't the only one talking. A very active financial press ferrets about hoping to uncover interesting, and sometimes scandalous, facts about the company. Companies are reluctant to highlight their own questionable accounting practices, but the financial press will not hesitate to do so. And the company will not generally compare itself to other firms in the same industry, but a good news article frequently does this. The only word of warning we offer is that writers for the financial press are paid to write exciting stories that people will be drawn to read; being accurate is desirable but not paramount. Frequently the financial press is the first to call attention to a firm's questionable accounting practices, but in our experience the accounting turns out to be bad only about half the time.

Most of the major financial portals on the web have links to recent news stories, along with the firm's press releases. The Yahoo! Finance portal provides access to a particularly wide range of sources. Other free sites that we recommend include Reuters and MSN Money. If you want to join the professionals, then a real-time subscription to Bloomberg or the Dow Jones News Service will give you timely and comprehensive access to both financial news and sports scores.

Lots of regional newspapers also write about companies in their own backyard, and the major news services may not pick up these stories. One way to be sure you haven't missed something big—and we hesitate to recommend this—is to check out the investment message boards for the company. Yahoo, Motley Fool, and several other sites sponsor boards where investors exchange views about particular stocks along with insults about one another's intelligence. The analysis offered by the average user of these boards is suspect, but you can benefit from the board's collective eyes and ears. If a great story about the company appeared in a local newspaper, or some other source you have overlooked, the odds are high that somebody on the message board has posted something about it. Look for message titles with headlines like "Did anyone else see the article on Hurricane Corporation in the Miami Herald?"

Analyst Research Reports

One final source for company-specific information is the research distributed by analysts working for the independent research firms and the research departments of brokerage houses. Analysts working for brokerage houses are referred to as sell-side analysts to distinguish them from the buy-side analysts who work directly for institutional investors. Buy-side research is used directly by the investor and is not typically made available to the public. Sell-side research is primarily produced for brokerage clients, and a number of services now collect and redistribute these research reports. The largest service is Investext, a division of Thomson Research. This is a subscription-based service that is offered through many business school libraries.

Sell-side research reports generally provide very precise and confident forecasts based on a rudimentary analysis of a company. Our experience suggests that students and other neophyte investors are often taken in by the apparent confidence with which these reports are written and their association with prestigious investment houses. Historically, however, the recommendations and price targets contained in these reports have been unreliable and overly optimistic. Moreover, sell-side analysts rarely charge a direct fee for the research they issue to clients. Instead, they generate revenue from two indirect sources. First, they help their brokerage business to generate commissions by attracting clients and encouraging them to trade. Second, the analysts often work for brokerage houses that are affiliated with investment banks. By issuing positive research on current and potential investment banking clients, sell-side analysts help to generate investment-banking business. As you can imagine, the fact that sell-side analysts generate revenue through these indirect sources poses a great conflict of interest. A strategy we recommend is to zero in on the research report of the analyst issuing the least favorable recommendation on a stock. This way, you are more likely to find insightful analysis rather than superficial hype.

Given the limitations of sell-side research discussed above, we encourage you to read this research with a healthy dose of skepticism. However, sell-side research does have its redeeming features. First, sell-side analysts tend to be industry specialists. A sell-side research report may give you some deep industry insights that you missed in your own industry analysis. Second, sell-side analysts are usually up to date on recent company news and guidance, so their reports are a good place to check that you have all the latest company-specific information. Third, sell-side research almost always contains earnings forecasts for the next year or so. One of the strongest catalysts for a stock price change is an earnings surprise, whereby a company announces earnings that differ from the consensus forecast of sell-side analysts. A number of services collect sell-side analysts' forecasts and construct consensus earnings estimates from these forecasts (the consensus earnings estimate is simply the mean or median estimate of the analysts following the stock). The leading service is Thomson Reuters and is available through the Yahoo! Finance portal.

There are also numerous independent research firms that sell their analyst research reports. Since our goal is to do our own analysis, we do not recommend relying too heavily on such reports.

2.3 MACROECONOMIC AND INDUSTRY DATA

Careful analysis of company-level data is where you are most likely to generate the best insights. However, a good understanding of the industry and macroeconomy is also useful for interpreting the past and forecasting the future. We have had many experiences where students have become excited about stocks that look "cheap" relative to past fundamentals, only to learn that the students have overlooked some key macroeconomic shifts. Examples include "cheap" oil services stocks in periods immediately following dramatic declines in the price of crude oil and "cheap" banking and home construction stocks in periods immediately following dramatic rises in interest rates. You don't have to be a guru macroeconomist to do sound equity analysis and valuation. But you do need to have a good idea of the macroeconomic factors that impact the company you are analyzing. And you should track the consensus view of where these macroeconomic factors are heading. Macroeconomic and industry analysis is covered in Chapter 3. In this section, we tell you where to collect the necessary data for your analysis.

The Global and Domestic Economy

A taxonomy for conducting macroeconomic and industry analysis is provided in Figure 2.3. At the broadest level, we have the global economy. As domestic economies become increasingly integrated, domestic economies are increasingly linked to the global economy. Global economic trends are measured by summing the trends in domestic economies. Countries with the largest domestic economies, such as the United States, Japan, and China, tend to dominate global economic trends. However, economic crises in smaller countries, such as those in Europe and Asia, can have a material impact on the global economy. There are a number of websites tracking the global economy. We recommend the Dismal Scientist, offered through Moody's economy.com website.

Armed with data on the global economy, you should next collect data on the domestic economy. The operations of most businesses are concentrated in a particular country and the health of this country's domestic economy is a key driver of profitability. Our discussion focuses on the U.S. economy.

FIGURE 2.3

Taxonomy for Conducting Macroeconomic and Industry Analysis

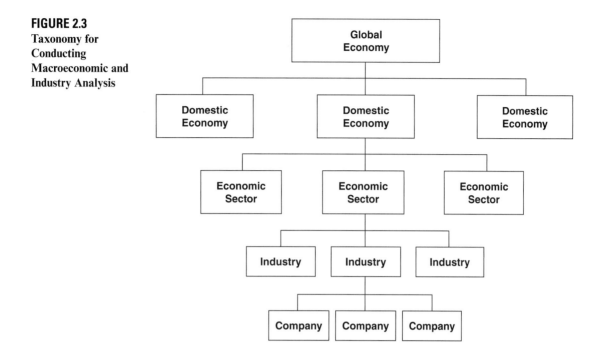

There is a wealth of free data available on the domestic U.S. economy, most of it made available courtesy of the U.S. government. A good starting point is the monthly *Economic Indicators* publication prepared by the Council of Economic Advisors for the Joint Economic Committee that is available from the U.S. government's gpo.gov website. If this report is too bland, sites such as Briefing.com provide monthly summaries.

Finally, you should keep track of major economic announcements by following an economic calendar of events. Briefing.com provides a good free economic calendar that includes descriptions, forecasts, and additional links for many economic statistics. We'll give you a framework for interpreting all of this macroeconomic data in Chapter 3.

Sectors and Industries

Economic sectors and industries are the next two levels in our taxonomy. Before we can discuss sources of data for analysis at these levels, we need to define what we mean by "sector" and "industry." An economic sector consists of a group of industries that engage in related activities. For example, "consumer goods" defines an economic sector consisting of firms that manufacture goods for consumers. Examples of industries included in this sector are automotive and tobacco. The production technologies are very different across these two industries, but it is their common customer base that places them in the same economic sector.

Within each sector are many industries. Industries are defined by the nature of the good or service that is provided by the business. Firms in the same industry provide similar goods and services and will typically use similar inputs and production technologies. Because of these similarities, common analysis techniques can be applied to firms in the same industry. Also, because firms in the same industry typically compete for market share, analysis of the competitive structure of input and output markets is usually conducted at the industry level. While the macroeconomic and sector-level analysis provides necessary background, the industry level is where we really get to understand the operating characteristics and competitive environment facing a company.

There are several competing classification systems for allocating firms to sectors and industries. While the similarities between systems outnumber the differences, it is important to use a single classification system consistently; otherwise, you can end up double-counting some companies and missing others altogether. We will use the **S&P/MSCI Global Industry Classification Standard (GICS)** system in this book. This is one of the more commonly used and comprehensive classification systems. It starts with 10 economic sectors, and then progressively divides them into 24 industry groups, 68 industries and 154 sub-industries. Figure 2.4 provides an overview of the GICS system. The system is based on an eight-digit GICS code, with the first two digits identifying the economic sector, the next two digits the industry group, the next two digits the industry, and the final two digits the sub-industry. Figure 2.4 shows the economic sectors and industry groups. The complete system is provided in Appendix A to this book. One place where you can find a company's GICS sector and code without requiring a subscription is the fidelity.com website. Simply select Research and then Stocks, load the company of your choice, and the resulting company snapshot will identify the GICS sector and code.

The best starting point to begin analyzing a new industry is the pertinent Standard & Poor's Industry Survey. These surveys are available through web-based subscriptions to S&P, available through many business school libraries. There is also a wealth of industry-specific information available on the web. Two good additional sources include Hoovers.com, which provides a wealth of industry information using its own classification system and the detailed industry links maintained by Polson Enterprises. See the end of this chapter for links.

In closing this section, we offer a final word of advice. The list of information given above may seem quite daunting. You may be asking, *"Do I really need to gather and read all of this every time I want to value a company?"* The answer is probably *Yes* if this is the first time you have ever studied the company and you know nothing about it, the economy, or the industry in which it operates. But a more typical situation is that you already have a good knowledge of general macroeconomic trends and may have good industry knowledge from following other companies operating in the same industry. With experience, you also should more quickly identify what is relevant and what is irrelevant, and be able to focus on the facts that will yield a better forecast.

FIGURE 2.4   **Overview of the Global Industry Classification (GICS) System**

Code	Sector	Subcode	Industry Group
10	Energy	1010	Energy
15	Materials	1510	Materials
		2010	Capital Goods
20	Industrials	2020	Commercial & Professional Services
		2030	Transportation
		2510	Automobiles & Components
		2520	Consumer Durables & Apparel
25	Consumer Discretionary	2530	Consumer Services
		2540	Media
		2550	Retailing
		3010	Food & Staples Retailing
30	Consumer Staples	3020	Food, Beverage & Tobacco
		3030	Household & Personal Products
		3510	Health Care Equipment & Services
35	Health Care	3520	Pharmaceuticals, Biotechnology, & Life Sciences
		4010	Banks
40	Financials	4020	Diversified Financials
		4030	Insurance
		4040	Real Estate
		4510	Software & Services
45	Information Technology	4520	Technology Hardware & Equipment
		4530	Semiconductors & Semiconductor Equipment
50	Telecommunication Services	5010	Telecommunication Services
55	Utilities	5510	Utilities

2.4   INPUTTING HISTORICAL DATA INTO *eVal*

The first step in building a valuation model is to enter the company's historical financial statement data into your valuation workbook. This data is the
foundation on which you will build your valuation model. The *eVal* software
provided with this book gives a standardized template in which to enter a
company's historical financial statement data. The default template contains
data for Kohl's Corporation for the five years ending January 31, 2010 and is
shown in Figure 2.5.

FIGURE 2.5 The *eVal* Financial Statements Worksheet Showing Historical Data for Kohl's Corporation

Company Name and Ticker	KOHL'S CORP		KSS	Link to Form 10-Ks	
Common Shares Outstanding	307,000	(in 000s at most recent fiscal year end)			
Estimated Price/Share=$43.63					
	Actual	Actual	Actual	Actual	Actual
Fiscal Year End (MM/DD/YYYY)	1/31/2006	1/31/2007	1/31/2008	1/31/2009	1/31/2010
Income Statement					
Sales (Net)	13,402,217	15,544,184	16,473,734	16,389,000	17,178,000
Cost of Goods Sold	(8,670,484)	(9,890,513)	(10,459,549)	(10,334,000)	(10,680,000)
Gross Profit	4,731,733	5,653,671	6,014,185	6,055,000	6,498,000
R&D Expense	0	0	0	0	0
SG&A Expense	(3,007,842)	(3,451,196)	(3,757,563)	(3,978,000)	(4,196,000)
EBITDA	1,723,891	2,202,475	2,256,622	2,077,000	2,302,000
Depreciation & Amortization	(307,710)	(387,674)	(452,145)	(541,000)	(590,000)
EBIT	1,416,181	1,814,801	1,804,477	1,536,000	1,712,000
Net Interest Expense	(79,383)	(74,427)	(98,712)	(140,000)	(134,000)
Non-Operating Income (Loss)	8,992	34,071	36,296	29,000	10,000
EBT	1,345,790	1,774,445	1,742,061	1,425,000	1,588,000
Income Taxes	(503,830)	(665,764)	(658,210)	(540,000)	(597,000)
Other Income (Loss)	0	0	0	0	0
Net Income Before Ext. Items	841,960	1,108,681	1,083,851	885,000	991,000
Ext. Items & Disc. Ops.	0	0	0	0	0
Minority Interest in Earnings	0	0	0	0	0
Preferred Dividends	0	0	0	0	0
Net Income (available to common)	841,960	1,108,681	1,083,851	885,000	991,000
Balance Sheet					
Operating Cash and Market. Sec.	286,916	620,400	663,671	676,000	2,267,000
Receivables	1,652,065	0	0	0	0
Inventories	2,237,568	2,588,099	2,855,733	2,799,000	2,923,000
Other Current Assets	89,503	192,541	204,485	225,000	295,000
Total Current Assets	4,266,052	3,401,040	3,723,889	3,700,000	5,485,000
PP&E (Net)	4,543,832	5,352,974	6,509,819	6,984,000	7,018,000
Investments	0	0	0	332,000	321,000
Intangibles	221,718	228,624	219,296	210,000	204,000
Other Assets	121,436	58,539	107,078	108,000	132,000
Total Assets	9,153,038	9,041,177	10,560,082	11,334,000	13,160,000
Current Debt	107,941	18,841	12,701	17,000	16,000
Accounts Payable	829,971	934,376	835,985	881,000	1,188,000
Income Taxes Payable	166,908	233,263	124,254	105,000	184,000
Other Current Liabilities	641,635	732,178	798,508	812,000	1,002,000
Total Current Liabilities	1,746,455	1,918,658	1,771,448	1,815,000	2,390,000
Long-Term Debt	1,046,104	1,040,057	2,051,875	2,053,000	2,052,000
Other Liabilities	185,340	235,537	372,705	407,000	488,000
Deferred Taxes	217,801	243,530	262,451	320,000	377,000
Total Liabilities	3,195,700	3,437,782	4,458,479	4,595,000	5,307,000
Minority Interest	0	0	0	0	0
Preferred Stock	0	0	0	0	0
Paid in Common Capital (Net)	1,586,485	123,861	(461,782)	(663,000)	(550,000)
Retained Earnings	4,370,853	5,479,534	6,563,385	7,402,000	8,403,000
Total Common Equity	5,957,338	5,603,395	6,101,603	6,739,000	7,853,000
Total Liabilities and Equity	9,153,038	9,041,177	10,560,082	11,334,000	13,160,000
Statement of Retained Earnings					
Beg. Retained Earnings		4,370,853	5,479,534	6,563,385	7,402,000
+Net Income		1,108,681	1,083,851	885,000	991,000
-Common Dividends	0	0	0	0	0
+/-Clean Surplus Plug (Ignore)		0	0	(46,385)	10,000
=End. Retained Earnings		5,479,534	6,563,385	7,402,000	8,403,000

The basic data input requirements for *eVal* are the historical income statement, the historical balance sheet, historical dividends and the number of shares outstanding at the end of the most recent fiscal year. All of these data items can be readily obtained from a company's annual financial statements. Unfortunately, companies do not create their financial reports using *eVal*'s standardized template; rather, each company chooses its own line items. This means that the data must first be mapped from the company's actual financial statements to our standardized template. This standardization process has important advantages and disadvantages. The most important advantage is that it provides a common and familiar framework for analyzing and valuing companies. For this reason, standardized financial statements are pervasive in practice. The most important disadvantage is that detailed information about many line items can be lost in the standardization process. For this reason, you *must* have a copy of the company's financial statements on hand so that you can figure out how the line items on those financial statements have been translated to the standardized financial statements.

There are two options for inputting data into *eVal*. The first is to manually enter it into the spreadsheet from a company's actual financial statements. This approach is tedious, but it has one very important advantage. You will have a full knowledge of the actual line items underlying each of the standardized line items, because you made your own mapping decisions. In addition, if you are building a model for one specific company, you might want to augment *eVal*'s line item definitions. For instance, you might augment the general description Other Current Liabilities with Customer Deposits. The second option is to obtain the standardized data directly from a data provider and then cut and paste this data into *eVal*. We provide all relevant standardized data for the cases covered in this book; you can find them under the Case Data tab in *eVal*. These two options—inputting the data manually or collecting it from a data service—are each explained in more detail below.

2.5 INPUTTING DATA MANUALLY

This approach requires you to manually enter the company's historical financial information into all of the yellow-shaded cells in the financial statements. All other cells in the financial statements are write-protected to prevent you from accidentally changing them. You can enter a maximum of five years of income statement and balance sheet data, but you don't have to enter all five years to use *eVal*. The minimum amount of data that we recommend is the company name, the number of shares outstanding and the financial statement data for each of the two most recent fiscal years.

You should enter all dollar and share amounts in thousands. Also, make sure to put the most recent year's financial statement data in the rightmost column and then gradually work back to the left for earlier years. Finally, you need to follow *eVal*'s conventions for positive and negative numbers. All amounts that increase net income, assets, liabilities, or equities are entered as positive amounts, while all amounts that decrease net income, assets, liabilities, or equities are entered as negative amounts. For example, costs and expenses such as Cost of Goods Sold are entered as negative numbers, even though they are usually shown as positive numbers in firms' actual financial statements. You can check your signing decisions by making sure that the subtotals of various line items computed in *eVal* are the same as the corresponding subtotals in your firm's actual financial statements.

You will have to exercise some judgment in mapping line items from the as-reported financial statements to the standardized line items in *eVal*. Many line items will have different names from those listed in *eVal*. For example, some firms refer to Cost of Goods Sold as Cost of Sales. Also, many companies report detailed line items that you will have to aggregate into a single line item in *eVal*. For example, some firms report marketing expenses and administrative expenses as separate line items, while *eVal* aggregates these expenses into the single line item SG&A Expenses. If a particular line item is not relevant, remember to enter the number 0 for that line item.

We refer you to Chapter 4 for a detailed discussion of the financial statements. This chapter should help guide your mapping from the actual financials to *eVal*'s standardized financials. The most important thing is to find a home for every single line item appearing on the as-reported financial statements. As you are doing this, you should remember the nature of the as-reported line items underlying each *eVal* line item so that you can meaningfully interpret ratios computed using these line items. *eVal* also has built-in alerts to warn you if your data input decisions seem unreasonable. For example, the message "Error! -Exp?" indicates that you have entered an expense as a positive number, when expenses should typically be entered as negative numbers. In some cases, you may actually mean to do this. For instance, if interest revenue and interest expense are netted together and the revenue exceeds the expense, then the amount of net interest expense should be entered as a positive amount. But generally the expense lines will be negative. The message "Error! A=L+E?" means that your balance sheet does not balance. This error is less forgivable—the entire financial analysis in *eVal* is suspect if this error is present. In sum, *eVal* will pick up some, but not all, data input errors, so you should exercise care and make sure that all the financial statement totals in *eVal* are the same as the corresponding totals in the as-reported financial statements.

eVal's Financial Statements worksheet comes preloaded with data for Kohl's Corporation. By way of illustrative example, section 2.8 below walks you through the process of manually inputting data from Kohl's. We suggest that you work through this section before manually inputting data on your own.

2.6 INPUTTING *eVal* CASE DATA

This book is supplied with a number of instructional cases. Many of these cases require you to analyze company data using the *eVal* valuation software. The cases sometimes relate to particularly interesting points in companies' histories. As such, we are interested in having you analyze the historical data that were available at the time of the case. To save you time inputting these historical data into *eVal,* we have coded and stored them along with the *eVal* software. Note that the cases provide you with the historical financial statements from which we obtained these data. Also, all of the case data are in *eVal*'s standardized format, so make sure you are able to reconcile these data back to the original financial statements.

The *eVal* case data is loaded by cutting and pasting the appropriate block of data from the Case Data worksheet to the location provided in the Financial Statements worksheet. The Case Data worksheet is located at the very end of the list of worksheets within the *eVal* workbook. Within that worksheet, you will find yellow-shaded data blocks for each of the relevant cases. The links at the top of the worksheet allow you to jump to the data blocks for specific cases. To load the data for a specific case, you first need to copy the data block (use your mouse to select the relevant block of cells and select copy from the Excel menu). Next, go back to the Financial Statements worksheet to paste the data. You will find the yellow-shaded paste location in cells B82:F116 at the bottom of the Financial Statements worksheet. You can either scroll down to this location, or you can use the Jump to Raw Data Input link at the top of the sheet to jump directly to this location. Then you simply need to paste the data block into this location. After doing this, scroll back up to the top of the sheet to see the standardized financial statements.

A final word of warning: To input data via this method, we recommend that you use an original copy of the *eVal* software (available at www.lundholmandsloan.com) rather than one that you have previously edited. If you have previously manually entered data into a particular workbook's financial statements, you will have overwritten the formulae that refer down to the data block and so the data in the data block will not populate the financial statements.

2.7 IMPORTING DATA FROM A STANDARDIZED DATA PROVIDER

There are a number of providers of standardized data. Unfortunately, these providers routinely make changes to both the agreements under which they distribute data and the format in which they distribute the data. As such, anything we write here could be out of date by the time you get to read it. We therefore provide an updated description of the options available for inputting standardized data on our accompanying website, www.lundholmandsloan.com. Please check there if you would like to input data from a standardized provider.

2.8 MANUAL INPUT OF DATA FOR KOHL'S CORPORATION

The Financial Statements worksheet contained in the default version of *eVal* comes pre-supplied with financial data for Kohl's Corporation and is reproduced in Figure 2.5. Recall that the data in *eVal* is standardized, and so this data has been derived from Kohl's Corporations 10-Ks and conformed to *eVal's* standardized financial statement template. Kohl's 10-K for the year ended January 31, 2010 is provided in a PDF document at www.lundholmandsloan.com. For convenience, we reproduce Kohl's reported income statement and balance sheet from this 10-K in Figure 2.6. By comparing Figures 2.5 and 2.6, you can see how the reported data was translated to *eVal's* standardized financial template.

Recall that to input data manually, the user must enter data in all of the yellow-shaded cells. Before entering a company's financial statement data, you must first enter some background information about the company including its name, exchange ticker, number of shares outstanding and most recent five fiscal year end dates. You can see the associated yellow-shaded cells at the top of *eVal's* financial statements worksheet in Figure 2.5.

The company name is straightforward and is listed on the front of the 10-K and at the top of each of its financial statements. In this case it is Kohl's Corporation. If you are wondering who Mr. or Ms. Kohl is, he is the now deceased

FIGURE 2.6
Kohl's Income Statement and Balance Sheet for the Year Ended 1/31/2010 from Form 10-K

KOHL'S CORPORATION CONSOLIDATED STATEMENTS OF INCOME (In Millions, Except Per Share Data)			
	2009	**2008**	**2007**
Net sales	$17,178	$16,389	$16,474
Cost of merchandise sold (exclusive of depreciation shown separately below)	10,680	10,334	10,460
Gross margin	6,498	6,055	6,014
Operating expenses:			
Selling, general, and administrative	4,144	3,936	3,697
Depreciation and amortization	590	541	452
Preopening expenses	52	42	61
Operating income	1,712	1,536	1,804
Other expense (income):			
Interest expense	134	132	82
Interest income	(10)	(21)	(20)
Income before income taxes	1,588	1,425	1,742
Provision for income taxes	597	540	658
Net income	$ 991	$ 885	$ 1,084
Net income per share:			
Basic	$ 3.25	$ 2.89	$ 3.41
Diluted	$ 3.23	$ 2.89	$ 3.39

See accompanying Notes to Consolidated Financial Statements

FIGURE 2.6
(*Continued*)

KOHL'S CORPORATION CONSOLIDATED BALANCE SHEETS (Dollars In Millions, Except Per Share Data)		
	January 30, 2010	January 31, 2009
ASSETS		
Current assets:		
Cash and cash equivalents	$ 2,267	$ 643
Merchandise inventories	2,923	2,799
Deferred income taxes	73	74
Other	222	212
Total current assets	5,485	3,728
Property and equipment, net	7,018	6,984
Long-term investments	321	333
Favorable lease rights, net	204	201
Other assets	132	117
Total assets	$ 13,160	$ 11,363
LIABILITIES AND SHAREHOLDERS' EQUITY		
Current liabilities:		
Accounts payable	$ 1,188	$ 881
Accrued liabilities	1,002	841
Income taxes payable	184	105
Current portion of capital leases	16	17
Total current liabilities	2,390	1,844
Long-term debt and capital leases	2,052	2,053
Deferred income taxes	377	320
Other long-term liabilities	488	407
Shareholders' equity:		

Common stock—$0.01 per value, 800 million
   shares authorized, 353 million and
   351 million shares issued
	4	4

Paid-in capital	2,085	1,971
Treasury stock, at cost, 46 million shares	(2,639)	(2,638)
Accumulated other comprehensive loss	(36)	(46)
Retained earnings	8,439	7,448
Total shareholders' equity	7,853	6,739
Total liabilities and shareholders' equity	$ 13,160	$ 11,363

See accompanying Notes to Consolidated Financial Statements

Max Kohl, who opened the first Kohl's supermarket back in 1946. The exchange ticker symbol is a little trickier. The SEC requires companies to list their exchange ticker(s) in Item 5 of the 10-K. You may recall that Item 5 contains information relating to the principal market on which the company's common stock is traded. You will find Item 5 on page 17 of Kohl's 10-K, where it explains that Kohl's trades on the New York Stock Exchange under the symbol KSS (note that the terms ticker, symbol and ticker symbol are used interchangeably). So we enter KSS in the cell immediately to the right of the company name.

The next piece of required data is the Common Shares Outstanding (in 000s at the most recent fiscal year end). The most straightforward place to find this information is the common equity section of the company's balance sheet on the 10-K. Figure 2.6 contains Kohl's balance sheet and information on common equity is reported near the bottom. Note that the amounts listed in the columns to the right of the balance sheet are the dollar amounts for the par value of common stock. These dollar amounts are NOT what we are after here. Instead, we want the actual number of physical shares outstanding, which is reported in the descriptions on the left of the balance sheet. You need to know a couple of tricks here. First, we want the number shares outstanding and NOT the number of shares that are authorized or the number of shares that are issued. What are the differences? Well, to be issued, a share must first have been authorized and to be outstanding a share must have been issued and not repurchased by the company as Treasury Stock. So we need to determine the number of issued shares and then subtract the number of shares held in treasury to arrive at the number of outstanding shares. In Kohl's case, the 10-K balance sheet lists "353 million and 351 million shares issued" (right next to the line item Common stock). 353 presumably refers to the number of shares issued at Jan 30, 2010, while 351 must refer to the number issued at January 31, 2009, so we want the former number. The balance sheet also lists "Treasury stock, at cost, 46 million shares." So the number of shares outstanding at January 30, 2010 is 307 million (353 million issued, less 46 million in treasury equal 307 million outstanding). We therefore enter "307,000" next to Common Shares Outstanding in *eVal*'s Financial Statements worksheet (remember that we enter amounts in 000s in *eVal*). At this point you may be concerned that the number of shares outstanding today may differ from the number of shares outstanding at the most recent fiscal year end. For example, the firm may have done a stock split or a stock repurchase since the most recent fiscal year end. But don't worry about this issue for now, as we will deal with it later.

Our next data input task is to enter the fiscal year ends for the most recent five years. You will find these dates at the top of the company's balance sheets on the 10-K. Note that a company only reports the most recent two years balance sheets in each 10-K, so you will have to access the most recent four years worth of 10-Ks to get the most recent five fiscal years. Like many retailers, Kohl's fiscal year closes at the end of January. We list the dates in yyyy/mm/dd format, with the earliest year on the left and the most recent year on the right.

We are now ready to start entering financial statement data, beginning with the income statement. We will concentrate on the fiscal year ended 2010/1/31, which is in the rightmost column of Figure 2.5. The income statement in Kohl's 10-K refers to this year as 2009 (see Figure 2.6). This income statement reports Net sales of $17,178 and Cost of merchandise sold of $10,680. These line items are transferred to the corresponding Sales (Net) and Cost of Goods Sold line items in *eVal*. There are several formatting issues to note here. First,

Kohl's 10-K lists the most recent fiscal year on the left, while *eVal* lists it on the right. Second, the amounts reported in Kohl's 10-K are in $millions, while the amounts in *eVal* are in $thousands, hence the amounts in *eVal* are multiplied by a factor of 1,000. Third, Cost of Goods Sold is entered as a negative amount in *eVal,* since it is an expense that causes Net Income to be lower.

The next reported line item in Kohl's income statement is Gross margin, which is simply the difference between Net sales and Cost of merchandise sold. This amount does not have to be input in *eVal,* since it can be computed by summing the first two line items. You can see this amount is listed in *eVal* as Gross Profit. You can use this line item to check that you entered the previous two line items correctly.

The next line item in the reported income statement is Selling, general, and administrative in the amount of $4,144. This amount is transferred to the SG&A Expense line item in *eVal.* There is an apparent inconsistency here, because the amount listed for this line item in *eVal* is (4,196,000). This inconsistency is resolved by noting that two lines further down Kohl's reported income statement is a line item called Preopening expenses in the amount of $52. Since there is no separate line item for preopening expense in *eVal's* standardized financial statements, this amount has been included in SG&A Expense ($4,144 + $52 = $4,196). Why do you think Kohl's chose to report preopening expense separately? It is probably because it is driven by new stores that are not yet generating sales. Hence, it is really an investment in the future rather than a current period expense. But accounting rules call for it to be expensed as incurred. Thus, Kohl's is reporting it separately from other expenses to make it easier for investors to appreciate the unusual nature of this expense. Between SG&A and preopening expense is Depreciation and Amortization in the amount of $590. This amount is transferred to the line item of the same name in *eVal.*

Note that around this point in the income statement, *eVal* lists two subtotals: EBITDA (which stands for earnings before interest, taxes, depreciation and amortization) and EBIT (which stands for earnings before interest and taxes). Both are common measures of income from operations, and we will talk more about them in Chapters 4 and 5. The income statement in Kohl's 10-K lists just one of these subtotals, Operating income, which corresponds to EBIT in *eVal.*

Next up is interest expense. This is listed as 134 in the 10-K and input as (134,000) next to the line item of the same name in *eVal.* Kohl's also lists interest income of (10). There is no corresponding line item for interest income in *eVal.* Instead, there is a catch all line item titled Non-operating income (loss). We input the interest income here in the amount of 10,000. Note that we enter it as a positive amount in *eVal* because interest income causes net income to go up. It is listed as a negative amount in Kohl's 10-K because they categorize it as an expense, when it is really income, so they treat it as a negative expense (do you ever get the sense that accountants are just messing with you?). This gets us to our next subtotal, which Kohl's 10-K refers to as Income before taxes and *eVal* refers to as EBT (which stands for earnings before taxes).

The final income statement item that we need to input is taxes. Kohl's 10-K lists a provision for income taxes of 597. We therefore input (597,000) next to Income Taxes in *eVal*. We have now input all the available income statement data for Kohl's. The standardized financial statements in *eVal* also have line items available for Other Income, Ext. Items and Disc. Ops. (which stands for extraordinary items and discontinued operations), Minority Interest in Earnings and Preferred Dividends. These line items are not applicable for Kohl's, and so we must input 0 next to each of these line items. The final amount for Net income on Kohl's 10-K is 991, while the corresponding amount in *eVal* is 991,000. We have successfully input Kohl's income statement.

Next up is the balance sheet. The first line item in the balance sheet on Kohl's 10-K is Cash and cash equivalents of 2,267 (yes, that is over $2 billion!). This is input in *eVal* as 2,267,000 next to the line item Cash and Market. Sec. (which stands for cash and marketable securities). The next line item is Merchandise inventories of 2,923, which is input as 2,923,000 next to the line item Inventories in *eVal*. Note that *eVal*'s balance sheet also has a line item for Receivables, but Kohl's does not separately report receivables, so we must input a 0 in *eVal* for Receivables. The remaining current assets on the 10-K are Deferred income taxes of 73 and Other of 222. *eVal*'s standardized balance sheet contains just one additional current asset line item, Other current assets, so we input 295,000 in *eVal* to reflect these final two current assets.

Moving on to noncurrent assets, the 10-K reports Property and equipment net of 7,018, which is input as 7,018,000 next to the line item PP&E (net) in *eVal*. This is followed by Long-term investments of 321, which are input as 321,000 next to Investment in *eVal*. Next is Favorable lease rights, net of 204. This is a type of intangible asset and so is input into *eVal* as 204,000 as Intangibles. The last asset category on the 10-K is Other assets in the amount of 132, which is input as 132,000 as Other Assets in *eVal*.

The next balance sheet category is liabilities, all of which map quite straightforwardly into the corresponding line items in *eVal*. Note that the line item Current portion of capital leases is a form of financing, and so it is input next to the line item Current debt in *eVal*. The final balance sheet category is shareholders' equity, which is trickier. First, note that Kohl's has no minority interest or preferred stock, so these line items are input as 0 in *eVal*. Second, Kohl's reports Common stock-$0.01 par value of 4, Paid in capital of 2,085 and Treasury stock of (2,639). These amounts are combined in *eVal*, and input as (550,000) next to the line item Paid in Common Capital (Net). Third, Kohl's reports Accumulated other comprehensive loss of (36) and Retained earnings of 8,439. These amounts are combined in *eVal* and input as 8,403,000 next to the line item Retained Earnings.

We have now completed the input of the income statement and balance sheet. The final piece of data we need to input is the amount of cash dividends declared on the common stock. You will find this amount in the Statement of Changes in Shareholders' Equity (see page F-5 in Kohl's 10-K) as part of the reconciliation of changes to the Retained Earnings account. In Kohl's case, there is no indication that any dividends were paid. If any dividends were declared, they would have to be listed here, so we simply set the amount of common dividends to 0.

2.9 CASES, LINKS, AND REFERENCES

Cases

- Building *eVal* (Part A)
- Create Your Own Standardized Data: A simple exercise that we encourage you try right now is to manually enter a single year's worth of data from the financial statements of a company of your choice into *eVal*'s standardized Financial Statements worksheet. What choices did you have to make? What type of information is evident in the original financial statements, but obscured by the standardization process? After doing this, you can also compare your standardization choices to those made by one of the data providers. For example, you can use the link to Yahoo! Finance below to enter a company ticker and navigate to the standardized financial statements. What did they do differently from you? Where they did things differently from you, who do you think made the best choices and why?

Links

The links referred to throughout this chapter are provided below, along with a brief description of the type of information that can be found. These links, along with the information that they provide, can change over time. Moreover, new and better sources of information become available. We therefore maintain an updated set of links at our website, www.lundholmandsloan.com.

Links to Company Information

- The Security and Exchange Commission:
  Home page: www.sec.gov
  Search for company filings:
  www.sec.gov/edgar/searchedgar/companysearch.html
  Description of SEC forms: www.sec.gov/info/edgar/forms/edgform.pdf
- Yahoo! Finance
  Home page: http://finance.yahoo.com/
  Company Index: http://biz.yahoo.com/i/

Links to Macroeconomic Information

- The Government Printing Office Federal Digital System
  Home page: http://www.gpo.gov/fdsys/
  Economic Indicators:
  www.gpo.gov/fdsys/browse/collection.action?collectionCode=ECONI

Code of Federal Regulations:
www.gpo.gov/fdsys/browse/collectionCfr.action?collectionCode=CFR

- Briefing.com
  Home page: www.briefing.com
  Calendar: http://www.briefing.com/investor/calendars/economic/
- Dismal Scientist
  Home page: http://www.economy.com/dismal/

Links to Industry Information

- Fidelity
  Home page: www.fidelity.com
  Links to company profiles:
  http://eresearch.fidelity.com/eresearch/landing.jhtml
- Polson Enterprises Industry Links
  How to Research an Industry:
  http://www.virtualpet.com/industry/howto/search.htm
  Links to Industry Portals:
  http://www.virtualpet.com/industry/mfg/mfg.htm
- Hoovers
  Home Page: www.hoovers.com
  Industry Overviews:
  www.hoovers.com/hooversdirectories/industryIndex-1.html

CHAPTER THREE

Understanding the Business

3.1 INTRODUCTION

After collecting the wealth of data described in Chapter 2, your next task is to weave it together in a meaningful way. Your goal is to develop a thorough knowledge of the macroeconomic environment, the industry structure, and the operations and strategies of the particular business you are studying. We encourage you to adopt a top-down approach. First, you should consider the general macroeconomic conditions. This will help you understand how the current economic climate affects the performance of each of the industries in which the business operates. Next, you should consider each of the industries in which the business operates. Most professional analysts concentrate on just one or two industries, and they know these industries like the back of their hand. So, if you are going to produce work of similar quality, you also will need to develop a thorough knowledge of each industry. The final stage is a detailed analysis of the operations and strategies of the business. What is the supposed source of competitive advantage in each of the industries in which the company operates, and what are the synergies between the different segments? We briefly review each of these steps below and refer you to the appropriate texts for a more detailed treatment.

Before devoting the next month to pouring over macroeconomic data and reading strategy textbooks, we also encourage you to use a healthy dose of economic intuition and common sense in your analysis. Macroeconomic and industry factors are only useful if you can draw a link between them and the particular firm you are studying. Also, the strategy literature has seen many fads over time—remember the "new economy"? Don't just join the herd and assume that any firm that pours resources into implementing the latest fad will have stellar growth and staggering profitability for the foreseeable future. Your goal at this stage is to develop a working understanding of the business you are studying and how it fits into the larger economy.

3.2 MACROECONOMIC ANALYSIS

A top-down approach to understanding a business must start with the global economy. Most domestic businesses have direct exposure to the global economy through their product markets, input markets, or foreign operations. Even businesses without direct exposure to global markets are increasingly sensitive to global factors as the world economy becomes more integrated. You need to understand the state of the global economy and the consensus among experts about where it is headed. You also should be aware of the state of the individual domestic economies that your business is exposed to and their individual sensitivities to the global economy. In particular, you should be aware of the expected economic growth rates, political risks, and currency risks in each of the domestic economies in which the firm operates. These factors can vary widely across countries. For example, expected growth is relatively low in large, mature markets such as North America and Europe. Expected growth rates are much higher in emerging markets, such as Asia and South America, but these economies often have the greatest political risks and currency risks.

Armed with a basic understanding of the global economic environment, you should next focus on the domestic economy. For many firms, operations and customers are concentrated in their home country and, consequently, the domestic economy is where you should begin your analysis. The overall state of the domestic economy and its future prospects can be summarized by a few key economic statistics. We review these below for the United States, but every government reports similar statistics.

Gross Domestic Product

Gross domestic product (GDP) is the most widely used measure of macroeconomic performance. It measures the market value of final goods and services produced domestically. Figures for GDP are released quarterly by the Commerce Department. These figures are typically expressed in real (i.e., inflation-adjusted) terms as an annualized quarter-to-quarter percentage change, which is referred to as the real GDP growth rate. The overall rate at which the economy is growing is an important determinant of the rate at which many businesses can grow, explaining why the GDP growth rate is such a closely watched statistic. Over the last 40 years, the real GDP growth rate has averaged about 3 to 4 percent in the United States, reaching highs of over 10 percent and lows of less than −5 percent. The most commonly used definition of an economic recession is two consecutive quarters of negative real GDP growth. Economists carefully monitor many leading indicators of GDP growth in an attempt to predict its future movements. Common leading indicators include unemployment insurance claims, consumer spending, consumer confidence, business orders, business productivity, and housing and construction activity.

Interest Rates

Interest rates reflect the cost of borrowing money and affect business performance in two important ways. First, interest rates determine the price that a firm must pay for its own capital. Other things equal, lower interest rates mean less interest expense and higher profits. Low interest rates also reduce the cost of capital, increasing the number of viable investment opportunities. For consumers, low interest rates also reduce the cost of current consumption relative to future consumption. For example, you have a greater incentive to buy a new car today if the cost of borrowing declines. A decline in interest rates tends to spur consumer spending, thereby increasing sales growth for many businesses. It is important to note that it is *changes* in interest rates that cause changes in consumer spending. If interest rates are low today, but have been low for many years, then consumers are not going to suddenly rush out today to increase their current consumption. However, if interest rates have been running at high levels in recent years and suddenly drop to more moderate levels, we will see an increase in consumption as the relative cost of current versus future consumption has just dropped. Interest rates reflect not only the cost of current versus future consumption, but also expectations concerning inflation and credit risk. We can abstract from the credit risk portion of interest by examining the interest rate on low-credit-risk borrowings such as the federal funds rate or the yields on the bills, notes, and bonds issued by the U.S. Treasury. Over the past 40 years, nominal (i.e., not inflation-adjusted) interest rates on low-risk borrowings have ranged from less than 2 percent to over 15 percent, with an average of about 7 percent.

Inflation

Inflation is defined as a general rise in price levels. Inflation creates the gap between real and nominal economic effects. In times of high inflation, businesses will generally find that they are better off in nominal terms because they are selling their goods for higher prices. But if those incoming dollars buy fewer goods and services, the businesses may actually be worse off in real terms. Armed with the inflation rate, it is possible to restate nominal dollars into real dollars and get a clearer picture of economic performance. Inflation has other more pernicious effects. In times of high and uncertain inflation, the risk from investing in financial assets increases and the credibility of the domestic currency is undermined in global financial markets. Faced with such risk, investors will take their capital to countries without such uncertainty or invest directly in commodities such as gold that provide a hedge against inflation. The inflation rate is most commonly measured using the rate of change in the Consumer Price Index (CPI), published monthly by the Bureau of Labor Statistics. The CPI measures the price of a basket of goods bought by a typical U.S. consumer. Over the past 40 years, the annual rate of inflation, as measured by changes in the CPI, has ranged from less than 0 percent to over 12 percent, and has averaged around 4 percent.

Foreign Exchange Rates

Foreign exchange rates describe how many units of one currency can be bought with a unit of another currency. Many of the inputs bought and outputs sold by domestic businesses are in transactions with foreign entities. As the relative value of the U.S. dollar rises, the cost of foreign inputs decreases and the revenue from foreign sales decreases. Thus, the impact of foreign exchange rate fluctuations on a business depends not only on whether exchange rates go up or down, but also on whether the firm is a net buyer or seller of goods and services denominated in a particular currency. Foreign exchange rates are driven by a complex variety of factors, including the relative productivity of capital and labor, relative inflation rates, and relative real interest rates.

Oil Prices and Other Key Commodity Prices

Commodity prices affect the costs of all businesses. The most important commodity price at the macro level is the price of oil. Oil is critical to the successful functioning of an industrialized economy. Oil prices tend to be volatile, due to the concentration of a large proportion of the world's oil reserves in a small number of countries. Increases in oil prices lead to increases in transportation and energy costs that affect nearly all businesses. Increases in oil prices also reduce the amount of income that consumers have to spend on other products. Other important commodity prices include natural gas and various metals. Obviously, different industries have different key commodity inputs: The price of steel is important for the auto industry and the price of palladium is important for the semiconductor industry. Make sure you identify the commodities that are important to the industry that you are studying.

Aside from the economic indicators above, other important factors to consider in your macroeconomic analysis are corporate hedging activities and the business cycle.

Hedging

A firm can effectively hedge its exposure to interest rates, foreign exchange rates, and most commodity prices. Consequently, two firms in the exact same business may have completely different exposures to these factors. For instance, one gold-mining firm may sell its entire production forward, so that its economic profits are unaffected by changes in gold prices, while another firm may not, so that its profits are tied closely to the price of gold. Similarly, financial institutions can alter their interest rate exposure by entering into various interest rate derivative contracts. Firms can also create natural hedges by the way they structure their business. For instance, a firm anticipating a large increase in receivables denominated in a foreign currency can arrange its operations in such a way that it also has a large increase in payables denominated in the same currency. The currency gains or losses on receivables will offset the gains or losses on the payables. The point is that, even if a firm's underlying business is exposed to changes in interest rates, foreign exchange rates, or commodity prices, you won't know its net exposure until you understand its real and financial hedging activities. Recall from Chapter 2 that Item 7A of Form 10-K requires disclosure of exposures to macroeconomic risks. This is the best place to learn about a company's net exposure to interest rate, currency, and commodity risks.

The Business Cycle

The *business cycle* is an important concept for understanding the current state and future prospects of the domestic economy. Historically, domestic economies have exhibited systematic periods of expansion (characterized by high GDP growth, low unemployment, and high consumer confidence) and contraction (characterized by low GDP growth, high unemployment, and low consumer confidence). While there is no guarantee that these cycles will continue, many macroeconomists believe that these cycles are a permanent feature of the economy. Hence, you should have a good sense of the current state of the business cycle as well as when and how it is most likely to change. The profitability of some sectors is much more sensitive to movements in the business cycle than others, as we will discuss below.

A Realistic Goal for Macroeconomic Analysis

If you set out to become an expert in all the factors that influence the global and domestic economies, you may never get to the point of analyzing your particular firm. Your goal should be to understand the general consensus about major macroeconomic factors. You don't need to develop your own independent forecasts of future GDP or interest rate movements, but you should understand what the experts are saying about these factors and how they might influence your firm's performance in the future.

3.3   INDUSTRY ANALYSIS

Before studying the detailed operations and strategies of an individual firm, it is first important to think about the industry that the firm resides in. Professional analysts tend to specialize in particular economic sectors and industries to achieve efficiencies in business analysis. Industry analysis has three primary objectives:

1. To understand the sensitivity of the industry to key macroeconomic factors.
2. To understand how the industry operates and the key performance metrics for evaluating these operations.
3. To understand the competitive structure of the industry.

We discuss each of these objectives in more detail below.

Sensitivity to Macroeconomic Factors

Recall from Chapter 2 that economic sectors represent groups of industries that have similar exposures to key macroeconomic factors. Figure 3.1 provides an overview of the sensitivities of each economic sector to three key macroeconomic factors: the GDP growth rate, interest rates, and oil prices.

The GDP growth rate is a key driver of profitability for all sectors of the economy. However, some sectors are much more sensitive to the GDP growth rate than others. For example, the materials, consumer goods, industrials, and information technology sectors all have high sensitivity to the GDP growth rate. Many of the industries in these sectors have high operating leverage (i.e., relatively high fixed costs), so small movements in economic activity have big impacts on profitability.

Increases in interest rates tend to have a negative effect on the profitability of all sectors, but some sectors are affected more than others. The industrials and information technology sectors are particularly sensitive to the reductions in corporate capital expenditures that accompany increased interest rates. The financial sector also suffers from the reduced borrowing activity associated with higher interest rates.

Increases in oil prices also tend to have a negative effect on the profitability of nearly all sectors. The one obvious exception is the energy sector, which consists largely of companies involved in the exploration, production, transportation, refining, and marketing of oil.

Industry Operation and Key Industry Ratios and Statistics

Firms in the same industry generally produce similar goods and services using similar production technologies. You should begin your industry analysis by

FIGURE 3.1
Sensitivity of Sector Profitability to Key Macroeconomic Factors

Sector	Macroeconomic Factor		
	GDP	**Interest Rate**	**Oil Price**
Energy	+ +	−	+ +
Materials	+ +	− −	− −
Industrials	+ +	− −	− −
Consumer Discretionary	+ +	− −	−
Consumer Staples	+	−	−
Health Care	+	−	−
Financials	+	− −	−
Information Technology	+ +	− −	−
Telecommunication	+	− −	−
Utilities	+	−	− −

Key: + + = strong positive relation; + = positive relation; − = negative relation; − − = strong negative relation.

figuring out how the industry operates. This involves finding the answers to questions such as: What is the nature of the production process that takes place in the industry? What are the key inputs in the production process? What is the nature of the marketing and distribution process? Is service after the sale a significant factor?

Once you understand how the industry operates, you should identify the key ratios and statistics that capture the financial health of the industry and firms within the industry. The particular metrics vary widely based on the nature of the industry's operations. In the oil production industry, for example, key statistics include oil prices, the current demand for oil, crude oil and petroleum inventories, oil refinery capacity utilization rates, and oil services equipment utilization rates. In contrast, in the semiconductor industry, key ratios and statistics include the semiconductor industry monthly global sales report, the semiconductor equipment book-to-bill ratio, wafer fabrication plant utilization rates, the purchasing managers' index, and business capital spending.

Competitive Structure of the Industry

Your study of the industry should include an assessment of the intensity of industry competition. As a benchmark, recall the old microeconomic concept of perfect competition. In a perfectly competitive market, there are many firms using the same production technology and facing the same input and output prices. In equilibrium, just enough firms enter the market to ensure that the equilibrium price provides a "normal" return on the invested capital to all firms in the market. In such a market, valuation is easy. In expectation, each firm simply generates a normal return on its invested capital. Thus, if we know the magnitude of the invested capital and the normal rate of return, we simply multiply the two together to forecast the expected profit. Indeed, this is exactly the logic that is applied to securities markets by efficient market theorists: In an efficient market, each investor is simply expected to earn a normal return on his or her investment. However, it is generally accepted that there are inefficiencies in the market for real assets. Firms in certain industries have been known to generate abnormally high returns for extended periods of time. For example, Coke and Pepsi have both sustained high profitability over prolonged periods, and they do so selling sugared water (with a touch of addictive caffeine)! When studying the industry, you should look for characteristics that might allow firms to generate abnormal profits over a prolonged period of time.

Famed strategist Michael Porter highlights five forces that determine the degree of competition in an industry:

1. Rivalry among existing firms
2. Threat of new entrants
3. Availability of substitute products

4. Bargaining power with suppliers
5. Bargaining power with customers

The first three forces relate to sources of direct competition. Let's apply these three forces to the restaurant industry, focusing particularly on chains of fast-food restaurants. Clearly there is intense rivalry among existing firms—next to every McDonald's is a Burger King, with Wendy's, Taco Bell, and Subway just around the corner. Similarly, new entrants face relatively low barriers to entry; patents are not available for food items, capital expenditures are relatively minor, and franchisees can help fund investment. The competitive pressure from substitute products depends entirely on how narrowly you define the industry. Customers of fast-food restaurants could switch to full-service restaurants at reasonably low cost. However, if the industry is more broadly defined as "restaurants," then the substitute product is cooking food at home. The switching costs here are somewhat higher, insofar as this requires a significant lifestyle change on the part of customers. Putting the three forces together, one would have to conclude that the fast-food restaurant industry is highly competitive, possibly even approaching the textbook definition of perfect competition.

The final two forces in Porter's framework relate to a company's relative bargaining position with its suppliers and customers. Both suppliers and customers can alter input and output prices in order to extract a firm's profits if they have a bargaining advantage. Consider the desperate situation of a small firm in the automotive parts industry, one that manufactures plastic parts. A few large corporations control the market for the raw plastic pellets that are used as inputs, leaving little room to negotiate a better price on the input side. And on the output side, the situation is even worse. The automotive firms have many alternative sources for plastic parts. They enjoy so much power over their suppliers that they occasionally give themselves price concessions on existing contracts. Without even consulting the supplier, they simply pay less than the full amount on their accounts payable, expecting that the supplier will either acquiesce or lose all business in the future.

As you analyze the industry, remember that less competition means that abnormal levels of industry profitability are easier to sustain. Of course, we also should remember that various regulatory bodies are charged with preventing business practices that restrain competition. In the United States, the Federal Trade Commission's Bureau of Competition and the U.S. Department of Justice's Antitrust Division are the pertinent regulatory bodies.

3.4 THE FIRM'S STRATEGY

Firm profitability is not solely a function of industry profitability. For example, McDonald's has been able to generate consistently high profits while operating in the highly competitive restaurant industry. What explains this anomaly? Strategists would say that McDonald's has developed a strategy for creating and sustaining competitive advantage. Strategy textbooks attempt to identify and categorize such winning strategies. Three common categories are cost leadership, product differentiation, and focus. A cost leadership strategy aims for low production costs and thin margins, with profits coming from a high volume as customers are attracted by the low price. Walmart successfully implemented such a strategy in the variety retail industry. Product differentiation is achieved by producing a product with unique attributes that are valued by buyers who will pay a premium price, resulting in higher profits. Revlon pioneered this strategy in the cosmetics industry. Finally, the idea behind focus is to develop a niche strategy that supplies one segment of the market with exactly what they want, be it low cost or a differentiated product. Apple successfully implemented such a strategy in the PC industry.

In evaluating a company's strategy, the most important point to keep in mind is that it is extremely difficult to sustain a competitive advantage. Each of the generic strategies described above will be difficult to sustain in the long run. A cost leadership strategy is vulnerable to imitation and to shifts in technologies that lead to new, lower-cost production methods. A differentiation strategy also is subject to imitation. Moreover, differentiation strategies are often short-lived fads. For example, the specialty retail and apparel industries are characterized by many differentiated brands that go in and out of style over time—in the market for denim jeans, Antik Denim is out and Rock & Republic is in, at least as of this writing. Finally, a focus strategy is subject to imitation and the risk that changes in market conditions will make the targeted segment nonviable.

The best source for information concerning a firm's strategy for achieving competitive advantage is the first section of a firm's 10-K filing with the Securities and Exchange Commission. This section must provide a description of the registrant's business. The applicable securities laws require the description of business to include:

> "Competitive conditions in the business involved including, where material, the identity of the particular markets in which the registrant competes, an estimate of the number of competitors and the registrant's competitive position, if known or reasonably available to the registrant. Separate consideration shall be given to the principal products or services or classes of products or services of the segment, if any. Generally, the names of competitors need not be disclosed. The registrant may include such names, unless in the particular case the effect of including the names would be misleading. Where, however, the registrant knows or has reason to know that one or a small number of competitors is dominant in the industry it shall be identified. The principal methods of competition (e.g., price, service, warranty, or product performance) shall be identified, and positive and negative factors pertaining to the competitive position of the registrant, to the extent that they exist, shall be explained if known or reasonably available to the registrant."

[Extracted from SEC Regulation S-K, Item 101(c)(1)(x)]

Thus, management is required to give its best shot at describing both the degree of industry competition and the firm's own perceived source of competitive advantage in Item 1 of the 10-K. However, you should always take management's ravings about their sources of competitive advantage with a grain of salt. Simply admitting that the firm doesn't really have any competitive advantage would probably not sit well with investors, so management will typically spin some sort of yarn. Your job is to check that the alleged source of competitive advantage is plausible and delivers superior financial performance.

Finally, you should remember that there are two elements of a successful strategy—profitability and growth. Profitability is essential. Unless a business is profitable enough to provide a competitive return on invested capital, it cannot justify its existence. Assuming that a business is profitable, growth becomes the multiplier that allows a strong return on capital to be converted into lots of dollars of profit. So your analysis of a business strategy should include both the profitability of the business and the growth potential of the business. You should also remember that while most managers would like to grow their businesses, growth generally results in declining profitability. Basic economics tells us that demand curves usually slope downward, so increasing supply leads to a reduction in price. Also, a strategy that is successful in one market may be difficult to replicate in another market. A classic example is Home Depot's attempt to replicate its do-it-yourself home improvement superstores in Mexico. The market for do-it-yourself home improvement was more limited in Mexico due to the smaller size of the Mexican middle class, making the business much less profitable.

Synergy Analysis

Not all firms operate a single business in a single industry. Corporate synergy analysis focuses on how firms can generate abnormal profits by bringing two or more businesses under the same corporate umbrella. Theories abound in this area. Synergies are created by leveraging proprietary assets, eliminating transaction costs, eliminating redundant overhead, increasing market power, or any number of other activities. The important point to remember here is that the free market is a very good disciplining mechanism, but it is eliminated when activities are brought inside a single firm. For instance, it could be that synergy is created when a sawmill company acquires a timber company, or it could be that the timber segment no longer harvests trees efficiently, because it no longer has to sell logs on the open market—the sawmill segment simply takes their timber as an input. Without the discipline of competing in an open market, the timber segment may respond to inefficient transfer prices or simply get lazy. Empire-building managers are often quick to identify the benefits of mergers but fail to appreciate the costs that can result from coordination and control issues that surface once market discipline is removed.

3.5   UNDERSTANDING KOHL'S BUSINESS

We will wrap up this chapter by applying what we have learned to Kohl's business. We will be focusing on the early months of 2010, around the time that Kohl's issued its 10-K for the 2009 fiscal year. Recall that Kohl's operates a chain of over 1,000 family-oriented department stores in 49 states. We will begin by studying the macroeconomic environment facing Kohl's in early 2010. Next, we will examine the key characteristics of the industry in which Kohl's operates. Finally, we will analyze Kohl's strategy within that industry.

The first quarter of 2010 marked the continuation of a slow economic recovery in the United States.[1] The annualized GDP growth rate had climbed from a low of –6.8 percent in the fourth quarter of 2008 to 3.7 percent by the first quarter of 2010. Unemployment had stabilized at around 10 percent, interest rates were at historically low levels and inflation was running at a tame 2 percent. This environment was driving a slow rebound in consumer confidence and retail activity. The consumer confidence index had climbed from a low of 27 in early 2009 to 59 by early 2010, but was still way short of 2007 levels of around 110. Retail sales were also improving from 2009 levels but were still down from their 2008 highs. The general consensus was that consumer spending would continue its slow climb to pre-recession levels, with more affluent consumers driving this climb.

Within the retail industry, sales were rebounding, and this rebound was particularly evident at high-end department stores. A *Standard & Poor's* survey of the retail industry described the situation as follows:

> "Although the broader economy remains weak, the business environment for department stores is stable, in our view. On a year-over-year basis, we noted improved store traffic trends, reduced discounting, and lower clearance levels, which we attribute to department stores having inventories in line with reduced demand, and to middle- and upper-income shoppers releasing pent-up demand and responding favorably to improved value propositions and fashion newness."[2]

Overall, our macroeconomic analysis points to a slow economic recovery that should lead to slow growth in retail sales, with high-end outlets showing stronger growth.

Next, we turn to our industry analysis. Kohl's is assigned a GICS code of 25503010. We can break this down using the complete GICS system that is listed in Appendix A. The first two digits, 25, refer to the economic sector Consumer Discretionary. The next two digits, 50, refer to the industry group Retailing. The next digits, 30, refer to the industry Multi-Line Retail. The

---

[1] The macroeconomic data discussed here is extracted from the *Standard & Poor's* publication "Industry Surveys: Trends and Projections" dated May 2010.

[2] Extracted from "Industry Surveys—Retailing: General," *Standard & Poor's*, May 27, 2010.

final two digits, 10, refer to the sub-industry Department Stores. Other large players in this GIC code include Macy's, Nordstrom, JCPenney, and Sears. Retail outlets offering a full assortment of general merchandise and extensive customer service characterize this industry

We begin our industry analysis by applying Porter's five forces to understand the competitive structure of the industry. Competition among existing firms is clearly intense in this industry. The big department store chains each have a presence in every major population center in the United States. When you jump in your car to go shopping, you probably have the choice of going to several department stores all within short driving distance of each other. Threat of new entry is limited by the economies associated with operating a department store chain. Centralized sourcing of merchandise, distribution and marketing all create economies of scale. Nevertheless, we should remember that Kohl's itself is a relative newcomer to the department store industry and didn't start its national expansion until the mid-1990s. Threat of new entry is therefore a longer-term threat if existing firms become inefficient or collusive. Competition from substitutes is intense. You may already have noticed that several of Kohl's major competitors have not been mentioned, including Target and Walmart. This is because the GICS system classifies such firms as General Merchandise stores since they also sell groceries. But they are clearly direct competitors for Kohl's. Other substitutes include specialty apparel retail outlets, such as The Gap and discount retailers such as Ross Stores. When we consider the totality of retail outlets selling similar products to Kohl's, competition is clearly intense. With respect to its bargaining position with customers and suppliers, Kohl's size puts it in a strong position. It sources its products from a variety of vendors, each accounting for less than 5 percent of net purchases. It sells its products to millions of relatively small customers, each simply paying the ticketed price at checkout.

Before analyzing Kohl's business strategy in detail, it is useful to summarize some of the key sources of competitive advantage in the department store industry. The basic business model in this industry involves sourcing product from manufacturers and wholesalers and reselling it at a markup to retail customers. Key sources of competitive advantage include:

1. *Product differentiation.* Successful product differentiation allows a company to sell its products at higher margins than its competitors. Important sources of product differentiation in the department stores include offering exclusive brand names and fashions, superior service, superior product range, and fostering customer loyalty.

2. *Cost leadership.* Successful cost leadership allows a company to offer lower prices than competitors and generate higher profits through higher turnover. Important sources of cost leadership in department stores revolve around maintaining a low-cost structure through an efficient store format, lean staffing levels, sophisticated information systems, and centralized buying, advertising, and distribution.

As you have probably realized, these two sources of competitive advantage involve a delicate trade-off. For example, providing superior customer service involves higher staffing levels. Companies in this industry therefore have to identify a strategy that strikes a trade-off between these sources and is sufficiently unique to woo customers from competitors.

Turning now to Kohl's Item 1 in their 10-K we read that:

> "We operate family-oriented department stores that sell moderately priced apparel, footwear and accessories for women, men and children; soft home products such as sheets and pillows; and housewares."

As you can see, Kohl's positions itself as a cost leader, though product differentiation also features in Kohl's strategy:

> "Our stores feature quality private and exclusive brands which are found 'Only at Kohl's' as well as national brands."

Kohl's also strives to do all this with the minimum frills:

> "An important aspect of our pricing strategy and overall profitability is a culture focused on maintaining a low cost structure. Critical elements of this low-cost structure are our unique store format, lean staffing levels, sophisticated management information systems and operating efficiencies which are the result of centralized buying, advertising and distribution."

Kohl's strives to attract fashion-conscious customers. In doing so, Kohl's differentiates itself from low-end retailers such as Walmart and discount retailers such as Ross Stores. At the same time, Kohl's has a strong focus on value pricing and maintaining a no-frills low-cost structure. This enables Kohl's to offer cheaper pricing than higher-end competitors such as Macy's or Nordstrom, and specialty retailers such as The Gap. Thus, Kohl's strikes a delicate balance between product differentiation and cost leadership, appealing to cost-conscious customers who are also interested in shopping for the latest fashions. Unfortunately, Kohl's also faces some fairly direct competition in this space, with Target being an obvious example.

The most delicate part of Kohl's strategy is continuing to sufficiently differentiate its product. Consumer tastes are fickle, and if Kohl's is perceived to have similar products to Walmart, it is unlikely to successfully compete with Walmart on the basis of a low cost structure alone. For this reason, it is crucially important that Kohl's continues to invest in developing and maintaining exclusive brands and appealing fashions. Failure to do so will result in eroding margins and obsolete inventory. We will talk more about how to detect these financial warning signs in Chapter 5. But the diligent analyst should also seek out information on the perceived attractiveness of Kohl's brands and fashions. Store traffic, same store sales and unseasonal sales are all potentially important sources of information.

Another important element of Kohl's strategy is its expansion plans. As we will discuss later in the book, the key to generating lots of value from a profitable strategy is growth. One store can only generate so much value. But by opening additional stores, new value is created as long as the stores are sufficiently profitable. If the new stores are as successful as the old stores and don't cannibalize the sales of the old stores, then the growth in value will be proportional to the number of stores opened. But most businesses run out of growth opportunities at some point, causing the value created by growth to decline or even turn negative. This is known to economists as "diminishing marginal returns to investment" and is discussed further in Chapter 8.

Kohl's discusses its expansion plans on page 5 of the 10-K:

> "Our expansion plans have been, and will continue to be, designed to achieve profitable growth. At the time of our initial public offering in 1992, we had 79 stores in the Midwest. As of year-end 2009, we operated 1,058 stores in 49 states and in every large and intermediate sized market in the United States. As a result of economic conditions throughout the United States, our store growth in 2009 was slower than in prior years."

As you can see, Kohl's has grown dramatically over the last 18 years, but is now on the verge of saturating all of its major markets in the United States. Thus, moving forward, growth will be more challenging for Kohl's. It must either expand domestically and run the risk of cannibalizing its existing stores or expand internationally and run the risk that its strategy won't be as profitable in foreign countries. Thus, Kohl's ability to create value through additional growth is questionable at this point. Kohl's limited growth opportunities also pose another interesting dilemma. It has historically invested its free cash flow into growing its store base. But as growth opportunities slow, Kohl's cash balance has been rising. Kohl's must now decide whether to keep hoarding cash, to invest it in something else, or to return it to stockholders. We will explore this issue in more detail in Chapter 6.

3.6 CONCLUSION

When you first examined the *eVal* software you were probably hoping that it would take all the hard work out of equity analysis and valuation. If so, you were sorely wrong. There is no substitute for a thorough understanding of the business underlying the equity security. Anyone who tries to convince you that you can accurately value a business by extrapolating past trends or applying fixed multiples to key historical financial statement variables is wrong. But the good news is that many investors do seem to use such simple rules to value equity securities. If enough of these investors trade using these simple rules, then they will have an impact on price. Armed with a thorough understanding of the underlying business, you will be in a position to determine when these simple rules give the wrong answer and take advantage of any associated security mispricing.

But there is still plenty of work to do before you are ready to value a firm. We still need to talk about how to use the financial statements to evaluate the effectiveness of the firm's strategy and how to develop good forecasts of the future financial statements. These forecasts are the ultimate drivers of your valuation. We turn to these tasks in the remaining chapters.

3.7 CASES, LINKS, AND REFERENCES

Cases

- Apple and the iFad (Questions 1–3)
- Boston Chicken, Inc. (Questions 1–3)
- Netflix, Inc. (Questions 1 and 2)
- Overstock.com (Questions 1 and 2)
- Sirius Satellite Radio? (Questions 1–3)

References

Further Readings in Macroeconomics

- *Principles of Macroeconomics,* by N. Gregory Mankiw (2008), is a good standard text on macroeconomics.

Further Readings in Strategy

- *Competitive Strategy,* by Michael Porter (1998), is a landmark book in the strategy literature. It lays out Porter's five forces for industry analysis and his three generic strategies for achieving competitive advantage.
- *Gaining and Sustaining Competitive Advantage,* by Jay Barney (2010), covers the basics of business strategy.

CHAPTER FOUR

Accounting Analysis

4.1 INTRODUCTION

Traditional valuation texts are usually very good at telling you how to value a business assuming that you already know the future cash flows. But, in practice, forecasting these cash flows is the most important and difficult task in conducting a valuation. Moreover, past cash flows are rarely a good indicator of either past performance or future cash flows. For example, successful growth firms often generate negative cash flows as they invest in their future business activities. The problem with cash flows is that they measure the distribution of value rather than the creation of value. For this reason, financial statements, prepared in accordance with generally accepted accounting principles (GAAP), have evolved to provide more useful information about value creation in a business. These statements provide a "language" for evaluating a firm's past performance and forecasting its future performance. It is the language that is spoken by the financial community, and it is the language that we will use throughout the valuation exercise.

At this point, you may ask yourself, "If accountants already measure value creation, what is left for the rest of us to do?" It turns out that financial statements are not designed to value a company. Instead, the financial statements are intended to provide information that is useful in helping others to conduct their own valuation. Since we are the "others" who actually get to do the valuation, we must understand three aspects of accounting information:

1. What information do financial statements provide?
2. How does this information help in valuation?
3. What are the key limitations of this information?

The purpose of this chapter is to address these questions.

We begin by reviewing the conceptual underpinnings of accounting. Our objective is not to teach you accounting. In fact, we assume that you already have a working knowledge of basic accounting principles. Instead, our objective is to discuss the nature of the information provided in the financial statements and how this information relates to firm value. We also discuss the limitations of financial statement information, including the potential for managerial manipulation.

4.2   THE UNDERPINNINGS OF ACCOUNTING

Although we assume you already know basic accounting principles, we fear that you may have lost the forest among the trees. So let's review the basics. The building blocks of accounting are assets and liabilities. Assets represent future benefits and liabilities represent future obligations. Accountants periodically identify and assign dollar values to a firm's assets and liabilities. The difference between the value of the assets and the value of the liabilities represents the accountants' value of the equity in the firm that belongs to the owners. The owners' equity is also referred to as the *net assets* or *book value* of the firm. This relation, rearranged and given as an equation, is

$$\text{Assets} = \text{Liabilities} + \text{Owners' Equity}$$

At the end of each accounting period, accountants prepare a *balance sheet* or *statement of financial position* listing and valuing the firm's assets and liabilities. Because this accounting equation must always hold, the balance sheet must always balance (hence its clever name!). The balance sheet and its relation to the other financial statements are illustrated in Figure 4.1.

If accountants were to recognize all assets and liabilities and record each item on the balance sheet at its fair market value, then the value of equity on the balance sheet would equal the fair market value of the firm. But accountants are adamant about the fact that they are not measuring the fair

FIGURE 4.1
Overview of Basic Building Blocks of Accounting

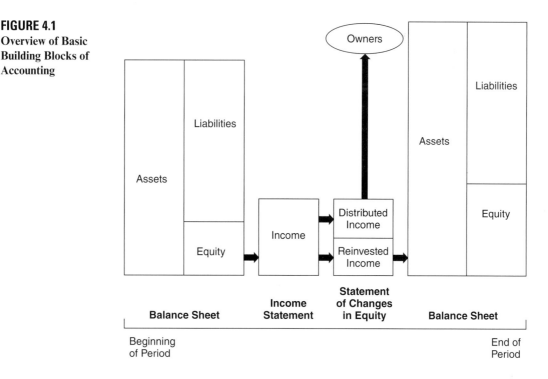

market value of every asset and liability, so the resulting value of equity is not a measure of the equity's fair market value. Instead, accountants ignore many future benefits and obligations altogether and value others at amounts having little connection with their fair market value. Why do accountants employ rules that result in incorrect valuations? It turns out that once we move away from simple examples such as bank accounts or lemonade stands, it would be impossible to reliably measure the fair market value of many assets and liabilities. The accountant may know the value of some equipment immediately after the company purchases it, but what about halfway through its useful life? And how should our humble accountant deal with the fact that the equipment will produce goods whose value is partially determined by the success of the firm's advertising campaign? In deciding what information to provide, accountants trade off relevance with reliability. We all want to know the present value of the cash flows associated with a firm's business activities. This would be very relevant information. But any attempt to measure this value would be highly subjective, and therefore quite unreliable. The historical acquisition costs of operating assets, on the other hand, can be measured reliably. Accountants view their role as providing the capital markets with reliable information, while leaving the forecasting of the unreliable but highly relevant stuff to us.

Given the limitations inherent in accounting, the primary role of accounting analysis is to determine which benefits and obligations have been ignored in the financial statements and which have been recognized but incorrectly valued. We start with the accounting rules governing the recognition and measurement of assets and liabilities. But before we start, we need to acknowledge that different countries have different accounting rules. For instance, the United States has its own Generally Accepted Accounting Principles, or U.S. GAAP, while Canada and most of Europe use International Financial Reporting Standards, or IFRS. Fortunately, for the purposes of this chapter, the distinction is not important. But because we know it best, our examples will come for U.S. GAAP.

Assets

Accountants define assets as probable future economic benefits obtained or controlled by a firm as a result of past transactions or events. This rather dry definition imposes two important hurdles for a future economic benefit to be recognized as an asset. First, the future benefit must be *probable*. Accountants have developed a long list of attributes to help determine whether a benefit is sufficiently probable to make it into the financial statements. Important examples of future benefits that are *not* deemed to be probable include those associated with most research and development and marketing activities. Second, the future benefits must have resulted from past transactions or events. The most important manifestation of this hurdle is that future benefits associated with selling goods and services cannot be recognized until the sale has actually been consummated (the realization principle). So future benefits associated with anticipated future sales revenues are not recognized. It is virtually certain that General Electric will generate millions of dollars' worth of sales during the next few years, but the accounting system does not recognize the value of these future transactions. And many start-up pharmaceutical companies have zero current sales (because they have not yet marketed their first drug) but are valued by the stock market as being worth millions of dollars. The market is valuing cash flows from anticipated future sales. Accountants ignore such future benefits.

So what future benefits are the accountants willing to recognize? There are three broad types of assets. First, there are cash and cash equivalents, which are valued quite simply at their face value. Second, there are amounts of cash owed to the firm as a result of past transactions or events (e.g., trade receivables and loans). These monetary receivables are generally valued using the net present value of the expected future payments. Third, there are future benefits acquired by the firm as part of a past transaction or event (e.g., marketable securities, inventory, property, acquired intangibles). If the acquired future benefits are financial assets, such as marketable securities, they are generally valued using their observed market value. If the acquired future benefits are nonfinancial assets, such as a truck or a building, they are generally valued at historical cost, adjusted downward to the extent that the anticipated future benefits have either been used up or impaired.

Overall, accountants do a good job at recognizing and valuing future benefits associated with financial resources but do a poor job at recognizing and valuing future benefits associated with operating resources. Accountants only recognize a subset of the future benefits associated with operating resources and they usually value these benefits based on what they cost rather than on the value of the cash flow streams they are expected to generate.

Liabilities

Liabilities are defined as the opposite of assets. Liabilities are probable future sacrifices of economic benefits arising from present obligations as a result of past transactions or events. The recognition hurdles imposed on liabilities correspond closely to those imposed on assets. The future sacrifices must be *probable*. Important examples of future sacrifices that are usually *not* deemed probable include the expected costs associated with unsettled litigation and third-party loan guarantees. The future sacrifices also must arise from present obligations as a result of past transactions or events. For example, we may have contracted with employees to purchase their services in the future. But we are not obliged to recognize a liability for the promised future payments until such time as we receive the promised services. Most liabilities are monetary in nature and are valued based on the present value of the promised payments. Obligations to provide future goods and services to customers represent an important exception and are valued based on the price paid by the customer to receive the future goods/services. While this sounds like a simple valuation rule, things can get tricky. For example, assume that a software company sells a software program bundled with a contract to service the software. The accountant must decide how to divide the selling price between the software program and the future service obligation. The latter is recognized as a liability on the balance sheet until the service envisioned by the contract has been provided.

Changes in Equity

Recall that equity is equal to the difference between assets and liabilities, so we don't need a separate set of recognition and measurement rules to determine the book value of equity. But it is useful to distinguish between two broad reasons why a firm's equity changes over time. One reason is that the owners of the firm can contribute new assets to the firm (e.g., equity issuances) or withdraw existing assets from the firm (e.g., dividends). Such transactions are recorded in the *statement of changes in equity*. The other reason is that the firm's business operations inevitably lead to changes in assets and liabilities. This is the miracle of value creation (or, in the case of negative net changes, the misfortune of value destruction). Through this second source of change, assets and liabilities not only provide the building blocks for the balance sheet, but also for the *income statement*. While the balance sheet lists the assets and liabilities of a firm at a point in time, the income statement measures changes in these assets and liabilities over a period of time. But it is important to remember that the income statement only reports changes in assets and liabilities resulting from the firm's business operations, and not those resulting from investing and financing transactions. Recalling that equity equals assets less liabilities, periodic income is the "plug" in the following equation:

$$\text{Ending Equity} = \text{Beginning Equity} + \text{Income} - \text{Net Distributions to Equity Holders}$$

and rearranging gives

$$\text{Income} = \text{Change in Equity} + \text{Net Distributions to Equity Holders}$$

This relation is known as the *clean surplus relation*—change in equity on the balance sheet plus distributions to equity holders represent income that is generated by the firm for its equity holders. The change in equity component of income is often referred to as *reinvested income* or *retained earnings,* while the distributions to equity holders' component of income is often referred to as *distributed income*. Intuitively, the income statement measures the net benefits generated by the firm's business operations over a period of time. And it does this using the same restrictive definitions of future benefits (i.e., assets) and future obligations (i.e., liabilities) as the balance sheet. Figure 4.1 illustrates the relation between the balance sheet, the income statement, and the statement of changes in equity.

FIGURE 4.2
Classification of Components of Income

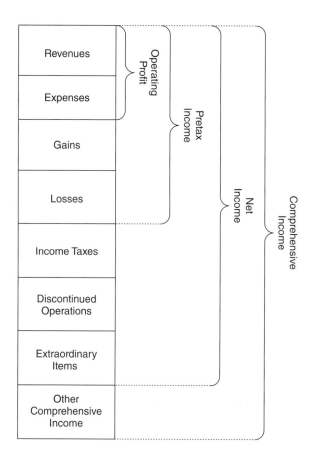

Armed with the balance sheet from the beginning of the period, the balance sheet from the end of the period, and the amount of net distributions to/from owners during the period, it is a simple matter to compute income. So what is the incremental role of the income statement? The real information in the income statement isn't just the bottom line; rather, it is the classification of the various changes in assets and liabilities into different components of income. The income statement provides insights into how the firm's business operations generated changes in assets and liabilities over the course of the period. The key components of the income statement are illustrated in Figure 4.2. Each of these components has a different definition that facilitates the interpretation of past performance and forecasting of future performance. We describe each component in more detail below.

Revenues

Revenues are defined as increases in assets or reductions in liabilities that arise from the provision of the goods and services in the course of a firm's operating activities. For the most part, revenues are simply the proceeds received by the firm in return for providing goods and services. Note that the goods and services sold must be part of the firm's intended operating activities. If a firm that is in the business of operating restaurants sells an entire restaurant, the proceeds from the sale will not be recorded as part of revenue, because the firm's intended operating activity is operating rather than selling restaurants. Instead, they will be reported as part of the gain or loss on the sale of the restaurant (more on this below).

A central question in accounting for revenues is establishing exactly when the revenues are earned. In what period do the associated assets increase in value? The general revenue recognition rule is called the *realization principle* and states that revenue is recognized when an exchange transaction has taken place, the earnings process is substantially complete, and collection of the proceeds is reasonably assured. While this sounds very reasonable, it clearly leaves room for interpretation. Consider a company that purchases land, does some minor improvements, subdivides it, and then sells plots to customers who pay 10 percent of the selling price and sign a 10-year mortgage for the balance. Is the selling price recognized as revenue when the firm purchases the land, when it finishes the minor improvements, when a customer pays the initial 10 percent, or when the customer pays off the mortgage? In most situations, the accounting rule is easy: Revenue is recognized when a sale is made and the customer takes possession of the goods. But even this seemingly simple rule has received its share of abuse, as we discuss later.

Sales transactions are the key driver of most other activities in a firm. Once a sale transaction occurs and revenues are recognized, the accounting rules attempt to measure the assets that are consumed in generating these revenues. Revenue recognition is the kick-off event for the measurement of income and, because of this, plays a central role in ratio analysis and forecasting.

Expenses

Expenses are defined as the mirror image of revenues: They are decreases in assets or increases in liabilities that arise from the provision of goods and services in the course of a firm's operating activities. As with revenues, the costs must be associated with the firm's intended operating activities. For example, the carrying value of a restaurant that is sold by a restaurant operating company would not be an expense (see discussion on gains and losses below).

Wherever possible, expense recognition rules attempt to match the consumption of specific assets to the production of specific revenues, but these rules frequently have to resort to ad hoc allocations of costs. For example, we might all agree that the cost of the raw materials used to produce finished goods should be matched against the revenue generated by the sale of the goods. But exactly how much property, plant, and equipment was consumed to convert the raw materials into finished goods? How much of the corporate Learjet was consumed in the production of the goods? What about the cost of deferred compensation to the sales force? What about interest on the money that was borrowed to purchase the equipment that was used to convert the raw materials into finished goods? There are a myriad of principles to provide guidance in this respect, but they can lead to poor matching and are also prone to manipulation, so you need to do your homework.

Operating Profit

The difference between a firm's revenues and expenses represents the profit associated with the firm's ongoing operating activities. This amount is often referred to as the *operating income* or *operating profit* of the firm and is the primary driver of firm value. If a firm can't generate a respectable operating profit, then it probably won't be around for very long.

An important role for the income statement is in distinguishing operating profit from the myriad of other, largely nonrecurring transactions and events that cause assets and liabilities to change. Revenues and expenses are intended to capture the financial consequences of a firm's ongoing operating activities. The remaining bits and pieces of income are discussed below. But just because an item is classified as revenue or expense does not rule out the possibility that it may be nonrecurring. Even the ongoing operations of a company are subject to nonrecurring demand and supply shocks. And it is not uncommon for companies to generate recurring sources of nonoperating income from investments they have made in other companies. Recall from Chapter 2 that the management discussion and analysis provided in Forms 10-K and 10-Q is required to identify any potentially nonrecurring components of revenue and expense. As you study a firm's income statement, think carefully about the extent to which each item is likely to be recurring.

Gains

Gains are increases in the net assets of a firm that occur in the normal course of business and contribute to the earnings of a firm but are incidental or peripheral to the firm's operating activities. Returning to our previous example of the restaurant-operating firm that sells an entire restaurant, if the proceeds from the sale exceed the carrying value of the restaurant sold, then we would report a gain. Since we are not in the business of selling restaurants, the proceeds and costs associated with the sale are not classified as revenues and expenses. Instead, they are netted and recorded as a gain in the income statement. By separating gains from revenues and expenses, we can discriminate between profitability that is directly associated with the firm's ongoing business operations and profitability that is due to incidental transactions and events. This distinction is very useful from a forecasting perspective, because these incidental transactions and events are much more likely to be one-off occurrences. Common examples of gains include proceeds from the sale of assets, awards from winning a lawsuit, and certain increases in the value of marketable securities.

Losses

Losses are decreases in the net assets of a firm that occur in the normal course of business and reduce the earnings of a firm but are incidental or peripheral to the firm's operating activities. If our restaurant-operating firm sells an entire restaurant and the proceeds from the sale are less than the carrying value of the restaurant sold, then we would report a loss. As with gains, losses are likely to be one-off occurrences, so it is useful to distinguish them from revenues and expenses. Transactions and events resulting in losses include asset disposals, legal settlements, asset impairments, and restructuring charges. The interest expense associated with debt financing is also included in this category.

As shown in Figure 4.2, revenues, expenses, gains, and losses combine to produce a firm's *pre-tax income*. All of the categories discussed thus far are presented on a pre-tax basis. Thus, the next step shown in Figure 4.2 is to deduct the applicable income taxes.

Other Items

There are a few other oddities on the income statement that are zero for most firms most of the time. Most of these items are nonrecurring. If a firm sells a major division or segment of its business, any operating income, gains, or losses related to that segment must be reported separately on the income statement as Discontinued Operations on an after-tax basis. There is also a separate line item reserved for extraordinary gains and losses. To be extraordinary, gains and losses must be both unusual in nature and infrequent in occurrence. However, U.S. GAAP define these terms so narrowly that even business losses associated with the September 11 terrorist attacks were not deemed to be extraordinary. So what can be put here? Gains and losses associated with natural catastrophes are allowed, so long as the natural catastrophes are sufficiently infrequent. For example, hurricane damage in Florida would not count, but hurricane damage in Idaho probably would. As shown in Figure 4.2, revenues, expenses, gains, losses, discontinued operations, and extraordinary items combine to produce a firm's net income. Net income measures the performance of the firm for the period, and includes all components of periodic performance, regardless of whether they are expected to recur.

Net income is the traditional *bottom line*. However, if the company has preferred stock, then any dividends declared on the preferred stock are deducted from net income to arrive at net income available to common stock. Similarly, if the company owns more than half but less than all of a subsidiary, then the claims of the non-controlling interests (also called the minority interests) are deducted from net income. The final result, net income available to common shareholders, is the real bottom line from a common shareholder's point of view.

The final component of the income statement is other comprehensive income. This component consists of a variety of other changes in equity that accountants could not bring themselves to include in net income. Remember that accounting is a political process, and corporations lobbied to keep the items in this section out of earnings. But because they involve changes in assets and liabilities that cause equity to change, they had to be put somewhere—hence this category. Examples include unrealized gains and losses on marketable securities, foreign currency translation adjustments, and minimum pension liability adjustments. These last adjustments make sure that we preserve the clean surplus relation, written precisely as:

Comprehensive Income Available to Common Equity
 = Change in Common Equity + Net Distributions to Common Equity Holders

On the bottom of the Financial Statements sheet in *eVal,* you will notice a line item titled Clean Surplus Plug (Ignore). We use this item to clean up the company's prior financial statements by putting all the other comprehensive income items here. But because these items are not expected to recur, we force it to be zero in the forecast financial statements. That's why we ask you to ignore the clean surplus plug. In addition, we use the shorthand "Net Income" for "Comprehensive Income Available to Common Equity;" typically, they are the same (or at least very similar) amounts.

4.3   ACCOUNTING INFORMATION AND VALUATION

By now, we should have driven home the point that the financial statements are not intended to yield a final measure of firm value. Instead, they provide information that assists in the determination of value. In this section, we explain why and how accounting information is useful. We'll be kind to accounting in this section, concentrating on the positive ways in which it provides information that facilitates valuation decisions. But accounting information also has many shortcomings, and we will discuss them in the next section.

In most businesses, the accounting system can be thought of as revolving around current and expected future *sales transactions*. The balance sheet measures the cumulative amount that has been invested in the past to generate future sales transactions. The income statement measures the expected benefits associated with sales transactions consummated during the current period. The sales transaction is the critical event that leads to the recognition and measurement of value in the financial statements. A sale triggers the recognition of revenues, representing the net assets created by the sales transaction, and expenses, representing the net assets used to generate the sales transaction. The difference between these revenues and expenses is recorded as operating profit in the income statement.

It is important to note that the operating income resulting from sales transactions during a period rarely coincides with the actual net cash receipts generated by these transactions during the period. The accounting rules that measure changes in assets and liabilities are collectively known as *accrual accounting,* and the differences between accounting income and cash receipts are referred to as the *accruals.* Differences between net income and the net cash receipts arise from changes in noncash assets and liabilities on the balance sheet (i.e., a completely cash-based accounting system would have no noncash assets or liabilities). But, over the long run, net income and cash flows will converge. Accrual accounting just changes the timing of the recognition of cash receipts and payments.

Accountants go to great lengths to make sure that the net assets resulting from a particular sales transaction include all the past and expected future cash consequences of that sales transaction. Some examples should make this clear:

- The expected future cash collections associated with credit sales are usually recognized in revenues in the period that the sales transaction occurs.
- The cash outflows associated with inventory purchases are usually not recognized as expenses until the inventory is sold.
- The cash outflows associated with the purchase of a factory are usually recognized as expenses gradually over the periods in which the factory is expected to generate sales.
- The present value of the expected future cash outflows associated with postretirement benefits earned by workers producing sales in the current period is usually recognized as an expense in the current period.

Although the financial statements do not attempt to measure the expected future cash consequences of future sales transactions, they nevertheless provide a rich source of information to help in forecasting the future cash flows associated with these transactions. Most firms operate in the same lines of business for many accounting periods and their competitive environments change slowly over time. Hence, by measuring the expected net benefits from current sales transactions, the financial statements provide useful information for forecasting the expected net benefits of anticipated future sales transactions. For example:

- Historical balance sheets provide a detailed breakdown of the investment that was required to generate historical sales.
- Historical income statements provide a detailed breakdown of the estimated net benefits of the firm's historical sales.
- The most recent balance sheet accumulates past investment that is expected to generate future sales.

Accounting Information and Value

To develop the link between accounting information and firm value, recall the basic valuation model we introduced in Chapter 1 (and will discuss in more detail in Chapter 10). Equity value V_0 is equal to the net present value of the future net cash distributions made by the firm to its stockholders:

$$\text{Value}_0 = \sum_{t=1}^{\infty} \frac{\text{Distributions to Equity}_t}{(1 + r)^t},$$

where r is the discount rate. Distributions to equity can be derived from the financial statements using the clean surplus relation. Recall from the clean surplus equation in the previous section that net income measures all changes in equity over a period except for Net Distributions to Owners. This gives us

$$\text{Distributions to Equity} = \text{Net Income} - \text{Change in Equity}$$

One important implication of this relation is that we cannot value a firm by simply discounting its net income. We first need to adjust for changes in equity. The intuition for this adjustment is simple. Net income is the result of accrual accounting and so may consist of cash receipts and disbursements relating to past or future periods. So whenever we record net income without an associated distribution to equity, we must also have added assets and/or removed liabilities from the balance sheet. By subtracting changes in equity from net income, we work back to cash distributions to equity. The increase in equity is also what we refer to in Figure 4.1 as *reinvested income*. Thus, if we can forecast the income statement and the beginning and ending balance sheets, we can easily solve for the implied forecast of distributions to equity required by our valuation formula.

By directing us to forecast income statements and balance sheets, accrual accounting organizes the forecasting process into three distinct tasks. First, we forecast future sales. The sales transaction is the trigger for recognizing benefits associated with a firm's ongoing business operations, and so the sales forecast is the starting point for forecasting income statements and balance sheets. Second, we forecast the other income statement components, many of which are driven by the forecasted sales. Third, we forecast the balance sheet components, many of which are driven by the forecasted sales. Each of these tasks is discussed in much greater detail in Chapters 7 and 8. For now, we simply want to emphasize that the past financial statements provide the starting point for forecasting the future financial statements, and the future financial statements are used to value the firm.

4.4   LIMITATIONS OF ACCOUNTING INFORMATION

Unfortunately, our love fest with accounting lasts only a short while. It's time to look at accounting's dark side. In order to think about the limitations of accounting, it is useful to introduce a "perfect accounting" benchmark. This benchmark should reflect what accounting would be like if we could overcome all its limitations. Let's start by considering a bank savings account. In a bank savings account, an initial amount is invested in order to generate a future stream of interest. Over a period of time, interest is earned on the account and contributions or withdrawals may be made from the account. The ending balance in a savings account is equal to the beginning balance plus interest earned less net withdrawals:

Ending Balance = Beginning Balance + Interest − Net Withdrawals

Rearranging gives:

Net Withdrawals = Interest − Increase in Balance

This equation is just the clean surplus relation applied to a savings account. There are a couple of interesting points to note here. Theoretically, you could value this savings account by discounting the expected future net withdrawals, just like our valuation equation tells us. But practically speaking, this is a cumbersome approach. Instead, common sense suggests simply looking at the current balance of the savings account. There are two reasons that this makes sense. First and most obviously, the bank typically stands ready to redeem the account for the amount of the current balance. Second, savings accounts typically offer a "normal" rate of return, which should in turn approximate the discount rate used in our valuation equation. In other words, we can think of a savings account as a zero net present value investment project, and we know that a zero net present value project is simply worth the amount of the initial investment, which in this case is the savings account balance.

The second point to note is that the key summary measure of investment performance for a savings account is the interest rate, computed as:

Interest Rate = Interest/Beginning Balance

Note that interest earned for the period is the numerator. It doesn't make sense to use the amount that was actually withdrawn during the period. Why? Well, the interest earned represents the amount we could theoretically withdraw at the end of the period while still keeping the savings account balance constant at its beginning-of-period level. So this is clearly the incremental amount that we have earned during the period.

At this point it is useful to ask whether a savings account must always be worth its current balance? Intuition suggests that the answer to this question is yes. So long as the bank is able to redeem the account for the amount of the current balance, this will clearly make the current balance the lower bound on the value of the account. But what if we find a savings account that pays a much higher interest rate than the current normal rate of return? It would be foolish to redeem this account for the current balance, suggesting that it must be worth something more than the current balance. In order to value such an account, we would need to use our valuation equation. We have created an example where the interest rate offered by the account exceeds the discount rate (i.e., we have a positive NPV investment). If we choose to redeem the account at its book value today, it will clearly only be worth the current balance. But if we choose to let the account earn this higher interest rate, it will be worth more than its current balance. The assumption of a much higher interest rate is somewhat unrealistic in the case of a savings account, where the rates offered tend to be competitive. We raise it here because a very profitable company is like a savings account offering an above market interest rate. The value of such a company will therefore exceed its book value.

Before we leave our savings account example, let's summarize the key lessons learned:

1. The investment in a savings account is always equal to the current balance of the account. This is because we can always redeem the account for exactly this amount.
2. The economic rate of return offered by a savings account always equals the interest earned for the period divided by the beginning balance. This is because withdrawing the interest earned for the period would leave the amount invested in the account unchanged from the beginning of the period.

The accounting for a savings account is pretty simple. The reason accounting works so well in this case is because we know exactly how much is invested in the account at any point in time. Now we will try to extend the same logic to an equity investment in a real company. Simply replace the savings account balance with the book value of equity and the interest earned with net income. The clean surplus relation given earlier is now written as:

$$\text{Distributions to Equity} = \text{Net Income} - \text{Increase in Equity}$$

Following the same procedure as we did for the savings account, we can also compute the rate of return on the equity investment as:

$$\text{Return on Equity} = \text{Net Income/Beginning Equity}$$

However, the return on equity (ROE) only measures the economic rate of return on the equity investment if the accounting rules correctly measure the amount of the equity investment at any point in time. While such measurements are easy with a savings account, they are almost impossible for an equity investment. We can't simply go and demand that our equity investment be redeemed at its book value. Recall that the book value isn't represented by a cash deposit, but by the net value of all the assets and liabilities recognized and measured under GAAP. For example, if a firm has invested substantial amounts in R&D then its book value will likely be understated because accountants don't allow past R&D investments to be recognized as assets.

To illustrate how ROE is affected by imperfections in accounting measurements, we will introduce some new notation. Suppose that, due to divine intervention, we could create the perfect accounting system. Let *Investment* denote the actual amount of investment and *Economic Income* denote amount of net income under this perfect accounting system. The clean surplus relation for this perfect accounting system would be:

Distributions to Equity = Economic Income − Increase in Investment.

The underlying economic rate of return is given by the Economic Rate of Return (ERR):

Economic Rate of Return = Economic Income/Beginning Investment

Now define ε as the *measurement error* in equity. It is the difference between the book value of equity, as computed by the imperfect accounting system, and the true value of the Investment, computed with our hypothetical perfect accounting system:

$$\varepsilon = \text{Equity} - \text{Investment}$$

Solving for the relation between accounting net income and economic income gives:

Net Income = Distributions to Equity + Increase in Equity

            = Distributions to Equity + Increase in Investment + Increase in ε

            = Economic Income + Increase in ε

So ROE can be expressed as:

ROE = (Economic Income + Increase in ε)/(Beginning Investment + Beginning ε)

Measurement error in equity has a two-pronged effect in distorting ROE relative to the economic rate of return. First, changes in the measurement error between two dates are reflected in the numerator. This is because accounting net income picks up the effects of any changes in the book value of equity between two periods. Second, the level of error at the beginning of the period is reflected in the denominator. The overall distortion in ROE relative to the economic rate of return (ERR) depends on the relative size of the numerator and denominator effects. Possible alternatives are listed in Figure 4.3.

A positive beginning ε causes ROE to be biased toward zero, because the denominator in the ROE calculation is overstated (and vice versa for a negative beginning ε). A positive change in ε causes a positive bias in ROE, because the numerator in the ROE calculation is overstated (and vice versa for a negative change in ε). If the sign of the beginning ε and the change in ε are the same, the two biases work in the opposite direction, and the overall bias in ROE is ambiguous (see the top-left and bottom-right cells of Figure 4.3). In this case, we need to quantify the errors in order to determine the exact nature of the bias.

At this point, you may be thinking that the above analysis is just an abstract exercise in algebra (if not, we suggest that you apply to an accounting Ph.D. program). So let's move from algebra to a simple example with real numbers in which perfect accounting is well-defined. We will then extend the

FIGURE 4.3   The Effects of Accounting Measurement Error (ε) on Beginning Equity, Net Income, and ROE, Along with Associated Accounting Scenarios

	Change in $\varepsilon < 0$ (Net Income Understated)	Change in $\varepsilon = 0$ (Net Income Correct)	Change in $\varepsilon > 0$ (Net Income Overstated)
Beginning $\varepsilon < 0$ (Equity Understated)	Effect Ambiguous Permanently conservative accounting with increasing investment	ROE > ERR Permanently conservative accounting with constant investment	ROE > ERR Reversal of temporarily conservative accounting; Permanently conservative accounting with declining investment
Beginning $\varepsilon = 0$ (Equity Correct)	ROE < ERR Origination of temporarily conservative accounting	ROE = ERR Perfect accounting	ROE > ERR Origination of temporarily aggressive accounting
Beginning $\varepsilon > 0$ (Equity Overstated)	ROE < ERR Reversal of temporarily aggressive accounting; Permanently aggressive accounting with declining investment	ROE < ERR Permanently aggressive accounting with constant investment	Effect ambiguous Permanently aggressive accounting with declining investment

Note: ROE is accounting return on equity (defined as net income divided by beginning equity), ERR is the true economic rate of return, and ε is the measurement error in accounting, defined as the book value of equity minus the true amount of investment.

example to illustrate how we could arrive at each of the scenarios identified in Figure 4.3.

Our simple example considers a firm that engages in business for five periods. In each period, the firm makes an initial investment of $100. This investment generates sales in the next period, and nothing thereafter. The proceeds from these sales are assumed to be collected in cash, and the firm is also assumed to incur additional cash operating costs in generating these sales. Sales are assumed to be 165 percent of the prior period's investment, and operating costs are assumed to be 55 percent of the prior period's investment. These are the only consequences of the investment. Thus, the firm invests $100 in each period in order to generate a net cash inflow of $110 ($165 − $55) in the next period. The economic income on this investment is therefore $110 − $100 = $10 and the economic rate of return is $10/$100 = 10%. We will assume that the firm invests $100 in each of the first four periods, and then ceases to make any further investments in period five and beyond. We also will assume that any surplus cash is immediately distributed to the owners of the firm.

Figure 4.4 presents a basic cash flow analysis for our simple example. Net cash distributions are –$100 in period one. This is the period in which the initial $100 investment is made, but since sales are not generated until the next period, cash sales and cash operating costs are both $0. Thus, in period one,

FIGURE 4.4
Cash Flow Analysis for Simple Example

	Period				
	1	**2**	**3**	**4**	**5**
Investment	100	100	100	100	0
Cash Flows:					
Cash from Sales	0	165	165	165	165
−Cash Operating Expenses	0	−55	−55	−55	−55
−Investment	−100	−100	−100	−100	0
= Net Cash Distributions	−100	10	10	10	110

the owners of the firm must invest $100 in the firm. In periods two through four, net cash distributions to the owners are $10 per period. This represents the excess of the $110 operating cash flows from the period's sales, less the $100 investing outflow to support the next period's sales. Finally, net cash distributions are $110 in period five. Since no new investment is made in period five, all operating cash flows are distributed to the owners. Note that net cash distributions provide an accurate measure of economic income in periods two through four, but are a poor measure of economic income in periods one and five. This is because there is a one-period lag between investing cash flows and operating cash flows. The main objective of accrual accounting is to match investment costs to the benefits that they generate, thus providing a superior measure of periodic performance. We next turn to Figure 4.5 to see how this is accomplished.

Panel A of Figure 4.5 presents the "perfect" accrual accounting scheme that exactly matches the cost of investment to the benefits generated. This accounting scheme perfectly captures the underlying economics of the business. Recall that a $100 investment in a given period generates $110 of cash flows in the subsequent period and is then "used up." The perfect accounting therefore adds an asset of $100 in the period the $100 investment is made, and then removes that asset in the following period. In accounting parlance, we *capitalize* the $100 investment in the period it is made and then expense (i.e., amortize) the asset as it is used up.

Each panel of Figure 4.5 employs a different set of accounting assumptions. The only potential future benefits or obligations in this example are the future benefits generated by the investment expenditure. It provides a future benefit, because it generates positive cash flows in the next period. Therefore, the only accounting issue that we need to consider is the amount of the investment to list on the balance sheet as an asset. In panel A, we employ perfect accounting and so the first row lists capitalized investment costs equal to $100 in each period that a $100 investment is made. The next row lists our accounting for capitalized operating costs. Note that since we assume that operating costs only generate a benefit in the period that they are incurred, none of these costs should be capitalized under a perfect accounting system (we will

FIGURE 4.5
Accounting
Measurement Error
Scenarios

Panel A. Perfect Accounting (All Investment Is Capitalized in all Years)

	Period				
	1	**2**	**3**	**4**	**5**
Accounting Assumptions:					
Capitalized Investment Costs	100	100	100	100	0
+ Capitalized Operating Costs	0	0	0	0	0
Balance Sheet:					
Assets = Equity	100	100	100	100	0
Accruals (Change in Assets)	100	0	0	0	−100
Measurement Error (ε):					
Ending ε	0	0	0	0	0
Change in ε	0	0	0	0	0
Income Statement:					
Sales	0	165	165	165	165
− Operating Expense	0	−55	−55	−55	−55
− Amortization Expense	0	−100	−100	−100	−100
− Investment Expense	0	0	0	0	0
= Operating Income	0	10	10	10	10
Return on Equity:		10.0%	10.0%	10.0%	10.0%

Panel B. Temporarily Aggressive Accounting (Perfect Accounting, Except That 120% of Investment Costs Are Capitalized in Period 3)

	Period				
	1	**2**	**3**	**4**	**5**
Accounting Assumptions:					
Capitalized Investment Costs	100	100	100	100	0
+ Capitalized Operating Costs	0	0	20	0	0
Balance Sheet:					
Assets = Equity	100	100	120	100	0
Accruals (Change in Assets)	100	0	20	−20	−100
Measurement Error (ε):					
Ending ε	0	0	20	0	0
Change in ε	0	0	20	−20	0
Income Statement:					
Sales	0	165	165	165	165
− Operating Expense	0	−55	−35	−55	−55
− Amortization Expense	0	−100	−100	−120	−100
− Investment Expense	0	0	0	0	0
= Operating Income	0	10	30	−10	10
Return on Equity:		10.0%	30.0%	−8.3%	10.0%

(*Continued on next page*)

FIGURE 4.5
Accounting
Measurement Error
Scenarios (*Continued*)

Panel C. Temporarily Conservative Accounting (Perfect Accounting, Except That 80% of Investment Costs Are Capitalized in Period 3)

	Period				
	1	2	3	4	5
Accounting Assumptions:					
Capitalized Investment Costs	100	100	80	100	0
+ Capitalized Operating Costs	0	0	0	0	0
Balance Sheet:					
Assets = Equity	100	100	80	100	0
Accruals (Change in Assets)	100	0	−20	20	−100
Measurement Error (ε):					
Ending ε	0	0	−20	0	0
Change in ε	0	0	−20	20	0
Income Statement:					
Sales	0	165	165	165	165
− Operating Expense	0	−55	−55	−55	−55
− Amortization Expense	0	−100	−100	−80	−100
− Investment Expense	0	0	−20	0	0
= Operating Income	0	10	−10	30	10
Return on Equity:		10.0%	−10.0%	37.5%	10.0%

Panel D. Permanently Aggressive Accounting (Perfect Accounting, Except That 120% of Investment Costs Are Capitalized in All Periods)

	Period				
	1	2	3	4	5
Accounting Assumptions:					
Capitalized Investment Costs	100	100	100	100	0
+ Capitalized Operating Costs	20	20	20	20	0
Balance Sheet:					
Assets = Equity	120	120	120	120	0
Accruals (Change in Assets)	120	0	0	0	−120
Measurement Error (ε):					
Ending ε	20	20	20	20	0
Change in ε	20	0	0	0	−20
Income Statement:					
Sales	0	165	165	165	165
− Operating Expense	20	−35	−35	−35	−55
− Amortization Expense	0	−120	−120	−120	−120
− Investment Expense	0	0	0	0	0
= Operating Income	20	10	10	10	−10
Return on Equity:		8.3%	8.3%	8.3%	−8.3%

FIGURE 4.5
Accounting
Measurement Error
Scenarios (*Continued*)

Panel E. Permanently Conservative Accounting (Perfect Accounting, Except That 120% of Investment Costs Are Capitalized in Periods)

	Period				
	1	**2**	**3**	**4**	**5**
Accounting Assumptions:					
Capitalized Investment Costs	80	80	80	80	0
+ Capitalized Operating Costs	0	0	0	0	0
Balance Sheet:					
Assets = Equity	80	80	80	80	0
Accruals (Change in Assets)	80	0	0	0	−80
Measurement Error (ε):					
Ending ε	−20	−20	−20	−20	0
Change in ε	−20	0	0	0	20
Income Statement:					
Sales	0	165	165	165	165
− Operating Expense	0	−55	−55	−55	−55
− Amortization Expense	0	−80	−80	−80	−80
− Investment Expense	−20	−20	−20	−20	0
= Operating Income	−20	10	10	10	30
Return on Equity:		12.5%	12.5%	12.5%	37.5%

use this row later, when we consider imperfect accounting systems). The next row lists the total assets of the firm, which are simply equal to the sum of the capitalized costs. This is the asset side of the balance sheet for the firm in our simple example. Since the firm has no future obligations, there are no liabilities, and so the liability and equity side of the balance sheet simply consists of an equity account with a balance equal in value to total assets (recall that we plug to equity to make the balance sheet balance).

The next three rows list various diagnostics for our accounting scheme. The first rows list the amount of accounting *accruals*. Recall that accruals are simply equal to the net change in noncash assets on the balance sheet. In our example, they are simply equal to the change in total assets (since we have no cash or liabilities on the balance sheet). Accruals are $100 in period one, $0 in periods two through four, and –$100 in period five. The positive accruals in period one arise because this is the first period we make an investment. The negative accruals in period five arise because this is the period in which we cease making investments. In the intervening periods, the originating accrual of $100 relating to the current period investment is exactly offset by the reversal accrual of –$100 relating to the prior period investment. The next two rows record the measurement error (ε) and the change in the measurement error respectively. We will use these two rows to see how our examples correspond to the scenarios identified in Figure 4.3. Panel A employs perfect accounting, so the amounts in both of these rows are zero in all periods. This corresponds to the center cell in Figure 4.3.

The next set of rows in panel A of Figure 4.5 presents the income statement corresponding to our perfect accounting system. The amounts in the income statement are all zero for period one, since we capitalize all of the period one investment and we don't have any other cash receipts or disbursements in period one (recall that these benefits come one period after the investment is made). In periods two through five, we generate cash receipts from sales of $165 and incur cash expenses of $55 (from our prior period investment). We also amortize 100 percent of the investment that was capitalized in the prior period, resulting in an additional expense of $100. Thus, we have operating income of $10 in each period. This is exactly equal to the economic income generated by our investment. The final row of panel A lists the return on equity, computed as current period operating income divided by prior period equity. The return on equity is 10 percent for periods two through five, which is exactly equal to the economic rate of return on investment. Thus, with perfect accounting, operating income equals economic income and return on equity equals economic rate of return.

Unfortunately, perfect accounting is the exception rather than the rule, so it's now time to consider imperfect accounting. We begin in panel B of Figure 4.5 by engaging in temporarily aggressive accounting. We will do perfect accounting in periods one and two. Then in period three we will do some aggressive accounting. We will then revert back to perfect accounting in periods four and five. The term *aggressive accounting* is applied to the situation where the net assets of the firm are overstated by either overstating assets or understating liabilities. Opportunistic managers can use temporarily aggressive accounting when they would otherwise fall short of important earnings targets, such as meeting bonus plan thresholds or meeting analysts' forecasts. To engage in aggressive accounting in our simple example, we will capitalize some of the operating costs incurred in period three. Recall that these costs all relate to the revenues generated in period three, and so a perfect accounting system should expense them all in period three. For the purposes of this example, we will capitalize an amount of these costs equal to 20 percent of the current period investment. Thus, we will be overstating our assets by 20 percent. The accounting assumptions shown at the top of panel B implement temporarily aggressive accounting by capitalizing $20 of operating costs in period three. This causes the period three balance sheet to be overstated by $20, showing total assets and equity of $120. The period three ε is therefore $20, and the change in ε for period three is $20 (since ε is zero in period two). This puts us in the center-right cell of Figure 4.3. Moving down to the income statement, operating expenses are understated by $20, causing operating income to be overstated by $20. This overstatement in operating income causes return on equity to be 30 percent, overstating the true economic rate of return by 20 percent. Note that even though we return to perfect accounting in period four, operating income and return on equity understate their "perfect" levels in period four. This is because we have to amortize an extra $20 worth of capitalized operating costs in period four. The period three ε is $20 and the period four ε is $0, so the period 4 change in ε is –$20. This puts us in the bottom-left cell of Figure 4.3. Since the numerator of return on equity is understated and the denominator is overstated, ROE must be understated. Note that the reversal of the aggressive accounting occurs in period four because we assume that the firm reverts to perfect accounting in this period. Thus, temporarily aggressive accounting has two consequences. First, it causes operating income and ROE to be overstated in the period in which the aggressive accounting originates. Second, it causes operating income and ROE to be understated in the period in which it reverses.

Although temporarily aggressive accounting must eventually reverse, in practice it may take more than one period for the reversal to occur. In panel B, we could have assumed that the firm capitalized another $20 of operating costs in period four, which would have delayed the reversal of the aggressive accounting to period five. Temporarily aggressive accounting is the most common type of accounting manipulation that occurs in practice. In fact, our example resembles the well-known accounting debacle at WorldCom. Managers at WorldCom capitalized almost $10 billion of operating costs in PP&E during 1999 and 2000, only to have it all reverse in 2001, precipitating WorldCom's bankruptcy.

Panel C of Figure 4.5 illustrates temporarily conservative accounting, which is just the flipside of temporarily aggressive accounting. The term *conservative accounting* is applied to the situation where the net assets of the firm are understated by either understating assets or overstating liabilities. Opportunistic managers can use temporarily conservative accounting to temporarily avoid regulatory scrutiny for excess profits or to create "cookie jar" reserves that can be used to boost future profitability. To engage in conservative accounting in our simple example, we immediately expense some of the current period investment. For the purposes of this example, we will expense an amount equal to 20 percent of the current period investment in period three. Thus, we will be understating our period three assets by 20 percent. The accounting assumptions shown at the top of panel C reflect this temporarily conservative accounting, with only $80 of the period three investment being capitalized. The period three balance sheet is understated by $20, showing total assets and equity of only $80. The period three ε is –$20, and the change in ε for period three is –$20. This puts us in the center-left cell of Figure 4.3. Moving down to the income statement, we have an additional investment expense of $20, causing operating income to be understated by $20. The understatement of operating income causes return on equity to be –10 percent, understating the true economic rate of return by 20 percent. We return to perfect accounting in period four, but operating income and return on equity overstate their "perfect" levels in period four. This is because amortization expense is only $80 in period four. The period three ε is –$20 and the period four ε is \$0, so the change in ε is \$20. This puts us in the top-right cell of Figure 4.3. Since the numerator of return on equity is overstated and the denominator is understated, ROE must be overstated. Thus, temporarily conservative accounting causes operating income and ROE to be understated in the period in which it originates and overstated in the period in which it reverses.

So far, we have considered temporarily aggressive/conservative accounting. Can accounting be permanently aggressive/conservative? It is unlikely that management could commit serious violations of GAAP that would never be detected by auditors. It is, however, possible that a company could engage in permanently aggressive or conservative accounting in a manner that is allowed or even required by GAAP. A good example is the GAAP requirement that research and development expenditures be immediately expensed. This accounting principle results in permanently conservative accounting. Examples of permanently aggressive accounting are less common, because GAAP are guided by the *conservatism convention,* which encourages the understatement, but discourages the overstatement, of assets. Nevertheless, managers have been creative over the years in exploiting loopholes in GAAP to structure transactions that receive permanently aggressive accounting. Employee retirement benefits are a good case in point. For many years, firms were not required to recognize a liability for nonpension retirement benefits. The result was an explosion in the use of such benefits to compensate employees. Accounting regulators in the United States finally addressed this GAAP loophole with the release of Statement of Financial Accounting Standard (SFAS) No. 106, which requires these liabilities to be estimated and recognized on the balance sheet. New types of permanently aggressive accounting are likely to be invented by tomorrow's generation of creative managers (no doubt with the eager assistance of their investment bankers and auditors). We will therefore examine the effects of both permanently aggressive and permanently conservative accounting.

Panel D of Figure 4.5 illustrates permanently aggressive accounting. This is achieved by capitalizing operating costs equal to 20 percent of investment in all periods. Consequently, assets and equity are equal to \$120 for all but period five (when investment ceases and both are equal to zero). Accruals are \$120 in period one (when investment commences), –\$120 in period five (when investment ceases), and zero in the intervening periods. Measurement error is 20 in periods one through four and 0 in period five, so the change in measurement error is 20 in period one, –20 in period five, and 0 in the intervening periods. Moving to the income statement, operating expenses are understated by \$20 in the first four periods and amortization expense is overstated by \$20 in the final four periods. The net result is that operating income is overstated by \$20 in period one and understated by \$20 in period five. In periods two through four, the understatement of operating expenses is exactly offset by the overstatement of amortization expense. Note that in every period, the change in measurement error equals exactly the amount by which accruals and operating income misstate their "true" levels from panel A. The final row of panel D lists the return on equity, which is 8.3 percent in periods two through four and –8.3 percent in period five. For periods two through four, the level of the measurement error is $20 and the change in measurement error is 0, so operating income is correctly stated and equity is overstated, resulting in the understatement of ROE. This corresponds to the bottom-center cell of Figure 4.3. For period five, the level of the measurement error from the prior period is still 20, but the change in the measurement error is –$20, putting us in the bottom-left cell of Figure 4.3 and causing an even more severe understatement of ROE.

Finally, panel E of Figure 4.5 illustrates permanently conservative accounting. This is achieved by capitalizing only 80 percent of investment in all periods. Consequently, assets and equity are equal to $80 for all periods except period five (when investment ceases and both are equal to zero). Accruals are $80 in period one (when investment commences), –$80 in period five (when investment ceases), and zero in the intervening periods. Measurement error is –$20 in periods one through 4 and 0 in period 5, so the change in measurement error is –$20 in period one, $20 in period five, and 0 in all of the intervening periods. Moving to the income statement, investment expense is overstated by $20 in the first four periods and amortization expense is understated by $20 in the final four periods. The net result is that operating income is understated by $20 in period one and overstated by $20 in period five. In periods two through four, the overstatement of investment expense is exactly offset by the understatement of amortization expense. The final row of panel E lists the return on equity, which is 12.5 percent in periods two through four and 37.5 percent in period five. For periods two through four, the level of the measurement error is –$20 and the change in measurement error is $0, so operating income is correctly stated and equity is understated, resulting in the overstatement of ROE. This corresponds to the top-center cell of Figure 4.3. For period five, the level of the measurement error from the prior period is still –$20, but the change in the measurement error is $20, putting us in the top-right cell of Figure 4.3 and causing an even more severe overstatement of ROE.

We'll finish this section by summarizing what we've learned about permanently aggressive and permanently conservative accounting. Aggressive accounting always overstates equity ($\varepsilon > 0$), while conservative accounting always understates equity ($\varepsilon < 0$). The effects on operating income are more complex and depend on the rate of growth in investment. Constant investment combines with aggressive and conservative accounting to correctly state operating income (as shown in periods two through four of our examples). Declining investment combines with aggressive (conservative) accounting to understate (overstate) operating income (as shown in period five of our examples). Increasing investment combines with aggressive (conservative) accounting to overstate (understate) operating income (as shown in period one of our examples). Thus, opportunistic managers in growing companies can boost income through the use of permanently aggressive accounting. But doing so also increases equity, resulting in an ambiguous effect on ROE. Figure 4.3 summarizes these effects.

4.5   COMMON SOURCES OF ACCOUNTING MEASUREMENT ERROR

So far, we've talked a lot about accounting theory, enjoyed some fancy algebra, and cooked up some simple examples. Now it is time to get practical and talk about some real world accounting errors. Recall from the accounting equation that equity is the difference between assets and liabilities. So measurement error in equity must arise from measurement error in the underlying assets and liabilities. We can divide the sources of measurement error into three broad categories:

1. Measurement error caused by GAAP.
2. Measurement error caused by lack of perfect foresight in the use of accounting estimates.
3. Measurement error caused by management's intentional manipulation of accounting estimates.

We discuss each of these sources of error in more detail below.

Measurement Error Caused by GAAP

The major source of measurement error introduced by GAAP is in the recognition and valuation of operating assets. Measurement error arises because investments made in operating assets are typically expected to generate uncertain benefits over multiple future periods. Because the timing and amount of these benefits are not known early in the life of an operating asset, measurement error is unavoidable. But worse still, the accounting rules for many types of investments often result in systematic and predictable measurement errors. Recall that GAAP accounting rules trade off relevance and reliability, with reliability often winning the day. Consequently, GAAP often require simple and objective procedures because they can be reliably computed and easily verified. Examples include the immediate expensing of certain investment expenditures and the use of mechanical depreciation and amortization schedules for others. We discuss the biases created by these simple procedures next.

Immediate Expensing of Internally Generated Intangibles

This is an example of an asset that GAAP ignores. Under GAAP, expenditures made on internally developed intangible assets are generally required to be expensed immediately. It is as if these expenditures produce no benefits beyond the accounting period in which they are incurred. Examples include most research and development expenditures, expenditures to develop patents, most advertising expenditures, and most administrative expenditures. Many of these expenditures clearly generate benefits that extend well beyond the period in which they are incurred, but, rather than attempt to estimate the unused amount of these investments, GAAP use the safe and reliable value of zero. So a firm gets to capitalize the cost of constructing a new building, but not the cost of developing a valuable patent. Immediate expensing of internally developed intangibles is a classic example of permanently conservative accounting. This accounting results in systematically negative measurement error in equity (because assets are understated) in all periods during which there has been a past expenditure on internally developed intangible assets that are still expected to generate future benefits.

As with other cases of permanently conservative accounting, the impact of this accounting distortion on net income relative to economic income depends on the growth rate in investment. If the firm is increasing its investments in internally developed intangibles, then immediately expensing the investment lowers net income relative to economic income. If investment is constant, there is no effect on net income. Finally, if investment is decreasing, net income is overstated relative to economic income.

The overall effect on ROE is also ambiguous. The systematic understatement of equity inflates ROE due to the denominator effect (i.e., it puts us in the first row of Figure 4.3). If we are in a period when investment on internally generated intangibles is increasing, income is understated and the numerator and denominator errors move ROE in the same direction, so the overall nature of the bias is ambiguous (i.e., we are in the top-left cell of Figure 4.3). But if we are in a period when investment is decreasing, income is overstated, equity is understated, and ROE is biased upward (i.e., we are in the top-right cell of Figure 4.3). Finally, if we are in steady state, ROE will be overstated (i.e., we are in the top-middle cell of Figure 4.3).

Depreciation and Amortization of Capitalized Operating Assets

Unlike internally developed intangible assets, GAAP generally allow for the capitalization of expenditures on tangible assets (e.g., property, plant, and equipment) and purchased intangibles (e.g., patents). The accounting for such expenditures at their inception is straightforward. Since these expenditures are investments that are expected to generate future benefits, the full amount of the expenditures is initially *capitalized* on the balance sheet as an asset. The difficult part is deciding how to subsequently reduce the value of the asset over the future periods in which it generates benefits. This process is known as *depreciation* for tangible assets and *amortization* for purchased intangible assets. Ideally, the depreciation/amortization method should reflect the flow of expected future benefits generated by the initial investment expenditure. However, implementing such a method would entail subjective forecasts of the future benefits. So GAAP generally sacrifice relevance for reliability, requiring firms to follow a predetermined depreciation schedule, with the most common method being straight-line, whereby the initial value of the asset is reduced in equal increments over the expected life of the asset.

The most common effect of these rules is to understate asset values by depreciating them too quickly. This leads to permanently conservative accounting, resulting in the same biases as for the immediate expensing of expenditures on internally developed intangibles. However, the degree of bias is not as great, because we simply depreciate the asset too quickly rather than expensing the entire asset immediately. One consequence of this is the so-called *old plant trap*. Firms with an old plant that has been almost completely depreciated will have low book values that result in high accounting rates of return. But once the old plant is replaced, book values will increase, causing accounting rates of return to fall. The old plant trap is sprung when investors mistake the high accounting rates of return for firms with old plants for high true economic rates of return.

An important exception to the above rules applies to the case of intangibles that are judged to have "indefinite" lives, with goodwill being the most common example. In such cases, current GAAP requires no amortization, but instead applies a periodic impairment test. We will talk more about asset impairments below. But for now we note that determining the value of such assets is an incredibly subjective process. Consequently, management typically defers impairments until there is clear evidence of a substantial decline in the value of the asset. The net result is that the accounting for intangible assets with indefinite lives often leads to temporarily aggressive accounting. We are left with something of a mismatch, with conservative accounting for many tangible assets and aggressive accounting for many intangible assets.

Asset Impairments

As discussed above, GAAP generally require that nonfinancial assets be carried at their amortized historical cost. This means that the carrying value of the asset represents a fraction of the amount that was originally invested in order to generate future benefits rather than a forecast of the value of the expected future benefits. However, GAAP also contain an important exception to this rule. If it is determined that an asset has been impaired, GAAP require that the asset be restated to fair value. The nature of the impairment tests depends on whether the asset is subject to amortization or falls into the special class of indefinitely lived intangibles that are not subject to amortization. In the former case, an impairment charge must be taken when the sum of the expected *undiscounted* cash flows from the asset is less than its carrying value. In the latter case, an impairment charge must be taken when the *discounted* sum of the expected future cash flows from the asset is less than its carrying value. The stricter test for indefinitely lived intangibles is a half-hearted attempt to counter the aggressive accounting that can result from not requiring such assets to be amortized.

Asset impairments are a manifestation of the aforementioned conservatism convention, and introduce a nasty asymmetry into asset valuations. If an asset's value falls significantly below its carrying value, it gets revalued downward based on its estimated fair value, but if the asset's value significantly exceeds its current carrying value, no upward revaluation is allowed. Hence, we cannot interpret book value as either an estimate of past investment or an estimate of fair value. Rather, it is something of a mongrel, representing a mixture of these two amounts.

From a practical perspective, we need to remember that firms with asset impairments have potentially flawed business models. Corporate managers often encourage investors to focus on net income before asset impairment charges, reasoning that these charges are nonrecurring and are not indicative of future performance. Moreover, while asset impairments often represent the reversal of past aggressive accounting, management often use the opportunity to take "big baths," booking a much larger impairment than is really justified. This is a form of temporarily conservative accounting. By writing down the value of an asset today, equity goes down and future expenses go down, so future income and ROE are overstated (see top-right cell of Figure 4.3). You also should remember that asset impairments are basically an admission by management that they have invested in unprofitable businesses. If asset impairment is recorded every time management makes a bad investment, it stands to reason that income and ROE before impairments will always look good, since they exclude the effects of all the bad investments. However, we should not draw the conclusion that management is doing a good job. We need to look at the aggregate performance of both the good and bad investments to draw overall conclusions about firm performance.

Omission of Contingent Liabilities

We have already discussed the fact that the accounting rules do not allow for the recognition of investments in internally generated intangibles as assets. The reason for this is that the future benefits are deemed to be so uncertain that they cannot be reliably measured. For the same reason, contingent liabilities also are not recognized on the balance sheet. A contingent liability is an expected future obligation that is not sufficiently probable or not reasonably estimable. Two common examples of contingent liabilities are ongoing litigation against a firm and potential environmental cleanup costs. Because liabilities are not recognized, net assets and equity are overstated. This results in permanently aggressive accounting, placing us in the bottom row of Figure 4.3. In the period that a contingent liability arises, measurement error increases, so net income is overstated and the impact on ROE is ambiguous (i.e., we are in the bottom-right cell of Figure 4.3). In subsequent periods, as long as the contingent liability remains contingent, equity will be overstated and there is no effect on net income, so ROE will be understated (we are in the bottom-center cell of Figure 4.3). Manufacturers of tobacco products represent good examples of companies with unrecognized liabilities. These companies have reported high past accounting profits, but these profits most likely overstate the companies' true economic profitability, because they ignore the cost of future litigation stemming from tobacco-related illnesses.

Measurement Error Caused by Lack of Perfect Foresight

The measurement of many assets and liabilities requires the estimation of future amounts. GAAP require that future amounts be measured with some minimum level of reliability before qualifying for recognition in the financial statements. However, this certainly doesn't mean that, just because accountants found the nerve to recognize and measure them, they have little estimation error. In fact, quite the opposite is often true. For example, employee postretirement benefit liabilities require forecasts of health care costs decades into the future. Even if management has made a good-faith estimate, we should recognize that the amount recorded on the balance sheet might differ greatly from the actual future obligations it represents.

If management has done a thorough job at estimating inherently subjective future amounts, then there is probably little that you can do to improve upon their estimates. However, it is very important that you understand the amount of potential estimation error involved in the various assets and liabilities presented on a company's balance sheets. Understanding estimation error is important for at least two reasons. First, the precision of forecasts based on financial statement data is directly related to the precision of the financial statement data themselves. Second, the inherent risk of a business is a direct function of the risk of its underlying assets and liabilities.

Unfortunately, there are only a few broad-brush rules we can give you for establishing the amount of potential measurement error associated with particular classes of assets and liabilities. For example, we can safely tell you that cash and short-term investments have little measurement error. For accounts receivable, however, the amount of potential measurement error can be very small or incredibly large. A bank that lends only to highly creditworthy customers will generally be able to measure its receivables with much less potential error than a firm that makes subprime loans. A detailed understanding of the nature of the assets and liabilities being measured and the techniques used to measure them is required to make a good assessment of the amount of potential measurement error. This can only be accomplished through a careful analysis of the financial statements and their notes.

Measurement Error Caused by Managerial Manipulation

The final source of error in the financial statements is introduced through intentional managerial manipulation (shock and horror!). Given the many estimates that GAAP entail, it is an inevitable fact that some managers will use this discretion to achieve their own short-term objectives. The most common type of managerial manipulation is temporarily aggressive accounting.

This allows management to temporarily boost earnings and ROE. Possible motivations include hitting key bonus thresholds, meeting analysts' earnings forecasts, and creating the illusion of a profitable business for the purpose of raising new capital. Temporarily aggressive accounting can be accomplished by overstating assets or understating liabilities. This results in either the over-statement of revenue (e.g., overstating receivables or understating deferred revenues) or understatement of expenses (e.g., overstating inventory or un-derstating pension liabilities). But temporarily aggressive accounting must ultimately reverse, so this type of *earnings management* is really about shifting income from one period to another.

The key to detecting temporarily aggressive accounting is to pin down the assets and liabilities over which management exercises the most discretion. This typically rules out things like cash, short-term investments, debt, and most payables. GAAP for these items are fairly rigid and there isn't much room for managerial manipulation.[1] As we advised in the previous section, you should devote extra attention to assets and liabilities that require the most estimation. This is where managers are most likely to perpetrate their dastardly deeds. Recall that Item 7 of the 10-K requires management to de-scribe their firm's critical accounting policies. This represents a good starting point for the identification of likely areas for earnings management. But you should not stop here since management is rarely dumb enough to tell you where the earnings management is taking place.

Another important technique in the detection of earnings management is to look for signs of temporarily aggressive accounting. Referring back to panel B of Figure 4.5, we see that accruals are inflated during periods of temporarily aggressive accounting. Therefore, high accruals are a good red flag for aggressive accounting. Unfortunately, high accruals do not always signal temporarily aggressive accounting. Accruals are also high in period one of panel B. This is because "true" investment is increasing in period one. High accruals can represent either the origination of temporarily aggressive accounting or growth in "true" investment. Without a detailed analysis, it is difficult to discriminate between these two determinants of accruals. We'll provide you with guidance on how to conduct a more detailed analysis in Chapters 5 and 6.

We will categorize common earnings management techniques based on how they impact on the income statement. Below, we briefly discuss each cat-egory, identifying the assets and liabilities that are most likely to be involved.

Revenue Manipulation

Revenue manipulation is the most common type of earnings management. The sales transaction is a key trigger for the recognition of future bene-fits under GAAP, so there is no better place to start looking for earnings

---

[1]There have nevertheless been cases where cash and short-term investments have been manipulated. The accounting scandals at Parmalat and Satyam are two such examples.

management. The asset most commonly involved in revenue manipulation is accounts receivable. A cash payment from a customer is a pretty good indication that the customer is committed to the transaction (although the revenue may still not have been earned—more on this below). However, when the customer has not yet paid, the balance lives in the accounts receivable, and there is greater uncertainty about whether the payment will be made. The customer may not be committed to the transaction, may not have the ability to make the contracted payment, or may not even know that the company recorded a transaction.

A common form of revenue manipulation is *trade loading* or *channel stuffing*, whereby product is shipped to a customer before the customer really needs it. This type of activity is most prevalent at the end of a reporting period. Management is effectively stealing from next period's sales in order to inflate this period's sales. Another form of revenue manipulation overstates the value of the net receivables by understating the allowance for uncollectible accounts. It is easy to increase the volume of sales transactions by granting more generous credit terms or by selling on credit to customers with lower credit quality. However, the cost of increasing sales in this way is the increased amount of expected uncollectible accounts. If accounts receivable is not adjusted downwards to reflect the increased expected uncollectibles, then accounts receivable, revenue, and earnings will all be overstated.

A variety of ratio analysis techniques can be used to identify firms that are potentially overstating revenue and accounts receivable, and we discuss them in Chapters 5 and 6. However, it is important to analyze these ratios in the context of the firm's business strategy and accounting policies. There have been examples of firms that have made strategic choices to loosen their credit terms that have paid off nicely. While unusually high receivables are an important red flag, they are not a definitive indicator of revenue manipulation.

Accounts receivable is not the only account that can be used for revenue manipulation. Suppose a customer pays in advance for a product or service, such as a subscription or a product that includes a servicing agreement. In such cases, GAAP require that revenue recognition should be delayed until the good or service is delivered to the customer. This creates a liability representing the future obligation of the firm to provide the promised goods/services. Common titles for such a liability are Unearned Revenue and Advances from Customers. In this case the total sales price is allocated to different periods based on subjective proration schedules. Unlike receivables, the collection of cash is already assured. It is simply the timing of the revenue recognition that is at issue. Nevertheless, understatement of the liability to provide future goods/services can be a powerful tool for revenue manipulation. For example, a firm can boost current period revenues by promising to provide enhanced future service or additional future products at discounted prices. If the cost of these future obligations is not recorded as a liability, then current period equity and earnings will be overstated.

Expense Manipulation

Whenever an asset is used up or a liability is created in the process of providing goods and services to customers, GAAP require an expense to be recognized. The theory is straightforward. However, like revenue recognition, there are many gray areas that open the door for earnings management.

Perhaps the biggest gray area is the "capitalize versus expense" decision. Whenever an asset is used up in a firm's operating activities, an expense must be recognized *unless* a new asset is created. In other words, there must be a future benefit that satisfies the criteria for recognition as an asset. Therefore, earnings can be manipulated by capitalizing costs that should really be expensed. This is exactly what we did in our aggressive accounting examples in panels B and D of Figure 4.5. It is also the means by which WorldCom perpetrated its famous earnings management scheme. WorldCom capitalized approximately $10 billion of its regular operating costs as part of Property and Equipment. Another common real-world example is the aggressive capitalization of costs incurred to develop and produce software. GAAP require that only costs incurred beyond the point of technological feasibility can be capitalized. But the determination of technological feasibility is subjective and lends itself to manipulation. In order to lower expenses, management can simply claim technological feasibility has been achieved. The auditor, not being an expert in software development, is in a poor position to question such a judgment. In an interesting twist on earnings management, Microsoft has been accused of understating income by expensing too much of its software development costs, regardless of technological feasibility. Following the permanently conservative accounting example from panel E of Figure 4.5, we should expect that when Microsoft slows its investment in new software, its earnings will predictably increase. A good check for expense manipulation of this kind is to compare the total proportion of costs that are capitalized by a firm with its industry counterparts. If a firm is capitalizing a very different proportion of its costs from other firms in the industry, it is more likely to be manipulating earnings. But remember that it is always possible that the firm really is different from its industry counterparts and its capitalization policies are appropriate.

Inventory accounting also lends itself to expense manipulation. In times of changing prices, the cost flow assumption used to account for inventory (FIFO, LIFO, etc.) can be very important in determining the cost of inventory that has been used up and therefore recognized as cost of goods sold. Management can time inventory purchases and change cost flow assumptions in order to manipulate earnings. They also can manipulate the allocation of joint costs. In a slaughterhouse that produces pork products, how should we allocate the cost of the pig between bacon and sausage? If we sell bacon more quickly than we sell sausage, we can temporarily boost earnings by assigning more costs to sausage, hence leaving these costs in inventory longer.

Yet another technique for manipulating earnings using inventory accounting is to purchase a diverse range of inventory and offer it for sale at a high markup. The firm makes big profits on the product that sells and leaves the product that doesn't sell in inventory. The problem here, of course, is inventory obsolescence. This type of earnings management is particularly prevalent in the specialty retail industry, where seasonal fashions are difficult to predict. By failing to write down the obsolete inventory on a timely basis, management can understate expenses.

Another avenue for expense manipulation involves noncurrent assets that are used up gradually over many periods, such as property, plant, and equipment. GAAP call for these assets to be depreciated, amortized, or impaired over time using a variety of rules. However, all of these rules provide management with considerable latitude in determining the periodic expenses recorded. An interesting example here is Blockbuster, a video rental chain. In the early years of video, Blockbuster depreciated its rental videos over a longer time period than its competitors. At the time, there was considerable uncertainty concerning the useful lives of rental videos, particularly because the demographics of video renters were changing rapidly as video players became more affordable. As a result, Blockbuster looked more profitable than its competitors, and so attracted more capital and was the leading player in this industry until Netflix came along and put them out of business.

Expense manipulation is not restricted to assets. Understating liabilities is another technique for understating expenses. Consider the accounting for warranty liabilities. When a firm sells a product with a warranty, the expected future costs of the warranty should be recognized as an obligation of the company at the same time that the sales transaction is recognized. This will result in an increase in liabilities and a decrease in equity and earnings. By understating or ignoring the warranty liability, management can overstate earnings. One spectacular example of expense manipulation in this vein involved Regina Company. Regina manufactured vacuum cleaners that were reputably so durable that they would last a lifetime. In fact, Regina offered a lifetime warranty on its products, but the high quality of its products meant that few warranty costs were ever incurred. Then, a new CEO boosted Regina's earnings and stock price by using cheaper components in the vacuum cleaners. The lower costs meant higher profits in the short run. But, as you would expect, costs associated with the lifetime warranty started to skyrocket, and Regina subsequently went broke. The higher expected warranty costs should have been recorded as a liability, and an associated expense recognized in the income statement. If this had been done, Regina would never have shown higher profits in the first place.

A final important area for expense manipulation is employee pensions and other retirement benefits. GAAP require these amounts be estimated, recognized as a liability, and charged off as an expense in the period that employees earn the right to these future benefits. There is huge subjectivity involved in estimating these amounts. What will be the ultimate amount of the benefits? What discount rate should be used to calculate the present value of the future benefits? Small changes in these assumptions can have huge impacts on the financial statements, so management has considerable leeway to manipulate earnings. Again, you should conduct an industry comparison of the accounting assumptions to determine whether a particular firm appears to be managing earnings.

In summary, most earnings management involves accruals that create associated assets or liabilities on the balance sheet. Consequently, the key to detecting earnings management is a careful examination of the balance sheet. So far, we have focused exclusively on traditional revenue and expense manipulation. However, there are other more subtle forms of financial statement manipulation. We provide a brief discussion of four of the most common forms below.

Related-Party Transactions

A key prerequisite for the recognition of many assets and liabilities on the balance sheet is a transaction with another party. The maintained assumption under GAAP is that these transactions represent arms-length business dealings. For example, if inventory is purchased, the underlying assumption is that the purchase price represents the fair market value at the date of purchase. Also, if a sale is made, the assumption is that the sale will not be reversed at a later date.

Given GAAP's heavy reliance on transactions with other parties, one possible technique for manipulating the financial statements is to engage in "sham" transactions with related parties. For example, a firm with an earnings shortfall could sell product to a customer with a verbal agreement that the sale will be reversed or the customer reimbursed in some other manner (e.g., future price discounts). Such practices are technical violations of GAAP, but they can be difficult to prove. Further, related-party transactions extend from earnings management to balance sheet management. A director may make a long-term loan to a company just before the end of a reporting period in order to create the impression of improved short-term liquidity on the balance sheet, and then reverse the loan shortly thereafter.

Fortunately, U.S. reporting requirements require that all material related-party transactions must be disclosed in the financial statements of the reporting entity. The nature of the relationship and the amount and nature of the transactions must be reported in the notes to the financial statements. Unfortunately, if management really wants to deceive you with related-party transactions, it is unlikely that they will say so in plain English in the financial statement footnotes.

Off-Balance-Sheet Entities

Off-balance-sheet entities have many similarities with related-party transactions. With off-balance-sheet entities, management creates a separate legal entity that is not required to be consolidated in the firm's financial statements.

Management nevertheless exercises influence over this new entity and uses the entity to manipulate the firm's financial statements. Management usually exercises influence over the off-balance-sheet entity by appointing related parties to the management of the entity or by being a key financier, supplier, customer, or guarantor of the entity. Once established, there are several ways in which the off-balance-sheet entity can then be used to manipulate the financial statements of the firm. For example, the off-balance-sheet entity may purchase goods and services from the firm at inflated prices, directly boosting equity and earnings. In many past cases, these purchases have been funded by loans from the firm itself and simply represent sham transactions designed with the sole intent of boosting earnings. Alternatively, a firm could boost revenue by using an off-balance-sheet entity to provide customers with loans for making purchases from the firm. If the firm itself guarantees these loans, then the risk associated with the loans is ultimately borne by the firm but is hidden from investors because the loans themselves are in the off-balance-sheet entity. Off-balance-sheet entities also can be used to hide financial leverage and other sources of risk from investors.

The analysis of off-balance-sheet entities can be extremely difficult. Firms that create such structures in order to manage the financial statements will go to great lengths to make it as difficult as possible for investors to figure out what is going on. Moreover, because we typically don't have financial information for these off-balance-sheet entities, we really don't have much to work with. The well-known rise and sudden fall of Enron was primarily attributable to the aggressive use of off-balance-sheet entities to boost earnings and hide risks from investors. The best advice we can give you here is that if you see any sign that off-balance-sheet entities are being used, you should make sure that you understand how they are being used. If you don't feel that you have enough information to make a meaningful assessment, you should assume the worst.

How do you know if any off-balance-sheet entities are out there? There are three potential disclosures in the notes to the financial statements that you should look for. First, there is the related-party note. This note must report any unconsolidated transactions with entities in which the firm has ownership, control, or significant influence. Second, there is the note relating to equity investments and other unconsolidated investments. You should ascertain whether any of these investments give the firm influence over the operating policies of the investee. Finally, there is the contingent liabilities note. If the firm has guaranteed the debt of any unconsolidated entities, then these guarantees should be identified in the contingent liabilities note.

Off-Balance-Sheet Financing

Off-balance-sheet financing is used to finance the acquisition of resources without showing the associated assets and liabilities on the balance sheet. By doing so, the firm usually hopes to create the impression that it has less financial risk than it really does. The most common type of off-balance-sheet financing is an operating lease. A firm enters into a contract in which it acquires the right to use an asset in return for periodic payments to the owner of the asset. If the contract covers a substantial portion of the useful life of the asset, then the economic substance of the transaction is identical to one in which the firm borrows money and then buys the asset. But because the legal form of the transaction is a lease contract, no assets and liabilities are recognized.

GAAP have developed a complex set of rules to determine whether leases can be kept off the books as operating leases or must be put on the books as capital leases (the future benefits and obligations associated with capital leases must be estimated and placed on the balance sheet). While we won't drag you through all the rules, suffice it to say that creative accountants have found ways to help management get whatever accounting treatment they want, regardless of the economic substance of the lease transaction. As a result, most leases remain off balance sheet.

Fortunately, figuring out the impact of operating leases is straightforward. Firms are required to disclose future minimum lease payments on most operating leases in the notes to the financial statements. By taking the present value of these payments, you can immediately get a good idea of how much off-balance-sheet financing is attributable to operating leases.

Operating leases are not the only way off-balance-sheet financing can be achieved. Any contract in which a firm acquires the right to use a resource and incurs future obligations in return represents off-balance-sheet financing. Other common forms of off-balance-sheet financing include take-or-pay contracts, sale of receivables with recourse, unconsolidated finance subsidiaries, joint ventures, and equity investments. You should be able to discover the existence of these and other off-balance-sheet financing techniques by studying the notes to the financial statements, particularly the investments and contingent liabilities notes.

Nonrecurring Charges and Pro Forma Earnings

A final form of financial statement manipulation that has become popular of late is the strategic use of nonrecurring charges, such as asset impairments, losses on the sale of long-lived assets, and restructuring charges. Because these charges are nonrecurring, it has become usual for management, analysts, and investors to focus on the recurring component of earnings that excludes such charges. This non-GAAP definition of earnings is often referred to as *pro forma* earnings in analyst reports and firms' press releases.

In recent years, the magnitude and frequency of nonrecurring charges has exploded. Moreover, firms have started to exclude recurring charges from pro forma earnings with the lamest of excuses. The idea is to reclassify as many recurring expenses as possible into a nonrecurring charge and, hence, report higher pro forma earnings. For example, if a firm writes down its fixed assets today in a nonrecurring impairment charge, recurring earnings will be higher moving forward, because the carrying value of these assets is lower and hence future depreciation expense will be lower. As a result, many firms consistently report large nonrecurring charges year after year. Management wins twice with this manipulation. First, they convince you to ignore the nonrecurring charge in the period that they take it, arguing that it is old news and irrelevant to the future. Second, expenses in the future are lower because of the write-down of assets in the current period. Ignoring expenses that management labels as nonrecurring is like evaluating a fund manager's performance after excluding the bottom 10 percent performers in her portfolio. You should determine what is really included in these charges and make a careful assessment of their implications for the soundness of the firm's financial health. A bad management team will blunder from one bad business decision to the next. Are the losses associated with each of these bad decisions nonrecurring simply because they relate to different business decisions? The answer is no.

4.6   APPLYING ACCOUNTING ANALYSIS TO KOHL'S

We'll wrap this chapter up by applying accounting analysis to Kohl's fiscal 2009 financial statements (shown in Figure 2.6). Let's start by computing Kohl's 2009 return on equity:

Kohl's 2009 Return on Equity = 2009 Net Income/2008 Equity = 991/6,739 = 14.7%

Note that we compute ROE for fiscal 2009 (i.e., the year ended January 30, 2010), by dividing net income for fiscal 2009 by the book value of stockholders equity at the beginning of fiscal 2009 (i.e., the end of fiscal 2008). We divide net income for the period by book value at the beginning of the period just as we would divide interest for the period by the balance in a savings account at the beginning of the period to compute the interest rate earned on the account.

At 14.7 percent, Kohl's 2009 ROE looks healthy, especially considering that the risk free rate in 2009 (estimated by the 10-year U.S. Treasury note yield) averaged around 3 percent. If we assume that there are no significant distortions in Kohl's accounting numbers, then Kohl's is clearly generating a relatively strong economic rate of return on its invested capital. But before jumping to this conclusion, we first need to evaluate the extent to which Kohl's accounting numbers reflect economic realty. Following the advice at the beginning of this chapter, we recommend a three-step process for doing this:

1. Verify the extent to which the accounting assumptions underlying the major reported assets and liabilities on the balance sheet reflect economic reality, quantifying any errors to the extent possible.
2. Identify significant economic assets and liabilities that are not reported on the balance sheet, quantifying them to the extent possible.

3. Identify line items on the income statement that are affected by the accounting distortions identified above, quantifying them to the extent possible.

Analyzing Kohl's Reported Assets and Liabilities

Since we just computed 2009 ROE using the book value of equity at the end of fiscal 2008, we will look at the amounts of Kohl's assets and liabilities at the end of fiscal 2008. A quick look at the asset side of Kohl's balance sheet reveals that the majority of Kohl's total assets of 11,363 are represented by three balance sheet line items; cash and equivalents of 643; merchandise inventories of 2,799; and property and equipment of 6,984. The later two should come as no surprise, since inventory and stores in which to sell the inventory are clearly necessary to operate a chain of retail stores. Nevertheless, we should make sure that the accounting assumptions underlying these amounts reflect economic reality and that the reported amounts look reasonable.

Before taking a more detailed look at inventory and property, let's briefly consider the first of the line items, cash and equivalents. You will see that the amount for this line item jumped from 643 in 2008 to 2,267 in 2009. Does Kohl's really need so much cash to run its business and why did the amount jump so much from 2008 to 2009? The accounting assumptions for cash and equivalents are pretty reliable, so as long as the auditors haven't been duped, the cash amounts should closely correspond to the underlying economic value. From an economic perspective, the key point to recognize is that it is likely that Kohl's doesn't actually need so much cash to run its retail business. Instead, this is excess free cash flow generated by the business that Kohl's management has decided to hold on to. Such a large cash balance will create a drag on Kohl's ROE, particularly in a year like 2009 when interest rates were so low. We can see this by noting that Kohl's interest income for 2009 (from the income statement) was only 10. So we can estimate the interest rate earned by Kohl's for 2009 as:[2]

Kohl's 2009 Interest Rate = 2009 Interest Income/2008 Cash = 10/643 = 1.5%

What you should realize here is that Kohl's ROE of 14.7 percent is weighed down by the fact that some of its capital is invested in cash earning only 1.5 percent. This means that the return on capital generated by its retail business must be even greater that 14.7 percent. We will revisit this issue again in Chapter 5 (where we will estimate the return on capital invested in Kohl's retail business) and Chapter 6 (where we will analyze what Kohl's management has been doing with its free cash flow).

---

[2]We emphasize that this computed interest rate is just an estimate. In fact it likely overstates Kohl's actual interest rate. Kohl's cash balance grew from 643 at the end of fiscal 2008 to 2,267 at the end of fiscal 2009. It is likely that this amount grew gradually over the course of the year, such that the average cash balance on which interest was earned during the year exceeded the balance at the beginning of the year.

Let's next take a look at Kohl's merchandise inventory in more detail. Note 1 to the financial statements states that:

> "Merchandise inventories are valued at the lower of cost or market with cost determined on the first-in, first-out (FIFO) basis using the retail inventory method ("RIM"). Under RIM, the valuation of inventory at cost and the resulting gross margins are calculated by applying a cost-to-retail ratio to the retail value inventory. RIM is an averaging method that has been widely used in the retail industry due to its practicality. The use of RIM will result in inventory being valued at the lower of cost or market since permanent markdowns are currently taken as a reduction in the retail value of inventory. We record an additional reserve when the future estimated selling price is less than cost."

There are no significant red flags here. These accounting assumptions are common in the retail industry and, correctly applied, they should not typically lead to significant accounting distortions. Nevertheless, there are at least two important areas of subjectivity in the application of these assumptions. First, the retail inventory method does not involve a physical inventory count. Instead, the ending inventory balance is estimated based on the difference between how much inventory was available for sale during the period (i.e., beginning inventory plus purchases) less how much was sold during the period. Retailers such as Kohl's typically track all this data at retail prices. But remember that inventory is carried at cost, so Kohl's management has to estimate the cost-to-retail ratio to translate ending inventory at retail to ending inventory at cost. Moreover, the amount of ending inventory at retail was backed out as the difference between inventory available for sale and actual sales. A common problem with this approach is that it doesn't account for inventory "shrinkage." Inventory rarely appears from thin air, but it often disappears due to events such as theft and unrecorded damage. For example, if Joe who drives the forklift in the warehouse drops a crate of glassware, he may decide to discretely dump it in the trash and hope nobody notices rather than inform his supervisor and get a black mark. On a more sinister note, the retail inventory method is also more susceptible to management fabrication of inventory purchases, because the auditor doesn't actually have to do a physical inventory count.

The other significant assumption for inventory involves the application of the "lower of cost or market rule," which involves management's assessment of whether the future estimated sales price of inventory items is less than cost. This is a subjective decision, and can basically involve an admission by management that they made money-losing purchasing decisions. Consequently, inventory write-downs are often not recorded on a timely basis.

For now, all we can do is note the subjectivity associated with the measurement of inventory and recognize the associated uncertainty concerning the extent to which the reported book values represent the economic values. In Chapter 5, we will provide you with some ratio analysis tools to help determine whether it looks like management may have used this subjectivity to misstate the carrying amount of inventory.

We'll now take a look at Kohl's other major asset line item, property and equipment. The amount for this line item stood at 6,984 at the end of fiscal 2008, making it Kohl's largest asset account. There are two significant accounting issues we need to investigate here. First, we need to make sure that Kohl's capitalization and associated depreciation and amortization accounting policies look reasonable. Second, we need to quantify the amount of any off-balance-sheet property. It is very common for retailers to lease retail space, and these leases are frequently structured as operating leases that are not required to be shown on the balance sheet even when the underlying economics of the leasing transactions look more like a purchase.

Note 1 to the financial statements explains Kohl's capitalization and depreciation/amortization policies under the heading Property and Equipment. Kohl's divides property and equipment into six categories and then uses straight-line depreciation/amortization over a range of useful lives for each category. These ranges are so wide that they leave a lot of uncertainty as to the effective useful lives being used. For example, buildings and improvements are depreciated over 8–40 years. From an economic perspective, 8 years seems short while 40 years seems long. But we don't know what point of this range they are effectively using. We can, however, estimate the average useful life across all categories. Total property and equipment <u>gross</u> of accumulated depreciation/amortization is listed as 9,449 at the end of fiscal 2008, while the associated depreciation/amortization for fiscal 2009 is 580 (see Note 1). The average useful life being used by Kohl's is therefore $9{,}449/580 \approx 16$ years. Since buildings and improvements make up over half of property and equipment balance, this average useful life seems reasonable. However, we should remember that it is not the physical life but the economic life of an asset that should determine the economic rate of depreciation. Do you find yourself shopping at dingy old stores in dilapidated neighborhoods or shiny new stores in up and coming neighborhoods? Chances are you frequent the latter, and these stores are also likely to be the ones generating the most profit. So from an economic perspective, we could argue that Kohl's depreciation policies are aggressive if we do not expect their stores to remain popular and profitable a decade from now. The accounting for Kohl's reported property and equipment looks reasonable, but you may have noticed that Kohl's is like many retailers in using operating leases to keep much of its property off balance sheet. We will consider the associated unreported assets shortly.

We have considered Kohl's major reported asset categories, so let's take a quick look at its liabilities. Kohl's has almost 5,000 of total liabilities with accounts payable (881), accrued liabilities (841) and long-term debt (2,053) representing the major line items. There is not much subjectivity involved in the accounting for these obligations, so we will not dwell here.

Analyzing Kohl's Unreported Assets and Liabilities

We have already noted that Kohl's uses operating leases for many of its stores, effectively keeping them off-balance-sheet. We will now quantify the associated unrecorded asset. The table in Note 4 to the financial statements at the top of page F-16 lists Kohl's minimum lease payments under operating leases (second column). We can infer from the reported amounts that Kohl's is committed to payments of around 460/year for about the next 24 years. Note 3 indicates that Kohl's borrowing rate has been around 7 percent. If we discount a 24-year annuity of 460 at 7 percent, we get a present value of over 5,000. You may recall from your accounting classes that what we have done here is a pro forma capitalization of Kohl's operating lease commitments, and it revealed that Kohl's has about $5 billion of property and equipment off-balance-sheet. This amount is almost as large as Kohl's on-balance-sheet property and equipment, and almost 50 percent of Kohl's on-balance-sheet total assets. Is this a good or a bad thing? Well if Kohl's continues to have a strong business and property prices rise, this is a good thing, because Kohl's has locked in the rights to use the leased property. On the other hand, if Kohl's business weakens or property prices drop, this is a bad thing, because Kohl's is obliged to make these lease payments just as it is obliged to make its debt payments. In fact, you should recall from your accounting classes that not only do these operating leases result in $5 billion off-balance-sheet property and equipment asset; they also result in a $5 billion off-balance-sheet debt liability. These off-balance-sheet assets and liabilities approximately cancel each other out such that there is no net effect on the book value of equity. But it is important to remember that they exist, because they make Kohl's more highly levered and hence more risky. This is because the benefits generated by the assets (i.e., the rights to use the leased stores) depend on the continued profitability of the stores, while the obligations represented by the liabilities (i.e., the minimum future lease payments) usually do not. We should keep this in mind when we analyze Kohl's financial leverage in Chapter 5.

Does Kohl's have any other significant economic assets that are not reflected on its balance sheet? One potential candidate is customer loyalty that has been created through Kohl's advertising programs. The associated costs are summarized in Note 1 at the bottom of page F-11 of Kohl's financials. We see that Kohl's spends almost 900 per year on advertising, expensing all of these costs when the associated advertisement is first seen. Do you think all the benefits associated with an advertisement expire as soon as the advertisement is seen? It is probable that some advertisements generate future sales, but it is very difficult to determine the frequency and duration of these sales. Nevertheless, the accounting used by Kohl's looks conservative because it very likely understates the expected future benefits from advertising. In order to gauge the potential magnitude of the understated asset, let's estimate its value using accounting estimates that are on the more aggressive side. Specifically, we will assume that the benefits from advertising are spread evenly over the three years after the initial expenditure. Kohl's likely makes these expenditures fairly evenly throughout the year, and so to simplify matters, we will assume that all expenditures are made in the middle of each fiscal year. This means that at the end of any given fiscal year, Kohl's unrecorded advertising asset is:

Unrecorded Advertising Asset =
      (2.5 years/3 years) × current-fiscal-year advertising expenditure
      + (1.5 years/3 years) × previous-fiscal-year advertising expenditure
      + (0.5 years/3 years) × two-fiscal-year-ago advertising expenditure.

Since Kohl's spends about 900/year on advertising, its unrecorded advertising asset at the end of any fiscal year using the above assumptions is about 1,350. An unrecorded asset of this magnitude represents over 10 percent of total recorded assets, but remember that it is based on fairly aggressive accounting assumptions.

    Kohl's also has another unrecorded asset with respect to its store preopening costs, as these are also expensed as incurred (see Note 1) but surely generate future benefits. However, we can see from the income statement that they only amount to about 50 each year, so even if we assume a 20-year life, we only come up with an unrecorded asset of about 500 (you should be able to verify this amount by adapting the formula we used for the unrecorded advertising asset).

    We have now completed our primary analysis of the balance sheet. As a useful check that we haven't missed anything significant, it is now worth scanning Kohl's remaining financial statement notes and MD&A. It turns out that we have already identified the major accounting issues, but we will briefly summarize some of the other interesting tidbits of information you will find here. Starting with the Notes, Note 1 under the heading of Cost of Merchandise Sold and Selling, General and Administrative Expenses provides some useful information concerning the allocation of certain costs between costs of goods sold and SG&A on the income statement. Since the allocation of these costs varies across companies in the retail industry, this information will come in useful when we do comparative ratio analysis in Chapter 5. Note 2 reveals that Kohl's has estimated losses of about $60 million on investments in auction rate securities, but that it expects these losses to be temporary and so has recorded them in other comprehensive income. Turning to the MD&A, the Contractual Obligations section identifies the unrecorded operating lease obligations that we have already considered. This section also identifies that Kohl's has over $3 billion of purchase obligations related to merchandise. This essentially represents unrecorded inventory and we may want to make sure that Kohl's isn't substituting purchase obligations for inventory purchases to mask obsolete inventory. Finally, the Critical Accounting Policies section largely repeats issues that we have already considered. The Impairment of Assets and Closed Stores Reserves paragraph is an interesting read. Kohl's reveals that while it hasn't experienced significant impairments or recorded significant reserves, the economic value of Kohl's property and lease commitments hinges on the continued success of its retail operations.

Analyzing Kohl's Income Statement

We have now covered Kohl's balance sheet and identified areas of subjective and potentially conservative/aggressive accounting. It is now time to turn to the income statement. Recall that accounting distortions on the income statement are created by changes in accounting measurement errors for assets and liabilities on the balance sheet. For example, if balance sheet inventory is overstated at the beginning of the period and correctly stated at the end of the period, then Cost of Goods Sold for the period will be understated. A good procedure for identifying distortions on the income statement is to consider each income statement line item in turn, determining which balance sheet accounts relate to that line item, and whether these balance sheet accounts have significant measurement errors at either the beginning or the end of the period. Note that in doing so, we should also consider any unrecorded economic assets and liabilities that may have changed over the period. If we identify any measurement errors, we should try and quantify their impact on the associated line item in the income statement. We will now apply this procedure to Kohl's income statement.

The first line item on Kohl's income statement is "Net sales." Sales transactions at Kohl's are transparent and are typically settled in cash at the time of the sale. Hence, there is little room for distortion here. If Kohl's had significant credit sales or frequently accepted payment in advance of delivering goods, we would have to worry about potential distortions created by incorrect measurement of the associated accounts receivable and deferred revenue accounts on the balance sheet. But Kohl's is primarily a cash business and these accounts do not feature on its balance sheet. The astute reader may have noticed that Kohl's does have an insignificant deferred revenue liability for gift cards and merchandise return cards. But this is a relatively small amount that is buried under "Accrued Liabilities – Various liabilities to customers" (see Note 1 under Accrued Liabilities). Further digging in the notes reveals that Kohl's does not recognize revenue on these cards until either the card is redeemed or has a low likelihood of redemption (see Note 1 under "Revenue Recognition"). We could argue that this accounting policy is conservative from an economic perspective, since the revenue and associated gross margin is reasonably assured and can be reasonably estimated at the time the card is issued. But since the associated balance sheet liability is relatively small and stable, it is very unlikely to introduce significant distortions into revenue.

The next income statement line item is "Cost of merchandise sold." The amount reported for this line item is a function of the amounts recorded for

"Merchandise inventory" and "Accounts payable" on the balance sheet. As discussed earlier, the measurement of inventory is an issue here. In Kohl's case, we should be particularly mindful of their use of the retail inventory method. Has the inventory balance been overstated due to the overstatement of margins or the understatement of shrinkage? Has obsolete inventory been written down? At this point, all we can do is note the potential for accounting distortions in this line item. We will introduce some ratio analysis techniques in Chapters 5 and 6 that will help indentify potential accounting errors in inventory and cost of goods sold.

The next line item is "Selling, general and administrative" (SG&A). The only significant balance sheet account associated with this line item is "Accrued liabilities," primarily via the "Payroll and related fringe benefits" sub-account (see Note 1 under Accrued liabilities). We aren't too concerned with this balance sheet sub-account, because the amount in it is relatively small and this balance sheet item is typically measured with high reliability. But recall there is another accounting issue to consider with respect to SG&A because it includes all advertising expenditures that have been incurred for the period. As we discussed earlier, these expenditures likely result in an unrecorded asset reflecting expected future benefits from advertising. If the estimated amount of this unrecorded asset has experienced a significant change during the period, then we should be sure to adjust SG&A accordingly. Since advertising costs have been relatively flat at around 900/year, our earlier balance sheet analysis identified an unrecorded asset of about 1,350/year. Because the estimated unrecorded balance sheet asset remains approximately constant over time, there should be no distortion to the associated annual advertising expense. But what if advertising expense had jumped from around 900 prior to fiscal 2009 to around 1,800 in fiscal 2009? Following our earlier accounting assumptions, the unrecorded asset would jump from:

$$
\begin{aligned}
\text{Unrecorded Asset at End of Fiscal 2008} &= (2.5 \text{ years}/3 \text{ years}) \times 900 \\
&\quad + (1.5 \text{ years}/3 \text{ years}) \times 900 \\
&\quad + (0.5 \text{ years}/3 \text{ years}) \times 900 \\
&= 1,350
\end{aligned}
$$

to

$$
\begin{aligned}
\text{Unrecorded Asset at End of Fiscal 2009} &= (2.5 \text{ years}/3 \text{ years}) \times 1,800 \\
&\quad + (1.5 \text{ years}/3 \text{ years}) \times 900 \\
&\quad + (0.5 \text{ years}/3 \text{ years}) \times 900 \\
&= 2,100
\end{aligned}
$$

By failing to record the increase in this asset, we would have overstated 2009 advertising expense by $2,100 - 1,350 = 750$ and hence understated 2009 operating income by 750. Note that misstatement of 750 simply represents the increase in the advertising expenditure for 2009 of 900 multiplied by the unexpired proportion of its economic life at the end of 2009 of (2.5 years/3 years).

The next line item is "Depreciation and amortization." This line item clearly depends on the "Property and equipment, net" asset on the balance sheet. If equipment is depreciated too slowly, then the balance sheet will be overstated and Depreciation and amortization expense will be understated. Following our balance sheet analysis, we should make sure that Kohl's stores are still operating profitably. If they are not, asset impairment will likely be required to reflect the shortened economic life of the stores and a corresponding write-down charged to net income. It is also important to remember that Kohl's keeps a lot of its property off the balance sheet through the use of operating leases. Thus, we need to consider impairments to both the on- and off-balance-sheet property.

The next line item is preopening expenses. As discussed earlier, while all store pre-opening costs are expensed as incurred, they should result in an economic asset that is tied to the economic life of the associated store. But as was the case for advertising costs, these costs have remained fairly constant in recent years, so the associated unrecorded asset should be fairly constant too. If there had been sharp trends in the amount of these costs, it would be important to estimate the change in the associated unrecorded asset and estimate the associated distortion to net income.

The final income statement line items involve interest and taxes. We'll skip interest. Other than some arcane accounting issues relating to capitalization of interest and amortization of debt premia and discounts, there is not usually a lot of action here, with Kohl's being a case in point. We will, however, spend a little time on taxes. As you should recall from your accounting classes, reported tax expense typically differs from the amount due to the relevant taxing authorities. This is because tax expense is based on the amount of tax that is ultimately expected to be paid on reported net income, rather than what is currently due. In Kohl's case, we see that they have a nontrivial deferred tax liability on the balance sheet that increased from 320 in fiscal 2008 to 377 in fiscal 2009. This must have arisen because Kohl's tax expense has been higher than its actual taxes due. This means that Kohl's must have been reporting more net income than taxable income. In other words, Kohl's has been using more aggressive accounting policies for tax purposes than for financial reporting purposes. This is not necessarily cause for alarm. It makes sense for a firm to pick the most conservative allowable accounting policies for tax purposes so as to minimize the present value of its tax liability. But it is useful to check which accounting policies cause the difference and determine whether the firm is using either aggressive accounting for tax reporting purposes or conservative accounting for financial reporting purposes. After all, most taxing authorities aren't naïve enough to specify unrealistically conservative accounting practices that minimize their collections. To understand the differing accounting policies underlying the deferred tax liability, study Kohl's tax footnote. This is Note 6 in Kohl's financials. The note opens by identifying Property and equipment as the cause of Kohl's deferred tax liability. Kohl's must therefore be depreciating property and equipment over a shorter life for tax purposes than for financial reporting purposes. Kohl's most likely chose the shortest allowable life for tax purposes. Thus, while we don't want to jump to the conclusion that the useful lives have been over-estimated for financial reporting purposes, we at least know that they are significantly longer than the minimum allowed by the taxing authorities.

This completes our accounting analysis for Kohl's. Let's close by sum-marizing the most important takeaways from this analysis. First, inventory and property and equipment are the most important balance sheet accounts for Kohl's. Both are large and potentially subject to measurement error. Any changes in the amount of this measurement error between adjacent periods will distort the income statement via cost of merchandise sold in the case of inventories, and depreciation and amortization expense in the case of property and equipment. While our accounting analysis did not reveal any obvious red flags in these areas, we should give special attention to these accounts when we conduct our ratio analysis in Chapter 5. Second, Kohl's has potentially unrecorded assets for advertising and store preopening costs. Kohl's expenses all such costs as they are incurred even though they are likely to generate future benefits. This conservative accounting will cause Kohl's book value of equity to understate actual invested capital. However, since the amounts of these expenditures have been fairly constant in recent years, the associated unrecorded assets will be fairly constant as well, and so recent years' net income should not be distorted. Finally, Kohl's has significant but offsetting unrecorded assets and liabilities relating to its operating leases. The offsetting nature of these unrecorded accounts means that they will cause little net error to book value of equity or reported net income. They do, how-ever, represent an important source of off-balance-sheet leverage.

4.7   CONCLUSION

You should take away three lessons from this chapter. First, the GAAP-based financial statements provide the universal language for evaluating past performance and forecasting future performance. Second, the financial state-ments only provide timely information on a subset of value-relevant events. The financial statements are not the accountants' attempt to value the firm. Rather, the goal of the financial statements is to provide people like us with information that is useful in conducting our own valuations. Third, while the financial statements are restricted to reasonably reliable information, lots of subjectivity is still involved in the estimation of assets and liabilities. This opens the financial statements to potential errors and managerial manipula-tion. A careful examination of a firm's assets and liabilities is the best starting point for identifying potential errors and manipulation.

To build a good valuation model, you must become intimately familiar with a firm's financial statements and the accounting policies underlying those financial statements. Are the accounting policies consistent with the firm's business operations and strategies? What important events are captured in the financial statements on a timely basis and what events are missing? Which assets, liabilities, revenues, and expenses are likely measured with the most error? Is there any evidence suggesting management is manipulating the financial statements? You need to answer all of these questions before you attempt to forecast the firm's future financial statements and produce a valuation.

4.8　CASES, LINKS, AND REFERENCES

Cases

- Apple and the iFad (Questions 4–6)
- Boston Chicken, Inc.
- EnCom Corporation (Stages 1 and 2)
- Netflix, Inc. (Questions 3–5)
- Overstock.com (Questions 3–6)
- Pre-Paid Legal Service

CHAPTER FIVE

Financial Ratio Analysis

5.1 INTRODUCTION

Valuing an equity security requires you to interpret and forecast a huge quantity of financial data. Ratio analysis provides a framework for doing this in an organized and systematic manner. By converting the financial statement data into ratios, we are converting data into information. For instance, margin analysis reveals how much profit a firm makes from each dollar of revenue it generates and turnover analysis reveals the amount of assets needed to generate each dollar of revenue. It is extremely important that you learn to identify a firm's performance in terms of the financial ratios presented here. This is the language that analysts and management use to discuss a company's performance, and we will use this language to construct forecasts of the future. Ratio analysis is traditionally applied to historical data to evaluate past performance, but we will also use it to evaluate the plausibility of our forecasted future financial statements.

5.2 TIME-SERIES AND CROSS-SECTIONS

Ratio analysis involves comparing individual ratios with their levels in prior years and their levels in other firms. Comparing a firm's ratios to their levels in prior years is called *time-series analysis*. Time-series analysis identifies changes in financial performance and helps to detect the underlying cause. It also helps you to see whether the firm's most recent performance is unusual, in which case it is unlikely to recur in the future, or whether it is just one in a series of normal outcomes. If you have a flair for quantitative analysis, you might be tempted to estimate a complicated time-series model of a firm's past ratios in order to predict their future values. We don't recommend such an approach. As a general rule, financial ratios don't follow mechanical time-series models. Instead, it is more important that you evaluate changes in ratios in the context of changes in the underlying business operations and strategies of the firm. *eVal* provides you with five years of historical data, which is about as far back as you should usually need to go in your time-series analysis.

Comparing a firm's ratios with the corresponding ratios in competitor firms is called *cross-sectional analysis*. This type of ratio analysis is also called *comparative analysis* (often shortened to *comps*). If management has done a consistently good job, then this will not be readily apparent in a time-series analysis. But it will be revealed by a cross-sectional ratio analysis with competitors. Does the company command a higher margin on its products? Is it the most efficient producer in its industry? Is it gaining market share from competitors? These are the types of questions that you can only answer by comparing a firm's financial ratios with competitor firms or the industry average. It isn't always easy, but you should try to triangulate a firm's ratios with its business strategy. If the firm is attempting to differentiate its product, it should enjoy higher margins than its competitors. If a firm is attempting to be a cost leader, it should have a higher asset turnover than its competitors. We'll discuss how different strategies influence particular ratios later in the chapter.

You can conduct cross-sectional analysis in *eVal* by loading a competitor firm into *eVal*, and then comparing ratios across the two firms. If you don't have any idea who a firm's closest competitors might be, you can get some help from the http://finance.yahoo.com website. Find your company by entering the ticker or name in the box at the top and then on the left-hand side of the page, Yahoo! gives a link to the firm's competitors. Note that some of these competitors may be private companies, in which case it will be difficult to obtain financial data for a cross-sectional analysis. You can also use cross-sectional analysis to gain insights into industry structure and bargaining power with customers and suppliers. For example, Priceline.com generates commissions by selling airline tickets. By studying margins in the airline industry, you can get a sense for the maximum commission rate that Priceline.com could plausibly charge the airlines.

Ratios Tend to Mean-Revert

From a valuation perspective, the main reason we want to study the historical performance of a firm's financial ratios is to guide us in forecasting the future values of these ratios. To this end, you should remember a common theme in the evolution of financial ratios over time—they tend to mean-revert. This means that if they are unusually high they tend to come down and if they are unusually low they tend to come up. For example, firms that experience an extremely high or extremely low return on equity (net income over common equity) in a given year probably had something unusual happen—a windfall gain on the sale of an asset, a write-off of inventory, a surprisingly successful advertising campaign, or an embarrassing product recall, to list just a few possibilities. In these cases it is unlikely that the extremely high or extremely low return will persist into the future, because the unusual event that happened once is unlikely to happen again. Later we will graph some common ratios to illustrate mean-reversion.

We don't want to oversell the power of mean-reversion. It is an observable tendency for many different ratios in a large sample of firms, but there are many exceptions. And, as we discuss below, how quickly and how completely a ratio mean-reverts varies greatly by both ratio and firm.

5.3 SOME CAVEATS

Despite their usefulness, ratios are also frequently misunderstood and abused. So before launching into a discussion of specific ratios, we offer some important caveats regarding ratio analysis.

There Is No "Correct" Way to Compute Many Ratios

Many people assign the same name to ratios that are computed quite differently. Consider the Return on Assets (ROA) ratio. The numerator (income) is sometimes measured on a before-tax basis and sometimes measured on an after-tax basis. It is sometimes measured on a before interest basis and sometimes on an after interest basis. It may or may not include any nonrecurring and/or nonoperating items for the period. The denominator (assets) usually represents total assets, but it is sometimes measured as net operating assets (in which case the ratio is sometimes referred to as the Return on Net Operating Assets). The key point here is that there are no standards like GAAP governing the computation of ratios. Basically, anything goes, and both management and sell-side analysts can be creative in coming up with ratios that put firms in the best possible light. Thus, when interpreting a ratio, you should make sure you understand how it was computed.

Ratios Do Not Provide Answers, They Just Tell You Where to Look for Answers

It is common to hear rules of thumb that attach certain interpretations to ratios falling in certain ranges. For example, a firm with an Interest Coverage ratio less than 2 is often deemed to be financially distressed, or a firm with an ROA less than the yield on the 10-year U.S. Treasury is deemed to be fit only for liquidation. Unfortunately, financial analysis is not that simple. There are many reasons why ratios can have unusual values—from accounting distortions to subtle differences in a firm's business environment. Ratio analysis guides you in your search for answers, but ratios themselves rarely provide the answers.

Managers Know That Investors Use Ratios

Managers are well aware that investors rely on ratios to summarize their firm's financial performance. Hence, they can and do use their discretion over accounting, operating, investing, and financing decisions to make their key ratios look more appealing. A common example is the use of operating leases and other off-balance-sheet financing techniques to reduce leverage ratios. It is therefore important to anticipate and undo the effects of any managerial window dressing of a firm's financial ratios.

5.4 A FRAMEWORK FOR RATIO ANALYSIS

With these caveats in mind, we will now describe how to conduct a comprehensive ratio analysis of a firm's financial performance. We encourage you to follow along by working through Kohl's ratio analysis, which is the default company in *eVal*. Recall that Kohl's is a department store chain located primarily in the Midwest and Midatlantic, but with some store presence in 49 states. It targets middle-income families with a niche strategy combining product differentiation with reasonable prices. Our analysis is based on financial statement data through fiscal 2009, which ended on January 31, 2010 for Kohl's.

Kohl's competes with other department stores, primarily selling moderately priced apparel. As contrasts, we will compare Kohl's with two other department stores, Nordstrom (JWN), which provides a more upscale retail experience, and Ross Stores (ROST), which is a closeout retailer. The standardized financial statements for Nordstrom and Ross Stores are available on the Case Data tab in *eVal*.

The results of *eVal*'s ratio analysis are displayed on the Ratio Analysis sheet. You will find it helpful to display Excel's formula bar so that you can see how the ratios in each cell have been computed. The formula bar can be displayed by selecting the Formula Bar menu item from the View menu in Excel.

Ratio analysis begins with the two pillars of firm value: *growth* and *profitability*. Growth measures changes in the magnitude of invested capital on which the firm is able to generate profitability. Profitability measures the return that a firm is generating on its invested capital. The key to value creation is to simultaneously achieve high growth and high profitability. Our ratio analysis starts with summary measures of each. We then examine the underlying drivers of profitability to learn more about its sources and sustainability.

5.5 GROWTH

The analysis of growth is relatively straightforward. Growth rates are commonly reported for a variety of financial statement line items and *eVal* reports growth rates for sales, assets, common equity, earnings and free cash flows. But *growth in sales* is the most commonly discussed growth statistic. Growth rates in assets, common equity, earnings, and free cash flows are closely related to the growth rates in sales. In fact, when sales growth and profitability reach steady state, the growth rates in all financial statement line items converge to the steady-state sales growth rate. However, during years when sales growth and profitability are fluctuating, the growth rates in the other line items will generally differ from the growth rate in sales. The intuition behind these differences is usually straightforward. For example, asset growth will differ from sales growth when a firm is building excess productive capacity in order to support future sales.

The final growth rate that we report in *eVal* is the *sustainable growth rate*. This ratio is computed as:

$$\text{Sustainable Growth Rate} = \text{Return on Equity} \times (1 - \text{Dividend Payout Ratio})$$

Given its current level of profitability and dividend policy, the sustainable growth rate is the maximum rate that a firm can grow without resorting to additional external financing. If a firm's forecasted sales growth rate exceeds its sustainable growth rate, be sure you understand how the additional growth will be financed. One possibility is through increased future profitability. However, if the increased profitability is not achieved, then the growth plans may have to be curtailed. Alternatively, the additional growth may be financed externally through the issuance of debt and/or equity. This introduces uncertainty, because capital markets must be receptive to the firm's growth plans if they are going to provide financing. A final option is for the firm to cut its dividend payout ratio. However, given that the dividend payout ratio is usually zero for growth firms, this final option is often not available.

Sales growth rates have very little memory; an unusually high growth rate this year rarely translates into a similarly high growth rate next year. To illustrate, Figure 5.1 takes all the firms in the U.S. economy between 1962 and 2009, computes their percentage sales growth each year, sorts them into five portfolios from low growth to high growth (labeled as year 0 on the figure), and then plots the median sales growth for each portfolio over the next

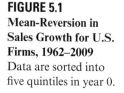

FIGURE 5.1
Mean-Reversion in Sales Growth for U.S. Firms, 1962–2009
Data are sorted into five quintiles in year 0.

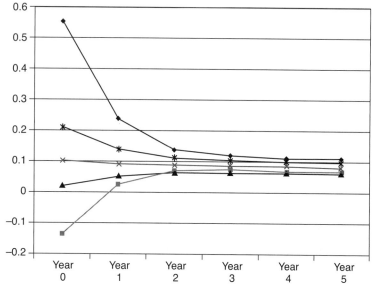

five years. The fact that all the lines snap back to the middle very quickly is something you should never forget.

Consider the top line. Firms in the highest portfolio have median sales growth of 55 percent in year 0. But in the very next year the median growth for these high flyers falls to 24 percent and after five years, their growth rate is barely distinguishable from all the other firms. If all you know about a firm is that they had huge sales growth last year, don't be too impressed. Remind yourself that sales growth mean-reverts very quickly.

Analyzing Kohl's Growth

Turning to *eVal*, you will notice at the top of the Ratio Analysis sheet that Kohl's sales growth pattern has followed the economy's pattern in the past few years. Fiscal 2006 and 2007 were very good years, both for Kohl's and the economy generally, as loose credit caused U.S. consumers to spend money they didn't really have. In fiscal 2008 a recession followed the financial crisis on Wall Street, and Kohl's sales declined, as did sales at most retailers, and then a recovery started in fiscal 2009. Figure 5.2 plots Kohl's sales growth rates for fiscal 2006–2009 along with the growth rates at Nordstrom and Ross Stores. Compared to Kohl's, Nordstrom's sales growth declined more steeply going into the recession, and was slower to recover, illustrating shoppers' substitution away from luxury goods during the recession. In contrast, note that sales growth at Ross Stores, our representative discount retailer, was positive through the entire period, and actually increased in the year of the recession. Basically, as household budgets became constrained, the Nordstrom shoppers started going to Kohl's, and Kohl's shoppers started going to Ross Stores. As the recession subsided (it officially ended in the third quarter of 2009), sales increased everywhere.

There is little relation between the growth rates of assets, common equity, and sales at Kohl's, as seen at the top of the Ratio Analysis, reproduced in

FIGURE 5.2
Sales Growth at Kohl's, Nordstrom, and Ross Stores

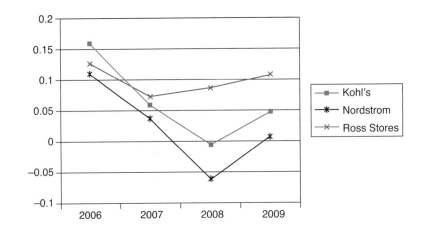

FIGURE 5.3
Growth Rates at Kohl's

Company Name	KOHL'S CORP				
	Actual	Actual	Actual	Actual	Actual
Fiscal Year End Date	06-01-31	07-01-31	08-01-31	09-01-31	10-01-31
Annual Growth Rates					
Sales		16.0%	6.0%	-0.5%	4.8%
Assets		-1.2%	16.8%	7.3%	16.1%
Common Equity		-5.9%	8.9%	10.4%	16.5%
Earnings		31.7%	-2.2%	-18.3%	12.0%
Free Cash Flow to Investors			-122.4%	#N/A	-109.7%
Sustainable Growth Rate			18.5%	13.8%	13.6%

Figure 5.3. Kohl's 2009 10-K report (page 20) indicates that from fiscal 2006 to fiscal 2009, Kohl's increased their store count steadily from 732 to 1058, or about 10 percent each year. The fact that the growth in total assets and common equity are more volatile than this illustrates that Kohl's is clearly not in steady state. As Kohl's grows, it needs to invest in assets other than stores and inventory. It also needs distribution centers, administrative offices, and computer systems, and these investments are "lumpy." Earnings growth each year at Kohl's is an amplified version of the sales growth pattern—earnings declined more rapidly than sales in the bad times and increased more rapidly than sales in the recovery. This reflects the fixed-cost/variable-cost structure of Kohl's, and will be discussed in the next section. Finally, if a growth rate is shown as #NA, as is the case for Free Cash Flow to Investors in fiscal 2008, this means that the value of the underlying series is negative at the beginning of the period, so a growth rate is not defined.

5.6   PROFITABILITY

While the analysis of growth is relatively straightforward, the analysis of profitability has endless nuance. The starting point for the analysis of profitability, and the ultimate ending point, is the *return on equity*, computed as:

$$\textbf{Return on Equity (ROE)} = \frac{\text{Net Income}}{\text{Average Common Equity}}$$

ROE is the accounting measure of the rate of return that the firm has provided to its common stockholders. It represents the amount of profit generated per dollar of book value of common equity. It is analogous to the interest rate that is generated by a fixed-income investment. However, accounting rates of return are complicated by two factors. First, the income-generating process for a firm is much more complicated and uncertain than for a fixed-income security. Second, as discussed in Chapter 4, GAAP accounting does not recognize many economic assets and liabilities. Consequently, common equity and net income are both distorted, causing ROE to provide a distorted measure of true economic performance. Our job is to understand these distortions and how they will resolve themselves in the future.

Because ROE is the ultimate accounting measure of a firm's profitability, it will be the focus of our financial analysis of the past and our forecasts of the future. We therefore devote most of the remainder of this chapter to the analysis of ROE.

Benchmarking the Return on Equity

ROE is one of the few ratios that can be compared to a well-defined benchmark. If you were considering investing in a fixed-income investment, you would compare its interest rate to the interest rates offered by like investments. Similarly, to evaluate firm profitability, you can compare the firm's ROE with its competitors' ROEs. Other things equal, the higher a firm's ROE, the greater the return generated per dollar of book equity invested in the firm. Moreover, to value a firm, you must estimate the firm's cost of equity capital. Loosely speaking, the cost of equity capital represents the expected return that an equity investment must generate to make it competitive with similar investment opportunities. So, accounting distortions aside, a firm with an ROE above its cost of equity capital is generating positive net present value for its equity holders. Thus, the cost of equity capital is a natural benchmark for a firm's ROE. Indeed, this is the logic behind some performance evaluation systems, such as Stern Stewart's EVA system.[1] Historically, the cost of equity capital has been estimated at about 10 percent for the average firm in the U.S. economy, so this is a crude benchmark you can use to assess a firm's ROE. Unfortunately, there are two key drawbacks with such comparisons. First, as we will see in Chapter 9, it is difficult to estimate a firm's cost of equity capital with any certainty. Second, as we have mentioned before, the vagaries of GAAP accounting rarely result in measures of net income and common equity that correspond with their economic counterparts. So, to make these constructs more meaningful, we need to do more work.

ROE is computed by dividing net income for the period by the average book value of common equity that was used to generate the net income. Ideally, we would like to use a time-weighted average of the equity that was invested during the year. But we generally only get to see balance sheets for the last day of each fiscal period, so we follow the common convention of dividing net income for the period by the simple average of the beginning and ending balances of common equity. This can lead to a distorted ratio when there have been large changes in common equity near the beginning or the end of the year. For example, if a firm doubled its common equity on the second day of the fiscal year, the average common equity calculation would understate the true magnitude of the equity base that was available for most

---

[1]Visit http://www.sternstewart.com to learn more about the EVA performance measurement system. A good understanding of the material in this book should help you develop your own performance evaluation system, and you'll be in a better position to understand the system's strengths and weaknesses.

FIGURE 5.4

Mean-Reversion in Return on Equity, U.S. Firms from 1962–2009

Data are sorted into five quintiles in year 0.

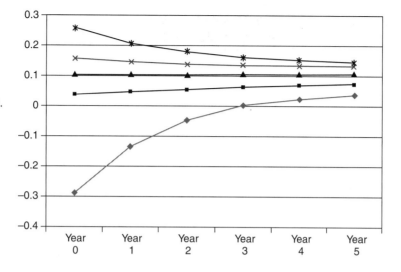

of the year, leading to an overstatement of ROE. This limitation arises any time we compute a ratio that compares flow variables (amounts generated over the course of the year—such as those found on the income statement) with stock variables (cumulative amounts present on the first or last day of the year—such as those found on the balance sheet).

Mean-Reversion in ROE

We stated earlier that many measures of financial performance tend to mean-revert, and ROE is no exception. Figure 5.4 shows the mean-reversion in return on equity for the entire sample of publicly traded firms between 1962 and 2009. Each year, we sort the firms into five groups from lowest to highest ROE and then we plot the median ROE for each of these groups over the next five years. As the plot shows, the highest groups move down over time and the lowest groups move up over time, consistent with the notion of mean-reversion. And note that the lines are reverting toward about 10 percent, the historical long-term average ROE in the U.S. economy.

There are a few other observations to take away from Figure 5.4. First, the drastic improvement in the lowest ROE group in year one is a bit misleading. If the firm goes bankrupt, it drops out of the sample, leaving only those firms who improved their performance enough to stay alive five more years and hence remain on the graph. Even with this selection bias, it takes this bottom group three years to get back to zero ROE. So they mean-revert, but slowly. Second, while the top two ROE groups decline and the bottom two groups improve, at no time do the lines completely converge. Even after five years the highest group has an ROE of about 15 percent and the lowest group has an ROE of about 5 percent. While mean-reversion over five years has definitely brought the two groups closer together, it has not eliminated the disparity in ROE.

Why does ROE tend to mean-revert? The short answer is competition. If a firm enjoys a high return on equity, this catches the attention of other firms. Existing rivals undercut the firm's prices and new firms enter the market. As the firm responds to these competitive threats with a price cut of its own, its profitability suffers, driving down the ROE. Why is the mean-reversion in ROE less than complete? For reasons we discussed in Chapter 3, many firms enjoy imperfect competition and are therefore partially shielded from competitive forces. In addition, accounting distortions can generate long-term disparity in ROE across firms. Firms in the pharmaceutical industry report among the economy's highest ROEs, but this is partly due to the fact that their most prominent economic asset—recent R&D expenditures—are expensed immediately. Because an asset is not recorded, assets and common equity are understated, causing ROE to be overstated.

It is reasonable to expect some components of income to be more persistent than others. For this reason we also compute *return on equity before nonrecurring items*. The idea is to exclude from the numerator items that are likely to completely disappear in subsequent years, thus providing a better indication of a firm's long-run sustainable ROE. We expect that ROE before nonrecurring items will mean-revert more slowly than regular ROE. Nonrecurring items are most commonly found in the extraordinary items and discontinued operations, other income, and nonoperating income line items on the income statement. Thus, *eVal* excludes these line items from the definition of net income used to compute ROE before nonrecurring items. Nonoperating income is a pre-tax item on the income statement, so it must be tax-adjusted before adding it back to net income. *eVal* does this by using the effective tax rate for the year. The resulting measure is as follows:

$$\text{Return on Equity (before nonrecurring)}$$
$$= \frac{\text{Net Income} - \text{After-Tax Nonrecurring Items}}{\text{Average Common Equity}}$$

where

After-Tax Nonrecurring Items = Ext. Items & Disc. Ops.
+ Other Income (Loss) + (1-tax) $\times$ (Nonoperating Income (Loss)), and
tax = effective tax rate = Income Taxes/Earnings before Taxes

You should remember that while *eVal* mechanically spits out ROE before nonrecurring items, it is only a general guide and you should engage in more detailed analysis in order to classify items as recurring or nonrecurring. For example, the Other Income line item sometimes includes earnings from equity affiliates, which may well be recurring. Also, nonrecurring items may be buried in other line items on the income statement, such as the effects of an inventory write-down, which will usually be hidden in the cost of goods sold (but can be recovered from the financial statement footnotes).

FIGURE 5.5
Basic Dupont Model

$$ROE = \text{Net Profit Margin} \times \text{Total Asset Turnover} \times \text{Common Equity}$$

$$= \frac{\text{Net Income}}{\text{Sales}} \times \frac{\text{Sales}}{\text{Total Assets}} \times \frac{\text{Total Assets}}{\text{Common Equity}}$$

Decomposing ROE—The Basic Dupont Model

It is very useful to decompose ROE into a few fundamental drivers of profitability. The Basic Dupont Model, pioneered by management at a predecessor of the Dupont Chemical Company, factors ROE into three components, as shown in Figure 5.5.

The Basic Dupont Model does a good job at highlighting the three key drivers of the accounting rate of return on equity. First, the *Net Profit Margin* measures the amount of net income generated per dollar of sales. Second, the *Asset Turnover Ratio* measures the amount of sales generated per dollar of assets. Third, the *Total Leverage Ratio* measures the amount of assets that are supported by a dollar of common equity. The product of the three gives the net income generated per dollar of common equity, which is just ROE.

The Dupont breakdown provides a variety of insights. First, if a firm can't earn a positive net profit margin, then it will generate a negative return regardless of how efficiently it utilizes its assets or how much leverage it applies. The first order of business at any hotdog stand is to sell the hotdogs for more than the cost of the meat and buns. The net profit margin extends this intuition all the way to the bottom line of the income statement—how much of each sales dollar remains after all expenses are deducted. Second, assuming the firm is making a net profit, the trick is to do so with the minimum investment in assets. If selling hotdogs requires an elaborate kiosk, or a fleet of home-delivery trucks, then the profit made might not be sufficient to justify the investment. Fortunately for the hotdog business, most stands run a large volume past a relatively inexpensive investment in assets; hence, the asset turnover is high.

Figure 5.4 illustrated the mean-reversion in ROE. The top panel in Figure 5.6 shows that most of this is due to mean-reversion in the profit margin, which makes sense if price competition is the driving force behind the mean-reversion. In contrast, the total asset turnover ratio and the total leverage ratios are remarkably stable, as seen in the second and third panels of the figure. These ratios are largely determined by the structure of the industry. It takes lots of equipment and a long time to construct buildings, for example, and so the construction industry necessarily has a slow asset turnover ratio. And, as we illustrate later in the chapter, financial institutions necessarily have lots of leverage. In fact, financial institutions dominate the top quintile of total leverage, which stands out from the rest, with a median value of about eight.

The first two components of the Basic Dupont Model capture the operations of the business. How does the firm use its assets to make sales, and how profitably can it convert the sales into net income? These two components tend to trade off against one another; if you multiply them together, you

FIGURE 5.6
**Mean-Reversion in
Net Profit Margin,
Total Asset Turnover
and Total Leverage,
U.S. Firms from 1962
to 2009**
Data are sorted into
five quintiles in year 0.

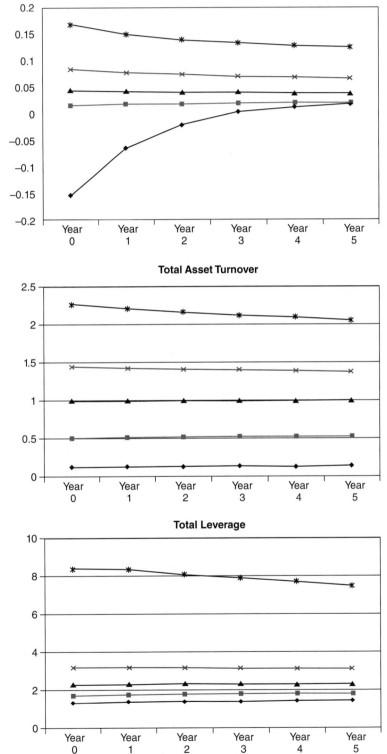

FIGURE 5.7
Trade-Off between Margin and Turnover for Nordstrom and Ross Stores in Fiscal 2006

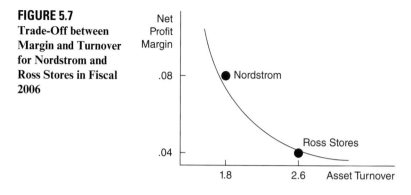

get Net Income/Average Total Assets, labeled the *return on assets*. We can characterize different firms and industries by the different trade-offs that are required between margin and turnover. Capital-intensive industries, such as construction and heavy equipment manufacturing, have low turnovers and must therefore charge higher margins to get a competitive return on assets. On the other end of the spectrum, high turnover discount retailers and fast food chains generally have razor thin profit margins and generate a decent return through high asset turnover. Within industries, we can also characterize firms based on the different margin and turnover trade-offs that they make. Firms that choose a cost leadership strategy, producing at the lowest possible cost and selling in large quantities, tend to have low margins and high turnover. On the other hand, firms that choose a product differentiation strategy, producing a premium product and selling in smaller quantities, tend to have higher margins and lower turnover.

As an example, consider the net profit margin and total asset turnover of Nordstrom and Ross Stores back in fiscal 2006 (well before the 2008 recession completely altered the retail landscape), as shown in Figure 5.7. For fiscal 2006, Nordstrom had a return on assets of about 13.8 percent and Ross Stores had a return on assets of about 11.1 percent—not exactly the same but reasonably close. How the two firms got to this similar return on assets was completely different. Nordstrom, the luxury retailer, had a net profit margin of 7.7 percent and an asset turnover of 1.8 while Ross Stores, the discount retailer, had a profit margin of 4.3 percent and an asset turnover of 2.6. These numbers reveal the very different strategies the two firms have. Nordstrom makes a significantly larger investment in assets—fancier inventory and fancier stores—and charges a premium for this. While Ross Stores keeps significantly less net income per dollar of sales, they make up for it by economizing on the stores and inventory; consequently, they generate significantly more sales per dollar of asset invested. While both firms would like to have a high margin *and* a high turnover, in practice this is very hard to achieve. If Ross Stores were to raise its prices in order to improve its margin, its sales volume would probably suffer, driving down its asset turnover. And if Nordstrom were to carry lower quantities of less expensive inventory in an effort in improve its asset turnover, its customers would probably be unwilling to pay its higher margins. The very nature of each firm's strategy dictates where they will be on the margin versus turnover trade-off.

The trade-off between margins and turnover plays out in a number of different business decisions. Putting inventory on sale lowers the profit margin but improves the asset turnover (assuming, of course, that the sale causes a buying frenzy among customers). Outsourcing production improves turnover, but lowers margins. Aging balsamic vinegar longer improves the quality and allows the vinegar-maker to charge a greater margin, but necessarily lowers the asset turnover.

The first two terms in the Basic Dupont Model determine the firm's return on total assets. The return on equity can be made larger than the return on assets by leveraging the assets. This effect is captured by the third factor in the Basic Dupont Model, Total Leverage. Imagine a firm whose assets are financed by a small amount of equity and a large amount of liabilities. The small equity base claims the entire return on assets and will therefore enjoy a very high return on equity.

Management has lots of control over the firm's leverage, so why don't all firms increase their ROE simply by borrowing more money? Ignoring for a moment the added risk that additional leverage brings, the more basic answer is that the additional debt comes with additional interest expense, and interest expense lowers net income and therefore lowers the Net Profit Margin. Thus, as Total Leverage increases, the Net Profit Margin decreases. Which effect dominates depends on whether the interest rate on the borrowed money is less than the pre-interest return that the firm earns with the borrowed money. This last effect is a weakness of the Basic Dupont Model; it doesn't cleanly separate operating decisions from financing decisions. For this, we must turn to the Advanced Dupont Model.

Decomposing ROE—The Advanced Dupont Model

The Advanced Dupont Model isolates operating performance more cleanly than the Basic Dupont Model by introducing a new measure of profitability: the *return on net operating assets* (RNOA). This core measure of operating performance is then adjusted for the effect of Leverage to arrive at the ROE. While this decomposition more cleanly separates operating and financing effects, it is also more complicated. Before we can present detailed definitions and computations, we need to associate each line item on the income statement and balance sheet with either operating or financing activities. What is operating and what is financing? The answer will not always be clear but as a guiding principle, financing activities relate to sources of capital, and typically come with some type of interest rate, while operating activities are ways in which a firm deploys capital to create value.

The income statement items are divided into Net Operating Income (NOI) and Net Financing Expense (NFE). Both amounts are net of tax, so that Net Income = NOI − NFE. The tax rate used is not arbitrary; it is the effective tax rate for the period, defined as Income Taxes/EBT (where EBT denotes earnings before taxes). The balance sheet assets and liabilities are divided into Net Operating Assets (NOA) and Net Financial Obligations (NFO), so that Common Equity = NOA − NFO. There will be some ambiguous items, but the general goal is to isolate the effects of operating activities from financing activities. The most important thing is to be consistent across classifications on the income statement and balance sheet. It would be wrong, for instance, to classify the interest on capital leases as part of Net Financing Expense but then classify the capital lease obligation as part of Net Operating Assets. Figure 5.8 illustrates how *eVal* has made these classifications. Remember,

FIGURE 5.8
Decomposing the Financial Statements into Operating and Financing Components

Income Statement

	Sales (Net)
−	Cost of Goods Sold
=	Gross Profit
−	R&D Expense
−	SG&A Expense
=	EBITDA
−	Depreciation & Amortization
=	EBIT
−	Interest Expense
+	Non-Operating Income (Loss)
=	EBT
−	Income Taxes
+	Other Income (Loss)
=	Net Income Before Ext. Items
−	Ext. Items & Disc. Ops.
−	Minority Interest in Earnings
−	Preferred Dividends
=	Net Income (available to common)

Balance Sheet

	Operating Cash and Market. Sec.
+	Receivables
+	Inventories
+	Other Current Assets
=	Total Current Assets
+	PP&E (Net)
+	Investments
+	Intangibles
+	Other Assets
=	Total Assets
	Current Debt
+	Accounts Payable
+	Income Taxes Payable
+	Other Current Liabilities
=	Total Current Liabilities
+	Long-Term Debt
+	Other Liabilities
+	Deferred Taxes
=	Total Liabilities
+	Minority Interest
+	Preferred Stock
+	Paid in Common Capital (Net)
+	Retained Earnings
=	Total Common Equity

Net Operating Income (NOI) =

	(EBIT + Non-Operating Income) × (1-tx)
+	Other Income (Loss)
−	Ext. Items and Disc. Ops.

Net Financing Expense (NFE) =

	Interest Expense × (1-tx)
+	Minority Interest in Earnings
+	Preferred Dividends

where the effective tax rate (tx) = Income Taxes/EBT.

Net Operating Assets (NOA) =

	Total Assets
−	Accounts Payable
−	Income Taxes Payable
−	Other Current Liabilities
−	Other Liabilities
−	Deferred Taxes

Net Financial Obligations (NFO) =

	Current Debt
+	Long-Term Debt
+	Minority Interest
+	Preferred Stock

Return on Net Operating Assets (RNOA) = $\dfrac{\text{NOI}}{\text{NOA}}$

Net Borrowing Cost (NBC) = $\dfrac{\text{NFE}}{\text{NFO}}$

eVal can't read and interpret the detailed financial statements, so some of the classifications are crude. You need to read the actual financial statements and adjust the data inputs or interpret *eVal* accordingly.

Having allocated the line items in the income statement and balance sheet into operating and financing components, we can now conduct our ratio analysis on each activity separately, and then examine how they come together to determine ROE. The two key ratios are shown at the bottom of Figure 5.8. They are

$$\text{Return on Net Operating Assets (RNOA)} = \frac{\text{Net Operating Income (NOI)}}{\text{Net Operating Assets (NOA)}}$$

and

$$\text{Net Borrowing Cost (NBC)} = \frac{\text{Net Financing Expense (NFE)}}{\text{Net Financial Obligation (NFO)}}$$

where

Net Financing Expense (NFE) = Interest Expense $\times$ (1-tax) + Preferred Dividends + Minority Interest in Earnings,

Net Operating Income (NOI) = Net Income + Net Financing Expense,

Net Financial Obligations (NFO) = Current Debt + Long-Term Debt + Minority Interest + Preferred Stock,

Net Operating Assets (NOA) = Common Equity + Net Financial Obligations, and

Effective Tax Rate (tax) = Income Taxes/Earnings Before Taxes

Each ratio associates the income statement flows with the balance sheet items that caused them. Consider the RNOA. In the numerator, NOI represents the after-tax income earned by the operating assets; equivalently, it is net income with the after-tax financing charges added back. In the denominator, NOA represents the operating assets used to generate the NOI. Equivalently, NOA is equal to common equity plus net financial obligations. Common equity and net financial obligations represent the sources of capital that are used to finance the net operating assets. The result is a measure of the firm's operating performance that abstracts from the manner in which these operations are financed. For instance, RNOA is not affected by the firm's level of debt, the interest rate it borrows at, or the tax shield that the interest creates. All these effects are isolated in the net borrowing cost (NBC), which associates the after-tax income statement flows that go to debt, minority interests, and preferred stock providers with the amount of capital they provided.

The absolute interpretation of the RNOA as a profitability measure is similar to the interpretation of ROE. The key difference is that the long-term hurdle rate for RNOA is the after-tax weighted average cost of capital—a blend of the cost of equity capital and debt capital that we will discuss in Chapter 9.

FIGURE 5.9
Advanced Dupont
Model

$$ROE = RNOA + Leverage \times Spread$$

$$= \frac{NOI}{NOA} + \frac{NFO}{Common\ Equity} \times (RNOA - NBC)$$

$$= \frac{NOI}{NOA} + \frac{NFO}{Common\ Equity} \times \left(\frac{NOI}{NOA} - \frac{NFE}{NFO}\right)$$

and

$$RNOA = Net\ Operating\ Margin \times Net\ Operating\ Asset\ Turnover$$

$$= \frac{NOI}{Sales} \times \frac{Sales}{NOA}$$

where ROE is Return on Common Equity, RNOA is Return on Net Operating Aassets, NBC is Net Borrowing Cost, NOI is Net Operating Income, NOA is Net Operating Assets, NFO is Net Financial Obligations, and NFE is Net Financing Expense, as defined in Figure 5.8.

A final word of warning about RNOA: In practice, there are many different definitions and terminologies used for RNOA. For example, it is not uncommon to use total assets in the denominator, in which case the measure is usually referred to simply as return on assets (ROA). Another common variant measures the numerator before taxes, in which case the measure is usually referred to as the pre-tax RNOA. Finally, the term return on invested capital (ROIC) is frequently used in place of the term RNOA. Recall that net operating assets are equal to invested capital (the sum of debt, minority interests, preferred stock and common stock). So the terms net operating assets and invested capital are often used interchangeably. The bottom line is that when you see a return on "something" you should make sure that you understand how it is computed before attempting to interpret it.

Putting all the pieces together, the Advanced Dupont Model decomposes ROE as shown in Figure 5.9.

Note that Leverage in this decomposition differs from the Total Leverage definition in the Basic Dupont Model. This measure of leverage only includes financial obligations in the numerator, whereas the Basic Dupont Model uses total assets. The Advanced Dupont Model describes ROE as RNOA plus an adjustment for the amount of Leverage the firm employs times the Spread between RNOA and NBC. To interpret this relation, first recall that RNOA measures a firm's operating performance. ROE, on the other hand, measures the return to the common equity holders after satisfying the claims of all the other capital providers that are funding the firm's operations. The common equity holders are the residual claimants on any operating earnings that remain after satisfying these other capital providers. Thus, if a firm's RNOA exceeds its net borrowing costs (NBC), then the ROE will exceed the RNOA because the common equity holders get more than a proportionate share in the net operating income. The extent to which ROE exceeds RNOA depends on the Spread between RNOA and the NBC, and the amount of Leverage the firm applies.

As simple illustration, consider a hypothetical bank that borrows funds at one rate, lends at another (hopefully higher) rate, and has no other revenues or expenses. The bank's RNOA is given by its lending rate (i.e., the rate it earns on its operating assets, which consist of its loan portfolio). The ROE generated for the bank's owners depends on its borrowing rate relative to its lending rate (i.e., its spread) and the proportion of its lending that is funded by debt. For example, if a bank lends at 10 percent, funds its lending with nine dollars of debt for each dollar of equity, and borrows the debt at 8 percent, then the bank's ROE is given by

$$\text{ROE} = 10\% + \frac{9}{1}(10\% - 8\%) = 28\%.$$

In this case the Leverage is 9 and the Spread is 2 percent, adding 18 percent to the RNOA of 10 percent to yield an ROE of 28 percent. Note that leverage does not always increase ROE relative to RNOA. If a firm has a negative spread, then additional leverage reduces ROE relative to RNOA. For example, assume that the bank in our example can only lend at 6 percent. In this case we have

$$\text{ROE} = 6\% + \frac{9}{1}(6\% - 8\%) = -12\%$$

Thus, higher leverage increases ROE when RNOA is greater than the cost of non-equity financing and reduces ROE when RNOA is less than the cost of non-equity financing. In other words, additional leverage makes the good times better and the bad times worse. This is just another way of saying that additional leverage increases the risk of the returns to common equity holders.

The next stage of the Advanced Dupont Model is to decompose RNOA into net operating margin and the net operating asset turnover, much like we did in the Basic Dupont Model:

$$\text{RNOA} = \text{Net Operating Margin} \times \text{Net Operating Asset Turnover}$$

where

$$\text{Net Operating Margin} = \frac{\text{NOI}}{\text{Sales}}$$

and

$$\text{Net Operating Asset Turnover} = \frac{\text{Sales}}{\text{NOA}}$$

Thus, RNOA is increasing in both the margin that a firm generates on its sales and the amount of sales that can be generated per unit of assets, just as in the Basic Dupont Model. The difference between the two models is that in the advanced model, the margin and turnover measures are based on cleaner measures of operating activities, and this has some important consequences. First, the net operating margin isn't polluted by interest expense, minority interest in earnings, or preferred dividends, as it was in the Basic Dupont Model. Second, the treatment of operating liabilities is very different between the two models. Imagine using operating cash to pay off an extra dollar of accounts payable on the last day of the year. Clearly this has no effect on the ROE. And no terms in the Advanced Dupont Model would change because the definition of NOA nets the operating liabilities against the operating assets. However, in the Basic Dupont Model, the Asset Turnover Ratio would increase because there is a dollar less of total assets (the dollar of cash is gone) and the Total Leverage would decrease because there is a dollar less total liabilities (because the dollar of accounts payable is gone). Again, because the Basic Dupont Model doesn't make a clean distinction between operating and financing, seemingly minor transactions can influence the ratios. The Advanced Dupont Model mitigates these distortions.

Financial Assets in the Advanced Dupont Model

eVal classifies all cash and marketable securities as part of net operating assets. Yet in many cases, these are really financial assets that are not directly tied to the operations. The firm needs to maintain some balance of cash to fund its ongoing operating activities, but this is rarely more than a few percent of sales. To pick an extreme example, Google at the end of June 2010 had over $30 billion in cash and marketable securities. This is more than 125 percent of its annual sales, and six times its balance of property and equipment. Google doesn't need to maintain this much cash for normal operations; rather, it is accumulating financial assets for future acquisitions (at least we think that's what they are up to). How should we deal with these financial assets in our Advanced Dupont Model? Ideally, we would net them against the Net Financial Obligations and we would net the investment income they produce against Net Financing Expense. They aren't really part of operations, so we should shuffle them into financing. *eVal* doesn't do this for a few reasons. First, we would be hard-pressed to specify for all firms at all times what the right amount of operating cash is, making it almost impossible to isolate the true financial assets. Second, without examining the as reported financial statements and footnotes, it is impossible to know where the investment income has been included on the income statement, and hence impossible to know the income statement line item where the data standardization process has allocated this income. It could be netted against Interest Expense and therefore included in that line item, it could be included in Non-Operating Income (Loss), or it could be netted against SG&A Expense. As we discussed in Chapter 2, you need to look at the as reported financial statements and make sure that *eVal*'s standardized income statement and balance sheet are in good order. Part of that exercise is making sure that the line item "Interest Expense" is only the interest outflow on the Current and Long Term Debt; any interest income should ideally be included in Non-Operating Income (Loss). An early indicator that your financial statements might have a problem in this regard is an extremely low (or even negative) Net Borrowing Cost.

FIGURE 5.10
Dupont Models
for Kohl's, Fiscal
2005–2009

Company Name	KOHL'S CORP				
	Actual	Actual	Actual	Actual	Actual
Fiscal Year End Date	06-01-31	07-01-31	08-01-31	09-01-31	10-01-31
Basic Dupont Model					
Net Profit Margin	0.063	0.071	0.066	0.054	0.058
x Total Asset Turnover		1.709	1.681	1.497	1.403
x Total Leverage		1.574	1.675	1.705	1.679
= Return on Equity		0.192	0.185	0.138	0.136
Advanced Dupont Model					
Net Operating Margin	0.067	0.074	0.070	0.059	0.063
x Net Operating Asset Turnover		2.257	2.222	1.931	1.834
= Return on Net Operating Assets		0.168	0.164	0.115	0.115
Net Borrowing Cost (NBC)		0.042	0.039	0.042	0.040
Spread (RNOA - NBC)		0.126	0.115	0.072	0.074
Financial Leverage (LEV)		0.191	0.267	0.322	0.284
ROE = RNOA + LEV*Spread		0.192	0.185	0.138	0.136

Decomposing Kohl's ROE

Let's take a look at what the Dupont models tell us about Kohl's ROE. You can locate this analysis in *eVal* by going to the Ratio Analysis sheet. We reproduce this analysis in Figure 5.10.

Kohl's ROE has steadily declined from 19.2 percent in fiscal 2006 to 13.6 percent in fiscal 2009, and its RNOA has declined from 16.8 percent to 11.5 percent over the same period. The Basic Dupont Model indicates that the decline in Kohl's ROE is a combination of declining net profit margins and declining total asset turnover ratios. The Advanced Dupont Model tells a similar story of declining net operating margins and net asset turnover ratios. Note that the spread between Kohl's RNOA and NBC is consistently over 7 percent, indicating that leverage helps to increase ROE relative to RNOA. Unfortunately, Kohl's financial leverage is generally less than 30 percent so the 7 percent spread translates into only about a 2.1 percent increase in ROE relative to RNOA. One wonders why Kohl's doesn't use more leverage, given its healthy spread. A probable explanation is that Kohl's has a lot of off-balance-sheet leverage in the form of operating leases for its stores. Thus, the reported leverage ratio of under 30 percent probably understates Kohl's economic leverage (more on this point later).

Turning to a cross-sectional comparison between Kohl's, Nordstrom, and Ross Stores, we see that in fiscal 2009 Kohl's ROE of 13.6 percent, while reasonable in an absolute sense, is far below the other two companies. Figure 5.11 gives the Advanced Dupont Model for the three companies in fiscal 2009. Nordstrom reports a healthy 31.7 percent ROE and Ross Stores rings in with an impressive 41.1 percent! Nordstrom's RNOA is only a bit larger than Kohl's, but with a leverage ratio of almost 2 and a spread of almost 10 percent, they get a huge boost from their leverage. Ross Stores, with almost no financial leverage, gets to their impressive ROE a completely different way. They earn a net operating margin as large as Kohl's and Nordstrom, yet they have a net operating asset turnover that is about three times larger than the other two

FIGURE 5.11

Advanced Dupont Model for Kohl's, Nordstrom, and Ross Stores in Fiscal 2009

Advanced Dupont Model	Kohls fiscal 2009	Nordstrom fiscal 2009	Ross fiscal 2009
Net Operating Margin	0.063	0.062	0.062
x Net Operating Asset Turnover	1.834	2.182	5.856
= Return on Net Operating Assets	0.115	0.135	0.366
Net Borrowing Cost (NBC)	0.040	0.037	0.039
Spread (RNOA - NBC)	0.074	0.099	0.327
Financial Leverage (LEV)	0.284	1.843	0.139
ROE = RNOA + LEV*Spread	0.136	0.317	0.411

companies, resulting in a RNOA of 36.6 percent. Ross Stores high margins are somewhat of a surprise. Following a discount retail strategy, it is supposed to have lower margins and make up for it with higher net operating asset turnover. And Nordstrom, following a luxury retail strategy, is supposed to have higher margins but pay for it with a slower asset turnover. And yet Kohl's, Nordstrom, and Ross Stores have almost identical operating margins. Consequently, Ross Stores cleans up by enjoying a high margin *and* a high asset turnover. We will explore the margins and turnover ratios of these three companies in more detail in the next section.

5.7   PROFIT MARGINS

The net operating margin used in the Advanced Dupont Model represents after-tax operating income divided by sales. In order to understand the drivers of net operating margin, we must look at each of the components of after-tax operating income as a proportion of sales. Note that the Forecasting Assumptions sheet in *eVal* expresses many of the income statement line items as a proportion of sales. Rather than repeating this analysis, our ratio analysis focuses on just a few key margins. If the bottom line net operating margin is unusual, then work your way down this list of intermediate margins to identify the underlying line items that are driving this behavior.

The starting point is the *Gross Margin*, which measures the difference between sales and cost of goods sold as a proportion of sales:

$$\text{Gross Margin} = \frac{\text{Gross Profit}}{\text{Sales}}$$

This is the first level of profitability—the mark-up on the product. For each dollar of sales, how much more can the firm charge over the cost of making or buying the product. It is generally all down hill from here, so if a firm can't generate a decent gross margin, there is not much point in looking any further. This is also the ratio to watch if you are worried about increased competition. If the firm is lowering its prices to retain market share, you will see it here.

The next key margin we report is the *EBITDA margin* that gives earnings, before interest, taxes depreciation, and amortization as a proportion of sales.

Another way to define the numerator is sales less cost of goods sold, R&D expense, and SG&A expense. The ratio is shown below:

$$\text{EBITDA Margin} = \frac{\text{EBITDA}}{\text{Sales}}$$

A firm may enjoy a large mark-up on its product, but it could be that its key costs aren't due to the actual production of the goods. For instance, the drug company Pfizer (ticker = PFE) has a gross margin of approximately 80–85 percent for the past few years. But the real costs at a pharmaceutical company are R&D and SG&A; the actual manufacturing of the drug is a relatively minor cost. Consequently, Pfizer's EBITDA margin is only about 38 percent. If you discover that the EBITDA margin is unusual, then you should go back to the detailed income statement to identify the specific line items that are responsible. Note that this ratio excludes depreciation and amortization, so it can be quite high for capital-intensive firms. Analysts often tout the EBITDA ratio, reasoning that depreciation and amortization represent noncash charges and are therefore irrelevant. But don't be tricked into relying too heavily on this ratio (as many Telecom investors were in the late 1990s). While depreciation and amortization are accounting adjustments, they nevertheless represent the allocation of real past capital expenditures. A capital-intensive firm may look great on an EBITDA basis, but sooner or later, it will have to reinvest real cash in its capital base in order to stay in business.

The *EBIT margin* is the EBITDA margin with the "DA" taken out. As such, it provides a useful summary measure of operating performance after deducting depreciation and amortization. The numerator is sales less all expenses except interest and taxes; hence the name Earnings Before Interest and Taxes:

$$\text{EBIT Margin} = \frac{\text{Earnings Before Interest and Taxes}}{\text{Sales}}$$

The net operating margin can fluctuate due to changes in leverage or tax rates. The EBIT margin abstracts from these effects, providing a clean measure of underlying operating performance.

As we move down the page from Gross margin to EBIT margin, the relation between sales and profits gets weaker. As sales increase, cost of goods sold will necessarily have to increase—the firm needs to pay for the goods that it is selling—so the gross margin is relatively stable over time. But an increase in sales does not necessarily mean that R&D expense will increase, as this is a much more discretionary expenditure. Similarly, administrative expenses bear no direct relation to sales. In the long run a firm needs these expenses to generate its sales, but in a given year there is no reason why they should vary in proportion to sales.

The final margin that we report is the *Net Operating Margin Before Nonrecurring Items.* This margin starts with net operating income but then adds back any nonrecurring expenses, adjusted for their tax consequences (specifically, it adds back tax-adjusted Nonoperating Income, Other Income, and Extraordinary Items and Discontinued Operations). Unusual behavior in this margin that does not show up in the EBIT margin is attributable to taxes, or costs of non-equity capital (specifically, tax-adjusted Interest Expense, Minority Interest in Earnings and Preferred Dividends).

$$\text{Net Operating Margin before nonrecurring items}$$
$$= \frac{\text{Net Operating Income} + \text{After-tax nonrecurring items}}{\text{Sales}}$$

Finally, any unusual behavior in the bottom line net operating margin that does not show up in the above margin is due to nonrecurring items. As mentioned above, *eVal* makes a leap of faith in classifying tax-adjusted Nonoperating Income, Other Income, and Extraordinary Items and Discontinued Operations as nonrecurring. You should identify the nature of these items from the Form 10-K and make sure you are confident that they are indeed unlikely to recur.

Economies of Scale and Operating Risk

Many young and growing firms have negative net operating margins. They all claim that this is a temporary situation and that once they grow past some critical size, they will be hugely profitable. Of course, many of them never achieve this dream and fail, but the ones that succeed do so because they experience economies of scale. A typical situation might be a firm with a positive gross margin but a negative EBITDA margin, due mainly to its SG&A expense. If the SG&A expense is composed of mostly fixed costs, then as sales grow, the SG&A expense does not increase proportionately, and eventually the EBITDA margin becomes positive. Moreover, expenditures on R&D and marketing have to be expensed immediately, but usually benefit future sales. Be on the lookout for such effects as you study a company's margins. If sales are growing and the margins are steadily improving, this is a sign that the firm is exploiting economies of scale. Alternatively, if a firm claims that it will not be profitable until it grows to some larger size, but its past sales growth has not generated any significant improvement in its margins, then you should be suspicious. The company's claims of great margins in the future may be nothing more than wishful thinking.

While a cost structure with a large fixed cost component helps achieve economies of scale, it also imposes *operating risk* (also referred to as *operating leverage*) on the company. If the sales volume is highly variable then in periods of low volume the firm will be stuck with its fixed costs and insufficient revenue to cover them; in periods of high volume it will easily cover its fixed costs and enjoy huge margins. In other words, the good times are really good and the bad times are really bad. As an example, consider a firm's decision to buy equipment or enter short-term rental contacts for the same equipment. Short-term rental contracts can be varied with sales, resulting in lower operating risk. For this reason managers often attempt to lower their operating risk by outsourcing many aspects of production. Frequently, however, they

FIGURE 5.12
Margin and Turnover
Analysis for Kohl's,
Fiscal 2005–2009

Company Name	KOHL'S CORP				
	Actual	Actual	Actual	Actual	Actual
Fiscal Year End Date	06-01-31	07-01-31	08-01-31	09-01-31	10-01-31
Margin Analysis					
Gross Margin	0.353	0.364	0.365	0.369	0.378
EBITDA Margin	0.129	0.142	0.137	0.127	0.134
EBIT Margin	0.106	0.117	0.110	0.094	0.100
Net Operating Margin (b4 non-rec.)	0.066	0.073	0.068	0.058	0.062
Net Operating Margin	0.067	0.074	0.070	0.059	0.063
Turnover Analysis					
Net Operating Asset Turnover		2.257	2.222	1.931	1.834
Net Working Capital Turnover		7.530	9.505	8.476	6.853
Avge Days to Collect Receivables		19.396	0.000	0.000	0.000
Avge Inventory Holding Period		89.043	94.985	99.863	97.778
Avge Days to Pay Payables		31.441	30.119	30.490	34.949
PP&E Turnover		3.141	2.777	2.429	2.454

find that there is little profit left over when they do this. No risk often means no reward. For example, most oil exploration companies rent exploration equipment from dedicated oil services companies. This lowers their operating risk. But when the price of oil is high, the oil services firms jack up their rental rates, cutting into the potential profits of the oil exploration companies.

Analyzing Kohl's Margins

Let's take a look at the breakdown of Kohl's margins. Margin analysis directly follows the Dupont Model on *eVal*'s Ratio Analysis worksheet. Kohl's margin and turnover analysis for fiscal 2009 is reproduced in Figure 5.12.

We see that the gross margin has increased slightly every year since fiscal 2005, adding .025 over the period. This is definitely good news, but it is only part of the story because the EBITDA margin decreased every year until it recovered slightly in 2009. By toggling to the Forecasting Assumptions worksheet we see that the main force behind the decline in the EBITDA margin is a steadily increasing ratio of SG&A to sales. So much for economies of scale at Kohl's. And the MD&A on page 24 of Kohl's fiscal 2009 Form 10-K doesn't offer much comfort. The increase in 2009 isn't due to increased advertising, which might generate future sales, or to process improvements. No, the main explanation given for the increase in SG&A is increased incentive compensation for non-hourly employees. While this is clearly good news for those lucky executives, it is not the direction investors like to see the ratio of SG&A to sales moving. There is no evidence of economies of scale at Kohl's. From fiscal 2005 to fiscal 2009 Kohl's sales increased 28 percent while the SG&A expenses increased 39 percent.

Earlier we compared Kohl's to Nordstrom and Ross Stores to illustrate the trade-off between margins and turnovers in the Dupont Model. We conveniently picked fiscal 2006 for this comparison, before the 2008 recession altered the retail landscape. If we roll the clock forward to fiscal 2009, we

FIGURE 5.13

Comparative Margins and Turnover Ratios for Kohl's, Nordstrom, and Ross Stores in Fiscal 2009

Margin Analysis	Kohls fiscal 2009	Nordstrom fiscal 2009	Ross fiscal 2009
Gross Margin	0.378	0.419	0.258
EBITDA Margin	0.100	0.133	0.101
EBIT Margin	0.100	0.097	0.101
Net Operating Margin (b4 non-rec.	0.062	0.061	0.062
Net Operating Margin	0.063	0.062	0.062
Turnover Analysis			
Net Operating Asset Turnover	1.834	2.182	5.856
Net Working Capital Turnover	6.853	4.002	15.731
Avge Days to Collect Receivables	0.000	84.132	5.062
Avge Inventory Holding Period	97.778	65.431	60.073
Avge Days to Pay Payables	34.949	46.926	41.005
PP&E Turnover	2.454	3.866	7.584

see some interesting changes, as shown in Figure 5.13. First, the basic value-luxury pricing structure remains the same: the gross margin is 41.9 percent at Nordstrom, compared to 37.8 percent at Kohl's and 25.8 percent at Ross Stores. But, as we noted earlier, in fiscal 2009 the net operating margin at the three companies is almost identical at around 6.3 percent. What happened between the gross margin and the net operating margin for these three companies? If we compare the EBITDA margins, we get the answer. The only relevant expense between the gross margin and the EBITDA margin for these companies is SG&A. By toggling to the Forecasting Assumptions sheet for Nordstroms and for Ross Stores, we see that Ross keeps this expense at 15.7 percent of sales, while Nordstroms reports 28.6 percent. Besides turning over their assets much faster than Kohl's and Nordstrom, Ross Stores spends much less on advertising and general administration. Ross Stores results are even more impressive if we note that their depreciation charge is included in SG&A while the other two companies report this amount separately. Adjusting Ross Stores financial statements in fiscal 2009 to move depreciation to its own line makes the adjusted SG&A/Sales ratio 13.5 percent. If you look at the time series of margins for Ross Stores, you see that as their sales steadily increased through the recession period, they managed to slowly increase their gross margin, while controlling their SG&A expenses and keeping their turnover high. Ross Stores delivered value to cost-conscious customers relative to the Kohl's and Nordstroms, but squeezed a few extra pennies out of them at the same time.

5.8   TURNOVER RATIOS

We now turn our attention to ratios measuring the amount of assets that the firm requires to generate its sales, known as turnover ratios. These ratios are also referred to as efficiency ratios, because they tell us how efficiently management is employing the firm's assets. A net operating asset turnover ratio of 2 indicates that $.50 of net operating assets are required to generate $1.00

of sales. We use turnover analysis to examine how the underlying operating asset and liability line items on the balance sheet contribute to the overall net operating asset turnover ratio. The basic approach is to compute a turnover ratio for specific groups of operating assets and operating liabilities. A common turnover ratio is the *Net Working Capital Turnover Ratio*, computed as

$$\text{Net Working Capital Turnover Ratio}$$
$$= \frac{\text{Sales}}{\text{Current Operating Assets} - \text{Current Operating Liabilities}}$$

In *eVal*, all the current assets are classified as operating and all the current liabilities except current debt are classified as operating. The net working capital turnover ratio measures how efficiently a firm is managing its working capital accounts. Ideally, a firm would like to generate sales with a minimum investment in working capital. Obviously this presents the firm with trade-offs. It is difficult to minimize the investment in inventory while still presenting the customers with a wide variety of choices and fast delivery. And all firms would like to collect on their sales immediately and pay their accounts payable very slowly, but customers often prefer to delay payments and suppliers often give incentives to pay early.

It is common to compute individual turnover ratios for the three most important components of working capital—receivables, inventories and payables—and there are a number of common modifications that are made to these ratios. First, they are often stated in the form of the average number of days that a dollar sits in the account. The relation between a turnover ratio and the average days outstanding metric is simply:

$$\text{Average Days Outstanding} = \frac{365}{\text{Turnover Ratio}}$$

For example, if we turn over our receivables 12 times per year, then the average receivable must have a life of approximately 365/12 = 30 days. Using this approach, the average days to collect receivables is given by:

$$\text{Average Days to Collect Receivables} = 365 \times \frac{\text{Average Accounts Receivable}}{\text{Sales}}$$

Similarly, the average inventory holding period is given by:

$$\text{Average Days to Sell Inventory} = 365 \times \frac{\text{Average Inventory}}{\text{Cost of Goods Sold}}$$

Note that we made an additional modification in computing the average inventory holding period; we replaced sales with cost of goods sold. This is because inventories are carried at cost, and so we want a flow variable that measures the cost of inventories consumed during the period. Lastly, the average days to pay payables is computed as:

$$\text{Average Days to Pay Payables} = 365 \times \frac{\text{Average Accounts Payable}}{\text{Purchases}}$$

where

Purchases = Cost of Goods Sold + Ending Inventory − Beginning Inventory

Note here that the denominator is measured using purchases. This represents the amount of payables that were added during the period, and so is directly comparable with the average balance in the payables account in the numerator.

The final turnover ratio that we report is property, plant and equipment (PP&E) turnover, computed as:

$$\text{PP\&E Turnover} = \frac{\text{Sales}}{\text{Average Net PP\&E}}$$

PP&E isn't literally consumed in the sale the same way that inventory is. Nonetheless, it is an asset that is necessary in the production of sales, albeit indirectly at times. In the very short run, Kohl's corporate headquarters and distribution centers could probably blow up and sales in the department stores wouldn't be affected, but in the long run headquarters and distribution centers are necessary. We want to know if the firm is using its PP&E efficiently. Does it have idle capacity? Does it invest too heavily in nonproducing assets, such as lavish headquarters and Learjets? Comparing the PP&E ratio of the firm with a few of its close competitors can frequently shed light on these questions.

Note that there are additional accounts, such as intangibles, that may also drive unusual turnover. You should identify and understand these accounts. For example, if a firm has engaged in an acquisition involving significant goodwill, this will typically drive the net operating asset turnover down relative to the company's competitors. However, this is not necessarily a bad sign, and competitors may have similar amounts of internally generated goodwill that is not recognized on their balance sheets.

Analyzing Kohl's Turnover

Referring back to Figure 5.12, we see that Kohl's net operating asset turnover has declined steadily from 2.257 in fiscal 2006 to 1.834 in fiscal 2009. Even if margins had remained steady over this period, this drop in asset turnover would have shaved almost three percent off RNOA. To understand this decline in Kohl's operating efficiency, we need to dig deeper into Kohl's use of the major assets on its balance sheet. For Kohl's, there are two: inventory and PP&E (i.e., stores).

Figure 5.12 shows that the days inventory increased from 89 days in fiscal 2006 to almost 100 days in fiscal 2008; the pants and shirts are in the stores 11 days longer in 2008 than in 2006. The trend reverses itself slightly in fiscal 2009, dropping to 98 days. Recall that over this period Kohl's has continued to grow the total number of stores by about 10 percent a year, and these stores need inventory. Thus, one possible cause of the slower inventory turnover is that Kohl's is beginning to saturate the market. The other cause of the increase in days inventory is quite different. The MD&A section of Kohl's 2009 10-K reports that in fiscal 2008, same-store sales declined a whopping 6.9 percent. This means that even at the stores that were open for two full years (i.e., the one used to compute annual same-store sales growth), 6.9 percent fewer sales dollars crossed the counter. Unless Kohl's kept 6.9 percent less stuff on the shelves in these stores, this will adversely impact the days inventory.

The second source of declining operating efficiency is the PP&E turnover ratio, which drops from 3.141 in fiscal 2006 to 2.454 in fiscal 2009. Given that PP&E makes up more than half the operating assets, this is a serious concern. As we just discussed, Kohl's continued to open stores throughout the recession period. Further, the MD&A reveals that they have recently added distribution centers which, while necessary to support sales and efficient inventory management, have no direct sales impact. The future will tell whether these were wise strategic investments or inefficient growth in lower-producing stores and unnecessary distribution centers.

Before leaving Kohl's time-series turnover analysis, we should ask ourselves whether we have considered all the balance sheet items that could have contributed to Kohl's significant reduction in NOA turnover. We've looked at inventory and PP&E, but Kohl's standardized balance sheet also shows a significant increase in Operating Cash and Marketable Securities in fiscal 2009. *eVal* treats cash as an operating asset although it is unlikely that Kohl's suddenly needs this much extra cash to operate its business. In fiscal 2009 Kohl's cut its capital expenditures to about half the previous level and instead kept the cash, possibly in a delayed response to the recession. If we reclassified "excess cash" as a financial asset, and estimated that Kohl's only needs operating cash equal to four percent of sales (consistent with prior years, as seen on the forecasting assumptions sheet), then we could move the rest out of the operating cash line item. Where we put the cash isn't really relevant at this point, but we could net it against their long-term debt. This would result in an adjusted net operating asset turnover ratio of 1.904—still lower than the previous year, but probably a better reflection of Kohl's true operating asset turnover.

Next, we compare Kohl's turnover ratios with the corresponding ratios for Nordstrom and Ross Stores, as shown in Figure 5.13. As we noted earlier, Kohl's net operating asset turnover is slightly slower than Nordstrom and considerably slower than Ross Stores. We might not expect Kohl's to keep up with Ross Stores, given Ross Stores' position as a discount retailer and their clearly stated strategy to quickly move inventory through sales and promotions. But why are Kohl's assets deployed less efficiently than Nordstrom? Comparing the working capital accounts reveals some interesting differences. First, Nordstrom's Days Inventory are significantly shorter than Kohl's, averaging 65 days in fiscal 2009, compared to almost 100 days at Kohl's. So Kohl's inventory stays in the stores 35 days longer than at Nordstrom. The only strategic reason for this would be that Kohl's feels they can charge a higher margin in return for holding more inventory; otherwise, it looks like

Kohl's is struggling with its inventory management. Working against Nordstrom's asset turnover ratio is the fact that they offer a private label credit card and, as a consequence, carry a significant receivable balance. In fiscal 2009, customers took on average 84 days to pay their Nordstrom credit card balance. Kohl's used to have a credit card program but sold it to Morgan Stanley in fiscal 2006, so they no longer have accounts receivable. Nordstrom's investment in receivables more than offsets Kohl's slow inventory turnover, and the small difference in their Days Payable isn't large enough to make much difference. In fact, if we add the Days Inventory, the Days Receivable, and subtract the Days Payable, we get an estimate of the length of the whole operating cycle: for Kohl's it is 63 days and for Nordstrom it is 103 days. While we might question Kohl's inventory management, their overall working capital management isn't the cause of their slower net operating asset turnover. It is due to long-term operating assets.

The only other significant operating asset for Kohl's and Nordstrom is PP&E, and this is where Kohl's loses the race with Nordstrom. PP&E make up about one half of Kohl's total assets and about one third of Nordstrom's total assets, so Kohl's fiscal 2009 PP&E turnover ratio of 2.454 is drastically lower than Nordstrom's ratio of 3.866. It is hard to imagine that Kohl's stores are so much plusher than Nordstrom's stores; the opposite is almost certainly true. The obvious interpretation is that Nordstrom generates more sales dollars per dollar of PP&E investment because of a combination of good merchandising and shrewd asset investments. Without discounting this conclusion, we offer two less economic explanations. The first is that both companies sell over the Internet and these sales bear no direct relation to the size of the PP&E investment. If Nordstrom does significantly more Internet business than Kohl's, this could enhance their PP&E turnover ratio. Unfortunately, Nordstrom doesn't break out the fraction of sales derived from the Internet, so we can't investigate this explanation any further. The second potential distortion in the PP&E turnover ratio is caused by the accounting measurement of PP&E. Both companies use a mix of leased stores, owned stores, and owned buildings on leased land. Of these, only the owned land and buildings appear in PP&E; the leased assets are expensed as part of SG&A when the lease payments are made. In fiscal 2009, Nordstrom leased approximately 49 percent of their stores while Kohl's only leased about 38 percent (as always, these juicy facts are gleaned from the MD&A section of the companies' 10-K filings). This will decrease Nordstrom's PP&E and increase their SG&A relative to Kohl's. And knowing this helps to reconcile the mystery that was posed at the start of this section: if Nordstrom is pursuing a luxury retail strategy, why is their net operating margin not significantly larger than Kohl's and their asset turnover ratios significantly smaller? If we correct for the different mix of leased versus owned stores between the two companies, we get closer to the ordering of margins and turnovers that we expected to see. But there is still evidence of a relative slippage in Kohl's turnover ratios.

5.9 LEVERAGE

In both the Basic and Advanced Dupont decompositions financial leverage makes the good times better and the bad times worse. As we analyze the firm's past, we can see how much leverage the firm employed, and whether it amplified superior or inferior operating performance. But leverage has a forward-looking feature that the previous ratios lacked. Leverage increases the riskiness of the expected future cash flows. Levered firms commit themselves to making fixed payments to creditors, and the common equity holders must ultimately surrender control of the firm to the creditors if these payments cannot be met. The more financial leverage a firm has, the greater the chance that unexpected poor performance will be amplified to the point that the firm cannot pay its creditors. The likelihood of defaulting on amounts owed to creditors is known as *credit risk*. Many of the ratios we discuss in this section form the basis for the debt covenants between the firm and its creditors. A firm may have great long-term potential, but if it runs into short-term liquidity problems, it may not live to see the long-term. For this reason the analysis of credit risk also includes a detailed examination of the firm's ability to meet its obligations in the next year or two. Our Dupont decompositions examined how financial leverage contributes to the level and variability of ROE; now we want to assess the amount of credit risk that the leverage imposes on the equity holders.

In this section we first discuss some summary measures of a firm's capital structure and short-term liquidity. We then discuss how these and other variables can be combined to make an explicit prediction of how likely it is that the firm will default on its debt.

Long-Term Capital Structure

A firm's capital structure—its mix of debt and equity—is the primary long-term driver of credit risk. The most common way to represent a firm's capital structure is the ratio of total debt to total common equity:

$$\text{Debt to Equity Ratio} = \frac{\text{End-of-Year Current and Long-Term Debt}}{\text{End-of-Year Common Equity}}$$

This ratio is similar to the definition of financial leverage used in the Advanced Dupont Model. It differs in that we exclude preferred stock and minority interests from the numerator, because these capital providers typically have fewer rights than debt holders in the case of a skipped payment. Because we want to assess risk at the most recent point in time, we also compute the debt-to-equity ratio based on the ending balances, rather than the average balances, as in the Advanced Dupont Model.

In the context of credit analysis, this ratio provides an overall indication of the extent of a firm's long-term credit commitments. Other things equal, higher debt-to-equity implies a higher probability of financial distress. The weakness of this ratio is that it fails to take into account the firm's ability to pay off its creditors. For example, firms with very stable and predictable cash flows, such as utilities and banks, frequently run very high debt-to-equity ratios. This is because they have stable cash flows from their customers (utility receipts and interest income), reducing the risk that they won't be able to meet their debt payments. Consequently, a high debt-to-equity ratio is not necessarily an indication of financial distress for firms with strong and stable cash flows.

Our next ratio is funds from operations to total debt, computed as:

$$\text{Funds from Operations to Total Debt} = \frac{\text{Funds from Operations}}{\text{Average Total Debt}}$$

where

Funds from Operations = Net Income + Depreciation & Amortization
+ Increase in Deferred Taxes + Increase in Other Liabilities
+ Minority Interest in Earnings + Preferred Dividends

Funds from operations represent the amount of working capital created or destroyed by the firms operations (it is computed as a subtotal in the Cash from Operations calculation on the Cash Flow Analysis worksheet in *eVal*). This measure directly compares the amount of debt with the flow of funds that will be used to service the debt. Thus, this measure overcomes the shortcoming described above for the debt-to-equity ratio. One benchmark for this ratio is the interest rate that the company pays on its debt. Unless funds from operations can comfortably cover interest payments, the probability of default is high. A potential shortcoming of this ratio is that working capital can be tied up in illiquid current asset accounts, such as prepayments and inventories. In reality, it will be difficult to pay creditors with these assets. Thus, a common variant of this ratio is the cash from operations to debt ratio. This ratio backs the noncash working capital accounts out of the numerator to get Cash from Operations (also computed on the Cash Flow Analysis worksheet in *eVal*):

$$\text{CFO to Total Debt} = \frac{\text{Cash from Operations}}{\text{Average Total Debt}}$$

This ratio is a useful check, but you should not interpret it too literally. Growth firms frequently run negative cash from operations as they invest in working capital to generate sales growth. This growth is not necessarily a bad thing, but we need to make sure that the firm has the necessary plans in place to finance this growth.

Short-Term Liquidity

The above ratios focus on the firm's capital structure to assess the credit risk created by the firm's long-run financial obligations. The next set of ratios focus on short-term liquidity. These ratios provide an indication of the firm's ability to meet its short-term cash commitments as they come due. The first ratio is the current ratio, measured as the ratio of current assets to current liabilities:

$$\text{Current Ratio} = \frac{\text{End-of-Year Current Assets}}{\text{End-of-Year Current Liabilities}}$$

Current assets represent the assets that the firm expects to convert to cash over the next 12 months. Current liabilities represent the obligations that the firm must satisfy over the next 12 months. A current ratio greater than one indicates that the company has enough current assets to meet its current liabilities. An obvious shortcoming of this measure is that, in the event of financial distress, some of the current assets may not be readily converted into cash at their book values. If no one is buying the company's inventory then it might not be worth its book value, and you can imagine the difficulty in converting prepaid rent back into cash. An alternative measure of the ability to meet current liabilities is the quick ratio:

$$\text{Quick Ratio} = \frac{\text{End-of-Year Operating Cash and Marketable Securities} + \text{Receivables}}{\text{End-of-Year Current Liabilities}}$$

This ratio restricts the numerator to cash, marketable securities and receivables, which are all likely to be converted into cash on short notice at close to their book values.

The next two ratios are called *interest coverage ratios*. These ratios provide an indication of the ability of a firm to cover its interest charges based on its ongoing operating profits. The first ratio uses EBIT (earnings before interest and taxes) in the numerator and interest expense in the denominator, while the second ratio replaces the numerator with EBITDA (earnings before interest, taxes, depreciation and amortization):

$$\text{EBIT Interest Coverage Ratio} = \frac{\text{EBIT}}{\text{Interest Expense}}, \text{ and}$$

$$\text{EBITDA Interest Coverage Ratio} = \frac{\text{EBITDA}}{\text{Interest Expense}}$$

The key difference between the ratios is the exclusion of depreciation and amortization expense from the numerator of the second ratio. The rationale for excluding depreciation and amortization is that they represent noncash charges, and therefore do not reduce the amount of cash available to meet interest payments. On the other hand, a firm must ultimately replace its depreciable assets in order to stay in business, and so it can also be argued that inclusion of these charges provides a more meaningful indicator of long-term solvency.

Analyzing Kohl's Leverage

In the Advanced Dupont decomposition for Kohl's we noted that they employed very little leverage when compared to Nordstrom. Figure 5.14 shows

FIGURE 5.14
Comparative
Leverage and
Liquidity Ratios for
Kohl's, Nordstrom,
and Ross Stores in
Fiscal 2009

Analysis of Leverage - Long-Term Capital Structure	Kohls fiscal 2009	Nordstrom fiscal 2009	Ross fiscal 2009
Debt to Equity Ratio	0.263	1.662	0.130
FFO to Total Debt	0.831	0.333	3.065
CFO to Total Debt	1.015	0.428	4.741
Analysis of Leverage - Short-Term Liquidity			
Current Ratio	2.295	2.013	1.466
Quick Ratio	0.949	1.405	0.733
EBIT Interest Coverage	12.317	5.635	77.305
EBITDA Interest Coverage	16.561	7.750	77.305

that at the end of fiscal 2009, Kohl's debt-to-equity ratio is 0.263 while at Nordstrom it is 1.662 (*eVal* computes a more detailed leverage analysis immediately following the turnover analysis on the Ratio Analysis worksheet). The low level of debt means that Kohl's has very little credit risk. Their CFO-to-Total Debt is greater than one—they could have paid off their entire debt balance with the most recent year's operating cash flows. An analysis of their short-term liquidity yields a similar conclusion. In fiscal 2009 Kohl's has more than twice as many current assets than current liabilities (i.e., the current ratio is greater than two). Their quick ratio is 0.949, meaning that they have enough cash and marketable securities on hand at the end of the year to almost pay off their entire debt balance. Finally, Kohl's EBIT interest coverage ratio is extremely healthy. They generated enough EBIT to make their interest payments 12 times over. Compare these values to Nordstrom, who has significantly more leverage. Nordstrom too is sitting on a pile of cash and marketable securities, so their quick ratio is 1.405 in fiscal 2009. Their coverage ratio is much lower than Kohl's, however, with an EBIT interest coverage of 5.635.

There is one accounting distortion that we should consider before concluding that Kohl's is financially healthy and has little credit risk. As discussed earlier, Kohl's leases about half of its stores and almost all of these leases are accounted for as operating leases, meaning that they do not show up as debt on the books. Nonetheless, these leases contractually commit Kohl's to significant fixed payments, much like interest on debt does. We can include the impact of operating leases on Kohl's credit risk by treating the operating lease payments just like interest in the coverage ratios. Specifically, we would add the payment back to EBIT in the numerator and to the interest in the denominator of the coverage ratios, creating an adjusted interest coverage ratio (often called a *Fixed Charge Coverage ratio*). Footnote 4 in Kohl's 10-K shows that the fiscal 2009 rent expense on operating leases was $498 million. Adding this back to EBIT and to net interest results in an adjusted ratio of 3.469. Kohl's all of a sudden doesn't look quite as safe.

5.10 MODELING CREDIT RISK

The analysis of leverage in the previous section gives us some interesting ratios, but it doesn't directly quantify the probability of default. Predicting the likelihood that a company will default on its debt is one of the most common uses of financial statement analysis. Every junior loan officer at every local bank requires financial statements from a commercial loan applicant and, if the loan is granted, then requires that financial statements be submitted on a regular basis in order to monitor the financial health of the company. The loan contract may contain covenants that limit subsequent borrowing or equity distributions by the company and establishes periodic tests of financial health. If the company fails a health test, then the loan is declared to be in technical default and it becomes immediately due and payable in full. The idea is that, if the company starts to look sufficiently sick, the bank can rush back in and grab assets before they are all gone.

Being in technical default on a loan doesn't necessarily mean the firm will fail, or seek bankruptcy protection, but these events are highly correlated. In any case, defaulting on a loan has enormous consequences; legal fees skyrocket, vendors may stop granting credit, and customers may stop buying goods and services. For example, when General Motors entered bankruptcy proceedings in 2009, the U.S. government pledged to honor new car warranties just to keep sales from plummeting. Interestingly, they did not pledge to honor existing warranties. Regardless of whether the firm can work out the default with its lenders or is forced into liquidation, default is a situation all parties wish to avoid.

Clearly lenders and company management want to avoid default, but who beyond this cares about estimating the likelihood of default? Investors in corporate bonds also care about the probability of default. Bond rating agencies specialize in issuing credit ratings for corporate debt to help bond investors assess credit risk. More surprisingly, in certain contexts the default probability can be an important input in pricing a firm's equity. If the firm defaults, the value of the equity is approximately zero, so the expected value of the equity is really the probability that it won't default times the value of the equity given that it continues as a going concern. For most firms the probability of default is so low that we ignore default when valuing the equity. But for a firm with a high probability of default, default should not be ignored. You can think of an equity investment in a troubled firm as an option—the default probability is the likelihood that the option ends up out of the money, in which case the equity holders can abandon their claim of the firm. We refer to this option as the abandonment option, and we discuss it in more detail in Chapter 12.

Estimating the Likelihood of Default

Broadly speaking, you should approach default forecasting in the same way as any other financial statement analysis topic: Use the past financial statements to get a clear understanding of the company's past financial performance and current financial position, and then forecast how you believe the firm will evolve in the future. But there are a few twists. First, for the purposes of assessing the risk of default, we don't really care how successful a firm is beyond the point where we are confident that it will avoid default. The difference between good financial performance and great financial performance matters when forecasting the cash distributions to equity holders, but makes little difference to the cash distributions to creditors. The maximum that creditors get is the agreed upon interest and principal payments. Second, we have a very specific notion of what unsuccessful is—failure to make contractual interest and principle payments or a violation of debt covenants.

The long-term capital structure and short-term liquidity ratios discussed earlier give you a qualitative feel for the firm's credit risk. In this section we attempt to attach specific probabilities of default to different levels of these and other ratios. Specifically, on the Credit Analysis sheet in *eVal*, there are six ratios that have been shown to be predictive of future default. Under each ratio we report the historical frequency that firms with a ratio near this value defaulted on their debt during the subsequent five years. As a benchmark, over the past three decades the probability that an industrial firm defaulted during a five-year period was about 5 percent, although this rate doubled in 2008–2009 due to the financial crisis.

Before proceeding with our model of default probability, we want to issue a word of warning. The actual covenants found in a typical loan contract are extremely detailed. They spell out exactly how each ratio will be measured, what line items will be included and excluded over what time periods, and what the consequences are for violating different hurdle rates for each ratio. By comparison, the ratios below are simple and standardized. For example, as illustrated by our discussion of Kohl's, these ratios ignore operating lease obligations that would typically be included in an actual covenant. You should consider the ratios below as a general guide for the types of ratios found in actual debt covenants, knowing that in practice the ratios are highly customized to each specific firm.

Figure 5.15 graphs each of the six ratios we use to build our model of default probability. The distribution of each ratio is computed for the entire sample of public firms between 1980 and 1999, excluding banks, insurance companies, and real estate companies (because their financial characteristics are so different from the majority of firms). For each ratio we sort this data into ten equal-sized groups, called deciles, and then plot the frequency that firms in each decile defaulted over the next five years.[2] Each graph also shows the cutoffs for each decile just above the axis; for instance, the value shown above deciles 5 and 6 is the median value of the ratio for the entire sample.

---

[2] The default probabilities associated with different levels of each ratio are taken from Falkenstein, Boral, and Carty (May 2000).

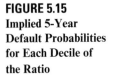

FIGURE 5.15
Implied 5-Year
Default Probabilities
for Each Decile of
the Ratio

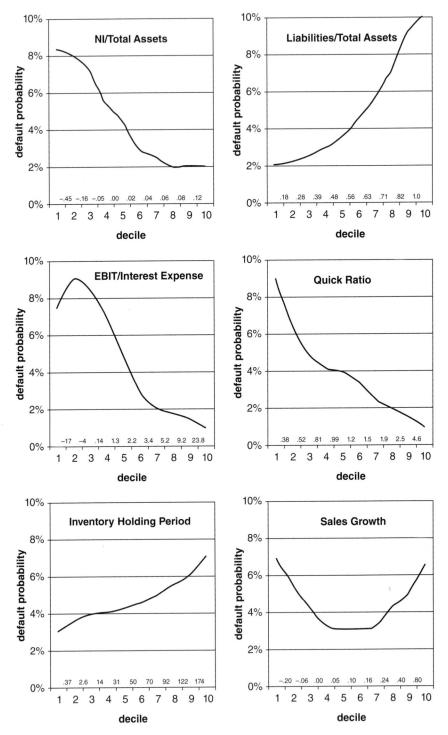

Profitability

For the purposes of predicting default, we measure profitability as the return on total assets before extraordinary items: (net income – extraordinary items)/ total assets. Regardless of the firm's other financial characteristics, if it is sufficiently profitable then it will generate enough cash each year to pay its creditors. But how much more likely is it for a firm to default on its debt when its profitability for the year is in the top 10 percent of all firms than if this ratio is in the bottom 10 percent? To get a feel for this, consider the top left graph in Figure 5.15. As expected, the graph slopes down—firms with higher levels of profitability are less likely to default on their debt. To quantify this, the graph shows that the median firm has a return on total assets of 2 percent, and an implied default probability of about 4 percent. However, the bottom decile of firms have return on total assets of less than −45 percent and the odds that they will default in the next five years jumps to over 8 percent, while the top decile of firms have a return on total assets of more than 12 percent and a default probability is only 2 percent. In other words, it is over four times more likely that a firm in the bottom decile will default than a firm in the top decile.

Leverage

The greater a firm's financial leverage the less the cushion that is available if profits fail to generate the necessary cash flow to pay creditors. Because some firms have negative equity (and this would mess up our graph), Figure 5.15 plots total liabilities/total assets rather than debt/equity, which is the more traditional measure of leverage. As a firm's leverage increases, the default rate increases steadily, starting at 2 percent for the firms in the lowest decile and increasing to 10 percent for firms in the highest decile.

Liquidity

If you have enough cash, or assets that will soon become cash, you can surely pay your bills, hence the importance of liquidity ratios in credit analysis. As we discussed earlier, it is difficult to pay debt holders with inventory and certain other current assets, so the quick ratio (cash, marketable securities and receivables divided by current liabilities) is the ratio we use to predict default. As Figure 5.15 shows, the quick ratio is predictive across the entire distribution, but the slope is steepest for the worst firms, those in the first two deciles. The default probability is 9 percent for firms with a quick ratio less than .38 but drops to 5 percent in the third decile, where firms have quick ratios between .52 and .81.

Interest Coverage

Interest coverage is typically computed in a very precise and complicated way in most debt covenants. But for our purpose, we simply graph EBIT/interest expense. Between the second and sixth decile, the slope of the interest coverage graph is very steep, showing that this ratio does a good job of discriminating winners from losers inside this region. The graph flattens out on the high end because it doesn't really make much difference if you are covering your interest eight times or ten times. On the low end the graph actually slopes up, which seems counter-intuitive. But for firms with negative EBIT, an increase in interest expense lowers the EBIT/interest ratio, which probably explains the unusual shape of the curve in the low region. As a crude benchmark, the median EBIT/interest ratio is 2.2.

Inventory

The inventory holding period is less predictive than the previous measures, as seen by its modest slope in Figure 5.15. We include it nonetheless because it captures information that is very different from the previous default predictors. Previously we described the inventory holding period as a measure of how efficiently the company manages its inventory. All else equal, a shorter holding period is better. In the context of default prediction, if the holding period is very long then, besides suggesting inefficient inventory management, it may indicate an even more serious problem. It could be that the firm is having trouble selling its inventory and, consequently, may suffer financial distress in the future. Firms in the lowest decile of this ratio are probably service firms that have little or no inventory, so the ratio doesn't really apply to them; as a benchmark, the median inventory holding period is about 50 days.

Sales Growth

Unlike the previous graphs, sales growth has a U-shaped relation with default probability, as seen in the bottom right graph in Figure 5.15. While this makes it more difficult to interpret, we include it because it captures information that is very different from the more traditional ratios. In the lowest deciles, sales are declining (i.e., negative sales growth), which is clearly a bad sign. But more curiously, the odds of default are also high for firms with the highest sales growth. The intuition is that the set of firms with rapidly growing sales includes a greater proportion of firms selling goods or services at a loss. Further, such rapid sales growth is more likely to be financed by additional borrowing, further increasing the risk of default. As a benchmark, the median annual sales growth for the sample is 10 percent, and this corresponds to the lowest default risk. Sales declines of more than 20 percent or sales growth of more than 80 percent imply twice as high a probability of default.

Final Thoughts on Credit Risk

As a summary statistic, the Ratio Analysis worksheet reports the simple average of the default probabilities from the six individual ratios. As seen at the bottom of this sheet, Kohl's faces very little risk of default. They are profitable and have a relatively low amount of financial leverage (remembering that the data does not include their leases), their quick ratio is almost 1, and they cover their interest expense more than 12 times. It isn't surprising, therefore, that the model estimates only a 3.2 percent chance that they will default in the next five years, well below the five percent overall average probability of default.

We stress once again that the ratios given here capture the spirit, but not the actual details, of the financial health tests specified in an actual debt contract. Further, if your forecasts imply that a poorly performing firm will turnaround and be wildly profitable in the future, then the implied default probabilities based on its historical performance don't really mean much.

5.11   CONCLUSION

Ratio analysis is an indispensable part of equity valuation and analysis. Ratios are the tools that you will use to evaluate financial performance. If you make a career in financial analysis, then you'll soon be reeling off the financial jargon we've introduced in this chapter with reckless abandon. But you should always remember the important caveats of ratio analysis. First, you should make sure you know how a ratio is computed before you start interpreting it. Second, ratios don't provide answers; they only guide you in your search for answers. Unusual ratios tell you which part of a firm's Form 10-K you need to delve into to get your answers. Finally, management knows that you'll be computing all these ratios, and they'll go to great lengths to make sure these ratios look nice. Be particularly skeptical of ratios that management flaunt in their press releases and be vigilant in your search for evidence of creative accounting.

5.12   CASES, LINKS, AND REFERENCES

Cases

- Interpreting Margin and Turnover Ratios
- Netflix, Inc. (Questions 6–9)
- Overstock.com (Questions 7–10)
- Royal Caribbean (Part A)
- Salton (Questions 2–5)
- A Tale of Two Movie Theatres
- Building *eVal* (Part C)

References

- Falkenstein, E., A. Boral and L. Carty (2000), "RiskCalc for Private Companies: Moody's Default Model," Moody's Investor Service Global Credit Research. Available online at http://papers.ssrn.com/sol3/papers.cfm?abstract_id=236011.

CHAPTER SIX

Cash Flow Analysis

6.1 INTRODUCTION

One of the novel features of accrual accounting is that firms can report oodles of accounting earnings in periods when they generate very little cash. As a simple example, a firm selling its goods on credit records sales revenue but doesn't actually receive any cash until and unless the customer pays. Many other transactions can also create large gaps between accounting earnings and cash flows. This is why companies like Enron and WorldCom were able to report healthy earnings one quarter, then go broke in the next. Their earnings turned out to be based on unrealistic accounting assumptions rather than actual cash flows. The fact that earnings and cash flows are different isn't, by itself, a sure sign of trouble. As we discussed in Chapter 4, the accrual accounting process was designed to generate more meaningful measures of periodic financial performance. Nonetheless, generating cash, not earnings, is the ultimate long-term goal of a business. Cash is what the firm needs to buy assets and pay creditors, and it is what standard valuation models tell us must ultimately determine the value of a firm.

This chapter describes how *eVal* creates pro forma statements of cash flows based on *eVal*'s standardized income statements and balance sheets. We then describe how to use the information in the resulting cash flow statements to evaluate the cash consequences of the company's operating, investing, and financing activities. Is the company generating positive cash from their operations? Is it reinvesting operating cash flow? If not, where is the free cash flow going? We'll also help you to evaluate whether the cash flow implications of your forecasted financial statements make sense. There is no point in assuming that a firm will raise gobs of new cash through an equity issuance at an extremely high price if the company's stock is currently out of favor with Wall Street.

Next, we'll show you how *eVal* employs the standardized financial statements to compute the inputs into discounted cash flow valuation models. We defer the technical development of the models to Chapter 10; here we simply describe how to compute the main inputs and discuss how they can be interpreted as measures of wealth distribution.

Finally, we'll finish with a discussion of how we can study differences between earnings and cash flows to evaluate the quality of earnings. You may recall from Chapter 4 that accounting distortions often cause earnings to temporarily deviate from cash flows, but that these distortions must ultimately reverse. Examining differences between earnings and cash flows can help us to identify such distortions and forecast their reversals. But how do we distinguish legitimate accruals from illegitimate distortions? While the only sure method is to corner the company's chief accounting officer in a dark alley, we offer some less reliable but more pragmatic alternatives.

6.2 THE STATEMENT OF CASH FLOWS

We begin with a brief review of how to construct a statement of cash flows. If this task is completely new to you, then we recommend you consult an intermediate accounting textbook. *eVal*'s pro forma statement of cash flows sets out to reconcile the beginning and ending balances in the Operating Cash and Marketable Securities line item given on the *eVal* Financial Statements sheet.[1]

You can intuitively think of the statement of cash flows as a categorized summary of all the transactions that ran through the company's bank account during the year. The statement of cash flows categorizes and summarizes these transactions by dividing them into operating, investing, and financing activities. To illustrate the logic behind the construction of this statement, we start with the basic accounting equation:

$$\text{Assets} = \text{Liabilities} + \text{Equity}$$

We next divide assets into cash and noncash assets, take the annual change in each term (denoted by Δ), and rearrange to get:

$$\Delta\text{Cash} = \Delta\text{Liabilities} + \Delta\text{Equity} - \Delta\text{Noncash Assets}$$

The statement of cash flows explains the change in cash on the left-hand side of the equation by decomposing the changes in liabilities, equity and noncash assets on the right-hand side of the equation. The statement organizes the changes in these accounts into three familiar categories: operating, investing, and financing. We have listed common transactions summarized in each of these categories in Figure 6.1. To consider some common examples, operating cash flows increase with (*i*) decreases in receivables (which

---

[1] We note that *Accounting Standards Codification 230,* "Statement of Cash Flows," requires a more restrictive definition of cash than the one used in *eVal*. The standard requires that only marketable securities representing short-term, highly liquid investments be classified as *cash equivalents.* We use a more general definition of cash equivalents that includes all marketable securities held as current assets. We do this both because these assets are typically readily convertible into cash and because some standardized financial statement databases do not distinguish between cash equivalents and other short-term marketable securities. As a practical matter, most companies with large "cash" balances put a sizeable portion in short-term marketable securities in order to generate more competitive returns than offered by bank accounts. For example, as of 9/30/2011, Microsoft has accumulated balances of cash and short-term investments of over $57 billion, and parks about $34 billion of this amount in marketable securities, including sizeable investments in government securities and corporate bonds.

FIGURE 6.1

Examples of
Common Transactions
Summarized in the
Statement of Cash
Flows

ΔCash	=	− ΔNoncash Assets	+ ΔLiabilities	+ ΔEquity
Operating Cash Flows	=	+ ↓Receivables	+ ↑Payables	+ Net Income
Investing Cash Flows	=	− ↑PP&E		
Financing Cash Flows	=		+ ↑Debt	− Dividends

is reflected as a decrease in a noncash asset in the above equation); (*ii*) increases in accounts payable (which is reflected as an increase in liabilities in the above equation); and (*iii*) net income (which is reflected as an increase in equity in the above equation). Investing cash flows and financing cash flows work similarly. Selling (purchasing) PP&E or issuing (retiring) debt increases (decreases) cash.

To see some of these computations in action, let's look at Kohl's pro forma statement of cash flows, shown on the Cash Flow Analysis sheet in *eVal* and reproduced in Figure 6.2. Note that the Operating section starts with Net Income at the top and ends with Cash from Operations at the bottom. In between these two amounts are all the adjustments necessary to convert net income to cash flow from operations. The first adjustment, adding back Depreciation & Amortization, seems obvious because these are noncash expenses. But note that our cash flow equation is still doing its work. Net income is a component of ΔEquity. Our equation indicates that ΔEquity only impacts ΔCash if it is not accompanied by an offsetting ΔLiabilities or ΔNoncash Assets. In the case of Depreciation & Amortization, there is an offsetting reduction in ΔNoncash Assets, with no net effect on cash.[2] In other words, the operating section of the statement of cash flows starts off with Net Income and then adjusts for all the components of Net Income that reflect offsetting changes in liabilities or noncash assets in order to arrive at cash from operations. After the adjustment for Depreciation & Amortization, there are adjustments for changes in other noncurrent assets and liabilities, leading to the subtotal Funds from Operations. This subtotal is the amount of working capital generated from operations; it makes no distinction between cash and other noncash sources of working capital. The final adjustments are for changes in all the noncash working capital accounts, leading to cash from operations of just over $2,101 million for Kohl's in fiscal 2009. We can see that while Kohl's generated net income of only $991 million, it managed to generate operating cash flows of $2,101 million. The main reasons for this difference are the noncash depreciation charge and the significant increases in accounts payable and other liabilities.

[2] You may encounter a classification issue related to Depreciation & Amortization in *eVal*. If the company lumps these expenses in with another line item, such as Selling, General, and Administrative or Cost of Goods Sold, then most standardized data providers will likely code Depreciation & Amortization as zero. The effect of this misclassification on the statement of cash flows is to understate cash from operations and overstate cash from investing.

FIGURE 6.2

Pro Forma Statement
of Cash Flows for
Kohl's

	A	B	C	D	E	F	G
1	**Cash Flow Analysis**	**($000)**					
2							
3							
4	Company Name	KOHL'S CORP					
5							
6		Actual	Actual	Actual	Actual	Forecast	Forecast
7	Fiscal Year End Date	1/31/07	1/31/08	1/31/09	1/31/10	1/31/11	1/31/12
8	Pro Forma Statement of Cash Flows						
9							
10	Operating:						
11	Net Income	1,108,681	1,083,851	885,000	991,000	1,046,887	1,093,460
12	+Depreciation & Amortization	387,674	452,145	541,000	590,000	604,888	632,501
13	+Increase in Deferred Taxes	25,729	18,921	57,549	57,000	17,528	17,692
14	+Increase in Other Liabilities	50,197	137,168	34,296	81,000	22,688	22,901
15	+Minority Interest in Earnings	0	0	0	0	0	0
16	+Preferred Dividends	0	0	0	0	0	0
17	=Funds From Operations	1,572,281	1,692,085	1,517,844	1,719,000	1,691,991	1,766,554
18	-Increase in Receivables	1,652,065	0	0	0	0	0
19	-Increase in Inventory	(350,531)	(267,634)	56,733	(124,000)	(135,898)	(137,172)
20	-Increase in Other Current Assets	(103,038)	(11,944)	(20,515)	(70,000)	(13,715)	(13,844)
21	+Increase in Accounts Payable	104,405	(98,391)	45,015	307,000	55,233	55,751
22	+Increase in Taxes Payable	66,355	(109,009)	(19,254)	79,000	8,555	8,635
23	+Increase in Other Curr. Liabilities	90,543	66,330	13,492	190,000	46,586	47,022
24	=Cash From Operations	3,032,080	1,271,437	1,593,315	2,101,000	1,652,751	1,726,946
25							
26	Investing:						
27	-Capital Expenditures	(1,196,816)	(1,608,990)	(1,015,181)	(624,000)	(931,174)	(961,844)
28	-Increase in Investments	0	0	(332,000)	11,000	(14,924)	(15,064)
29	-Purchases of Intangibles	(6,906)	9,328	9,296	6,000	(9,465)	(9,573)
30	-Increase in Other Assets	62,897	(48,539)	(922)	(24,000)	(6,137)	(6,195)
31	=Cash From Investing	(1,140,825)	(1,648,201)	(1,338,807)	(631,000)	(961,720)	(992,676)
32							
33	Financing:						
34	+Increase in Debt	(95,147)	1,005,678	5,424	(2,000)	96,147	97,048
35	-Dividends Paid to Minority Interest	0	0	0	0	0	0
36	-Dividends Paid on Preferred	0	0	0	0	0	0
37	+Increase in Pref. Stock	0	0	0	0	0	0
38	-Dividends Paid on Common	0	0	0	0	0	0
39	+/-Net Issuance of Common Stock	(1,462,624)	(585,643)	(201,218)	113,000	(681,779)	(724,931)
40	+/-Clean Surplus Plug (Ignore)	0	0	(46,385)	10,000	0	0
41	=Cash From Financing	(1,557,771)	420,035	(242,179)	121,000	(585,632)	(627,883)
42							
43	Net Change in Cash	333,484	43,271	12,329	1,591,000	105,399	106,387
44	+ Beginning Cash Balance	286,916	620,400	663,671	676,000	2,267,000	2,372,399
45	= Ending Cash Balance	620,400	663,671	676,000	2,267,000	2,372,399	2,478,786
46							
47							

Intro | Financial Statements | Ratio Analysis | **Cash Flow Analysis** | Credit Analysis | Forecasting Assumptions | Valuation Parameters | Residual Income Valuati

The Operating section of the cash flow statement is the trickiest section to understand; the line items in the Cash from Investing activities and Cash from Financing activities sections are relatively straightforward. Note that *eVal* displays a cash outflow as a negative number. For example, in the most recent year, Kohl's invested $631 million, mostly in capital expenditures on PP&E. Kohl's also raised a relatively small amount of cash by issuing new stock (this relates to employee stock option exercises). The net effect of Kohl's operating, investing, and financing activities is a Net Change in Cash of approximately $1,591 million in fiscal 2009.

The pro forma statements of cash flows shown in *eVal* are unlikely to exactly match the statements in the 10-K. One reason is that our definition of cash may not match the company's definition.[3] A second reason is that we construct the cash flow statements based only on the information from the standardized income statements and balance sheets, so our classification of items into operating, investing, and financing activities may be less accurate than those on the 10-K. A third reason is that the company may have restated its prior year balance sheet, and *eVal* is attempting to prepare the statement using the original balance sheet.[4] The company's published statement of cash

[3] See footnote 1 for details.

[4] This turns out to be the case for Kohl's in its fiscal 2009 Form 10-K. The comparative balance sheet for January 31, 2009 is slightly different from the one originally reported in the fiscal 2008 Form 10-K (with the latter being used in *eVal*).

flows is the most accurate source of information about past cash activity. We construct pro forma statements for both the past and the forecasted future so that you can see a time series of cash flow data computed on a consistent basis.

6.3   EVALUATING A FIRM'S PAST CASH FLOWS

The statement of cash flows is the starting point for evaluating the firm's past cash flows. Recall from Chapter 2 that the MD&A section of the 10-K includes a required discussion of the firm's liquidity and capital resources. It is useful to review this discussion and have it close at hand while conducting your cash flow analysis. You should then work your way through each of the three sections of the statement of cash flows.

Evaluating Cash from Operations

The first section reports cash from operating activities. The first port of call is to see whether cash from operations is positive or negative. Positive cash from operations is generally good news. The company's operations are generating cash flow that can be either reinvested in the business or paid out to debt and equity holders. We'll find out exactly what the firm is doing with its cash flow in the next two sections. Negative cash from operations is a more mixed signal. One reason for negative cash from operations is that the company's operations are performing poorly. To see whether this is the case, check the company's net income. If net income is also negative, then poor operating performance is a likely explanation. In this case, you need to establish whether the company is going to be able to turn its operating performance around, and whether it has sufficient financial resources to complete the turnaround. A second reason for negative cash from operations is that the company is investing in working capital. Investments in working capital, such as receivables and inventory, reduce cash from operations but do not reduce net income. That is why they are subtracted from net income to arrive at cash from operations. Investments in working capital can be good or bad. If a company is investing in working capital to grow a business on which it is generating healthy economic performance, the increase in working capital is good. On the other hand, if the increase in working capital is not accompanied by healthy growth in the underlying business, it is more likely to be bad. For example, if a company's products are not selling, inventory will increase, and will probably have to be written down in the future. But growth in working capital without accompanying growth in operations is not always a bad signal. For example, assume that a company implements a successful new credit program for its customers. Receivables will increase even if sales are flat, as customers take advantage of the new credit program. If the interest generated by the credit plan is sufficient to provide the company with a healthy return on its incremental investment in receivables, the program is justified.

There are a couple of other things to check before moving on from the operating section. First, if there is a big gap between net income and cash from operations, you should make sure that you understand what is driving this gap. Recall from Chapter 4 that the difference between net income and cash flows represents accounting accruals, and this is where accounting distortions are most likely to lurk. We'll talk more about how to identify accounting distortions in section 6.6. For now, you should just realize that a big gap raises a red flag about earnings quality. What is a big gap? As a rule of thumb, if the difference between net income and cash from operations is greater than 5 percent of total assets, then you should follow the advice in section 6.6.

The second thing to check is the extent to which cash from operations is distorted by unusual one-time items. For example, a big one-off tax payment can temporarily depress operating cash flows. Or a cash receipt from the settlement of a major legal dispute can temporarily inflate cash flows. It is useful to separate these one-time items from recurring cash flows to evaluate the long-run cash-generating ability of the firm's operations.

Evaluating Cash from Investing

The second section of the statement of cash flows reports cash from investing activities. While cash from operating activities is usually positive, cash from investing activities is usually negative. This is because most firms require ongoing capital expenditures to maintain their operating activities. For example, a trucking company must buy new trucks to replace spent ones that are taken out of service. A useful way to check whether a company is increasing or decreasing its investment base is to compare its capital expenditures in the investing section to the depreciation add-back in the operating section. If capital expenditures are greater than depreciation, then the company is growing its capital base. Growth in a company's capital base can be evaluated in much the same way as growth in working capital. If the growth in the capital base is accompanied by profitable growth in the firm's operations, all is usually well. But growth in the capital base that is not accompanied by profitable growth in the firm's operations should raise a red flag. Either the company is using its capital less efficiently or accounting distortions are inflating capital and earnings. We'll provide you with more advice for identifying such distortions in section 6.6.

Apart from capital expenditures, you'll also find cash expenditures on investments and intangibles in this section. For investments, you should make sure you understand exactly what they are. At one extreme, they could be low-risk investments, such as treasury bonds. At the other extreme, they could represent investments in shady off-balance-sheet entities that could disappear overnight. Purchased intangibles most frequently relate to goodwill associated with the acquisition of other businesses. For acquisitions, you should follow up and make sure that the acquisitions make good economic sense. Do the earnings of the acquired company justify the price that was paid for the acquisition? All too often, companies generate healthy cash flows from their existing operations only to squander them by overpaying for acquisitions. Some managers would rather build an empire for themselves than return cash to equity holders.

As a final check on the investing section of the statement of cash flows, you should see whether the sum of operating and investing cash flows is positive or negative. The sum of operating and investing cash flows is frequently referred to as *free cash flow*. This is the cash flow that is free to be distributed to the debt and equity holders. If free cash flow is negative, then the company has to either dip into cash reserves or raise new capital to finance its operations. In this case, you should check that the company's operations have sufficient potential to warrant additional infusions of capital. If not, the company is unlikely to survive.

Evaluating Cash from Financing

The third and final section of the statement of cash flows reports cash from financing activities. This section tells us what the firm has been doing with its free cash flow. If free cash flow is positive, then the firm is probably distributing free cash flow to debt and/or equity holders. Such cash distributions are what give debt and equity securities value in the first place, so it is a good sign to see that a company is distributing free cash flow. If free cash flow is negative, then the firm is probably funding the shortfall by issuing new debt and equity securities. If the company is primarily issuing equity, this is usually a sign that there is uncertainty about its ability to produce positive free cash flow in the near future and so debt providers are staying away.

Note that we qualified our statements about the relation between free cash flow and financing activities using the word *probably*. The reason for this qualification is that a firm can use its cash reserves to bridge the difference between free cash flow and cash from financing activities. For example, firms with positive (negative) free cash flow can add to (subtract from) their cash reserves rather than engaging in financing activities. The last few lines of the statement of cash flows indicate whether this is the case. If a firm is funding negative free cash flows by using up its cash reserves, you should determine how long it could continue to do this before it runs out of cash. The ratio of negative free cash flows to cash reserves is often termed the *cash burn rate;* the reciprocal of the cash burn rate provides an estimate of how long it will be before cash runs out. On the other hand, if a firm is squirreling away positive free cash flows as cash reserves, you should understand management's motives. Are they too selfish to pay this money back to investors? Are they empire builders who are planning value-destroying acquisitions? Firms that try to sell themselves as "growth" stocks are particularly reluctant to pay cash back to investors, because this basically amounts to an admission that they have run out of growth opportunities. Be wary of managers who hoard free cash flow.

Evaluating Kohl's Past Cash Flows

We'll now apply the above discussion to the evaluation of Kohl's cash flows. You should have a copy of the Liquidity and Capital Resources section of Kohl's MD&A from its fiscal 2009 10-K close at hand. The relevant section starts on page 26 of the 10-K. Recall that *eVal*'s pro forma statements of cash flows can be accessed on the Cash Flow Analysis worksheet, or we refer you back to Figure 6.2. As discussed earlier, the cash flow amounts reported by *eVal* will differ somewhat from the corresponding numbers reported in Kohl's Form 10-K, and so we round the numbers to the nearest billion.

Both cash from operations and net income are positive and have grown over the last year. Kohl's operating activities are generating a healthy stream of cash flows. Note that cash from operations is significantly larger than net income in fiscal 2009 ($2 billion versus $1 billion). Inspection of the other line items in the operating section indicates that this difference is primarily attributable to the depreciation and amortization add-back and to increases in accounts payable and other current liabilities. Page 27 of Form 10-K discusses how improved inventory management and the negotiation of extended payment terms with vendors enabled accounts payable to grow more quickly than inventory. Thus, it appears that improved working capital management has contributed to the unusually large gap between cash from operations and net income in fiscal 2009.

Turning next to the investing section of the statement of cash flows, we see that Kohl's reduced its capital expenditures in fiscal 2009. Capital expenditures amounted to $0.6 billion in fiscal 2009. From the operating section, we see that depreciation and amortization is also $0.6 billion. Kohl's therefore had a flat net capital base in fiscal 2009. Page 28 of the 10-K indicates that Kohl's opened only 56 new stores in 2009, down from 75 in 2008. Kohl's also indicates that it expects store growth to slow to 30 in 2010, but that overall capital expenditures should increase to around $0.9 billion on increased store remodels. How should we interpret the reduction in the rate with which Kohl's is opening new stores? Recall from our earlier discussion of Kohl's strategy in Chapter 3 that Kohl's is starting to saturate its primary markets. The slowdown in growth therefore reflects a measured decision on the part of Kohl's management to avoid either cannibalizing sales in existing markets or venturing into unknown territory. While this seems like a sensible move, it nevertheless suggests that Kohl's will have difficulty maintaining its historical sales growth rate, and we should keep this in mind when trying to forecast future sales growth.

Summing the cash flows across the operating and investing sections, we see that Kohl's generated free cash flow of approximately $1.6 billion. This resulted from a combination of strong profitability, good working capital management, and modest growth. What did Kohl's do with this free cash flow? To help answer this question, we next turn to the financing section of Kohl's statement of cash flows. The financing section indicates that Kohl's generated relatively little cash from financing in fiscal 2009. Most of this financing came from stock option exercises. Moreover, Kohl's didn't give any significant free cash flow back to its investors. Instead, it simply added it to its now significant cash balance. Kohl's cash balance started the year at $0.643 million and ended the year at $2.267 billion. What does Kohl's intend to do with this spare $2 billion and change? The MD&A provides few clues. Page 30 indicates that Kohl's expects to generate a further $800–$900 million of free cash flow in 2010, so management clearly doesn't appear to intend to use it to fund future store expansions. This raises the concern that as Kohl's growth slows, management may hoard free cash flow rather than distributing it to investors. Unless Kohl's management find something useful to do with this cash, we should hope that they will soon begin paying a dividend and/or repurchasing stock in order to distribute it to investors.

6.4 EVALUATING A FIRM'S FUTURE CASH FLOWS

After you forecast the company's future income statements and balance sheets, you get the future statements of cash flow for free. *eVal* constructs these pro forma statements using the procedure described in section 6.2. You should evaluate the forecasts of future cash flows in much the same way that you evaluated the past cash flows. In addition, you should make sure that the future cash flow forecasts make economic sense. For example, it is unrealistic to think that a firm could finance a long string of negative future operating cash flows by issuing short-term debt. Creditors usually like to see a healthy stream of future cash to facilitate the timely repayment of debt.

As before, begin your evaluation with forecasted cash from operations. If it is significantly negative into the distant future, you should ask yourself whether the firm is really going to continue its operations. It doesn't make sense to continue losing money forever. Either the firm will ultimately generate positive operating cash flows or it will cease operations. You need to figure out which alternative is more likely and then adjust your forecasted financial statements accordingly. Even if cash from operations is only forecast to be negative for a few years, you still need to ask yourself whether the company will be able to raise sufficient financing to keep itself afloat until positive operating cash flows arrive. While you might forecast that cash flows will be huge and positive in 10 years, other investors may disagree. Unless you are personally prepared to provide the firm's entire financing needs in the meantime, it may not survive long enough to reach that glorious day.

Your evaluation of forecasted cash from investing should ask similar questions. First, you should make sure that your capital expenditure plans are consistent with those espoused by management in the Liquidity and Capital Resources section of MD&A in the most recent 10-K. Second, if you have forecast that the firm is going to have significant capital expenditures, you should make sure that financing is likely to be available. If the firm's operations are forecast to be unprofitable, the firm may have a tough time convincing investors to provide financing to fund additional capital expenditures.

If you are forecasting that a firm will generate positive free cash flows, what do your forecasts imply about where the money will go? Will the firm pay down debt, will it increase dividends or will it simply let its cash balance pile up? How do the implied financing cash flows compare with the firm's historical financing activities, and with management's plans outlined in the MD&A? It would be foolish, for instance, to make forecasts that imply that the firm will pay large dividends in the near future when the firm has publicly stated that it has no intention of doing so. You should be particularly wary of firms with a record of wasting free cash flows on unsuccessful projects. Make sure that you don't inadvertently assume that such firms will stop this behavior and start graciously paying out all of their free cash flow as dividends.

6.5   CONSTRUCTING DCF VALUATION INPUTS

Chapter 10 covers valuation models, one of which is the standard discounted cash flow (DCF) model. Unfortunately, the cash flows reported in the statement of cash flows do not correspond exactly with the inputs to the DCF model. For this reason, *eVal* provides a separate set of *free cash flow* computations right after the statement of cash flows on the Cash Flow Analysis sheet. Recall from our discussion in section 6.3 that the sum of cash from operations and cash from investing can be loosely referred to as *free cash flow*. The key difference between this measure of free cash flow and the measures of free cash flow used in DCF valuation models is that valuation models tailor their cash flow metrics to the stakes(s) being valued. For example, if we are valuing equity, we only want to consider free cash flow that is distributed to equity holders. The free cash flow measure computed from the statement of cash flows shows *all* free cash flow, regardless of whether it is paid to equity holders, paid to debt holders, or held in cash reserves. The stakes most commonly valued are common equity and all invested capital (the sum of debt, minority interest, preferred stock, and equity). We present computations for the corresponding measures of free cash flow below.

Free Cash Flow to Common Equity

The *free cash flow to common equity* is simply the net cash distributions to common equity holders. If this amount is negative in a particular year, it means that common equity holders have contributed more cash to the firm than they have received. This is the input to the most basic valuation model—the DCF to common equity—alluded to in Chapters 1 and 4. We can compute this amount several different ways, and, if we do so properly, we will always get the same answer. Because different people prefer different computation methods, *eVal* computes the amount in all the common ways and

FIGURE 6.3

Free Cash Flow to
Common Equity for
Kohl's

	A	B	C	D	E	F	G
1	Cash Flow Analysis	($000)					
2							
3							
4	Company Name	KOHL'S CORP					
5							
6		Actual	Actual	Actual	Actual	Forecast	Forecast
7	Fiscal Year End Date	1/31/07	1/31/08	1/31/09	1/31/10	1/31/11	1/31/12
47							
48	Free Cash Flow to Common Equity						
49							
50	Net Income	1,108,681	1,083,851	885,000	991,000	1,046,887	1,093,460
51	- Increase in Common Equity	353,943	(498,208)	(637,397)	(1,114,000)	(365,108)	(368,529)
52	+/-Clean Surplus Plug (Ignore)	0	0	(46,385)	10,000	0	0
53	=Free Cash Flow to Common Equity	1,462,624	585,643	201,218	(113,000)	681,779	724,931
54							
55	Computation based on SCF:						
56	+Cash From Operations	3,032,080	1,271,437	1,593,315	2,101,000	1,652,751	1,726,946
57	-Increase in Cash	(333,464)	(43,271)	(12,329)	(1,591,000)	(105,399)	(106,387)
58	+Cash From Investing	(1,140,825)	(1,648,201)	(1,338,807)	(631,000)	(961,720)	(992,676)
59	+Increase in Debt	(95,147)	1,005,678	5,424	(2,000)	96,147	97,048
60	-Dividends Paid to Minority Interest	0	0	0	0	0	0
61	-Dividends Paid on Preferred	0	0	0	0	0	0
62	+Increase in Preferred Stock	0	0	0	0	0	0
63	+/-Clean Surplus Plug (Ignore)	0	0	(46,385)	10,000	0	0
64	=Free Cash Flow to Common Equity	1,462,624	585,643	201,218	(113,000)	681,779	724,931
65							
66	Financing Flows:						
67	+Dividends Paid	0	0	0	0	0	0
68	-Net Issuance of Common Stock	1,462,624	585,643	201,218	(113,000)	681,779	724,931
69	= Free Cash Flow to Common Equity	1,462,624	585,643	201,218	(113,000)	681,779	724,931

demonstrates that they are, indeed, the same. Figure 6.3 shows *eVal*'s free cash flow to common equity computations for Kohl's.

The first method of computation uses the clean surplus relation, as discussed in Chapter 4. Free cash flow to common equity is computed as net income less the increase in common equity. The computation is illustrated below using Kohl's forecasted fiscal 2010 results from *eVal* (the first forecasted year, shown in black).

$$\text{Free Cash Flow to Common Equity} = \text{Net Income}$$
$$- \text{Increase in Common Equity}$$
$$681{,}779 = 1{,}046{,}887 - 365{,}108$$

In this case, common equity holders are forecast to receive 681,779 from the company. Now we'll show you how we can arrive at the same answer using the amounts already computed in our statement of cash flows. The next method of computation in *eVal* backs into free cash flow to common equity by taking the aggregate free cash flow from the firm's operating and investing activities and then subtracting cash that is either retained in the firm or paid out to non-equity capital providers. We start with the cash from operations and then subtract the increase in the cash balance. This adjusts for any cash flow that was retained in the firm. Next, subtract net cash outflows from investing (shown as negative on the statement) and add (subtract) any cash that was received from (distributed to) debt, minority interests, or preferred stockholders. What's left must have been paid out to common equity holders. You will note that the answer on the Cash Flow Analysis sheet is exactly the 681,779 we computed above.

The final computation is the most intuitive. Simply look in the Financing section of the statement of cash flows and pick out the two items that are cash transactions with the common equity holders—Dividends Paid and Net Issuance of Common Stock. Once again we see that common equity holders are forecast to receive 681,779 from Kohl's during the year. We also see that the entire amount comes from a negative entry next to the Net Issuance of Common Stock. This means we are forecasting that Kohl's will repurchase 681,779 of stock in fiscal 2010.

Now that Kohl's growth is slowing but its operations are still profitable, Kohl's is forecast to generate significant free cash flow. Rearranging the clean surplus relation produces a useful heuristic for understanding whether a firm is expected to generate positive or negative free cash flow:

$$\text{FCF to common} = \text{NI} - (\text{CE}_{end} - \text{CE}_{beg})$$
$$= \text{CE}_{beg}\,(\text{NI/CE}_{beg} - (\text{CE}_{end} - \text{CE}_{beg})/\text{CE}_{beg})$$
$$= \text{CE}_{beg}\,(\text{ROE} - \text{Growth Rate in CE})$$

where

FCF to common = Free cash flow to common equity

NI = Net Income

CE = Common equity at either the beginning (beg) or end of the period

ROE = Return on beginning common shareholders' equity

This means that free cash flows to common equity should be positive (negative) whenever ROE is greater (less) than the growth rate in common equity. In Kohl's case, ROE is around 14 percent, while its growth rate is only around 5 percent, so FCF to common is positive.

We have already touched on the pluses and minuses of free cash flow to common equity as a measure of firm performance and equity value. It is a measure of wealth distribution, not a measure of wealth creation. As such, in any given period it is a poor measure of firm performance. In the long run, however, this is what the common equity holders actually get as a return on their investment. In this sense, it is final arbiter of equity value.

Free Cash Flow to Investors

Free cash flow to all investors is the net amount of cash distributed by the firm to all providers of capital: debt holders, minority interests, preferred stockholders, and common equity holders. This is the primary input to the traditional DCF model. The traditional DCF model also involves another wrinkle. The cash savings from the tax deductibility of interest payments on debt are *not* included in free cash flow to investors. The reason for their exclusion is *not* that these tax savings don't increase free cash flow—they do. Rather, it is because there is a tradition of valuing these cash inflows by reducing the discount rate that is applied to all other cash flows. The tradition involves the computation of another beast called the *weighted average cost of capital,* which we'll get to in Chapter 9. This all seems unnecessarily convoluted to us, but who are we to argue with tradition? *eVal* reports computations using this traditional method so that you can communicate with brainwashed B-school graduates who don't know any different. But we can assure you that

FIGURE 6.4
Free Cash Flow to All Investors Computation for Kohl's

Cash Flow Analysis	($000)					
	A	B	C	D	E	F / G
Company Name	KOHL'S CORP					
		Actual	Actual	Actual	Actual	Forecast / Forecast
Fiscal Year End Date		1/31/07	1/31/08	1/31/09	1/31/10	1/31/11 / 1/31/12

	B (1/31/07)	C (1/31/08)	D (1/31/09)	E (1/31/10)	F (1/31/11)	G (1/31/12)
Free Cash Flow to all Investors						
Net Operating Income	1,155,183	1,145,266	971,947	1,074,623	1,132,413	1,182,890
- Increase in Net Operating Assets	449,090	(1,503,886)	(642,821)	(1,112,000)	(461,255)	(465,577)
+/-Clean Surplus Plug (Ignore)	0	0	(46,385)	10,000	0	0
=Free Cash Flow to Investors	1,604,273	(358,620)	282,741	(27,377)	671,158	717,314
Computation based on SCF:						
Cash From Operations	3,032,080	1,271,437	1,593,315	2,101,000	1,652,751	1,726,946
-Increase in Operating Cash	(333,484)	(43,271)	(12,329)	(1,591,000)	(105,399)	(106,387)
+Cash from Investing	(1,140,825)	(1,648,201)	(1,338,807)	(631,000)	(961,720)	(992,676)
+Interest Expense	74,427	98,712	140,000	134,000	137,049	143,305
-Tax Shield on Interest	(27,925)	(37,297)	(53,053)	(50,377)	(51,523)	(53,875)
+/-Clean Surplus Plug (Ignore)	0	0	(46,385)	10,000	0	0
=Free Cash Flow to Investors	1,604,273	(358,620)	282,741	(27,377)	671,158	717,314
Financing Flows:						
+Dividends on Common Stock	0	0	0	0	0	0
+Interest Expense	74,427	98,712	140,000	134,000	137,049	143,305
-Tax Shield on Interest	(27,925)	(37,297)	(53,053)	(50,377)	(51,523)	(53,875)
+Dividends on Preferred Stock	0	0	0	0	0	0
+Dividends Paid to Minority Interest	0	0	0	0	0	0
-Net Issuance of Common Stock	1,462,624	585,643	201,218	(113,000)	681,779	724,931
-Net Issuance of Debt	95,147	(1,005,678)	(5,424)	2,000	(96,147)	(97,048)
-Net Issuance of Preferred Stock	0	0	0	0	0	0
=Free Cash Flow to Investors	1,604,273	(358,620)	282,741	(27,377)	671,158	717,314
Traditional Computation of FCF:						
EBIT	1,814,801	1,804,477	1,536,000	1,712,000	1,804,138	1,884,555
-Taxes on EBIT	(693,689)	(695,507)	(593,053)	(647,377)	(682,190)	(712,599)
+Increase in Deferred Taxes	25,729	18,921	57,549	57,000	17,528	17,692
= NOPLAT	1,146,841	1,127,891	1,000,496	1,121,623	1,139,476	1,189,648
+Depreciation & Amortization	387,674	452,145	541,000	590,000	604,888	632,501
+Non-Operating Income (Loss)	34,071	36,296	29,000	10,000	10,465	10,934
+Other Income (Loss)	0	0	0	0	0	0
+Ext. Items & Disc. Ops.	0	0	0	0	0	0
=Gross Cash Flow	1,568,586	1,616,332	1,570,496	1,721,623	1,754,829	1,833,083
-Increase in Working Capital	1,126,315	(463,919)	63,142	(1,209,000)	(144,639)	(145,994)
-Capital Expenditures	(1,196,816)	(1,608,990)	(1,015,181)	(624,000)	(931,174)	(961,844)
-Increase in Investments	0	0	(332,000)	11,000	(14,924)	(15,064)
-Purchases of Intangibles	(6,906)	9,328	9,296	6,000	(9,485)	(9,573)
-Increase in Other Assets	62,897	(48,539)	(922)	(24,000)	(6,137)	(6,195)
+Increase in Other Liabilities	50,197	137,168	34,295	81,000	22,688	22,901
+/-Clean Surplus Plug (Ignore)	0	0	(46,385)	10,000	0	0
=Free Cash Flow to Investors	1,604,273	(358,620)	282,741	(27,377)	671,158	717,314

you get exactly the same valuation if you instead use the more direct approach of including these cash savings in free cash flow and leaving the discount rate alone.

As with the free cash flow to common equity, we can compute free cash flow to all investors a number of different ways and always get the same answer. Figure 6.4 shows *eVal*'s computations of free cash flow to all investors for Kohl's. The first computation makes use of the relation between net operating income and changes in net operating assets, and is analogous to the clean surplus relation that we used to determine the free cash flow to common equity above. We simply redefine net income as net operating income and common equity as net operating assets. Recall from Chapter 5 that the advanced Dupont decomposition defines net operating income and net operating assets by isolating the income statement and balance sheet items that are associated with the firm's operating and investing activities. Here, we use the same approach to calculate the free cash flow generated by the firm's operating and investing activities. We define net operating income and net operating assets exactly as given in Chapter 5. Recall that net operating income is defined before the tax savings accruing from the tax deductibility of interest on debt. We simply apply the firm's effective tax rate to earnings before interest and taxes, thus deducting how much tax the firm would have had to pay assuming it had no debt. As mentioned above, we'll incorporate any tax savings by reducing the discount rate in the valuation computation. Using Kohl's fiscal 2010 forecasts as an illustration, we can now write:

Free Cash Flow to Investors = Net Operating Income
− Increase in Net Operating Assets

$$671{,}158 = 1{,}132{,}413 - 461{,}255$$

Intuitively, this calculation starts with operating income that is available to all providers of capital and then deducts all amounts that are reinvested in the firm as opposed to being distributed to capital providers.

The next two methods of computing free cash flow to investors make use of measures already computed in the statement of cash flows. The first of these methods starts with cash from operating and investing activities, subtracts cash that is retained in the firm, adds back interest expense, and subtracts out the tax savings from interest. The reason that interest is added back is that interest is a cash flow to debt holders and not an operating expense. Accountants don't appreciate this distinction and so leave interest expense in the operating section rather than shifting it to the financing section of the statement of cash flows. The tax savings of interest are added back to conform to "the tradition." The next method takes the most direct route: It simply picks the appropriate cash flows out of the financing section of the statement of cash flows, again correcting for the misclassification of interest and the subtraction of tax savings on interest. Note that in all cases we get 671,158 of free cash flow to investors for Kohl's fiscal year 2010.

There is one more common method of computing free cash flow to investors, which we label the "traditional" approach, because it is the recipe used in most finance textbooks. This approach starts with EBIT (i.e., earnings before interest and taxes) and then replicates many of the adjustments found in the operating and investing sections of the statement of cash flows. The traditional folk derived this method long before firms were required to report a statement of cash flows, and many of them still prefer to use this method rather than using the statement of cash flows as a shortcut. The general logic behind this approach is to start with EBIT, adjust for taxes, add back noncash charges (e.g., depreciation), subtract net changes in working capital, and subtract investment expenditures. Note that we don't have to worry about adding back interest expense or subtracting tax savings on interest. This is because we started out with EBIT, which is earnings before interest and taxes, and then applied the effective tax rate to EBIT, essentially ignoring the tax savings from interest. Adding back deferred taxes to the result of the above computation gives us *NOPLAT,* which stands for *net operating profit less adjusted taxes.* If you get out a large piece of paper and pour a tall cup of coffee, you can reconcile this last method with all the other more direct methods. The pieces are all the same; the jigsaw puzzle is just put together in a different order.

Just as we did for free cash flow to equity, we can rearrange the clean surplus relation for free cash flow to all investors to yield the following heuristic.

$$FCF = NOA_{beg} (RNOA - \text{Growth Rate in NOA})$$

where FCF is now free cash flow to all investors.

This heuristic tells us that FCF to all investors should be positive (negative) when RNOA exceeds the growth rate in NOA. Since Kohl's RNOA is around 11 percent and it is only growing net operating assets at around 4 percent, it is forecast to have positive FCF.

6.6 CASH FLOWS AND EARNINGS QUALITY ANALYSIS

Recall from Chapter 4 that accounting distortions arise from imperfections in the accrual accounting process. Accrual accounting involves the recognition of estimated future benefits and obligations in the financial statements. Many accrual accounting estimates are subject to measurement errors. These errors can arise from limitations of GAAP, unintentional managerial forecasting errors, and intentional managerial manipulation. The examples we constructed in section 4.4 of Chapter 4 indicate that accounting distortions often lead to systematic patterns in accruals and earnings. For example, temporarily aggressive accounting causes accruals and earnings to be temporarily high, while temporarily conservative accounting causes accruals and earnings to be temporarily low. Recall that accruals are simply the difference between earnings and cash flows. Equivalently, accruals also manifest themselves as changes in assets and liabilities on the balance sheet. Now that we are armed with a good understanding of accruals, we are in a position to use this knowledge to help us identify accounting distortions. We refer to this process as earnings quality analysis, because we are primarily concerned with identifying the impact of accounting distortions on earnings.

The main goal of earnings quality analysis is to distinguish between "good" accruals, which represent accurate estimates of expected future benefits and obligations, and "bad" accruals, which do not represent future benefits and obligations and are thus accounting distortions. There are two simple *red flags* that we can use to isolate suspect accruals. First, if a firm's accruals are unusually large, accounting distortions are more likely to be at work. Second, if the unusually large accruals relate to balance sheet accounts that typically consist of less reliable accrual estimates, accounting distortions are even more likely at work.[5] For example, a big increase in accounts payable is unlikely to be due to an accounting distortion, because accounts payable can be measured with a high degree of reliability. On the other hand, a big

---

[5] The technique of earnings quality analysis that we describe here is supported by extensive academic evidence. It doesn't just represent our own opinions (though our opinions are almost as good as fact). We list the most relevant academic studies as references at the end of this chapter.

increase in inventory is more likely to be due to an accounting distortion, because inventory is measured with a relatively low degree of reliability. A big increase in inventory may signal a build up in obsolete inventory, meaning that inventory is overvalued and an inventory write-down is overdue.

In order to help you use these red flags more effectively, we need to give you more guidance on what represents an unusually large accrual and which accrual categories are measured with low reliability. As a rule of thumb, whenever any individual line item on the balance sheet changes by more than 5 percent of net operating assets, it represents a large accrual and warrants further investigation. Figure 6.5 provides guidelines on the relative reliability of different categories of accruals.

As a general rule, balance sheet items that are financial in nature are measured with a high degree of reliability, while balance sheet items that

FIGURE 6.5   **Accrual Reliability Assessment by Accrual Category**

Accrual Category	Associated Balance Sheet Items in *eVal*	Reliability Assessment	Illustrative Examples
Change in Noncash Current Operating Assets	Receivables; Inventories; Other Current Assets	Low	Category is dominated by receivables and inventory. Receivables require the estimation of uncollectibles and are a common earnings management tool (e.g., channel stuffing). Inventory accruals entail subjective cost flow assumptions, allocations, and write-downs.
Change in Current Operating Liabilities	Accounts Payable; Income Taxes Payable; Other Current Liabilities	Medium	Category is dominated by payables, which represent short-term financial obligations of the company that can be measured with a high degree of reliability. But can also include more subjective accruals, such as deferred revenue and warranty liabilities.
Change in Noncurrent Operating Assets	PP&E; Investments; Intangibles; Other Assets	Low	Category is dominated by PP&E and intangibles. Both PP&E and internally generated intangibles (e.g., capitalized software development costs) involve subjective capitalization decisions. Moreover, PP&E and intangibles involve subjective amortization and write-down decisions.
Change in Noncurrent Operating Liabilities	Other Liabilities; Deferred Taxes; Minority Interest	Medium	Category includes long-term payables, deferred taxes and postretirement benefit obligations. Best characterized as a mixture of accruals with varying degrees of reliability.
Change in Financial Assets and Liabilities	Cash & Marketable Securities; Current Debt; Long-Term Debt	High	Category consists of financial assets and liabilities with reliably determined book values.

are operational in nature are measured with a lower degree of reliability. Figure 6.5 therefore begins by classifying all of the standardized balance sheet items in *eVal* as either operating or financial. This classification mirrors the classification we used in Figure 5.8, but with one important exception. Our objective in Chapter 5 was to distinguish between balance sheet items that are used in the firm's operations versus those that are not. Our objective here is to distinguish between balance sheet items that are financial in nature versus those that are not. In Chapter 5, we classified cash and marketable securities as part of operations, because firms typically need cash and marketable securities to facilitate their operations. But for the purpose of evaluating earnings quality, cash and marketable securities are financial assets that can be measured with a high degree of reliability. We therefore classify cash and marketable securities as financial assets. This results in the following modified definition of net operating assets:

Modified Net Operating Assets (NOA*)
= Total Assets − Cash and Marketable Securities − Total Liabilities
− Current Debt − Long-Term Debt

We reiterate that this definition of operating assets differs from the definition used in Chapter 5 only in that it excludes cash and marketable securities. We refer to this measure as NOA* to distinguish it from the NOA measure developed in Chapter 5.

We next classify the operating items based on whether they are assets versus liabilities. Operating assets are generally measured with less reliability than operating liabilities, because operating liabilities primarily relate to financial obligations that are the result of a contractual commitment (e.g., accounts payable or deferred revenue). Thus, we classify operating assets as low reliability and operating liabilities as medium reliability. Finally, it is useful to distinguish between current and noncurrent items. Noncurrent items involve estimates in the more distant future, and hence tend to be less reliable. Figure 6.5 summarizes these reliability assessments and provides illustrative examples.

You should remember that Figure 6.5 summarizes general rules and not absolute truths. There have been some famous accounting scandals involving distortions in the measurement of supposedly high reliability accruals. For example, a well-known accounting scandal at the Italian food company Parmalat involved the overstatement of the cash balance (but it also involved Italian auditors and American bankers). Nevertheless, the vast majority of accounting manipulations involve the overstatement of operating asset accounts. Therefore, the change in operating assets provides a good summary measure of the amount of low reliability accruals that are included in earnings.

This claim is supported by the results of a research study of accounting enforcement actions undertaken by the SEC.[6] The study examines over

---

[6]See Richardson, Sloan, Soliman, and Tuna (2006). The implications of accounting distortions and growth for accruals and profitability, *The Accounting Review* 81: 713–743.

100 cases where the SEC alleged that firms had overstated their earnings in violation of GAAP. To examine whether these manipulations were perpetrated through the overstatement of operating assets, the researchers decomposed the return on net operating assets into a cash component and an operating accrual component:

$$\text{RNOA} = \frac{\text{FCF}}{\text{NOA}^*_{beg}} + \frac{(\text{NOA}^*_{end} - \text{NOA}^*_{beg})}{\text{NOA}^*_{beg}}$$

where

FCF = Free cash flow to all investors,

NOA* = Modified net operating assets at either the beginning (beg) or end of the period, and

RNOA = Net operating income divided by beginning net operating assets.

They then tracked the behavior of each of the components around the year of the alleged earnings management. Figure 6.6 summarizes their results. As you can see, RNOA declines slightly in the year of the manipulation and then falls sharply thereafter. The operating accrual component of RNOA, labeled ACC on the figure, increases in the year of the alleged manipulation and then decreases sharply thereafter. The cash component (not shown in Figure 6.6) must therefore decrease in the year of the alleged manipulation and level off thereafter. The clear message emerging from the figure is that accruals and RNOA are temporarily overstated in the year of the alleged manipulation and then reverse in the following years. This is exactly the scenario we labeled as *temporarily aggressive accounting* back in Chapter 4 (see panel B of Figure 4.5 and associated discussion). The increase in accruals in the year of the alleged manipulation is a clear signal that accruals are temporarily inflated in that year. This should have tipped smart investors off to the precipitous earnings declines in the following year.[7]

To assist you in identifying accounting distortions and low-quality earnings, *eVal* computes various accrual metrics. You will find these metrics under the caption "Analysis of Earnings Quality" at the bottom of *eVal*'s Cash Flow Analysis worksheet. The analysis begins by reporting the current and noncurrent portions of the operating accrual component of RNOA, defined as follows:

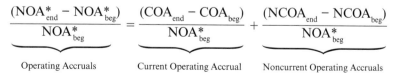

$$\underbrace{\frac{(\text{NOA}^*_{end} - \text{NOA}^*_{beg})}{\text{NOA}^*_{beg}}}_{\text{Operating Accruals}} = \underbrace{\frac{(\text{COA}_{end} - \text{COA}_{beg})}{\text{NOA}^*_{beg}}}_{\text{Current Operating Accrual}} + \underbrace{\frac{(\text{NCOA}_{end} - \text{NCOA}_{beg})}{\text{NOA}^*_{beg}}}_{\text{Noncurrent Operating Accruals}}$$

---

[7]An obvious question to ask at this point is whether stock prices act as if investors understand that high operating accruals signal low earnings quality. Academic research shows that firms with high accruals do tend to have future earnings declines, but that investors don't appear to fully anticipate these earnings declines, resulting in predictably low future stock returns. For more details, see the References section at the end of this chapter.

FIGURE 6.6
Plots of RNOA and the Operating Accrual Component of RNOA (ACC) for Firms Subject to SEC Enforcement Actions
Year 0 Represents the Year that a Firm was Subject to an SEC Enforcement Action for an Alleged Earnings Overstatement. The solid (dashed) line reflects the mean (median) of the respective variable.

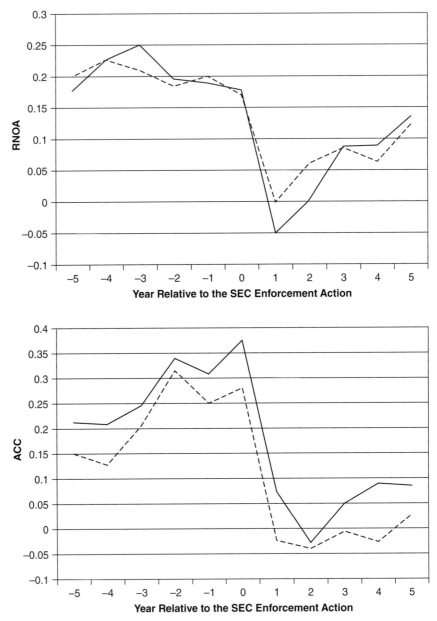

where

COA = Current Net Operating Assets, defined as Current Assets − Cash and Marketable Securities − Current Liabilities + Short-Term Debt, and

NCOA = Noncurrent Net Operating Assets, defined as Total Assets − Current Assets − Total Liabilities + Current Liabilities + Long-Term Debt

FIGURE 6.7   **Percentile Cutoffs for the Historical Distributions of Accrual Components**

Accrual Component	50th percentile	75th percentile	90th percentile
Operating Accruals	0.08	0.20	0.38
Current Operating Accruals	0.01	0.05	0.11
Noncurrent Operating Accruals	0.02	0.06	0.14
Sales Growth (%)	0.09	0.21	0.39
Growth in NOA Turnover	0.01	0.09	0.20

If any of these components are unusually large, you should identify the balance sheet items that are responsible for the change and look for any evidence that the change is attributable to accounting distortions. What constitutes unusually large in this context? Using data from thousands of firms over the past 50 years, Figure 6.7 reports the cutoffs that would place a firm above the 50th, 75th, and 90th percentiles for each of these measures. At a minimum, you should conduct a detailed investigation of the underlying accruals for any component that come in above the 90th percentile. To assist you in flagging these cases, *eVal* shades cells above the 90th percentile in orange.

Let's see how this quality of earnings analysis works out for Kohl's. Figure 6.8 reproduces *eVal*'s analysis of earnings quality for Kohl's fiscal 2009 financial statements. We can see that both the current and noncurrent components of operating accruals are negative in fiscal 2009, so there are no red flags here. Looking back to fiscal 2007, however, we see that noncurrent operating accruals are positive and large enough to set off our red flag alert. If we check back to the Financial Statements worksheet, we find that the PP&E balance was responsible, increasing by over $1 billion in fiscal 2007. If you investigate further by reading Kohl's 10-K for fiscal 2007, you will find that Kohl's spent over $1.5 billion on new capital in that year, opening over 100 new stores. We therefore have a satisfactory explanation for the growth in PP&E. Since Kohl's existing stores are highly profitable, this is likely to represent a sound investment that will lead to future profit growth. In retrospect, however, this wasn't such a great time to grow, as a recession was just around the corner.

Our analysis of Kohl's earnings quality raised a red flag in fiscal 2007, but we have a reasonable explanation for the red flag. This leads us to the broader question of what are the other common explanations for unusually large accruals. Other than bad accounting distortions, there are two good explanations. First, recall from the examples we considered in Chapter 4 that *legitimate* growth in investment leads to increased net operating assets and hence high accruals. This is exactly what we saw at work in Kohl's in fiscal 2007. How do we distinguish between legitimate growth in investment and illegitimate accounting distortions? Legitimate growth in investment should be accompanied by legitimate growth in sales. Thus, we should check that the sales growth rate is commensurate with the operating asset growth rate and that the

FIGURE 6.8

Analysis of Earnings Quality for Kohl's

◇	A	B	C	D	E	F	G
1	**Cash Flow Analysis**	**($000)**					
2							
3							
4	Company Name	KOHL'S CORP					
5							
6		Actual	Actual	Actual	Actual	Forecast	Forecast
7	Fiscal Year End Date	1/31/07	1/31/08	1/31/09	1/31/10	1/31/11	1/31/12
117							
118	Analysis of Earnings Quality						
119	(Red Shading = Quality Flag)						
120	Current Op. Accruals/NOA	(0.214)	0.070	(0.010)	(0.047)	0.005	0.005
121	+ Non-Current Op. Accruals/NOA	0.099	0.172	0.094	(0.012)	0.041	0.040
122	= Operating Accruals/NOA	(0.115)	0.242	0.084	(0.059)	0.046	0.045
123							
124	Sales Growth	0.160	0.060	(0.005)	0.048	0.046	0.045
125	- NOA Turnover Growth	(0.237)	0.172	0.090	(0.102)	0.000	(0.000)
126	- Interaction	(0.038)	0.010	(0.000)	(0.005)	0.000	(0.000)
127	= Operating Accruals/NOA	(0.115)	0.242	0.084	(0.059)	0.046	0.045
128	Fiscal Year	2006	2007	2008	2009	2010	2011

sales themselves are not the product of revenue manipulation. For example, if there is a disproportionate increase in credit sales, we should make sure that the firm is not artificially inflating receivables in order to boost revenues.

The second legitimate explanation for increased accruals is a reduction in net operating asset turnover, whereby more assets are required to produce the same level of sales. A legitimate reduction in operating asset turnover occurs when more economic investment is required to produce the same level of sales. Examples include a shift to a more capital-intensive production process, offering longer credit terms to customers and insourcing operations that were previously outsourced.

Accounting distortions most often manifest themselves as reductions in operating asset turnover, so distinguishing between legitimate reductions in operating asset turnover and illegitimate accounting distortions can be tough. Nevertheless, we can offer a couple of good pointers. First, a legitimate reduction in operating asset turnover will usually be the result of an important strategic shift in the way that management conducts business. If you see no evidence of such a shift, then accounting distortions are likely at work. Second, as discussed in Chapter 5, a successful strategic shift to lower operating asset turnover should be accompanied by higher margins. It makes no sense to sacrifice turnover unless the reward is higher margins. Perhaps the most classic signal of an accounting distortion is declining inventory turnover in conjunction with flat or declining margins. This is a strong signal that inventory is overvalued and overdue for a write-down.

In order to help you distinguish between these two alternative explanations for high accruals, *eVal* decomposes operating accruals into a sales growth component and a turnover component, as shown below:

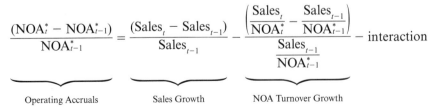

$$\underbrace{\frac{(NOA_t^* - NOA_{t-1}^*)}{NOA_{t-1}^*}}_{\text{Operating Accruals}} = \underbrace{\frac{(Sales_t - Sales_{t-1})}{Sales_{t-1}}}_{\text{Sales Growth}} - \underbrace{\frac{\left(\dfrac{Sales_t}{NOA_t^*} - \dfrac{Sales_{t-1}}{NOA_{t-1}^*}\right)}{\dfrac{Sales_{t-1}}{NOA_{t-1}^*}}}_{\text{NOA Turnover Growth}} - \text{interaction}$$

This algebraic decomposition and its associated "interaction" term are pretty nasty, and so we omit them for brevity, but we can assure you that the decomposition holds. It demonstrates that operating accruals increase one-for-one with sales growth and decrease one-for-one with NOA turnover growth. This decomposition serves two purposes. First, accounting distortions are more likely to reside in the NOA turnover growth component than the sales growth component, so a large NOA turnover growth component is an important red flag for accounting distortions. Second, as outlined above, the factors driving legitimate growth in accruals differ across the two components, so pinpointing the appropriate component will guide your search for explanations.

We refer you again to Figure 6.7 for the cutoffs for each of these accrual components and Figure 6.8 for the decomposition at Kohl's. Note that this decomposition involves subtracting NOA turnover growth from sales growth, so positive (negative) values for NOA turnover growth are listed as negative (positive) amounts in *eVal*. In other words, decreases in NOA turnover growth cause an increase in accruals. As before, *eVal* flags accrual components that are above the 90th percentile. This time, we see no red flags. There was nevertheless a big reduction in NOA turnover in fiscal 2007. This was no doubt attributable to the large number of stores that were opened in that year, as discussed earlier. We can see that the rate of sales growth lagged the rate of investment in new stores, causing a significant decline in NOA turnover.

We've just gone through a lengthy analysis of earnings quality for Kohl's without identifying any major problems. For the purpose of comparison, let's look at another company where there are some problems. Figure 6.9 shows *eVal*'s analysis of earnings quality for WorldCom through the end of fiscal 2001. You may recall that WorldCom seemed to be doing just fine until early in 2002, when the firm announced it had discovered some accounting irregularities. The firm filed for bankruptcy soon thereafter and ultimately wrote down assets by $70 billion (you'll excuse us for rounding to the nearest $10 billion). Most of the write-down related to asset impairments. The key accounting manipulations used by the company to prop up its sagging profitability in 2000 and 2001 involved the capitalization of operating costs in PP&E. The amounts incorrectly capitalized were approximately $2 billion in 2000 and $3 billion in 2001. You'll remember that this is exactly the kind of temporarily aggressive accounting that we modeled in Chapter 4. Wall Street analysts were caught off guard by these accounting distortions. Let's see if *eVal*'s analysis of earnings quality could have alerted us to their presence.

Figure 6.9 shows multiple flags for WorldCom's accrual components in 1998. Operating accruals, noncurrent operating accruals, sales growth, and NOA turnover growth are all excessively high. The search for explanations for these accruals reveals that WorldCom engaged in a number of strategic acquisitions in that year. In particular, WorldCom acquired MCI late in 1998. The acquisitions boosted operating assets substantially. Sales also increased, but to a lesser extent, because WorldCom acquired MCI late in 1998 and so only booked a few months of MCI sales in fiscal 1998. In 1999, sales growth

FIGURE 6.9

Analysis of Earnings
Quality for WorldCom

	A	B	C	D	E	
1	**Cash Flow Analysis**	($000)				
2	Go To User's Guide	View Statement of Cash Flows		View FCF to Investors Computations		
3		View FCF to Equity Computations		View Analysis of Earnings Quality		
4	**Company Name**	WORLDCOM INC NEW				
5						
6		Actual	Actual	Actual	Actual	Fo
7	**Fiscal Year End Date**	12/31/1998	12/31/1999	12/31/2000	12/31/2001	12/3
117	**Analysis of Earnings Quality**					
118	**(Red Shading = Quality Flag)**					
119	Current Op. Accruals/NOA	(0.094)	(0.006)	0.018	0.003	
120	+ Noncurrent Op. Accruals/NOA	2.174	0.064	0.143	0.087	
121	= Operating Accruals/NOA	2.080	0.058	0.161	0.090	
122						
123	Sales Growth	1.262	1.038	0.089	(0.100)	
124	- increase in NOA Turnover	0.362	(0.481)	0.067	0.211	
125	- Interaction	0.456	(0.499)	0.006	(0.021)	
126	= Operating Accruals/NOA	2.080	0.058	0.161	0.090	
127	**Fiscal Year**	1998	1999	2000	2001	
128						
129						
130						
131						
132						
133						

User's Guide / Data Center / Financial Statements / Ratio Analysis \ Cash Flow Analysis / Forecastin

Ready

is again high and NOA turnover drops. This is because 1999 includes a whole year's worth of sales from MCI. Thus, the red flags in 1998 and 1999 are primarily explained by the MCI acquisition. *eVal* also flags WorldCom's noncurrent operating accruals in 2000. It is difficult to come up with legitimate explanations for these accruals. Noncurrent operating accruals are 14.3 percent, while sales growth is only 8.9 percent and current operating accruals are only 1.8 percent. Further inspection of WorldCom's financial statements reveals that the high accruals are entirely attributable to an increase in PP&E of approximately 30 percent. So why did PP&E increase by 30 percent when sales increased by only 8.9 percent? The only explanation offered in the MD&A accompanying WorldCom's fiscal 2000 10-K is that "primary capital expenditures include purchases of transmission, communications and other equipment." This explanation is incomplete, as it does not mention any strategic shifts that would explain why PP&E is growing so much more rapidly than sales. Accounting distortions are therefore a likely explanation.

Finally, *eVal* flags WorldCom's NOA turnover growth in 2001. The amount shown is 0.211, indicating that NOA turnover declined by 21.1 percent in 2001. Inspection of the other accrual components for 2001 reveals that sales fell by 10 percent, while noncurrent accruals were up 8.7 percent. Inspection of WorldCom's financial statements indicates that the high accruals are primarily attributable to a 4 percent increase in PP&E and a 9 percent increase in intangibles. The 9 percent increase in intangibles is explained by WorldCom's acquisition of Intermedia Communications in July 2001. But why did PP&E increase by 4 percent when sales declined by 10 percent? Again, the only explanation offered in the MD&A accompanying WorldCom's fiscal

2001 10-K is that "primary capital expenditures include purchases of transmission, communications and other equipment." With hindsight, we know that these unexplained increases in PP&E were attributable to accounting manipulations. The fact that no legitimate explanation was provided for these accruals by WorldCom's management should have provided an early warning sign that WorldCom's earnings quality was suspect. The lesson to be learned from this example is that large operating accruals lacking legitimate explanations are the calling card of accounting distortions (and, yes, the bad pun is intentional).

6.7   CONCLUSION

Every so often a writer in the financial press will get upset about accrual accounting and declare that "cash is king," implying that we should use cash-based measures of financial performance over accrual-based measures. We take a more balanced view. Accrual accounting is designed to measure wealth creation in a more accurate and timely manner than simply recording cash receipts and disbursements. For most companies most of the time, these measures add information. Further, we don't have to choose between cash flows and earnings—we can have both. By using two different systems to examine a company's activities, we learn much more about what really happened in the past, and we generate more informed forecasts of the future.

6.8   CASES, LINKS, AND REFERENCES

Cases

- Building *eVal* (Part B)
- Turnaround at Bally Total Fitness?
- Sirius Satellite Radio (Questions 1–14)

Links

- WorldCom's Form 10-Ks are available at http://www.sec.gov. Hit the search for company filings link, then enter the CIK code 0000723527. The company was renamed MCI, but this is the company that you want. The filing dated 2002-03-13 is the last one before the accounting scandal broke.

References

- Richardson, S., M. Soliman, R. Sloan, and I. Tuna. (2006). The implications of accounting distortions and growth for accruals and profitability. *The Accounting Review* 81:713–743.
- Sloan, R. (1996). Do stock prices fully reflect information in accruals and cash flows about future earnings? *The Accounting Review* 71: 289–315.

CHAPTER SEVEN

Structured Forecasting

7.1 INTRODUCTION

Forecasting the future financial statements represents the ultimate goal of all the analysis we have discussed thus far. You may go on to be an All-Star analyst on Wall Street, or you may go on to manage your uncle's convenience store, but regardless of where in the business world you work, at some point you will need to forecast the future income, the future assets necessary to produce the forecasted income, and the future mix of debt and equity necessary to fund the assets. In short, while we focus on equity valuation in this text, everyone in business needs to forecast future financial statements at some time. The next two chapters are aimed at teaching you how to go about this task.

From a theoretical perspective, equity valuation requires forecasts of the future cash distributions to equity holders. From a practical perspective, however, most analysts focus on forecasting net income. We begin this chapter by reconciling these two perspectives. We lay out a forecasting framework that builds forecasts of the complete set of financial statements in a systematic manner. This framework highlights the joint role of income statement and balance sheet forecasts in generating forecasts of cash distributions to equity holders.

We next discuss broad issues that arise in constructing forecasts for the purpose of valuing equity securities. Should we forecast quarterly financial statements or annual statements? How many years into the future do we need to forecast? What are reasonable assumptions for forecasts that are in the distant future? What balance sheet item should we use as the "plug" that equates assets to liabilities and equity? We close the chapter by showing you how *eVal* guides you through the forecasting process. With these preliminaries covered, Chapter 8 provides more detailed advice about forecasting each of the line items in the financial statements.

7.2 A SYSTEMATIC FORECASTING FRAMEWORK

The cash distributions a firm pays to its equity holders are the result of a complex and interrelated set of operating, investing, and financing activities. The only sound way to proceed is to first forecast each of these underlying activities and then aggregate their financial implications into a forecast of the ultimate distributions to equity holders. We do this by building forecasts of both the income statement and the balance sheet. By forecasting both financial statements, we can take important interactions into consideration. A good example of the interplay between balance sheet forecasts and income statement forecasts is forecasted interest expense. Your forecast of interest expense on the income statement clearly depends on the amount of debt you forecast on the balance sheet. But the amount of your debt will also depend on your forecasts of the firm's net operating assets and capital structure. And your forecast of the net operating assets clearly depends on your forecast of sales growth. If we are going to keep track of all these interactions we clearly need to develop a systematic approach to forecasting.

Figure 7.1 illustrates our solution to this forecasting puzzle. The process begins with a forecast of sales. Sales are the primary input to the forecasting

FIGURE 7.1
Systematic Forecasting Framework

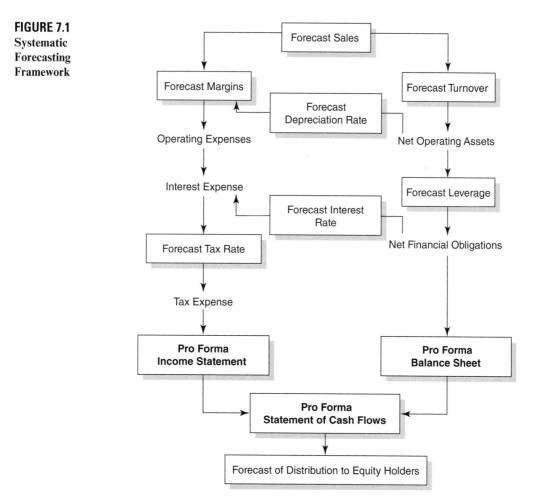

process for two reasons. First, recall that the sales transaction is the trigger for the recognition of value creation under GAAP. We forecast operating income by first forecasting sales and then forecasting all of the operating expenses necessary to generate the sales. Second, the sales forecast is our basic statement about how rapidly the firm will grow. This in turn drives our forecasts of the required levels of net operating assets to generate the sales growth and the required amounts of capital to finance the acquisition of the operating assets.

This two-pronged forecasting sequence is illustrated in Figure 7.1. On the left side of the figure we move from the sales forecast to the operating expense forecast by making assumptions about operating margins. On the right side of the figure we move from the sales forecast to the net operating asset forecast by making assumptions about turnover ratios. And the right side of the figure should pay attention to what the left side is saying! For example, growth in cost of goods sold typically requires growth in inventory. More generally, you should see that the forecasting process is like applying the Dupont ratio analysis in reverse. Instead of starting with the individual line items in the financial statements and then expressing them as ratios, we forecast the ratios directly and then back into what this implies for the individual line items in the forecast financial statements.

Armed with forecasts of operating expenses, and net operating assets (i.e., operating assets less operating liabilities), the next task is to forecast the net financial obligations. Our forecast of net operating assets indicates the total amount of invested capital that is required to support the future business activities. But we still need to forecast the mix of equity and non-equity financing that the firm will use to finance the forecasted level of invested capital. That is, we need to forecast the firm's future leverage. By applying leverage assumptions to the net operating assets, we obtain the required amount of non-equity forms of financing, such as short-term debt, long-term debt, minority interest, and preferred stock. At this point, you may be tempted to forecast common equity and thus complete the balance sheet. However, we have run out of degrees of freedom. We have forecast every item on the balance sheet except for common equity. Since the balance sheet must balance, we have already made an implicit forecast for common equity. Common equity is the plug that is found by subtracting the liabilities from the assets. This is an important point and one to which we return later in the chapter.

We have now forecasted all the line items on the balance sheet. We refer to this forecasted balance sheet as a *pro forma* balance sheet to distinguish it from the actual balance sheets that the firm reported in the past. We still have more work to do on the pro forma income statement. The three items we have omitted are depreciation expense, interest expense, and tax expense. We could not forecast depreciation earlier because it clearly depends on the amount of assets on the balance sheet, so we needed to forecast the asset balance first. Similarly, we couldn't forecast interest or taxes, because interest expense clearly depends on the amount of debt financing and tax expense clearly depends on the magnitude of the interest expense tax deduction. We needed the balance sheet forecast of debt before we could construct these income statement forecasts. By applying our forecast of the interest rate to the amount of forecasted debt financing, we generate an interest expense forecast. By deducting our interest expense from our forecast of operating earnings, we generate a forecast of earnings before taxes. Applying a tax rate forecast to earnings before taxes gives our tax expense forecast.

At this point, we are pretty much done forecasting the income statement. You may note that there are still a number of income statement components that we haven't mentioned: items such as gains and losses in other income, extraordinary items, and discontinued operations. By their very nature, these items are nonrecurring and difficult to forecast. Therefore, ignoring them (i.e., assuming that they are zero) is often the best that we can do. One final item to consider for your income statement forecasts is preferred dividends. If preferred stock is one of the non-common-equity sources of financing represented on the balance sheet, then there will typically be a stated dividend on this stock that should be incorporated in your income statement forecasts. Recall that we are trying to value the common equity, so we must deduct cash distributions to preferred stock holders in order to derive the net cash distributions to common stock holders. The same holds true for minority interest, it typically comes with "minority interest in earnings" as shown on the income statement.

We now have both our pro forma balance sheet and our pro forma income statement. Armed with these two statements, the preparation of our pro forma statement of cash flows is a mechanical task. You should remember from your introductory accounting class that a statement of cash flows can be prepared using the information in the income statement and the beginning and ending balance sheets, so there is nothing left to forecast (if this is news to you, go back to Chapter 6). And, by referring to the financing section of the statement of cash flows, we can see how our pro forma income statements and balance sheets determine the cash distributions to common equity holders. It is worth emphasizing that we need information from both the pro forma income statement and the pro forma balance sheet to extract our forecasts of distributions to common equity holders. We can see this by recalling the clean surplus relation that we first introduced in Chapter 4:

$$\text{Distributions to Equity} = \text{Net Income} - \text{Increase in Equity}$$

We get the net income forecast from the pro forma income statement, but this alone isn't sufficient for our valuation model. To solve for cash distributions to common equity holders, we also have to deduct the increase in common equity, which is extracted from the beginning and ending balance sheets. This latter adjustment takes account of additional capital that is required to fund the net operating assets of the business. Wall Street analysts often miss this subtlety, focusing almost exclusively on net income. But the clean surplus relation makes it clear that we should be concerned with both how much income is generated *and* how much additional capital has to be invested to generate this income.

7.3 FORECASTING QUARTERLY VERSUS YEARLY FINANCIALS

Exchange-listed firms in most countries are required to prepare financial statements on a quarterly basis. However, for the purpose of building financial forecasts for input into a valuation model, quarterly forecasting is overkill. The value of a firm is determined by its results over the next 10 or 20 years, not the next few quarters. And in addition to providing unnecessary detail, quarterly forecasting requires careful consideration of seasonal effects in financial data. For example, retailers' sales and profits are usually greatest in the fourth quarter, which covers the end-of-year holiday period. A quarterly forecasting interval requires us to build these seasonal patterns into our forecasts. But given that our value estimate will be determined by many years of forecasts, detailed knowledge of the quarterly numbers has little impact on the final answer. As a consequence, most valuation models, including *eVal*, use an annual interval for building financial statement forecasts. For simplicity, this annual interval typically corresponds with the fiscal year that the company uses for financial reporting purposes.

Despite the use of an annual measurement interval in most valuation models, the quarterly financial statements are still useful. The most recent quarterly financial statements provide the most current information on a firm's performance and financial position. If we are currently in a firm's fourth fiscal quarter and we are attempting to forecast the income statement for the full fiscal year, then we should obviously use the financial statements from the first three quarters as a starting point. But it is very important to be aware of any seasonal effects in the data before extrapolating financial statement data from earlier quarters to later quarters. There are two useful techniques for incorporating seasonal patterns in income statement forecasting. The first is to sum together the most recent four quarters of financial statements. By doing so, you will have abstracted from any seasonal effects. The cumulative results for the four most recent fiscal quarters are often referred to as the *trailing twelve months* (TTM) or *last twelve months* (LTM) results. The second technique is to perform *year-over-year* (YOY) comparisons for the most recent quarters. This involves comparing the most recent quarters in the current fiscal year to the corresponding quarters in the previous fiscal year. For example, we compare the third fiscal quarter of the current year to the third fiscal quarter for the previous year. By doing so, we control for any seasonal patterns in the firm's performance. Similar considerations apply to forecasting the balance sheet for the end of the current fiscal year. While the most recent quarterly balance sheet is the timeliest, it may also reflect seasonal patterns in net operating asset balances. For example, most retailers build up inventory during the third fiscal quarter and run it down during the fourth fiscal quarter. If you simply extrapolate the third quarter inventory balances into the future you will overstate the inventory necessary to sustain the annual sales. YOY comparisons of quarterly inventory changes are the best technique for controlling for such seasonal patterns.

Another role for quarterly financial statements in valuation is in assessing the ongoing performance of the company relative to your previous forecasts. You may not want to wait until the end of the year to find out whether or not a company is meeting your forecasts. Indeed, quarterly earnings announcements are one of the most important catalysts for a stock price revision, suggesting that market participants use information in the quarterly financial statements to update their forecasting models. For this reason, it is very useful to prepare explicit quarterly forecasts through the end of the current fiscal year.

7.4   FORECASTING HORIZON

Theoretically speaking, the valuation of an equity security requires us to estimate and discount all the future cash distributions for the infinite future. But, practically speaking, this would require way too many columns on our spreadsheet. Instead, we select a finite horizon over which to prepare explicit forecasts for each year and then we assume that after this point the financial statement line items settle down to a constant growth rate. In this way, we describe an infinite series of future cash distributions without having to explicitly derive an infinite number of pro forma financial statements. Oddly enough, the period at the end of the finite forecasting horizon is known as the "Terminal Period" even though the business itself is not expected to terminate. In later chapters, we will discuss how valuation formulas deal with the infinite series of future cash distributions. What we need to concern ourselves with in this chapter is the selection of an appropriate finite forecasting horizon.

The forecasting horizon should begin with the fiscal year that we are currently in and extend out to the point where we can no longer make a better forecast than to simply assume that all the financial statement line items will grow at the same rate as sales. To be more precise, the terminal period should begin when our forecasts meet the following four conditions. First, sales must settle down to a constant growth rate. Second, margins must remain constant. This condition, combined with the constant sales growth rate, ensures that operating expenses on the income statement grow at the same constant rate as sales. Third, turnover ratios must remain constant. This condition, combined with the constant sales growth rate, ensures that the net operating assets on the balance sheet grow at the same constant rate as sales. Fourth, financial leverage ratios must remain constant. This condition, combined with the constant sales growth rate, ensures that the financial obligations on the balance sheet grow at the same constant rate as sales. Together, these four conditions ensure that all the items in the income statement and balance sheet will grow at the same constant rates as sales. As a result, cash distributions to equity holders will also grow at this same constant rate.

It is important to note that we do not expect all of these conditions to literally hold beyond the forecasting horizon. In reality, sales growth rates, margins, turnover and leverage ratios are all constantly changing and we expect them to continue to change beyond the forecasting horizon. But what is crucial is that we don't expect them to deviate from this constant growth rate in a systematic way. In other words, our forecasts in the terminal period should be unbiased estimates of where we expect these ratios to be in the long run.

How far out do we need to build explicit financial statement forecasts before it is reasonable to assume that things will settle down to this constant long-run equilibrium? It all depends on the nature of the business and the amount of information that is available to build the forecasts. At one extreme, we could be looking at a company in a mature industry with a well-established product, stable demand, a stable production technology, and stable input prices. Moreover, assume that the company offered no forward-looking information about expansion plans, there were no discernable industry trends, and you generally had every reason to believe that "more of the same" is the best description of the future. In such an extreme case it is reasonable to assume that the sales growth rate, margins, turnover and leverage ratios will remain constant at their recent levels. In this simple case, the finite forecasting period is non-existent and the first year in the forecast period is the terminal period. We generate the forecasted financial statements by naively extrapolating the past sales growth rate, margins, turnover and leverage ratios into the infinite future. This process is called "straight lining" because if sales growth, margins, turnover and leverage ratios did all stay constant at their current levels they would plot against time as a straight line. Straight lining is the default forecasting assumption built into *eVal*. We make this choice because, in the absence of additional information, it is the best that we can do. We'll take a closer look at *eVal*'s default forecasting assumptions at the end of this chapter.

In most circumstances, however, straight lining is a very naïve forecasting technique. Instead, we should use what we have learned from our analysis of the past to build more sophisticated forecasts of the future. The length of the forecast horizon depends on how far into the future we can reasonably predict variation in the sales growth rate, margins, turnover and leverage ratios before they settle down to their long-run expected steady-state values. Sales growth won't settle to a steady growth rate until industrywide sales stabilizes and the firm's market share in the industry stabilizes. Thus, firms in start-up industries or firms that are gaining market share from competitors are likely to require longer forecasting horizons. Margins are a function of a firm's competitive advantage in the marketplace. Because it is very hard to sustain a competitive advantage for a long period of time, our forecast horizon should be long enough to capture the erosion of any competitive advantage, assuming this is what you believe will happen. Margins are also subject to systematic accounting distortions. For example, a growing company in an R&D–intensive industry will tend to have its margins temporarily depressed due to the immediate expensing of R&D. Your forecast horizon needs to be long enough to allow any temporary accounting distortions to play out.

Turnover ratios tend to be fairly stable over time, being dictated primarily by the production technology of the firm. However, rapidly growing firms often enjoy economies of scale that lead to increasing turnover ratios as they grow, so you need to anticipate when these economies will be exhausted. Leverage ratios are typically more stable. A firm's target capital structure generally balances the cost of different types of capital, taking into account the tax benefits of debt and the risk of financial distress. Various factors can cause the actual capital structure to deviate from the target capital structure in the short run, but it is typically quite straightforward for a firm to get back to its target capital structure within a few years.

The above analysis points to two key determinants of the forecast horizon. First, it must be long enough for sales growth to settle down to its steady-state level. Second, it must be long enough for any anticipated erosion of any abnormal profits resulting from competitive advantage in the marketplace. In other words, the forecast horizon must be long enough for any abnormal sales growth and abnormal profits to dissipate. For this reason, the forecast horizon is sometimes referred to as the *competitive advantage period*. *eVal* gives you 10 years of finite-horizon forecasting columns before the terminal period. You can start the terminal period earlier simply by straight lining your forecasts earlier. Why no more than 10 years? We have found that both students and practicing security analysts are biased toward overestimating how long firms can sustain their competitive advantage. Typically, when a firm has a new product or new service innovation that enables it to generate abnormally high profits, analysts get excited and extrapolate the abnormally high profits far into the future, not realizing that other firms will be quick to imitate the innovation and compete away the abnormal profits. There are some rare exceptions to this rule, such as Microsoft, Coca-Cola, and McDonald's, but these are very unusual cases. In these exceptional cases, the firm has usually created a key proprietary asset that gives it some degree of monopoly power. If this is truly the case then it is reasonable to assume that the firm will sustain its abnormal profits indefinitely, and we can incorporate the abnormal profitability into the terminal value computation. We caution, however, that cases of indefinitely sustainable competitive advantage are rare.

7.5 TERMINAL PERIOD ASSUMPTIONS

Now that we are finished with the forecast horizon, we are ready to talk about the terminal period forecasting assumptions. Recall from the discussion above that the terminal period is the period in which we expect sales growth, margins, turnover and leverage ratios to settle down to their constant steady state levels. The assumptions that we make about the levels of these variables will drive the terminal value computation and can have a great impact on our overall valuation results. It is therefore important that we choose plausible values for these terminal assumptions. This section provides some guidelines for plausible assumptions or, failing that, describes what assumptions might be considered ridiculous.

The first, most important, terminal value assumption is the terminal sales growth rate. We can offer you some pretty tight guidelines for this one. If a company were to grow faster than the rest of the economy forever, then it would gradually become a larger and larger proportion of the total economy. Past some point, it would basically take over the whole economy, and then the world, and then the universe! It therefore stands to reason that the terminal growth rate cannot be greater than the long-run expected economywide growth rate. Conversely, if a company were to grow more slowly than the economy forever, then it would gradually become a smaller and smaller proportion of the whole economy and eventually disappear. If your company produces a product that you think will eventually become obsolete, then such an assumption is reasonable. This is effectively the same as assuming the company is a finite-lived project. The most common terminal assumption is that the company will grow at the long-run expected economywide growth rate. This way, the company will maintain its size relative to the overall economy indefinitely.

Historically, the annual growth rate in the U.S. economy, as measured by the nominal GDP growth rate, has averaged around 6 percent, composed of roughly 4 percent real growth and 2 percent price inflation. However, the financial crisis of 2007–2008 sent both real growth and inflation plummeting into negative territory, albeit briefly. The long-term forecasts from the Congressional Budget Office and the Federal Reserve at the end of 2010 put real growth at 2–3 percent and inflation at 1–2 percent. So, in most cases, a terminal sales growth rate forecast should fall between 3 and 5 percent. If you want to think of the firm as a finite-lived project (or you are evaluating some specific finite-lived project), you can set the terminal growth rate to −100 percent in *eVal* and this will kill the firm (or project) in the terminal year. We use 3 percent as the default terminal value for Sales Growth in *eVal*. Finally, for reasons to be discussed in Chapter 9, your terminal Sales Growth assumption cannot exceed your cost of equity capital; if it does, you will get error messages.

Next, we must consider the terminal assumptions for margins, turnover and leverage ratios. Unfortunately, it is not possible to give tight guidelines for each of these assumptions. Recall from Chapter 5 that a company can trade off these performance drivers in an infinite number of ways. For example, more outsourcing will lead to higher turnover and lower margins, while greater product differentiation will lead to lower turnover and higher margins. This makes generalized guidelines impossible. Fortunately, we can offer more precise guidelines on the overall combination of assumptions that you choose. As demonstrated in Chapter 5, margin, turnover, and leverage ratios combine to give return on equity (ROE). ROE is an accounting measure of the rate of return on investment, and competition tends to force rates of return toward the cost of capital. In fact, if the following two conditions are satisfied, then the terminal ROE should be identical to the cost of equity capital:

1. The firm is operating in a long-run competitive equilibrium, and
2. The accounting ROE provides a good measure of the economic rate of return on investment.

Under these conditions, the terminal margin, turnover and leverage assumptions must combine to give an ROE that is equal to the cost of capital.

What are plausible levels for ROE when we relax these assumptions? Let's relax the first assumption and consider a firm that has a source of competitive advantage that is sustainable indefinitely. In this case, the terminal ROE will be greater than the cost of capital. How much greater depends on how much of a competitive advantage the company is able to sustain. Here again, we caution that it is very difficult to sustain competitive advantage indefinitely. Make sure that you have a very good case for such a scenario before incorporating it into your valuation model. Finally, you should remember that a terminal rate of return that is more than about 10 percent above the cost of equity capital is simply unrealistic (we refer you back to Figure 5.4 to see just how unrealistic). Even if competition fails to drive away the abnormal return, the Federal Trade Commission and Department of Justice will prevent the abnormal return from becoming too large (as Microsoft found out).

Now let's relax the assumption that accounting ROE provides a good measure of the economic rate of return. As discussed in Chapter 4, there are many reasons why accounting rates of return can provide distorted measures of the economic rate of return. In Chapter 4, we classified these distortions according to whether they were temporary or permanent. Temporary accounting distortions reverse, and we simply need to extend the forecast horizon until these distortions have reversed. For example, if a firm is depreciating equipment too slowly, we simply need to forecast out as far as the equipment is retired, and then use more appropriate accounting assumptions for any new equipment. Permanent accounting distortions, in contrast, do not reverse. Even in steady state, these distortions lead to systematic misstatements in book value. Recall that permanently conservative accounting is quite common. GAAP require many investments that generate cash inflows over multiple future periods to be expensed in the period that they are incurred. The most common examples of such expenditures are R&D, marketing and administrative expenditures. Note that while the impact of immediate expensing washes out of the income number in steady state, it still causes book value of equity to understate invested capital. That is, the numerator of ROE is unbiased in steady state, but the denominator is systematically understated.

In the face of such accounting distortions, the best way to figure out whether your terminal ROE is reasonable is to do a pro forma capitalization of all expenditures that generate future benefits but are immediately expensed under GAAP. This requires you to identify all such expenditures, determine the period over which they are expected to generate future benefits, and then capitalize and amortize them over this period. Once you have done this, you should check that the resulting pro forma ROE is within a plausible range of the cost of capital, given any sustainable competitive advantage. An example helps illustrate the importance of making the pro forma adjustments. Pharmaceutical companies have historically generated ROEs that average about 30 percent, whereas the cost of capital in this industry has only been in the range of 10–15 percent. Is this evidence of monopoly profits? Possibly, but first we need to consider that pharmaceutical companies' annual R&D expenditures have averaged around 25 percent of the book value of equity. Now let's assume that these R&D expenditures generate benefits evenly over the next 12 years, so at any given point there is an average of 6 years worth of R&D investment missing from book value. This means we have omitted from book value capitalized R&D equal to about 150 percent of book value (25 percent per year times an average of 6 years). Hence, if ROE based on as-reported numbers is

$$\text{ROE} = \frac{NI}{BV} = 30\%,$$

then pro forma ROE (ROE′) is equal to

$$\text{ROE}' = \frac{NI}{BKV(1 + 1.5)} = 12\%$$

which is in line with the cost of equity capital. No monopoly profits here!

Forecast Horizon and Terminal Value Assumptions for Kohl's

As discussed in Chapter 3, Kohl's long record of strong growth ended abruptly in 2008 and is expected to be more anemic moving forward. In Kohl's 2009 10-K filing they estimated sales growth of 4–6 percent for the next few years. In the next chapter we develop a detailed forecast for Kohl's that results in near-term sales growth of 5.1 percent and a terminal growth rate of 4.5 percent after 10 years. The detailed forecasts also have Kohl's increasing their ROE steadily from 13.6 percent to 18.7 percent, largely due to increased leverage, over a 10-year period. This is considerably higher than the 10 percent estimate of Kohl's cost of equity capital given in Chapter 9. Can the difference be justified by a sustainable competitive advantage or a continuing accounting distortion? We don't see a long-term accounting distortion for Kohl's, but we do see some competitive advantage. The retail market in the United States is being taken over by "big box" formats such as Kohl's, and smaller chains are being driven out of business. This implies a certain amount of monopoly power in the future to the surviving large companies. Consequently, we believe that Kohl's will be able to hang onto its operating margin.

7.6   THE BALANCE SHEET *PLUG*

When we build a forecast of the balance sheet that contains 20 line items, we have only 19 degrees of freedom. In other words, since the balance sheet must balance, the forecasts for the first 19 line items determine the forecast for the 20th line item. Generally, regardless of the number of line items on the balance sheet, the forecast of one line item will always have to be set to make sure that the balance sheet balances. We call this line item the balance sheet *plug*. But which line item should we select for the balance sheet plug? The net operating assets are determined by the level and nature of the firm's business activities and should therefore definitely require explicit forecasts, making them unsuitable as a plug. This leaves line items relating to financing activities. These line items are more suitable as a plug, because management can generally adapt them as circumstances require. In other words, management typically decides on their desired level of operating and investing activities and then picks a set of financing activities that provide sufficient capital to fund the operating and investing activities.

While most analysts would agree that the net operating assets should be forecasted directly, there is less agreement on which particular financing line item should be used as a plug. Some analysts use cash as the plug (with a negative cash balance representing a bank overdraft). This has two shortcomings:

1. It assumes that management will make no attempt to establish a financing policy that keeps their cash balance at the minimum level necessary to sustain their operating activities. This is a somewhat naïve financing policy (but then again, it seems to be the one that Apple is using).
2. In the case of a bank overdraft, it presupposes that management would be able to secure an overdraft. In the case of a financially distressed firm, this may not be a reasonable supposition.

The other common choice is to plug to common equity. The appeal of this choice is that the common stockholders are the residual claimants of the firm and are thus the natural group to soak up any surpluses or deficits in the firm's financing activities. But this approach also has two shortcomings:

1. In the case of a financing surplus, plugging to common equity assumes that management will pay a big dividend or make a big stock repurchase. But many managers instead choose to either keep surplus cash or to reinvest it in new projects.
2. In the case of a financing deficit, plugging to common equity assumes that the firm will issue new equity. As with a bank overdraft, this presupposes that management would be able to access capital markets on acceptable terms.

There is no perfect answer to this problem. *eVal* plugs to common equity, but we warn you not to take the results of this assumption blindly. You should look at the plug amount and ask yourself whether the implied amount of stock issued or repurchased really represents what you think management will do. If not, then you need to iterate back through the other line items in your forecasting model until you get a complete set of satisfactory forecasts. For instance, if you really believe that management will build a large cash balance rather than make distributions to investors (like Apple has), then turn up the forecasted cash until the plug to common equity implies no cash distributions to investors.

7.7   FORECASTING WITH *eVal*

Now let's take a look at how *eVal* guides you through the forecasting process. Start *eVal* and open the Forecasting Assumptions worksheet as shown in Figure 7.2. Reading across the columns of this worksheet you will see five years of historical data on each of the forecasting assumptions and 11 years of forecast data shaded in yellow. Your job is to fill in these yellow cells.

We will give you lots of detailed advice on filling in the yellow cells in the next chapter; for now we just want you to become familiar with the overall way that *eVal* organizes your forecasting inputs. Reading down the rows of this worksheet, you will see each of the forecasting assumptions laid out following the forecasting framework outlined in Figure 7.1. We begin with the sales growth rate assumption. If you look at the default forecasting

FIGURE 7.2

Forecasting Assumptions Sheet in *eVal*

Fiscal Year End Date	Actual 2006-01-31	Actual 2007-01-31	Actual 2008-01-31	Actual 2009-01-31	Actual 2010-01-31	Forecast 2011-01-31	Forecast 2012-01-31
Implied Return on Equity		0.192	0.185	0.138	0.136	0.130	0.130
Sales Growth		16.0%	6.0%	-0.5%	4.8%	4.6%	4.5%
Cost of Goods Sold/Sales	64.7%	63.6%	63.5%	63.1%	62.2%	62.2%	62.2%
R&D/Sales	0.0%	0.0%	0.0%	0.0%	0.0%	0.0%	0.0%
SG&A/Sales	22.4%	22.2%	22.8%	24.3%	24.4%	24.4%	24.4%
Dep&Amort/Avge PP&E and Intang.		7.5%	7.3%	7.8%	8.2%	8.2%	8.2%
Net Interest Expense/Avge Net Debt		6.7%	6.3%	6.8%	6.5%	6.5%	6.5%
Non-Operating Income/Sales	0.1%	0.2%	0.2%	0.2%	0.1%	0.1%	0.1%
Effective Tax Rate	37.4%	37.5%	37.8%	37.9%	37.6%	37.6%	37.6%
Minority Interest/After Tax Income	0.0%	0.0%	0.0%	0.0%	0.0%	0.0%	0.0%
Other Income/Sales	0.0%	0.0%	0.0%	0.0%	0.0%	0.0%	0.0%
Ext. Items & Disc. Ops./Sales	0.0%	0.0%	0.0%	0.0%	0.0%	0.0%	0.0%
Pref. Dividends/Avge Pref. Stock		0.0%	0.0%	0.0%	0.0%	0.0%	0.0%
Balance Sheet Assumptions							
Working Capital Assumptions							
Ending Operating Cash/Sales	2.1%	4.0%	4.0%	4.1%	13.2%	13.2%	13.2%
Ending Receivables/Sales	12.3%	0.0%	0.0%	0.0%	0.0%	0.0%	0.0%
Ending Inventories/COGS	25.8%	26.2%	27.3%	27.1%	27.4%	27.4%	27.4%
Ending Other Current Assets/Sales	0.7%	1.2%	1.2%	1.4%	1.7%	1.7%	1.7%
Ending Accounts Payable/COGS	9.6%	9.4%	8.0%	8.5%	11.1%	11.1%	11.1%
Ending Taxes Payable/Sales	1.2%	1.5%	0.8%	0.6%	1.1%	1.1%	1.1%
Ending Other Current Liabs/Sales	4.8%	4.7%	4.8%	5.0%	5.8%	5.8%	5.8%
Other Operating Asset Assumptions							
Ending Net PP&E/Sales	33.9%	34.4%	39.5%	42.6%	40.9%	40.9%	40.9%
Ending Investments/Sales	0.0%	0.0%	0.0%	2.0%	1.9%	1.9%	1.9%
Ending Intangibles/Sales	1.7%	1.5%	1.3%	1.3%	1.2%	1.2%	1.2%
Ending Other Assets/Sales	0.9%	0.4%	0.6%	0.7%	0.8%	0.8%	0.8%
Other Operating Liability Assumptions							
Other Liabilities/Sales	1.4%	1.5%	2.3%	2.5%	2.8%	2.8%	2.8%
Deferred Taxes/Sales	1.6%	1.6%	1.6%	2.0%	2.2%	2.2%	2.2%
Financing Assumptions							
Current Debt/Total Assets	1.2%	0.2%	0.1%	0.1%	0.1%	0.1%	0.1%
Long-Term Debt/Total Assets	11.4%	11.5%	19.4%	18.1%	15.6%	15.6%	15.6%
Minority Interest/Total Assets	0.0%	0.0%	0.0%	0.0%	0.0%	0.0%	0.0%
Preferred Stock/Total Assets	0.0%	0.0%	0.0%	0.0%	0.0%	0.0%	0.0%
Dividend Payout Ratio	0.0%	0.0%	0.0%	0.0%	0.0%	0.0%	0.0%

assumptions for sales growth, you will see that it makes a smooth progression over the forecast horizon from its value in the most recent historical year to a terminal year rate of 3 percent. If you change the sales growth forecast for the first year of the forecast period, *eVal* automatically smoothes between this new growth rate and the terminal growth rate. The default *eVal* formula for most line items is similar, smoothing between the value in the first forecast period and the value in the terminal forecast period. Therefore, one approach to quickly entering the forecasting assumptions is to forecast the first year and the terminal year and let the formulas smooth out everything in between. Or you can enter the first few years of forecasts and let the formulas smooth from the last year you entered to your terminal year forecast (play with it a bit—you'll soon get the hang of it!). Because *eVal* starts with the most recent year, you should be particularly wary of unusual changes in this year—go back and read the MD&A again!

The remaining income statement assumptions forecast the operating margins. The default assumption for most of the income statement items is to simply straight line their values from the most recent historical year. The exceptions to this rule are Other Income/Sales and Extraordinary Items and Discontinued Operations/Sales. These line items typically contain nonrecurring amounts, so a better default forecasting assumption is that they will be zero in all future periods. Of course, you should always take a close look at the exact nature of the items that have appeared here in the recent past and make your own assessment about the likelihood that they will recur in the future.

The balance sheet assumptions are listed further down the sheet and are presented in four groups. The working capital assumptions are basically forecasts of the turnover ratios, except that we put the balance sheet item in the numerator and divide by the corresponding flow variable (sales or cost of goods sold). This is basically the reciprocal of the turnover ratio. We have found that it is much more intuitive to put the balance sheet item in the numerator when we are trying to forecast the balance sheet item. Note also that we are forecasting the ending balance of the item rather than an average over the period (unlike the turnover ratios in *eVal*'s Ratio Analysis sheet that are based on average balance sheet amounts). While algebraically possible, forecasting the average balance and then backing into the implied ending balance can cause the forecasted ratios to oscillate in very disconcerting ways. Consistent with the way in which we compute turnover ratios, we express inventory and payables as a percentage of cost of goods sold and all of the other working capital accounts as a percentage of sales.

The next two groups of balance sheet forecasting assumptions are the noncurrent operating asset and noncurrent operating liability assumptions. As with the working capital assumptions, we forecast the ending balance of each of these line items as a percentage of sales. These assumptions fill out the asset side of the balance sheet and the operating portion of the liabilities (i.e., the net operating assets). All that is left on the balance sheet are the financial obligations and equity, which are determined by your financing assumptions. The debt, minority interest and preferred stock assumptions are statements about the firm's leverage, expressed as a proportion of total assets. Having forecasted the assets, the liabilities, and the preferred stock, the common equity balance is determined; it is the *plug* that we discussed earlier.

Notice that you are allowed to forecast the dividend payout ratio. You may wonder how the ending balance in common equity can be determined if you are free to forecast any dividend you like. Doesn't a dividend reduce the common equity balance? Technically, yes, but since the common equity balance is already determined by your other assumptions, *eVal* adjusts the implied stock issuances or repurchases to exactly offset any dividend that you forecast. That is, your forecasted dividends reduce retained earnings, but *eVal* increases the balance in paid in capital by exactly the same amount so as to leave common equity unaffected. Play with it a bit and you will see what we mean.

eVal provides you with a few diagnostics to help judge the plausibility of your forecasting assumptions. First, up at the top of the Forecasting Assumptions worksheet you will find the Implied Return on Equity. Recall from section 7.5 that while it is difficult to provide plausible bounds for each of the individual balance sheet and income statement assumptions, they should all combine to give a return on equity figure that is within a plausible distance of the cost of capital. Second, by clicking on the Ratio Analysis and Cash Flow Analysis tabs, you can see the complete ratio and cash flow analyses implied by your assumptions. Do these forecasted ratios jibe with your views about the firm's future? One particularly important item to look at in the cash flow analysis is Net Issuance of Common Stock. As we discussed earlier, this is the amount computed by *eVal* in order to balance your balance sheet. A positive amount indicates the amount that will have to be raised through issuance of new stock; a negative amount indicates the amount that will be used to repurchase stock. You should ask yourself if the market conditions are conducive to raising new stock? Does management intend to use excess cash for stock repurchases? If not, then you need to iterate back through your forecasting assumptions until you have a more plausible scenario.

Suppose management told you that they expected the balance in PP&E to be $100 million next year. To hit this amount on your forecasted balance sheet might be a bit tough—you would have to keep changing the PP&E/Sales forecast until you hit exactly $100 million on the financial statements. It might be tempting at this point to simply toggle over to the Financial Statements sheet and type in $100 million. While possible, we caution against this approach. By forecasting a balance directly, you overwrite all the checks and balances built into *eVal*. Further, even if you are sufficiently careful to keep your balance sheet balancing, it is very easy to enter individual line items that don't appear unreasonable, but together imply crazy financial statement ratios (see the Amazon case at the end of the book for an example). As one small check, *eVal* will generate an error message if your balance sheet no longer balances, which is what would happen if all you did was change PP&E to $100 million.

7.8 FORECASTING EPS

The forecasts discussed so far are all firm-level forecasts. However, investors in public corporations rarely buy the entire firm. Instead, they buy shares representing fractional interests in the firm. For this reason, it is common practice to express certain key forecasts on a *per-share* basis. Expressing forecasts on a per-share basis allows for direct comparisons with stock prices, which are also expressed on a per-share basis. Not surprisingly, the most common component of the financial statements to be expressed on a per-share basis is earnings. Earnings is the key accounting summary measure of firm performance and so it is useful to know just how much earnings a company is generating per share of outstanding common stock. Earnings-per-share (EPS) is the most commonly published forecast by security analysts. Moreover, the extent to which reported quarterly EPS differs from the consensus analyst forecast of EPS is probably the single most important determinant of firm-specific movements in stock price.

Given the prevalence of EPS forecasts in practice, it is useful to construct the forecasts of EPS implied by your forecast financial statements. By doing so, you can quickly evaluate whether your forecasts are more optimistic or pessimistic than the forecasts of other analysts following the firm. In theory, the computation of EPS forecasts is quite simple. We simply divide forecast earnings by the forecast weighted-average number of shares outstanding for the period. In practice, however, the forecasting of the weighted average number of shares outstanding is troublesome. There are two distinct problems:

1. Forecasting the number of shares that will be issued and/or repurchased between now and the end of each future forecasting period.
2. Forecasting the number of common stock equivalents that will be outstanding at the end of future forecasting periods.

The first problem arises because we do not know the future prices at which any stock issuances and repurchases will take place. Our forecasted financial statements tell us how many dollars of common equity we expect the firm to issue or repurchase in each future forecasting period. But in order to compute the associated number of shares, we need to know the prices at which these transactions will take place. This introduces a strange circularity into our computations. Remember that one of the main goals of financial statement forecasting is to figure out the value of a share of stock. But in order to forecast EPS, we first need to forecast the future price of a share of stock. If we already knew the latter, we probably wouldn't bother with the former! Fortunately, there is a pragmatic and internally consistent solution to this circularity problem. *eVal* simply assumes that your forecasts of the future financial statements of the firm are correct and appropriately incorporated in the firm's stock price. The future stock price is then computed by taking the current intrinsic stock price generated by your forecasted financial statements, compounding it at the cost of equity capital, and subtracting any cash dividends paid. The computations are mundane and automated in *eVal,* so we won't bother with a more detailed description of them here.

The above solution is fine if the current market price of the stock is close to the intrinsic price generated by your forecasting model. But what if the current market price of the stock is very different from the price implied by your model? In this case, either your forecasting model is wrong, or the market price is wrong. If you conclude that the former is the case, then you should go back to the drawing board and build a better forecasting model. If you conclude that the latter is the case, then you have identified a mispriced stock. But before computing EPS forecasts, you need to consider the possibility that the firm could issue or repurchase shares of common stock in the future at a market price that differs from intrinsic value. Firms with mispriced stock can influence their own EPS (and intrinsic share price) by engaging in strategic transactions in their own stock. Firms with overpriced stock can increase EPS (and intrinsic share price) by issuing stock, while firms with underpriced stock can increase EPS (and intrinsic share price) by repurchasing stock. This is a complicated topic, and we defer a more complete discussion to Chapter 12. At this point, you should simply be aware that the procedure used by *eVal* to compute EPS does not consider such effects.

The second problem in computing EPS concerns the fact that analysts and investors most commonly forecast *diluted* EPS. If you are an accounting geek, you will remember that EPS comes in two varieties—basic and diluted. Basic EPS simply involves dividing earnings by a time-weighted average of shares outstanding. Diluted EPS involves dividing earnings by a time-weighted average shares outstanding plus common stock equivalents related to potentially dilutive securities, such as employee stock options and convertible bonds. These potentially dilutive securities represent contingent claims on common equity, and incorporating them helps in figuring out what is likely to be left for the existing common stockholders. Unfortunately, the forecasting of future common stock equivalents is very complicated and difficult to do with much accuracy. We therefore focus on forecasting basic EPS. We can, however, offer you some simple practical advice if you want to forecast diluted EPS. Take a look at the firm's most recent financial statements. The income statement should report both basic and diluted EPS. If these two numbers are very similar, then potentially dilutive securities are probably not that big of a deal, and so ignoring them is reasonable. If these two numbers differ by 5 percent or more, then common stock equivalents are important and should be considered. A good base case forecasting assumption is that the number of common stock equivalents related to potentially dilutive securities remains constant in the future. But if you are looking at a firm that

FIGURE 7.3

EPS Forecaster Sheet

Company Name	KOHL'S CORP		
Common Shares Outstanding at BS Date	307,000		
Equivalent Shares at Valuation Date	307,000		
Forecasted Price at Valuation Date	$39.79		
	Forecast	Forecast	Forecast
Fiscal Year of Forecast	2011-01-31	2012-01-31	2013-01-31
Net Income	1,046,887	1,093,460	1,140,301
Common Equity Issued (Repurchased)	(681,779)	(724,931)	(769,408)
Forecasted Price at Year End	$43.77	$48.15	$52.96
New Shares Issued (Repurchased)	(15,576)	(15,056)	(14,527)
Shares Outstanding at End of Year	291,424	276,368	261,841
Forecast EPS	$3.50	$3.85	$4.24
Consensus Analyst Forecast of EPS			
Forecast Five Year Growth Rate in EPS	10%		
Consensus Analyst Forecast of Growth Rate			

Although not a necessary input for eVal, you find the analyst forecasts for your co yellow-shaded cells for comparison purpo

To obtain analyst forecasts, click here

plans to restructure its employee stock option plan or refinance its convertible debt, you need to pull out your intermediate accounting text and burn some midnight oil.

To make the above discussion more concrete, let's take a look at the EPS forecasts for Kohl's using the default forecasting assumptions in *eVal*. The EPS forecasts and associated computations are contained in the EPS Forecaster worksheet. This worksheet is reproduced in Figure 7.3 using a valuation date of January 31, 2010 and the default forecasting assumptions, with the result of an intrinsic value estimate of $39.79/share. The key financial statement inputs to this sheet are the number of common shares outstanding at the most recent balance sheet date, the forecasted price of the company (based on *eVal*'s current forecasting assumptions), the forecast of net income for each future year, and the amount of common equity that is forecast to be issued (repurchased) in each future year. You can follow the formulas in the respective cells to trace each of these inputs back to their source worksheets.

The first computation in the EPS Forecaster worksheet is the forecast of the price at the end of each future year. The price is computed by taking the price at the end of the previous year, multiplying by one plus the cost of capital to reflect the expected return for the year, and subtracting the forecast dividend-per-share for the year. For our example, this works out to be $39.79 \times (1+.10) - 0 = \$43.77$/share. The assumption is that this is the future price that shares will be issued or repurchased at. Armed with the forecasted price-per-share, the computation of EPS is straightforward. We first divide common equity issued (repurchased) for the year by forecast price for the year to obtain the number of new shares issued (repurchased) for the year. Next, we compute shares outstanding at the end of each year by adding (subtracting) shares issued (repurchased) for the year to the outstanding balance from the previous year. Finally, we divide net income by the average number of shares outstanding for the year to arrive at our EPS forecast.

In our example, the implied $681,779 thousand stock repurchase translates into 15,576 shares repurchased, reducing the shares outstanding from 307,000 thousand to 291,424 thousand. The forecasted income of $1,046,887 divided by the average of the beginning and ending shares outstanding results in an EPS forecast of $3.50.

If all this work seems too pedantic just to get the denominator to your EPS calculation, then you can simply type the forecast number of shares directly into the EPS Forecaster worksheet (using, for example, the number of shares outstanding). The EPS Forecaster sheet stands alone, so changes here will not flow back to other parts of your *eVal* model.

One of the most important functions of the EPS Forecaster worksheet is to allow you to compare your EPS forecasts with the consensus analyst forecast. We provide a link at the bottom of the EPS Forecaster worksheet that takes you directly to the consensus earnings estimates provided at Yahoo .com. Whenever possible you should compare your forecasts to the consensus analyst EPS forecasts for each of the next two years, and for the five-year growth rate in EPS.

7.9 SUMMARY AND CONCLUSION

Forecasting is where the rubber meets the road in equity valuation. A valuation is only as good as the forecasts that support it. And good forecasts only come from a careful synthesis of the findings from your business, accounting, and financial analyses. It is important that you forecast the complete financial statements and that you use a systematic forecasting framework that maintains internal consistency in the resulting statements. It is also important that your forecasting assumptions lead to economically plausible statements about the future.

So far we have talked about forecasting from the 30,000-foot level. The next chapter gets down to the nitty-gritty of forecasting the individual line items on the financial statements.

7.10 CASES, LINKS, AND REFERENCES

Cases, links, and references relating to material in this chapter are presented at the end of Chapter 8 and should be reviewed after reading Chapter 8.

Forecasting Details

8.1 INTRODUCTION

The last chapter described our general framework for forecasting a firm's future financial performance. In this chapter we give more specific guidance about how to come up with a reasonable forecast for each specific line item. Obviously, we can't tell you what to forecast in every circumstance; rather, we try to give you a list of things to think about.

As you proceed through the income statement and balance sheet assumptions, you may be plagued by the following two thoughts. The first is that there is always more you could do to develop a better forecast of each item. There is an endless amount of data available—maybe a little more hunting will identify the perfect indicator of the future for the particular variable you are trying to forecast. The second doubt is that, even after all your hard work, you still feel uncertain about the resulting forecast. Both of these feelings are legitimate, but there is nothing we can do about them; the world is an uncertain place. We offer you a framework to guide you through the forecasting process and we offer you some guidance about what reasonable forecasts might be, but we don't have the crystal ball that perfectly predicts the future.

This chapter will walk you through the individual income statement and balance sheet assumptions that *eVal* uses to construct the forecast financial statements. For some of the forecasts it may help to build a more detailed model and then plug the forecasting assumptions implied by the detailed model into the appropriate income statement or balance sheet assumption in *eVal*. The easiest way to do this is to build your more detailed model further down the Forecasting sheet, or add a new sheet to *eVal*, and then link the result back to the appropriate yellow-celled forecasting assumption.

8.2 FORECASTING SALES GROWTH

If God offers to fill in one row of your spreadsheet, this is the one to ask for. Sales growth, or the lack of it, is a huge driver of value. You should bring everything you can to bear on this forecast. *eVal* shows the firm's past history of sales growth but this is only a starting point. Extreme levels of sales growth tend to mean-revert very quickly. Recall from Figure 5.1 that firms in the top quintile of sales growth averaged 55 percent, but the same firms only averaged 24 percent sales growth the next year. So just because sales growth has been high in the past doesn't mean that sales growth will be high in the future.

Obviously we can't give you a recipe for forecasting sales that will apply to all companies in all situations. What follows is a basic approach along with a list of things that you should consider for most companies. One approach is to start by forecasting industry sales growth. With this as a benchmark, you can then ask if the firm is likely to increase or decrease its share of industry sales. This exercise starts with macroeconomic data and works down to a firm-specific forecast. As we will see, such an approach works well when the firm is a large player in the industry. Alternatively, if the firm's industry is ill-defined, or the firm is a very small part of the industry, then it might be better to start at the firm level and only look to other companies for a few key comparisons.

Forecasting Industry Sales Growth

To build a forecast of industry sales growth, go back to Chapter 2 and look over the list of available macroeconomic data. What are the key drivers of sales in your industry? More importantly, what are the key indicators of *future* sales? For example, the aging of the baby boomers is a very predictable phenomenon that has huge implications for the health care sector. You could study past trends in personal expenditures on health care as a function of the median age of the population. As another example, suppose you are studying a house-building company in the south. The demand for houses is a function of many things, including age demographics, migration patterns across geographic regions, and interest rates. Governments around the world collect detailed statistics on all of these variables. You could estimate the relation between these variables and past housing demand in the south and then extrapolate this model to estimate the demand for future housing.

Building a model of industry sales that predicts the future is no easy task. And, even if you find a set of variables that predicts industry sales very well, your particular firm may buck the trend. Nevertheless, we encourage you to spend some time on this task. Even if your work doesn't result in a great predictor of industry sales, the exercise will help you identify the key drivers of sales and this should help to keep your long-term sales forecasts reasonable. Also keep in mind that your goal is to predict future sales, not explain past sales. A macroeconomic variable that moves concurrently with industry sales will make for a beautiful graph, but unless you can generate decent forecasts of the variable, it won't be much help in forecasting future sales. For example, it turns out that the return on the S&P 500 is a great concurrent predictor of demand for cruise vacations; apparently, when the market is up, the cruising segment of the population splurges on a great vacation. While this observation makes for a great graph, it is completely useless for predicting future demand for cruise vacations, unless you think you can predict future movements

FIGURE 8.1

Estimating Industry and Firm Sales from Macroeconomic Data

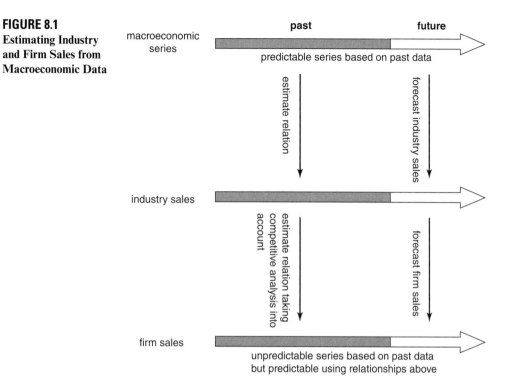

in the S&P 500. And if you can reliably predict future movements in the S&P 500 then you really don't need this book!

Figure 8.1 illustrates how you might think about linking macroeconomic data to industry sales and firm-specific sales. For this to be a useful exercise, you need two key relationships to be very strong. You need the macroeconomic data to be predictable in the future and you need the links between the macroeconomic data, the industry sales, and the firm sales to be strong. If both of these conditions are true then you can build a sales forecast by first predicting the macroeconomic series, then forecasting industry sales from the macro prediction, and then forecasting firm sales from the industry prediction. Demographic trends, for example, are very predictable macroeconomic phenomena. It would be foolish to ignore these trends if your firm's customers come from a particular slice of the demographic pie. In addition, a number of macroeconomic trends are linked to GDP growth. While GDP growth isn't a simple series to predict, economists put so much effort into forecasting it that you can get decent forecasts from the web (check out the Congressional Budget Office or the Conference Board links at the end of the chapter). As an example, personal consumption expenditures on durable goods (e.g., washing machines) tend to grow rapidly as the economy comes out of a recession. If the GDP forecasts indicate a recession is ending, then this is a powerful indicator of a large increase in sales of durable goods in the immediate future. On the other hand, business investment in fixed goods takes much longer to start growing after a recession, so your prediction for an equipment supplier might be much more subdued.

Once you have a forecast of industry sales growth, the next task is to predict how this will relate to your particular firm's sales growth. At this step you need to consider the intensity of competition from alternative sources for the same products or services. Who are the firm's competitors and how intensely are they competing? The link between industry sales and firm sales is obviously stronger if the firm makes up a significant fraction of the industry. The link is weakest when the firm is small or when the industry is growing rapidly.

As an example, the growth in grocery store sales in the United States is remarkably stable, ranging between one and four percent in the last decade. No matter how much advertising stores put in the local newspapers, people can only eat so much. Grocery store sales would probably mirror population growth perfectly except that grocery stores have expanded their product lines to include pharmacies and home goods. Further, the past decade saw larger grocery store chains swallow up many smaller ones. The result is that Kroger, the largest grocer in the United States, grew sales at an average rate of about 6 percent in the past decade, roughly double the industry rate. Over the same period Whole Foods grew more than twice as fast as Kroger, as Americans discovered "whole" food. Kroger, which accounts for more than 13 percent of total grocery sales in the United States, can only deviate from the industry rate by so much because it is such a large part of the industry. Whole Foods, on the other hand, accounts for only about one percent of grocery sales, and so is far less governed by the overall industry growth rate.

The firm-specific facts that we discuss in the next section are typically the main drivers of sales for small and growing firms. In addition, firms with winning strategies may generate unusually large sales growth in the short run by stealing market share from other firms. But in the long run even these companies can't escape the economic forces of the industry.

Firm-Specific Influences on Sales Growth

There are many useful predictors of future sales that come from the firm itself. One significant indicator of future sales is the firm's current and future investments in operating capacity, especially in new sales locations or new products. Firms make investments to generate future income so, assuming the firm isn't making bad bets, these investments will be harbingers of future sales. As an example, you can divide retail sales growth into growth from opening new stores and growth from increased sales at existing outlets (with the latter known as same-store or comparable-store sales growth). California Pizza Kitchen can grow rapidly by opening up new restaurants all over the country, but the very nature of a restaurant puts severe limits on the amount of sales growth that can be generated from the existing locations. Only so many people can squeeze into one booth. Retail companies frequently disclose their plans for new store openings over the next few years and you should use this information to estimate the contribution that new stores will make to total sales growth. You can then combine this with an estimate of the more modest contribution that same-store sales growth will make to arrive at the total sales growth rate.

This same logic extends well beyond forecasting in the retail sales business. Most investments are made to generate a sequence of future sales. When newly invested capital starts producing output, there should be a big burst of new sales, followed by a reasonably steady stream of future sales from that investment. It is therefore useful to distinguish between the large bursts of sales growth that come from newly invested capital and the much lower growth in sales, if any, that comes from the continued operation of previously invested capital.

You can frequently gain some useful information from the segment disclosure footnote in the financial statements. This footnote describes sales, profits, and investments by major product lines and geographic regions. This information can help focus your attention on the largest sources of sales for the firm and help to identify where they are investing for the future. The firm's MD&A (capital resources section) is also a good source of information about the firm's future growth prospects.

Forecasting future sales is very important but very difficult. Take this part of the forecasting task seriously, but also be mindful that some fraction of future sales is inherently unknowable. Floods, pestilence, technological innovation, and the inherent fickleness of the consumer all combine to make sales a truly random variable. Use all of your collected wisdom to make educated guesses, and to put reasonable bounds on your estimates, but then move on.

Finally, we would like to repeat the warning from the previous chapter. Do NOT make the terminal year forecast of sales growth very large—7 percent might be a maximum. Think about what it would mean to forecast a large growth rate into perpetuity; as the company grows faster than the world economy it would slowly but surely take over the entire planet. So unless you mean to forecast this type of world domination, don't use a big sales growth forecast in the terminal period.

A Sales Forecast for Kohl's

We will illustrate our approach to forecasting sales using Kohl's. Since Kohl's is only a small part of a huge industry, the macro approach to forecasting sales might not be very fruitful, at least for the next few years. In the short run, we should forecast their sales based on estimates of their new store growth. However, in the long run Kohl's will be subject to the undeniable fact that the clothing and accessories industry is a relatively stable and slowly growing industry. We will start by looking for the drivers of industry sales growth to guide our terminal period forecast but then develop our

FIGURE 8.2

Clothing and Accessories Industry Sales Growth Drivers

Source: Bureau of Census Retail Sales Survey and Bureau of Economic Analysis NIPA Tables

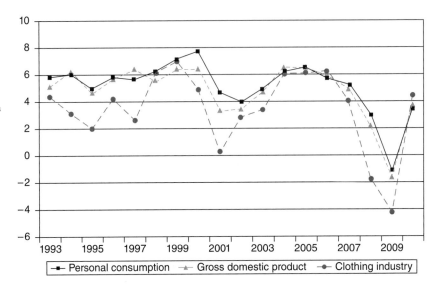

more immediate sales forecasts for Kohl's based primarily on company-specific data.

Figure 8.2 illustrates how sales growth in the clothing and accessories industry is related to growth in the gross domestic product and particularly to growth in personal consumption expenditures. While growth in clothing and accessories sales is more volatile than growth in personal consumption expenditures or GDP, all three series basically move together and average to about the same amounts over time. In addition, consumer expenditure survey data from the Bureau of Labor Statistics shows that the percent of personal consumption expenditures on apparel has remained between 3.8 and 4.1 percent over the past few years. Forecasted growth in GDP is therefore likely to be a good predictor of growth in the clothing and accessories industry.

The Congressional Budget office estimated that nominal GDP growth (real GDP growth plus price inflation) was 3.8 percent in 2010 and would fall to 3.7 in 2011 and then increase to about 4.5 percent in 2012 and remain there. Given the correspondence between GDP growth and growth in the clothing and accessories industry, we can use this as our industry forecast. Although Kohl's may grow faster or slower than the industry in the short run, we will assume that it eventually will be governed by these industry growth forecasts.

Turning to company-specific information, we learn from Kohl's 10-K that they currently have 1,058 stores spread across the United States, having opened about 58 stores per year since their initial public offering in 1992. They also state that they opened 54 stores in 2009, expect to open 30 new stores in 2010, and plan to continue opening stores at this more modest rate into the future. So one estimate for Kohl's is that they will grow their stores by 2.8 percent for the next few years (30/1,058). Another approach might be to estimate how many stores a fully built-out system would contain. We note that in the Midwest, Kohl's most developed region, they are averaging 5.1 stores per million people. Extrapolating to the United States population of 305 million, this suggests a mature system of about 1,555 stores (as a point of comparison, Target has 1,740 stores). This would imply about 4 percent growth in stores over the next 10 years.

New stores certainly contribute to growth in sales, but in the retail environment an equally important statistic is the growth in sales from stores that have been open at least a year, known as comparable store sales, or simply "comps." In their 2009 MD&A Kohl's discloses that their comps were 0.4 percent, the result of a 1.4 percent improvement due to the closure of their competitor Dillard's and a 1.0 percent reduction due to cannibalized sales from their own existing stores by newly opened stores. The net result of 0.4 percent comp growth is the result of a simple calculation, but the two underlying causes cannot be verified. How could they possibly know that a new customer walked through their door because her favorite Dillard's closed, or a former Kohl's customer *didn't* walk through the door because a new Kohl's opened closer to her home? Nonetheless, if we believe that Kohl's management has this type of insight, then we might want to use the fact that they forecast in the MD&A that 2010 comp growth will be 1–3 percent, and total sales growth will be 4–6 percent.

There are many ways to weave the new store growth estimate and the comparable store growth estimate together into a forecast of future sales. If we are willing to assume that old stores and new stores generate sales at the same rate then a valid approach is to simply compound the two growth rates together. That is

$$\text{Total Sales Growth} = (1 + \text{growth rate in stores})$$
$$(1 + \text{growth rate in comps}) - 1$$

Figure 8.3 shows the estimated and corresponding actual sales growth rates at Kohl's for the past four years, where the estimate is made by inserting the actual store growth and comp growth statistics into the formula above. Notice that the actual sales growth is a bit less than the estimated growth in each year, suggesting that perhaps the new stores do not reach maturity instantly, as the model above assumes. However, given that Kohl's is planning on slowing their new store growth considerably, the complication of estimating separate sales for new versus old stores is unlikely to yield a significant improvement.

Putting all this together, we forecast that new store growth will be 3 percent per year for the next 10 years, and comp growth will be 2 percent per year for the next 10 years, for a compounded growth rate for sales of 5.06 percent. We will round up to 5.1 percent in *eVal*. After 10 years we forecast that the terminal growth rate in sales will equal the estimated growth in GDP of 4.5 percent.

FIGURE 8.3
Kohl's Estimated and
Actual Sales Growth
Rates

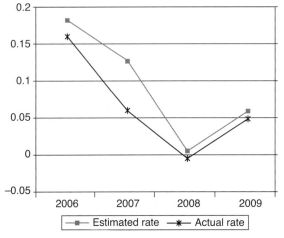

8.3 EXPENSE FORECASTS

As a roadmap to the expense forecasts, Figure 8.4 shows the Income Statement Assumptions section of *eVal*'s Forecasting Assumptions sheet. Having
completed the sales growth forecasts, now it is time to think about how expenses are going to eat away at those revenues.

Many expenses move directly with sales, such as Cost of Goods Sold and
Selling, General and Administrative expenses, and so we forecast these expenses as a percentage of sales. However, just because the forecast input is
a percentage of sales doesn't mean that you should forecast it as a *constant*
percent of sales. Firms may enjoy economies of scale as they grow or they may
implement cost management programs; both would lower these expense ratios.
In addition, remember that a sales price increase has the same effect as lowering expenses when it comes to forecasting expenses as a percent of sales.

FIGURE 8.4 **Income Statement Assumptions for Kohl's**

Fiscal Year End Date	Actual 07-01-31	Actual 08-01-31	Actual 09-01-31	Actual 10-01-31	Forecast 11-01-31	Forecast 12-01-31
Implied Return on Equity	0.192	0.185	0.138	0.136	0.130	0.128
Income Statement Assumptions						
Sales Growth	16.0%	6.0%	-0.5%	4.8%	5.1%	5.1%
Cost of Goods Sold/Sales	63.6%	63.5%	63.1%	62.2%	62.0%	62.0%
R&D/Sales	0.0%	0.0%	0.0%	0.0%	0.0%	0.0%
SG&A/Sales	22.2%	22.8%	24.3%	24.4%	24.4%	24.4%
Dep&Amort/Avge PP&E and Intang.	7.5%	7.3%	7.8%	8.2%	8.5%	8.9%
Net Interest Expense/Avge Net Debt	6.7%	6.3%	6.8%	6.5%	6.5%	6.5%
Non-Operating Income/Sales	0.2%	0.2%	0.2%	0.1%	0.0%	0.0%
Effective Tax Rate	37.5%	37.8%	37.9%	37.6%	37.6%	37.6%
Minority Interest/After Tax Income	0.0%	0.0%	0.0%	0.0%	0.0%	0.0%
Other Income/Sales	0.0%	0.0%	0.0%	0.0%	0.0%	0.0%
Ext. Items & Disc. Ops./Sales	0.0%	0.0%	0.0%	0.0%	0.0%	0.0%
Pref. Dividends/Avge Pref. Stock	0.0%	0.0%	0.0%	0.0%	0.0%	0.0%

In some cases, the account balances rather than sales levels are the drivers of the income statement items. For example, there is a very strong relation between the Debt on the balance sheet and the Interest Expense on the income statement—the debt balance times the interest rate equals the interest expense. So for interest expense and some other items, the forecast of the income statement item is based on its relation to a specific balance sheet item.

When forecasting a firm's expense ratios you should always compare them with their industry peers. You can often find these statistics at Yahoo! Finance.

Cost of Goods Sold

The ratio of Cost of Goods Sold (COGS) to sales describes how much of every sales dollar is spent directly on providing the product or delivering the service. When forecasting this item think about how the firm's products or services are viewed in the product market. Can they charge a price premium over their competitors? Is this premium sustainable in the long run? The effects of competition are first seen in this line item: As a firm is forced to lower its prices in response to competitors' price reductions, this ratio will increase. Are there manufacturing efficiencies to be gained that will lower production costs? As the firm grows, do you anticipate it getting sufficiently large that it can demand lower prices from its suppliers (as Walmart does)? Much of the ratio analysis of profitability that we discussed in Chapter 5 is designed to help you forecast this item. In addition, you may find some guidance for this forecast by reading the firm's MD&A and earnings announcements. Note that the discussion in the MD&A may be pitched in terms of the Gross Profit Margin, defined as

$$\text{Gross Profit Margin} = 1 - (\text{COGS/Sales})$$

Finally, remember that a pure price increase, with no other changes, will increase the gross profit margin, which reduces the COGS/Sales ratio.

Along with the firm's own past, the COGS/Sales ratio of a few close competitors is a good place to start when forecasting this ratio. If the firm has a low COGS/Sales ratio relative to its peers then you need to think about whether or not it can sustain this advantage. If you are analyzing a young firm with no clear cost structure exhibited in the data, then using a more mature firm's COGS/Sales ratio in your forecasts is a good idea. If the firm has exhibited some economies to scale that have caused the COGS/Sales ratio to decline in recent years then ask yourself how much longer you expect this trend to continue. If you believe that economies of scale are a significant factor for your firm, then you should refer to the discussion about estimating them in the section on Selling, General and Administrative expenses below.

Research and Development Expenses

While there is no necessary relation between Research and Development (R&D) expenses and sales, many firms budget their R&D expenditures in exactly this way. For instance, Gillette has a stated goal of growing R&D expenditures at the same rate as sales, so the ratio of R&D to sales should remain constant for Gillette. Be particularly cognizant of the stage in a firm's life cycle when forecasting this item. Start-up firms will invest a much larger fraction of their sales in R&D with the intent of bringing this percentage down over time. Also, there may be a relation between the firm's R&D spending and the price premium implied in your COGS forecast. A firm whose strategy is to continually develop new products and sell them at a premium will have a higher R&D to sales ratio and a lower COGS to sales ratio than a firm who copies other firms' products and sells them at a discount. For example, a hallmark of IBM is its research and development activity—it has produced the largest number of patents granted per year for any firm in the world for the last 17 year's running. This strategy is reflected in its ratios: IBM's ratio of R&D Expense to sales has been within a tenth of 6 percent every year for the past five years, and its gross margin hangs around 45 percent. In contrast, Dell Computer invests only 1 percent of its revenue in R&D but its gross margin is only 17 percent—clearly a different strategy than at IBM.

You should be aware of opportunistic accounting related to R&D on software. Software development costs can be capitalized as an asset once the product is "technologically feasible"—whatever that means, so these expenditures will not show up in R&D expense immediately. Given the vagueness of this definition, companies have considerable flexibility when choosing whether to allocate software expenditures to R&D, in which case they are expensed immediately, or to software development, in which case they are classified as an asset and then amortized to expense over a number of years.

Selling, General and Administrative Expenses

Selling, General and Administrative (SG&A) expenses have some components that move directly with sales, such as commissions paid to the sales force, and other components that are only weakly related to sales, such as the clerical staff salaries. Over short horizons, many costs in this category are almost completely fixed, like rent on facilities, property taxes, or utility bills for the administrative headquarters. The fixed components will give this ratio economies of scale, so it may decline as a percentage of sales as sales grow. Working against this effect, however, is the fact that many of these expenditures are highly discretionary. For example, when sales are high the firm may invest in management training programs but when sales are low they may cut back on these types of discretionary expenditures. Examine how this ratio has changed in the past in response to changes in the sales growth rate for evidence of economies of scale. In addition, the MD&A discussion might give you some clues about future movements in this ratio. In particular, cost-cutting initiatives are frequently aimed at this line item.

If you believe there are significant economies of scale in SG&A or any other line item, you may want to quantify the effect more precisely. To do this, start by plotting the percentage change in SG&A on the percentage change in

FIGURE 8.5
Economies of Scale
and "Sticky Costs" in
U.S. Economy from
1979–1998 (adapted
from Anderson,
Banker, and Jana-
kiraman (*Journal of
Accounting Research*
2003). Both scales are
in percentage changes.

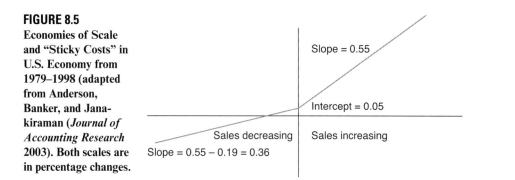

sales each year and then examine the chart for two patterns. Assuming there is a discernable upward pattern, is the slope significantly less than one? If so, then your company is exhibiting economies of scale in SG&A. Next, does it appear that the slope of the line is flatter when the percentage change in sales is negative? If so, then SG&A is exhibiting "sticky" costs. It is often harder to cut costs in bad times than it is to increase costs in good times. Consequently, when sales are declining, economies of scale cause costs to hang around and "sticky" costs hang around even more. Both effects are illustrated in Figure 8.5. The figure shows the result of the following estimation:

$$\% \text{ change in SG\&A} = a + b \times \%\text{change in Sales} + c \times \text{Indicator if Sales}$$
$$\text{declined} \times \%\text{change in Sales} + \text{error}$$

If $b = 1$ then there are no economies of scale and costs increase in direct proportion to sales. More commonly $b < 1$, meaning that the firm enjoys economies of scale. If $c < 0$ then the slope of the line is even lower for sales decreases, capturing the "sticky" cost phenomenon.

We tend to think of economies of scale as a good thing—when sales increase costs do not increase as rapidly. However, when sales decline the sword cuts the other way—costs do not decline as rapidly. And the "sticky cost" phenomenon shown in Figure 8.5 makes matters even worse. As the figure illustrates, a 10 percent reduction in sales is estimated to result in only a 3.6 percent reduction in SG&A. It is this effect that often brings on bankruptcy, as illustrated in the "Tale of Two Movie Theaters" case at the end of the textbook.

Depreciation and Amortization

The ratio of Depreciation and Amortization to Average (Net) Property, Plant and Equipment (PP&E) and Intangibles is forecasted based on the relation between the balance sheet amounts and the income statement amounts. For firms using straight-line depreciation and replacing assets at roughly the same rate as they depreciate them, this ratio is approximately constant and equal to one over *half* the average useful life of the assets. Why half? Because in steady state, the assets are roughly halfway through their useful life, so net PP&E is roughly half gross PP&E. But remember that this rule only applies for stable firms. For a growing firm, the ratio is smaller, because the existing assets are less than half way through their useful life, and hence less than half depreciated. But you should make sure that as the firm's growth rate slows, you trend this forecasting assumption to one over *half* the average useful life of the assets.

Another problem that frequently arises when forecasting Depreciation and Amortization is that the line item is not shown on the income statement and so is coded as zero by the standardized data providers. For example, Intel doesn't list depreciation/amortization expense on their income statement and consequently you get a ratio of 0 percent for this item when loaded into *eVal* (from the Case Data sheet). If you get the actual financial statements you can typically find the depreciation and amortization amounts on the Statement of Cash Flows but this is of only limited value, because you don't know the income statement line item that the company lumped these expenses into. They could be included as part of COGS, as part of SG&A or, most likely, divided between these two line items. If you know which line item contains the depreciation and amortization expense then you can correct the financial statements in *eVal* by moving the balance to the "depreciation and amortization" line item. Otherwise, all you can do is skip this item and pick it up implicitly in your forecasts of COGS and SG&A.

To forecast the Depreciation and Amortization expense ratio, you need to think about the type of assets that the firm must deploy to generate sales and how long these assets are expected to last. The footnote that describes the firm's accounting policies typically gives the useful lives of their major types of assets. If the firm primarily uses just one type of asset, then this disclosure is a great guide for your forecast (e.g., if the asset has a 10-year useful life and is in steady state, then you should forecast 20 percent), but more commonly all you learn is that buildings have a 20–40 year life, equipment has a 5–10 year life, and computers have a 2–4 year life. In addition, the intangible asset goodwill is not amortized at all. Instead it is treated as a permanent asset (like land) and each year the accountants ask if it has been "impaired." The consequence of this accounting treatment is that it is virtually impossible to forecast when the consumption of goodwill will show up as an expense in the financial statements. Practically speaking, all you can do is try and match the forecast impairment of the goodwill to its expected future life.

Interest Expense

The ratio of Interest Expense to Average Debt is the firm's average interest rate on all of its debt. The past rate at which the firm has borrowed is a good indicator of their future borrowing rate, unless you forecast a large change in either the firm's default risk or macro level interest rates. You may also want to read the debt footnote and see what rate the firm has borrowed at most recently. As a reminder, we warned you in Chapter 5 to beware of interest income that is netted against the company's interest expense. This will make the past interest expense look extremely low when computed as a percent of average debt. If this is the case, then you should find the amount of interest income and move it into the nonoperating income line item on the financial statements. Another complication arises if a firm has convertible debt. Convertible debt carries a lower interest rate because of the value of the conversion option. The easiest method of dealing with this problem is to assume that the firm will issue straight debt in future years at the going market rate of interest (see Chapter 12 for more detail on this issue).

Nonoperating Income

Nonoperating Income includes such things as dividends or interest income received on investments, the write-down of assets, and other miscellaneous income. Because this item represents a mix of many things, none of which have obvious drivers, we ask you to forecast it as a percent of sales with the idea that the amounts for these items vary roughly with the firm's size. If the past amounts of nonoperating income are significant then you should go back to the actual financial statements and figure out what is in this item.

If the nonoperating income is interest or dividends from a financial asset you need to think about whether that asset will exist in the future. For example, a firm might have an unusually large cash balance if it has recently raised capital but not yet spent it, and this cash balance will generate some interest income. If you believe that the cash will soon be invested in operating assets, then the interest income will soon disappear. Alternatively, the asset might be an investment in another company that was made for strategic reasons and is not expected to change in the near future. In this case, the dividend income or equity method income is likely to continue into the future, but will bear no relation to the level of company sales. In this case you will want to forecast the nonoperating income as a dollar amount and then express this amount as a fraction of sales. The general point is that income rarely falls from the sky, even nonoperating income; rather, it takes assets to produce it. Make sure that you know where these assets are on the balance sheet—they may be in Cash and Marketable Securities, they may be in Investments or they may be lumped in with something else—and keep track of the relation between the balance of these assets and your forecast of nonoperating income.

Other items that frequently show up as part of nonoperating income are asset write-downs, impairment charges, and restructuring charges (note that expenses are entered as negative numbers in *eVal*). While all of these charges sound like one-time events, it is actually quite common for companies to record expenses like these year after year. If you see a string of impairment and restructuring expenses in a firm's past financial statements, then it is very likely that they will continue in the future. In effect, the company is moving normal operating charges into this line item, hoping you will ignore them. If this is the case, then your forecasts should treat them as recurring expenses. In addition, if you anticipate a significant asset write-down in the future, possibly because you believe the company's accounting is currently too aggressive, then you should work out more precisely how the write-down will affect this ratio.

Effective Tax Rate

A firm's Effective Tax Rate is the ratio of the tax expense to earnings before income taxes (EBT). As a ballpark figure, the statutory federal tax rate for most firms in the United States is 35 percent. (The lowest corporate tax rate among the G7 nations is in Canada at 15 percent.) To this, you add a few percentage points for state and local taxes and possibly deduct a few percentage points for the tax advantages that come from having foreign operations, if your company should be so lucky. The firm's tax footnote contains a great table that explains why the effective tax rate differs from the statutory rate. In accounting language, the items appearing in this table are called "permanent differences" to distinguish them from the "timing differences" that create deferred taxes, as discussed later. You should look through this table with an eye for things that might change in the future. For example, if a company is planning to move its operations from California, with a flat corporate tax rate of 8.84 percent, to Wyoming, with no state corporate income tax, it will save 8.84 percent on its effective tax rate (but it will give up the ocean view).

If the firm is losing money (pre-tax), then its current effective tax rate may be a very poor indicator of its future tax rate. Suppose, for example, that you are examining a young company that has yet to show a profit. The company's losses create net operating loss carryforwards that can be used to reduce taxes in the future if and when it becomes profitable, but can only be booked as assets in the year of the loss under strict conditions. So our young company will probably have an effective tax rate close to zero. But if you forecast that the company will become profitable, then you need to trend the effective tax rate toward the statutory tax rate. We hate to send you there, but the only place you can learn about all this stuff is in the tax footnote. Grab your flashlight and carry a stick.

Minority Interest

Minority Interest, also called Non-Controlling Interest, represents the claim on the income of the consolidated firm of minority shareholders in subsidiaries. For most firms this is zero because they own 100 percent of their subsidiaries, so there are no minority shareholders to make a claim, and you can skip to the next item. However, ignoring this line item for firms that actually have a minority interest can lead to big mistakes, so we include a line for it on *eVal*'s Forecasting Assumptions sheet. For an example, load Verizon into *eVal* from the Case Data sheet and note that minority interest is almost 49 percent of after-tax income. Verizon owns 55 percent of Verizon Wireless, while Vodafone owns the other 45 percent minority portion of the joint venture. Consequently, the consolidated Verizon after-tax income includes 100 percent of Verizon Wireless, but because they don't actually own all of Verizon Wireless, they need to show the minority interest expense. We ask you to forecast the minority interest amount as a percent of after-tax income. But since the size of the minority interest claim varies with the subsidiaries income and not the parent company's income, there is no necessary reason that this line item will remain constant. It is generally very difficult to get much information about the subsidiaries income, however, so this scaling variable is the best we can do. If the subsidiary's income moves roughly with the parent's income, then this percentage will be fairly constant.

Other Income

Other Income is a bit of a catchall line item. This item differs from nonoperating income because it is after tax. You might find the after-tax effects of investment gains/losses or equity method investments here. If this item is nonzero then you really need to read the actual financial statements to figure out what the company or standardized data providers have put here and whether you believe it will continue in the future. As with nonoperating income, we ask you to forecast this as a percent of sales simply to capture the idea that these items tend to increase with the size of the firm, not because sales is really the driver of these costs. This line item is also a good place to tuck any major adjustments that you might make to the financial statements. For instance, if you want to forecast a large write-off, possibly because you think the company's accounting practices are aggressive, then you can enter the after-tax effect on this line item and keep it nicely separated from the rest of your forecasts.

Preferred Dividends

The ratio of Preferred Dividends to Average Preferred Stock is quite similar to the ratio of Interest Expense to Debt discussed earlier. This ratio gives the preferred dividend payout percentage, which can usually be found in the financial statement footnotes, or can be inferred from the statement of shareholders' equity. For some firms you may notice that their balance sheet shows preferred stock outstanding yet shows 0 percent for this ratio in the past data. This occurs because some standardized data providers do not give the preferred stock dividend in their database, so our default entry is zero. If you see a historical balance of preferred stock, then you should get the firm's complete financial statements to look up the historical dividend percentage and input the preferred dividends manually on the Financial Statements sheet in *eVal*. Note that the dividend on preferred stock is distinct from the dividend on common stock, which we will discuss shortly.

Some Final Thoughts about Forecasting the Income Statement

The results of your income statement assumptions are forecasts of the firm's entire sequence of future income statements. For each line item, you should think once again about the transition from the firm's most recent historical performance to its performance in the next few years, and then its transition to your terminal year forecasts. As a rough guide, you might think of the near-term performance as being driven by firm-specific activities, such as a rapid expansion plan or a cost-cutting initiative, while the long-term performance as being driven by industrywide and economywide forces, such as the GDP growth rate. Do your forecasts paint a reasonable picture of how the firm might evolve? You will undoubtedly feel more confident about your near-term forecasts than your long-term forecasts; this is simply the reality of forecasting in an uncertain world.

You aren't completely done with your income statement assumptions. These assumptions combine with your balance sheet assumptions to generate implied financial ratios and cash flow forecasts, and these forecasts might be implausible. If this is the case, as it often is after just the first pass, then you need to revisit your income statement assumptions once again.

Expense Forecasts for Kohl's

As an example, we will develop a set of expense forecasts for Kohl's. In framing these forecasts, you may want to refer back to the ratio analysis of Kohl's in Chapter 5.

As noted in Chapter 5, Kohl's has shown a steady improvement in its gross margin over the past few years. They attribute the most recent margin improvement to a shift in sales mix to more private labels and exclusive brands that command higher margins. While Kohl's expects this trend to continue, we note that they are probably getting to the top of their potential margin given that Nordstrom has a gross margin of 41.8 percent, and is clearly higher on the fashion food chain than Kohl's. In the MD&A, Kohl's management forecasts that the gross margin will improve 20 to 30 basis points, so we forecast that the COGS/Sales ratio will drop from 62.2 percent in fiscal 2009 to 62 percent in fiscal 2010 and then remain constant thereafter. Margins significantly higher than this would surely invite entry and imitation from competitors.

In contrast to the steadily improving gross margin's, Kohl's SG&A/Sales ratio has gotten worse each year. This, combined with generally increasing sales, shows that Kohl's has not been enjoying any economies of scale in SG&A. In fact, the past data exhibit dis-economies to scale! Further, as we noted in Chapter 5, the most recent increase in SG&A/Sales was attributed to increased compensation expense. It is unlikely that this was a one-time event, so we forecast that Kohl's will maintain their SG&A/Sales ratio at the 2009 rate of 24.4 percent. It would be nice to forecast some improvement in this item, but Kohl's is coming out of a recessionary period where it is likely that any costs that could be cut already have been cut. In the 2009 MD&A, Kohl's says that they expect SG&A to increase 4–5 percent and Sales to increase 4–6 percent. Together this might suggest a slight improvement in the SG&A/Sales

ratio. But given the complete lack of economies of scale in the past data, we aren't buying it; we forecast 24.4 percent to the terminal period.

Kohl's ratio of Depreciation and Amortization to the average balance of *net* PP&E and Intangibles is 8.2 percent in the most recent year and has fluctuated between 7.3 percent and 8.2 percent over the past five years. Although Kohl's has added significantly to assets in the past few years, it expects to slow its growth considerably in the future. As they mature, the accumulated depreciation should approach the 50 percent level of a stable company (i.e., the assets are, on average, half way through their useful lives). From the financial statement footnotes we learn that the ratio of depreciation and amortization expense to average *gross* PP&E is about .06, implying that the assets have on average about a 17-year useful life. Given that the bulk of the PP&E is buildings, which have a relatively long life, this seems like a reasonable estimate. When Kohl's is in steady state and its asset mix is approximately halfway through its useful life at all times, the ratio of Depreciation and Amortization to *net* PP&E will be one over half of the useful life, or approximately 12 percent. We forecast that this ratio will increase smoothly from its current level of 8.2 percent to a terminal value of 12 percent. Note that you can enter this quickly by putting 12 percent in the terminal column and letting *eVal* do the smoothing in between.

Kohl's most recent Interest Expense as a percentage of the average Debt balance is 6.5 percent and has fluctuated in the narrow range of 6.3 percent and 6.8 percent in the past few years. Their debt footnote shows that almost all their borrowing is plain vanilla senior debt with no call provisions or convertibility provisions that might complicate the picture, and with a weighted average interest rate of 6.55 percent. Kohl's stated in their MD&A that they can fund their planned store growth with existing cash flows, and therefore have no intentions of borrowing more in the immediate future. Consequently, it seems very likely that their effective interest rate will remain right around 6.5 percent.

The $10 million of nonoperating income for Kohl's in fiscal 2009 is due to interest income on their cash and cash-equivalents, and on their long-term investment in auction-rate securities (backed by your student loans!). Although *eVal* shows this amount as a percent of sales on the forecasting assumptions sheet, sales are clearly not the driving force behind interest revenue. We forecast that this amount will go to zero and remain there in the future. It has never been more that .2 percent of sales, and as Kohl's settles into a mature slow-growth phase they can manage their cash balance to a lower level with the result that interest revenue will disappear. As discussed later, the auction-rate securities became illiquid in the aftermath of the financial crisis, but the interest continues to be paid by the United States government. Kohl's intention is to slowly liquidate these securities or hold them to maturity when they can be redeemed at par.

Finally, Kohl's effective tax rate is 37.6 percent and has never deviated from this amount by more the a few tenths of a percent. From a tax perspective,

Kohl's is a simple business. They have no foreign operations, their mix of stores across different states (and state tax rates) isn't changing much in the future, and they don't make the kind of investments that generate large investment tax credits (like R&D). Consequently, we see no reason why this rate should change in the future. The tax footnote reveals details of an ongoing game between Kohl's and the taxing authority. Every year they are audited and every year some adjustment is made. This is common for any large corporation. But, at the end of the day, any adjustment that might be required is insignificant to Kohl's effective tax rate.

8.4 BALANCE SHEET FORECASTS

The next set of assumptions construct the balance sheet forecasts. They are organized into assumptions about the net operating assets, consisting of working capital, other operating assets and other operating liabilities; and assumptions about financial obligations. The net operating assets are forecasted as a percent of sales (or as a percent of COGS) because these assets generate the sales. In contrast, the financial obligations are forecasted as a percent of total assets. As a guide to the balance sheet assumptions, Figure 8.6 shows the forecasting assumptions sheet in *eVal*.

FIGURE 8.6 **Balance Sheet Assumptions for Kohl's**

Balance Sheet Assumptions					
Working Capital Assumptions					
Ending Operating Cash/Sales	4.0%	4.1%	13.2%	13.2%	13.2%
Ending Receivables/Sales	0.0%	0.0%	0.0%	0.0%	0.0%
Ending Inventories/COGS	27.3%	27.1%	27.4%	27.4%	27.4%
Ending Other Current Assets/Sales	1.2%	1.4%	1.7%	1.7%	1.7%
Ending Accounts Payable/COGS	8.0%	8.5%	11.1%	11.1%	11.1%
Ending Taxes Payable/Sales	0.8%	0.6%	1.1%	1.1%	1.1%
Ending Other Current Liabs/Sales	4.8%	5.0%	5.8%	5.8%	5.8%
Other Operating Asset Assumptions					
Ending Net PP&E/Sales	39.5%	42.6%	40.9%	40.9%	40.9%
Ending Investments/Sales	0.0%	2.0%	1.9%	1.9%	1.9%
Ending Intangibles/Sales	1.3%	1.3%	1.2%	1.2%	1.2%
Ending Other Assets/Sales	0.6%	0.7%	0.8%	0.8%	0.8%
Other Operating Liability Assumptions					
Other Liabilities/Sales	2.3%	2.5%	2.8%	2.8%	2.8%
Deferred Taxes/Sales	1.6%	2.0%	2.2%	2.2%	2.2%
Financing Assumptions					
Current Debt/Total Assets	0.1%	0.1%	0.1%	0.1%	0.1%
Long-Term Debt/Total Assets	19.4%	18.1%	15.6%	15.6%	15.6%
Minority Interest/Total Assets	0.0%	0.0%	0.0%	0.0%	0.0%
Preferred Stock/Total Assets	0.0%	0.0%	0.0%	0.0%	0.0%
Dividend Payout Ratio	0.0%	0.0%	0.0%	0.0%	0.0%

8.5   WORKING CAPTIAL ASSUMPTIONS

Working capital requirements are driven largely by the operating cycle of the firm. Consequently, all the forecast assumptions in this section are linked to either sales or COGS. A firm's past working capital requirements, and your forecasts of its future requirements, are a statement about the firm's operating efficiency. An improvement in operating efficiency means the firm can generate the same level of sales with fewer net assets tied up in working capital.

Operating Cash

Every firm requires some amount of operating cash. A typical amount might be 3 percent of Sales, but firms vary widely in their holdings of cash and cash equivalents. If your firm has traditionally held a large amount of cash relative to their peers, then they probably don't need all this cash for daily operations; rather, part of the balance is really an investment in financial assets. As we discussed in Chapter 5, if the past operating cash balance appears larger than you think necessary for operations, you need to get the actual financial statements and make an estimate as to how much of the line item is really operating cash and how much is an investment in financial assets. Once you have an estimate of the amount of true operating cash and the amount of financial assets, you have a few choices about how to proceed. Assuming you think the firm is going to hang onto the financial assets, you can continue to forecast a high ratio of operating cash to sales and then include the interest income from the financial assets in nonoperating income. Alternatively, you can reclassify the financial assets into the 'Investments' line item and forecast its balance separately. (Recall that, despite the title, *eVal* classifies nonoperating income as operating and not financing.)

A bolder alternative for dealing with excess cash is to effect a pro forma liquidation of it in the first forecast period. For example, assume that a firm has been recently running its cash balance at 10 percent of sales, but only reasonably requires cash equal to 3 percent of sales in order to run its operations smoothly. Within *eVal* you can simply choose to set the operating cash/sales assumption to 3 percent for all future years. Because equity is the plug on the balance sheet, this will effectively force a large cash distribution to equity holders in the first year of the forecast period, either in the form of a stock repurchase or a cash dividend (the latter requiring you to also change the dividend payout assumption). On the surface this might seem absurd since it is probably unlikely that the firm will distribute the cash next period. But, from a valuation perspective, so long as the firm is generating a competitive return on its excess cash balance, the present value of a future stream of interest income should be equivalent to the liquidation value of the cash, and so either approach should yield a similar valuation. From a pedagogical perspective, liquidating the excess cash immediately has the advantage of getting it out of the picture so that we can focus on forecasting the operating variables.

For this reason, the liquidation alternative is a common choice in a traditional discounted cash flow valuation. We nevertheless caution that if the firm is not expected to generate a competitive return on its cash balance, or if it is instead expected to waste the cash buying other assets that yield a poor return (corporate jet anyone?), then the liquidation alternative will overvalue the excess cash balance.

Receivables

The ratio of Receivables to Sales depends directly on the company's credit policy and its customers' ability to pay. A ratio of 0.25, for instance, means the average receivable was outstanding for one quarter of a year, or about 90 days. This is approximate because sales and collections fluctuate through the year, but you get the idea. Insofar as receivable credit is effectively granting the customer an interest-free loan, this is an important strategic decision the firm makes, and one you should think carefully about when forecasting. If the firm's past values of this ratio are constant then this reflects a consistent collections policy that is unlikely to change in the near future. However, if the ratio is changing significantly or differs drastically from competitors' ratios, then you will need to investigate further. Ask yourself, "What is the firm's relative bargaining power with its customers?" A small firm that supplies a large firm might see a favorable Receivables to Sales ratio disappear quickly when economic times get tight.

A good example of this phenomenon is the "Can Salton Swing?" case at the end of the chapter. Salton used to be the sole maker of the famous George Foreman Grill ("it's a lean, mean grillin' machine!"). They sold the bulk of their grills to a few large retail chains, like Kmart and Walmart, who are not generally known for the generous terms they provide their suppliers. Indeed, as the George Foreman Grill became a small appliance hit between 1998 and 2001, Salton saw the average time it took to collect its receivables go from 41 days to 73 days and its inventory holding period go from 113 days to 143 days as these big customers slowly put on the squeeze.

Inventories

The ratio of Inventories to COGS is very similar to the Receivables ratio, except that both the numerator and the denominator are computed using historical costs rather than selling prices. The other principle difference is that the company can acquire inventories without selling them, which would increase the numerator without the commensurate increase in the denominator. For that reason an increasing Inventory to COGS ratio is traditionally considered to be a warning sign that the company is having trouble selling its goods. Of course, the common retort is that they are stocking up for a new product release that will send sales skyrocketing. When forecasting this ratio think about why it might differ from its historical past. Do you anticipate the company implementing a just-in-time inventory handling system and thus lowering the required amount of inventory? Alternatively, do you anticipate that the firm's customers or suppliers have so much bargaining power that they will force the firm to hold the inventory for increasingly long periods? Was there some unusual event in the most recent fiscal year that caused the ratio to differ significantly from its normal level?

As discussed in Chapter 4, a firm attempting to manipulate its income upward may delay the recognition of expenses by failing to write off obsolete inventory. Effectively they hold this expense in inventory for too long, with the result that the inventory turnover ratio falls. Later, when they write the inventory off, the ratio instantly improves. If you see evidence of this behavior in the inventory turnover ratio, you might want to investigate the firm's inventory accounting a bit further.

Other Current Assets

Other Current Assets include tax refunds, prepaid expenses, and other miscellaneous items. We ask you to forecast this item as a percent of sales because it tends to increase with the size of the firm, so this ratio should be fairly stable. However, if this is a large amount you really need to look at the published financial statements and see what is included in this line item and decide if it does indeed move with sales.

Accounts Payable

The ratio of Accounts Payable to COGS is the mirror image of the Receivables ratio for the firm's suppliers (with respect to their accounts with the company). It reveals how quickly the firm is paying for the inventory it purchased and sold. Since this is an interest-free loan to the firm, the higher this ratio, the more free credit the company is receiving. You may forecast that the ratio will increase if you believe that the firm has sufficient power over its suppliers that it can delay paying its bills. When times get tight in the automotive industry, for example, the Big 3 automakers don't renegotiate the contract terms with their suppliers—they simply delay paying their suppliers for long periods.

Taxes Payable and Other Current Liabilities

Taxes Payable frequently shows up as a current liability simply because the firm owes taxes as of the end of the fiscal quarter but they don't have to pay them until a later date. Other Current Liabilities includes dividends declared but not yet paid, customer deposits, unearned revenue and other miscellaneous liabilities that will be paid within a year. We ask you to forecast these items as a percent of sales because they tend to increase with the size of the firm, so this ratio should be fairly stable. But, as with Other Current Assets, if the amounts in these categories are significant, you should read the financial statements to see precisely what they are and decide if you think the past ratios are good predictors of the future.

8.6 OTHER OPERATING ASSETS AND LIABILITIES

The key issue for this set of assumptions is determining the size of the firm's future investment in long-lived assets necessary to produce the forecasted sales. Consequently, these items are forecasted as a percent of sales. Your forecasts of these ratios are a statement about the firm's expected production technology. If the firm outsources much of its production, its investment in assets will be significantly smaller than the investment that is necessary for a more vertically integrated operation. Of course, since outsourcing captures a smaller portion of the value chain, the firm should earn correspondingly smaller margins.

PP&E

To forecast the ratio of PP&E to Sales you should consider the firm's existing capacity relative to your forecast of sales growth. Firms tend to add capacity in large lumps, so as you analyze the firm's past ratio of PP&E to Sales, be aware of whether the past ratio amounts were generated by assets operating at full or partial capacity. A good source of information for forecasting this item is the discussion of liquidity and capital resources in the MD&A; in fact, firms often give estimates of future capital expenditures here. And capital-intensive industries, such as steel or automaking or airlines, often give capacity utilization statistics included in their Selected Data Schedule (Item 6 on the 10-K). Finally, you can get industry-level statistics on growth rates in investments in different classes of assets from the Bureau of Economic Analysis Fixed Asset tables.

It is common for PP&E to rise rapidly during a company's early years and then remain relatively constant thereafter. But note that this pattern does not imply that the *ratio of PP&E to Sales* will rise and then flatten out. If the company's sales are also rising rapidly in the early years, this ratio could remain constant throughout the growth and maturity phases of a firm's life cycle. What you really need to think about is whether there are significant economies to scale that the firm will enjoy as it grows. As California Pizza Kitchen expands across the country its investment in PP&E will necessarily grow at the same rate as sales because there are very few scale economies in a restaurant chain (i.e., having a restaurant in Nebraska has little effect on the investment required to open a restaurant in Oregon). Alternatively, after Iridium put the necessary satellites in place for its global phone system, sales grew significantly without significant additional investment in PP&E.

Suppose you are lucky enough to have the firm tell you their planned future capital expenditures (and you believe them). Given the beginning balance of PP&E, your forecasted amount of depreciation, and the company's estimate of its capital expenditures, the ending PP&E amount is determined (equivalently, your forecast of ending PP&E determines capital expenditures). The easiest way to get this information into *eVal* is to play around with your PP&E/Sales forecast until the capital expenditures line on the Cash Flow Analysis sheet corresponds with the company's estimate.

Investments

Investments are primarily made up of equity holdings by the firm in other companies. If this amount is significant for your company, then read the financial statements and figure out exactly what this investment represents. We forecast this item as a percent of sales but there may be no structural reason for the size of the investment to be related to sales. Consider two examples. About 10 percent of Coca-Cola's total assets are investments in other companies, primarily bottlers of Coke. We would expect that the scale of the bottling companies would rise and fall with sales of Coke, so forecasting as a percent of consolidated sales is probably a good idea. In contrast, Apple Computer holds over $25 billion in long-term marketable securities at the end of fiscal 2010, which is about a third of their total assets. The footnotes reveal that these investments are roughly half in government securities and half in corporate securities, with a combined average interest rate of 3.44 percent. These investments do not play a role in supporting Apple's sales and so their ratio to sales could vary substantially over time.

Intangibles

Intangibles are all those assets that can't be physically touched. To be recognized in the accounting system, the intangible must usually have been acquired in an arm's length transaction by the firm. So *purchased* patents, copyrights, licenses, and trademarks would be included, but *internally developed* versions of the same things are not. What you really need to forecast is *purchased* intangibles but, unfortunately, companies that purchase lots of intangible assets generally develop lots of them internally as well. To make matters worse, the biggest purchased intangible is "goodwill," defined to be the excess of the purchase price in a corporate acquisition over the fair market value of the identifiable assets (tangible and intangible) received. Because it is only created by an acquisition, goodwill tends to arrive in large and unpredictable lumps. Goodwill, plus the rather arbitrary distinction between purchased and internally developed intangible assets, makes forecasting intangibles very difficult. As with investments, there is no particular reason why this item should remain a constant percent of sales; we use this ratio only because larger firms tend to have more intangibles than smaller firms.

Intangible assets without specific lives, like goodwill, are not amortized. Rather, the firm performs periodic impairment tests to see if the fair value is less than the book value. How the firm decides when an intangible has become impaired is rather arbitrary. Basically, if the future cash flows related to the intangible look bleak, then an expense is recorded to write the asset down. These large expenses often get recorded only after everyone knows something bad has happened. For example, Quaker Oats bought Snapple at the end of 1994 for approximately $1.7 billion, and Snapple was on the Quaker Oats books for $1.7 billion at the end of 1996. Although management repeatedly mentioned the poor performance of the Snapple brand in the 1996 10-K filing, they concluded that they did not believe a write-down was necessary at that time. The loss was not recognized until 1997 when they sold the Snapple brand for a mere $300 million.

Other Assets and Other Liabilities

Other Assets includes many items; some examples are long-term receivables, preopening expenses for retail stores and pension assets. Other Liabilities include pension liabilities and other miscellaneous noncurrent liabilities. See the financial statement footnotes for specifics if your firm has a significant amount for these items.

Deferred Taxes

To forecast deferred taxes you need to think about the firm's tax timing differences. You may have noticed that when we forecasted the firm's effective tax rate, we considered permanent differences that caused the rate to differ from the federal statutory rate of 35 percent, but did not take into consideration the timing of the tax payments. Timing differences arise because the taxing authority's rules for when a deduction can be taken differ from the financial accounting rules for when an expense is recognized. For example, a firm might have accelerated tax deductions because of an investment in a certain type of asset. In this case, not only does the firm get to deduct the cost of the investment, but they also get to deduct most of it in the first few years of the asset's useful life. Accountants capture the net effect of these timing differences in the balance of deferred taxes, so named because accelerated deductions today mean higher taxes tomorrow when the deductions run out. The firm's specific deferred tax items are described in the footnotes to the financial statements. A common source for deferred tax liabilities is the timing difference between depreciation on PP&E and the tax deductions for these investments. Early in the life of an asset this will result in deferred tax liabilities (representing the future increase in tax payments when the accelerated tax deductions for the PP&E are exhausted); later this effect will reverse and the liability will shrink back to zero. But as long as the firm is replacing its assets, this liability will remain. If the firm maintains its assets at a fixed level then the deferred taxes will remain a constant percentage of total assets; the ratio will increase slightly if the asset base is growing. But if you forecast that the firm will shrink its asset base, this ratio will fall dramatically. This is because, without new acquisitions of assets, new tax deductions are not generated, causing tax payments to increase and the liability to fall.

Some Final Thoughts about Forecasting the Net Operating Assets

The key statistic coming out of the working capital, other asset and other liability assumptions is the Net Operating Asset Turnover ratio (defined as Sales over Net Operating Assets), which is given on the Ratio Analysis sheet in *eVal*. This statistic summarizes your forecasts of the net operating assets that a firm will need to put in place in order to create the sales that you forecasted. Because a firm's asset turnover is largely determined by its production technology, this ratio does not usually change radically over short periods. Therefore, if your forecasts show this ratio changing dramatically, go back and make sure that you have good reasons for the specific forecasts you have made.

Forecasting Net Operating Assets for Kohl's

Recall from Chapter 5 that Kohl's delivered a lower RNOA than Nordstrom and Ross Stores largely because of their slower net operating asset turnover. The question in this chapter is whether we expect Kohl's to close the gap with the other two companies. We begin with line-by-line forecasts for Kohl's operating assets and then consider what this implies for their future net operating asset turnover ratio.

Kohl's investments in new stores have been slowing in recent years, and Kohl's has been hoarding the resulting free cash flow. The cash balance grew from a constant 4 percent of sales in 2005–2008 to 13.2 percent of sales at the end of fiscal 2009. They certainly don't need this much cash to operate the business, so we bring the level back to 4 percent in our forecasts. This is also consistent with the levels at Nordstrom and Ross Stores prior to the recession. In addition, we have a management forecast of next year's cash from operations that we can use later to validate our cash balance forecast.

Kohl's biggest working capital account is inventory. Kohl's talks extensively about its inventory management policy in the 2009 10-K. Management believes that their new distribution centers, plus some diligent work on their own part, will help improve their inventory management. Working against this optimism is the observation from Chapter 5 that their days inventory have increased from 89 days to about 100 days in the past few years. The net result is that we do not forecast any drastic change in this ratio going forward. Assuming that 2009 was anomalous because of the drastic decline in store sales, we forecast the ending inventory/COGS ratio to equal 26.6 percent, the average of 2005–2008 levels. This implies a 97-day inventory holding period.

The second biggest working capital item is accounts payable. The ratio of accounts payable to COGS has increased significantly in 2009 to 11.1 percent. The probable cause is that Kohl's could successfully squeeze their suppliers during economic hard times by extending the time they took to pay. We forecast that this trend will continue. Both Ross Stores and Nordstrom have averaged about 12 percent in the past, so we forecast 12 percent for Kohl's going forward.

The next biggest working capital item is "Other Current Liabilities," which are mostly gift cards that Kohl's has sold but have not yet been redeemed. This liability should have a constant relation with sales, and it has been relatively stable in the past, so we see no reason to change it going forward. Similarly, we leave the remaining working capital accounts at the same level as 2009.

The biggest asset for Kohl's is Property, Plant and Equipment (PP&E). As you may recall from Chapter 5, this was the asset that caused Kohl's to report a net operating asset turnover ratio that was significantly lower than Nordstrom and Ross Stores. If we thought that Kohl's stores was still maturing, then we might be able to forecast an improvement in this ratio. Unfortunately, it doesn't take long for a retail establishment to hit steady state. Further, a large part of the recent increase in PP&E was due to new distribution centers. While these are necessary investments, and will hopefully improve the inventory turnover ratio in the future, they do not generate sales. As a consequence, we do not foresee any significant improvement in the PP&E/Sales ratio going forward. We have one juicy detail that we can use to make a very accurate PP&E/Sales forecast: Kohl's discloses in the MD&A that they expect capital expenditures to total about $900 million in 2010. This, combined with our earlier forecast of $627.431 million depreciation and a beginning balance of $7,018 million, we can solve for an ending balance of PP&E of $7,290.569 million. Dividing this ending balance by the forecast of $18,054.087 million for sales gives a ratio of 40.4 percent, which is very close to the 40.9 percent ratio from the previous year.[1]

At this point we also get a nice reality check on our forecasts. Kohl's discloses that they expect that cash from operations less capital expenditures will total approximately $900 million in 2010, so cash from operations should be about $1,800 million. If we toggle to the cash flow analysis sheet in *eVal*, we see that our forecasts imply cash from operations of just over $1,850 million. This means our working capital forecasts, including our ending cash balance forecast, look reasonable.

The remaining operating assets and liabilities are not particularly consequential. Kohl's 10-K shows that the investments line item is composed of auction rate securities, and their discussion of this item reveals that they intend to slowly liquidate these investments as the market becomes more liquid or as they mature. We therefore forecast that the balance of Investments/Sales will decrease to zero over 10 years. The 10-K also shows that the intangibles line item is composed of favorable lease rights. These arrived on the balance sheet as Kohl's bought out the lease rights on other stores that they later remodelled and opened under their own name. Because the major growth phase of Kohl's appears to be over, we do not expect any new investments in these assets. Consequently, we also reduce this line item to zero over 10 years. We leave the remaining operating assets and liabilities at the same ratio to sales as in 2009.

The net results of the operating asset forecasts is a net operating asset turnover ratio of approximately two in the next year and very small improvements thereafter. This is an improvement over 2009 but is still not as good as the ratio at Nordstrom or Ross Stores.

---

[1] Excel geeks can find this quickly by using Goal Seek to make the Capital Expenditures cell on the cash flows sheet equal $900,000 thousand by changing the Ending PP&E/Sales cell on the Forecasting Assumptions sheet.

8.7   FINANCING ASSUMPTIONS

The main consideration for this set of assumptions is the firm's long-term capital structure. What mix of debt and equity will the firm employ to support the level of net operating assets that you have forecasted? The optimal capital structure for a firm takes into account the risk that debt financing brings with it, as well its tax advantages. Volumes have been written in corporate finance textbooks about optimal capital structure. When forecasting this item you should examine the firm's capital structure in the recent past, and the capital structure of other firms in the same industry. In the liquidity section of the MD&A, firms will sometimes discuss their target capital structure; if so, you should consider this in your forecasts. Each of the items in this section is forecasted as a percent of total assets.

Current Debt and Long-Term Debt

Current debt is short-term borrowing plus the current portion of long-term debt that is due within a year. Long-term debt, combined with the current debt above, is the firm's total debt financing. These liabilities, unlike the other noncurrent liabilities above, are represented by contractual interest-bearing claims to debt capital providers. As such, they are financing liabilities rather than operating liabilities. Details of a firm's debt contracts are given in the footnotes to the financial statements. Particularly noteworthy are the discussion of short-term borrowing, the allocation of total debt to current and noncurrent portions, and the schedule of future maturities of existing debt.

Minority Interest

Minority interest, also called non-controlling interest, represents the claim of shareholders in the firm's partially owned subsidiaries. There is no immediate reason why this amount should remain a constant percentage of Total Assets other than larger firms tend to have larger minority interests, if they have them at all. You could make a more informed estimate of this amount if you knew that the firm intended to acquire a less-than-100 percent interest in another company, or if you knew the firm would not be making any more acquisitions of less than 100 percent, so that this amount might decline as a fraction of total assets. But, in all honestly, it is hard enough to forecast a firm's future acquisition activity without having to also estimate the percentage of ownership they will acquire when they acquire less than 100 percent.

Preferred Stock

Preferred stock is more like long-term debt than equity when it comes to forecasting the value of the firm's common equity. Details of the preferred stock holdings can be found in the financial statement footnotes. You may want to forecast that this item remains a constant dollar value, rather than a constant percentage of total assets, unless the firm specifically says that it intends to continue issuing preferred stock.

Some Final Thoughts on Forecasting the Financing Ratios

The end result of this set of forecasts will be a leverage ratio, defined either as total capital to equity or debt to equity. Like the net operating asset turnover ratio, these ratios tend to be very stable for a firm over time, probably because the optimal capital structure of a firm is driven by fairly stable economic factors. Do not fall into the trap of believing (and forecasting) that a firm will increase its return on equity simply by borrowing to increase its leverage. Remember that more debt begets more interest expense; increasing leverage only increases ROE if the return the firm earns on the new capital exceeds the after-tax cost of debt. Note that the Forecasting Assumptions sheet in *eVal* automatically takes this into account—you forecast the interest rate in the income statement assumptions and this amount is applied to the forecasted debt balance.

You have now constructed the forecasted balance sheets for your company. The turnover ratio assumptions determine the net operating assets and the financing assumptions determine the financial obligations. The common equity is therefore determined: common equity = net operating assets − financial obligations.

Dividend Payout Ratio

The dividend payout ratio shown historically is the percent of net income that is paid out as cash dividends. But note that your preceding forecasts completely determine future net income and future total common equity. Hence, your forecasting assumptions already imply the net amount of flows to or from common equity holders. The dividend payout ratio assumption determines what retained earnings will be, but with a compensating adjustment to paid in capital that sets common equity to the level implied by your previous forecasting assumptions. That is, since the future equity balances are already determined, this assumption can only change the composition of the equity. Nonetheless, it is a useful item to forecast, because later, when performing a cash flow analysis, you will be asked to think about the reasonableness of the firm's implied stock issuance activity, and the more that a firm pays out in dividends, the more it needs to issue in new equity to finance future growth.

Forecasting Kohl's Financial Obligations

As noted in Chapter 5, Kohl's currently has a relatively low debt to equity ratio, less than 0.3. Our comparison firms do not help much with this statistic: Ross Stores has a debt/equity ratio of less than 0.2 while Nordstrom has a ratio of 1.67 (recall that it was this leverage that helped Nordstrom deliver an ROE of over 30 percent). Kohl's management might be tempted to raise their ROE by increasing their leverage, given that they have a positive spread between RNOA and the net borrowing cost. But a significant increase in leverage would likely cause their future borrowing rate to increase as well. There is no discussion in Kohl's MD&A about changes in leverage, and it has been relatively constant for the past few years. In fact, they disclose that they have no plans for additional borrowing in 2010, and plan to pay off $400 million in debt using cash from operations in 2011. For this reason, we have little choice but to make our forecasts so that there is no change in the dollar amount of total debt in 2010 and it drops by $400 million in 2011. For convenience, we zero out the current portion of debt and run our forecasts through the long-term portion. This results in ratios of 17.3 percent and 13.3 percent in 2010 and 2011, respectively. Beyond this point, we believe that as Kohl's reaches a mature stage of slow growth, it will slowly raise its leverage ratio to enjoy some benefits of financial leverage. We increase the ratio of debt to total assets to 30 percent over 10 years, a level that approaches Nordstrom's current leverage ratio.

8.8   PRO FORMA ANALYSIS OF FORECASTS

Wait! You aren't done yet! Once you get to the bottom of *eVal*'s Forecasting Assumptions sheet you have completed your *first pass* at forecasting a complete set of financial statements. However, you now need to do some ratio and cash flow analysis on these future financial statements to see how reasonable they really are. Go back to the Ratio Analysis and Cash Flow Analysis sheets in *eVal* and look at what your forecasts imply for the future ratios and cash flows? Is this what you meant to forecast? Are the implied ROEs and margins consistent with industry norms? If the turnover or leverage ratios are changing significantly, make sure that this is what you really mean, because typically these ratios are relatively stable over time.

Pro Forma Analysis of Kohl's Forecasts

If you have been busy inputting the Kohl's forecasts that we have made in the previous sections then you can now examine the implications of those forecasts by returning to the Ratio Analysis and Cash Flow Analysis sheets. From the Cash Flow Analysis sheet we already noted that our forecasted cash from operations is approximately equal to the amount given by Kohl's in their MD&A discussion. Beyond that, the big thing that jumps out from the Cash Flow Analysis sheet is the $2,500 million stock repurchase that our forecasts imply. Basically, the forecasts imply more than $900 million in excess cash flow after the capital expenditures. In addition, we forecast an approximately $1,600 million reduction in the cash balance. Is this reasonable? It might seem excessive, but we note from the 10-K that Kohl's board of directors authorized a $2,500 million stock repurchase plan in 2008, of which only $261 million has been used. If the board believes the stock is undervalued, they might well undertake a large stock repurchase. Another way to get to the same point would be if Kohl's initiates a regular cash dividend. If you still feel this implied cash distribution to the equity holders is unreasonable then you might want to adjust the forecasts. The next most reasonable alternative would be to forecast an early retirement of long-term debt, which Kohl's also discusses as a possible use of excess cash.

From the Ratio Analysis sheet, the summary measure of note is the slow but steady increase in the forecasted return on equity from 13.6 percent to 18.7 percent over ten years. Given that the current values of Ross Stores and Nordstrom (41 percent and 32 percent, respectively), this increase does not seem unreasonable. Further, the advanced Dupont analysis shows that the improvement is mostly due to the increase in financial leverage; the RNOA increases very little over the forecast period. None of these amounts seem unreasonable, so we are content with our forecasts.

8.9 CASES, LINKS, AND REFERENCES

Cases

- The Home Depot, Inc.
- Forecasting for the Love Boat: Royal Caribbean Cruises in 1998
- Netflix, Inc. (Questions 10 and 11)
- Overstock.com (Questions 11–14)
- Sirius Satellite Radio (Questions 15–18)
- Hogs and Chestnuts: Who Profits When the Chinese Eat?
- The Eighty-Minute Forecast

Links

- Bureau of Economic Analysis—www.bea.gov
  In addition to GDP data this site's fixed asset surveys describe, by industry, quantities of fixed assets by industry, amount spent, net holdings, average age, etc. of investments in many classes of assets. For example, it gives the amount the electrical machinery industry spent on metalworking machinery (lots) versus farm tractors (very little).
- Bureau of Labor Statistics—www.bls.gov
  This is a good source for wages and productivity statistics and also has fascinating surveys on consumer spending patterns.
- Congressional Budget Office—www.cbo.gov
  This is a good source for economic forecasts of GDP and its major components.
- Conference Board—www.conference-board.org/
  This site has leading indicators for GDP growth and some interesting consumer confidence data.
- Yahoo! Finance — http://finance.yahoo.com/
- *eVal* website — www.lundholmandsloan.com

References

Nissim, D. and S. Penman (2001). Ratio analysis and equity valuation: From research to practice. *Review of Accounting Studies* 6: 109–154.

CHAPTER NINE

The Cost of Capital

9.1 INTRODUCTION

The forecasted financial statements describe an infinite series of future cash distribution. In order to combine all these distributions into a single estimate of present value, we need a discount rate, commonly referred to as the firm's *cost of capital*. This chapter explains what it is we are trying to estimate with the cost of capital and it gives some advice on how to go about making the estimate. But we should be frank at the outset: There are no good answers to these questions. None of the standard finance models provide estimates that describe the real world data very well. The discount rate that you use in your valuation has a large impact on the result, yet you will rarely feel very confident that the rate you have chosen is the right one. The best we can hope for is a good understanding of what the cost of capital represents and some ballpark range for what a reasonable estimate might be.

This chapter is closely linked to the next chapter on valuation models. You can probably read either one first: Your choices are to read about the discount rate used in the valuation models without yet fully understanding the models, or you can read about the models without yet fully understanding the discount rate, one of the most important inputs for the models. *eVal* calculates the firm's equity value using both the residual income model and the free cash flow model. For both models, it computes the value of the equity directly by discounting the residual income or cash flow each period by the cost of equity capital. *eVal* also gives you the option to compute the value of the firm to all investors, both equity and non-equity capital providers combined. Computing the value of the equity directly only requires one valuation input: the cost of equity capital. However, computing the value to all investors requires that you also estimate the cost of capital for all other non-controlling interests, such as debt capital, preferred stock or minority interests, and then weight these pieces correctly to derive a weighted average cost of capital. We begin with the cost of equity capital because it is conceptually the easiest to describe, and it is a necessary input to any equity valuation model.

9.2 COST OF EQUITY CAPITAL

At its most basic level, the cost of equity capital is the expected rate of return that equity investors could earn on their next best alternative investment with an equivalent level of risk (i.e., the opportunity cost of the equity capital).

The "equivalent risk" portion of this statement is where the problem lies. What is the correct measure of risk? Risk has something to do with investors' distaste for the uncertainty in future payoffs, but how should we quantify this distaste? Should we quantify risk only by reference to the volatility of the company's underlying cash flows, or should we rely on stock price volatility to infer risk? Should our measure of risk take into consideration the fact that we may or may not hold a diversified portfolio of equity securities? How we estimate the cost of equity capital—the expected return on an investment with "equivalent risk"—depends on the answers to these and other questions.

What Is Risk?

The discount rate that we use in our valuation model serves two purposes. It must account for the time value of money and it must account for the riskiness of the investment. The time value of money, absent any risk, is a straightforward concept. It is why bank's pay interest on savings accounts and charge interest on even relatively risk-free loans. If risk was not an issue, we could use the risk-free interest rate; say the yield on a 10-year U.S. Treasury bond, as our cost of equity capital. Unfortunately, risk is very much an issue.

The forecasted financial statements are your best estimates of how the future will unfold for the company, but it is certainly possible that the actual outcomes could be better or worse. And, even if reality plays out exactly as you forecasted, the market may still not value the firm as you think it should. In short, the payoff to investing in any equity is uncertain. Further, investors generally dislike uncertainty. (What would you rather have: $1 million for sure or a 50/50 gamble between $0 and $2 million?) A fundamental measure of risk would quantify the amount of uncertainty and the investors' distaste for different levels of uncertainty, and then combine these measures in a model of investor decision making. But, while developing a fundamental measure of risk works great on paper, in practice it is very difficult to quantify an investment's level of uncertainty and extremely difficult to quantify investors' distaste for it. Consequently, the standard approach sidesteps the issue by looking at how the market has historically compensated investors for bearing risk. We don't attempt to measure the fundamental risk directly; rather, we measure the compensation that was offered in exchange for bearing it.

Because investors dislike uncertainty, they will only hold a risky security if they are compensated for doing so. Higher-risk investments must offer higher expected returns. We quantify risk as the additional expected return beyond the risk-free rate that the security offers. The idea is simply that the risk-free rate captures the time value of money, so everything else in the expected return must be compensation for risk. To measure the expected return for different levels of risk, we identify different *risk classes* or *risk factors* and then compute the average past-realized returns for firms in each class. The amount by which the average return in a risk class exceeds the risk-free rate is the *risk premium* for firms in that risk class. The trick, then, is to identify risk classes that group together firms with similar fundamental risk, even though we are punting on actually measuring the fundamental risk itself.

One issue that plays a big part in any discussion of risk is the idea of diversification. A particular equity investment may feel very risky because your estimates of the firm's future cash flows seem quite uncertain, but if the company is only one investment in a large portfolio, then even though its individual payoffs may seem risky, this risk could be diversified away in the portfolio. Consider, for instance, a small hardware store chain in Wisconsin whose cash flows are particularly susceptible to the local Wisconsin economy. If you hold this investment in a portfolio of stocks that include hardware stores in many other states, then when one state's economy is down, another state's economy may be up, so that the average of all the investments is less volatile than any one investment. Diversification lowers risk. Before you conclude that a particular company has uncertain cash flows and is therefore very risky, think about the source of the uncertainty. If the source can be diversified away in a portfolio, then the market is probably not willing to compensate investors for bearing the risk.

As a practical answer to the question "what is risk?" we offer two models that identify classes of firms that are considered similarly risky. The first model is the capital asset pricing model (CAPM) and the second model is based on the size of the firm.

Capital Asset Pricing Model

Our first pass at quantifying risk is derived from the *capital asset pricing model* (CAPM). Without diving into a semester-long class on the subject, the CAPM says that a firm's expected stock return is given as

$$r_e = r_f + \beta(r_m - r_f),$$

where

r_e is the expected stock return for the firm; equivalently, it is the firm's cost of equity capital,

r_f is the risk free rate of return,

r_m is the expected return for the whole market, and

β is "beta," the firm's sensitivity to the market's return.

One assumption underlying the CAPM is that every investor holds a mix of the risk-free bond, which returns r_f, and the entire market portfolio, which while uncertain, returns r_m in expectation. The only source of risk that cannot be diversified away in the market portfolio is variation in the market return and, consequently, the only thing that distinguishes one equity security from another is β, the degree to which the security moves with the market. Firms with high β's are more risky than firms with low β's and firms with the same β are equally risky. Putting it all together, the firm's cost of equity capital r_e

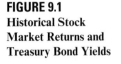

FIGURE 9.1

Historical Stock Market Returns and Treasury Bond Yields

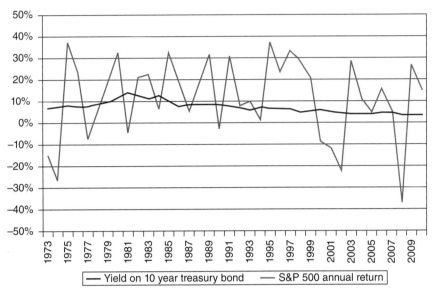

is the sum of compensation for the time-value of money r_f and compensation for bearing risk, where the amount of risk a firm engenders is captured by β, and the amount of compensation the market is expected to deliver per unit of risk over and above the risk-free rate is $(r_m - r_f)$. This last amount is referred to as the market risk premium.

To use this model, you need an estimate of the risk-free rate, an estimate of the market risk premium, and a firm-specific estimate of beta. The risk-free rate, measured by the yield on the 10-year U.S. Treasury Note, has ranged between 2 and 5 percent during the last five years, but has been over 10 percent at times, as seen in Figure 9.1. To get the latest yield on the 10-year Treasury Note, go to http://finance.yahoo.com/indices?e=treasury (see the Last Trade for the CBOE Interest Rate, 10-Year T-Note).

The expected market risk premium $(r_m - r_f)$ is much more difficult to estimate. This is the amount investors expect to earn as compensation for bearing the risk of owning the market portfolio. The average of the difference between the S&P 500 return and the annual yield on the 10-year Treasury bond between 1973 and 2010 is 4.25 percent. But, as seen in Figure 9.1, while the risk-free rate changes very little over time, the realized returns on the S&P 500 have fluctuated wildly, ranging from 37 percent in 1995 to −37 percent in 2008, with a standard deviation of 18.5 percent. If we use the entire United States stock market (rather than just the S&P 500), and set the time period to be 1929 to 2001, we get an average risk premium of 6.7 percent. If we average over 16 countries with historical stock return data from 1900–2001, we get a 5.4 percent average risk premium with a standard deviation of 14.6 percent (Dimson, Marsh, and Staunton, 2003). None of this should make you feel very confident about your estimate of the expected risk premium.

Estimating the firm-specific beta, β, is also fraught with difficulty. It is typically estimated by regressing the realized r_e on the realized r_m for the past five years of monthly returns. What we are shooting for is a measure of how closely the firm's equity price moves with the broader market. Since the market movement is the only source of risk that is priced in the CAPM, a firm with a stronger sensitivity to the market is a riskier investment. As a benchmark, a firm that perfectly tracked the market would have a β of one; a β of 0.5 would be very low and a β of 1.5 would be very high, by historical standards. The trouble with estimates of firm-specific beta is that they change drastically over time for no apparent reason. For example, IBM's beta estimate was 1.5 in 1966 and 0.85 in 1969; it was 0.51 in 1995 and 1.2 in 1998. Surely IBM's fundamental risk didn't change this much during these two three-year periods. Because of this instability, it is not uncommon to use the average beta in the firm's industry rather than the firm-specific estimate. Table 9.1 gives the average beta by industry for 100 industries, computed over the past five years of monthly data.

Another source for beta estimates, computed for individual stocks over the most recent five-year horizon, is Yahoo! Finance. Enter the company ticker symbol and select Key Statistics from the resulting menu. For example, as of May 2011, the beta for Kohl's is given on the Yahoo! Finance Key Statistics page as 0.88. In contrast, Table 9.1 lists the industry average beta for Apparel as 1.35 and the industry average beta for Retail Stores as 1.33. Is Kohl's significantly less risky than the Retail Stores or Apparel industry averages, or is the firm estimate of 0.88 downward biased? If we use a risk-free rate of 3 percent, a market premium of 5 percent and a beta of 0.88, we get a cost of equity capital for Kohl's of 7.40 percent, but if we substitute in a beta of 1.35, we get a cost of equity capital of 9.75 percent. This is a huge variation! It seems unlikely that Kohl's is significantly less risky than its industry average so for the next chapter, we will use a cost of equity capital of 10 percent. But we aren't overly confident in this estimate, and nor should you be overly confident in your cost of equity capital estimates derived from the elegant CAPM model.

A more scientific reason to question the CAPM estimate is that it fits the actual data very poorly. The CAPM says that the only systematic thing causing different firms to have different stock returns is their beta. So you would think that if you estimated firms' betas at a point in time and then tracked the subsequent stock returns, you should find that firms with higher beta estimates would, on average, have higher subsequent stock returns (as compensation for the extra risk). Unfortunately, many studies have shown that this relation is weak to non-existent. Further, you may ask yourself, why are we relying on market prices to tell us about the firm's risk in the first place? The whole premise of this book is that securities can be mispriced, and we can discover the mispricing by our careful analysis. Finally, there is a difference between the realized risk premium over the past 85 years in the United States and the expected risk premium going forward. Back in 1926, it would have been difficult to know that the U.S. economy would turn out to be such a huge success story. Part of the difference between the market return and the

TABLE 9.1 Industry Average Betas

Source: Damodaran Online and Valueline.

Industry Name	Number of Firms	Average Beta	Industry Name	Number of Firms	Average Beta
Advertising	28	1.79	Machinery	114	1.22
Aerospace/Defense	63	1.15	Maritime	53	1.37
Air Transport	40	1.21	Medical Services	139	0.88
Apparel	48	1.35	Medical Supplies	231	1.02
Auto Parts	47	1.78	Metal Fabricating	30	1.44
Automotive	19	1.50	Metals & Mining (Div.)	69	1.33
Bank	418	0.75	Natural Gas (Div.)	32	1.25
Bank (Canadian)	7	0.86	Natural Gas Utility	27	0.65
Bank (Midwest)	40	0.96	Newspaper	13	1.71
Beverage	34	0.92	Office Equip/Supplies	24	1.45
Biotechnology	120	1.13	Oil/Gas Distribution	12	0.97
Building Materials	47	1.33	Oilfield Svcs/Equip.	95	1.48
Cable TV	24	1.43	Packaging & Container	27	1.06
Canadian Energy	10	1.14	Paper/Forest Products	37	1.52
Chemical (Basic)	17	1.28	Petroleum (Integrated)	23	1.21
Chemical (Diversified)	31	1.51	Petroleum (Producing)	163	1.36
Chemical (Specialty)	83	1.37	Pharmacy Services	19	0.96
Coal	25	1.59	Pipeline MLPs	11	0.85
Computer Software/Svcs	247	1.06	Power	68	1.34
Computers/Peripherals	101	1.27	Precious Metals	74	1.18
Diversified Co.	111	1.22	Precision Instrument	83	1.27
Drug	301	1.11	Property Management	27	1.20
E-Commerce	52	1.14	Public/Private Equity	8	2.18
Educational Services	37	0.79	Publishing	23	1.30
Electric Utility (Central)	23	0.78	R.E.I.T.	6	1.29
Electric Utility (East)	25	0.73	Railroad	14	1.28
Electric Utility (West)	14	0.75	Recreation	52	1.50
Electrical Equipment	79	1.32	Reinsurance	8	0.98
Electronics	158	1.13	Restaurant	60	1.33
Engineering & Const	17	1.65	Retail (Special Lines)	143	1.54
Entertainment	75	1.72	Retail Automotive	15	1.44
Entertainment Tech	31	1.39	Retail Building Supply	8	0.92
Environmental	69	0.85	Retail Store	38	1.33
Financial Svcs. (Div.)	230	1.37	Retail/Wholesale Food	29	0.74
Food Processing	109	0.87	Securities Brokerage	25	1.25
Foreign Electronics	9	1.14	Semiconductor	115	1.56
Funeral Services	5	1.22	Semiconductor Equip	14	1.79
Furn/Home Furnishings	30	1.67	Shoe	18	1.31
Healthcare Information	26	0.94	Steel (General)	19	1.59
Heavy Truck/Equip Makers	8	1.94	Steel (Integrated)	13	1.72
Homebuilding	24	1.39	Telecom. Equipment	104	1.04
Hotel/Gaming	52	1.76	Telecom. Services	85	1.01
Household Products	22	1.17	Telecom. Utility	28	1.03
Human Resources	24	1.44	Thrift	181	0.70
Industrial Services	137	0.96	Tobacco	13	0.73
Information Services	26	1.10	Toiletries/Cosmetics	15	1.27
Insurance (Life)	31	1.39	Trucking	33	1.20
Insurance (Prop/Cas.)	67	0.92	Utility (Foreign)	5	0.99
Internet	180	1.11	Water Utility	12	0.70

risk-free rate over this period is simply due to good luck. For this reason, we are inclined to use the estimate of 5.4 percent for the market risk premium, taken from the Dimson, Marsh and Staunton study.

The Size Model

Our second pass at quantifying the risk of an "equivalent investment" is quite simple. Firms of similar size, as measured by their market value, are considered to be in the same risk class. That is, the firm's expected return is

$$r_e = r_f + r_{size},$$

where

r_e is the expected stock return for the firm; equivalently, it is the firm's cost of equity capital

r_f is the risk-free rate of return

r_{size} is the expected return in excess of the risk-free rate for the firm's size-matched portfolio.

This model is motivated by the empirical observation that small firms have historically generated higher returns than large firms, so the higher return, it is argued, must be compensation for higher risk. The knock on this model is that there is no good explanation for why the size of the firm should drive its non-diversifiable risk. A large firm may have more resources to adapt to changing conditions than a small firm, but isn't a portfolio of small firms very much like a single large firm with many divisions? Table 9.2 describes 25 stock portfolios, ranked by their market value at the beginning of each year, and gives various statistics about the risk and return that each portfolio has averaged between 1963 and 2008. The first column gives the average market value in each portfolio for 2008, so you can use this column to look up where in the table a particular firm might land.

The main observation from Table 9.2 is that the average annual returns shown in the third column are almost monotonically increasing; as firms get smaller their average returns get bigger. The largest firms shown in portfolio 1 have averaged 10.97 percent annual returns while the smallest firms shown in portfolio 25 have averaged 21.63 percent annual returns. The second column shows that the CAPM model would also conclude that large firms are less risky than small firms, with beta increasing steadily across the portfolios. But the change in beta is far too small to account for the large change in portfolio returns. In fact, the fifth column reports the portfolio return in excess of the return predicted by the CAPM model, and shows a 9-percent difference between the largest and smallest firms.

After you find what portfolio your firm resides in (approximately), there are two ways to use Table 9.2 to develop a cost of equity capital estimate. The first is to simply use the historical size risk premium from the fourth column and add it to your estimate of the risk-free rate. However, if you still have some lingering love for the CAPM model, the second approach is to figure out the CAPM cost of equity capital and then add the excess return shown in the fifth column. For example, Kohl's market capitalization as of May 2011 is approximately $15 billion, and was about $12 billion at the end of 2008. This

TABLE 9.2 **Returns and Risk Premiums by Size Portfolio**

Source: CRSP and Duff and Phelps Risk Premium Report 2009.

Portfolio Rank by Size	Average Mkt Value ($ mil) in 2008	Beta Computed since 1963	Average Annual Return since 1963	Average Risk Premium over Long-Term Treasury Bonds	Premium over CAPM Return
1	127,995	0.86	10.97	3.93	0.64
2	36,587	0.92	11.25	4.21	0.67
3	21,569	0.97	10.11	3.07	−0.65
4	16,126	0.98	11.63	4.59	0.83
5	12,369	0.97	11.34	4.3	0.59
6	9,399	1.04	12.6	5.56	1.58
7	7,150	1.03	13.32	6.28	2.31
8	5,597	1.04	12.43	5.39	1.4
9	4,775	1.11	14.12	7.08	2.83
10	3,948	1.07	12.76	5.72	1.6
11	3,418	1.15	14.87	7.83	3.43
12	2,933	1.12	12.76	5.72	1.41
13	2,675	1.09	13.64	6.6	2.41
14	2,346	1.12	14.81	7.77	3.46
15	2,086	1.16	13.58	6.54	2.07
16	1,808	1.15	15.21	8.17	3.75
17	1,558	1.19	16.55	9.51	4.96
18	1,347	1.19	15.45	8.41	3.83
19	1,172	1.2	15.13	8.09	3.5
20	997	1.26	16.11	9.07	4.24
21	838	1.25	17.22	10.18	5.39
22	697	1.26	15.71	8.67	3.84
23	515	1.23	17.05	10.01	5.29
24	331	1.27	17.78	10.74	5.85
25	111	1.29	21.63	14.59	9.65

Data from 1963 to 2008.

would but Kohl's somewhere between the 4th and 5th portfolios. The size model would assign them a risk premium of somewhere between 4.3 percent and 4.6 percent. This amount, added to our risk-free rate estimate of 3 percent, would give a cost of equity capital of somewhere between 7.3 percent and 7.6 percent. Alternatively, we could start with our CAPM estimate of approximately 10 percent and add another 0.59 percent to 0.83 percent to end up with an estimate between 10.59 percent and 10.83 percent.

Does size really measure risk? Should you set your discount rate higher for smaller firms? The empirical evidence in Table 9.2 would certainly say yes. However, the evidence is taken from market prices and this raises two questions. First, by using the market value to sort firms into size portfolios we could be inadvertently inducing the result we are looking for. To state the question cleverly, are small firms riskier or are riskier firms small? Because we determined "big" or "small" by their market value, maybe the fundamental risk of a firm is causing market participants to give it a small market value. There is some comfort that this isn't the case, however. If we sorted firms on the basis of their accounting book value instead of their market value we get results that look very much like those in Table 9.2.

The second problem that using market values to assess size arises if markets are inefficient. In particular, suppose that there is no difference in the fundamental risk of large or small stocks, but market participants consistently undervalue small stocks. In most years, the small stocks would outperform the large stocks, as some of the mispricing is corrected. Their market value would increase and they would move out of the lowest-size portfolio, and a new crop of small stocks would be born to take their place. If this were the case, then we would see small stocks generating larger returns than large stocks, but it wouldn't be because they were any riskier than large stocks; it would be because the market was mispricing the small stocks. This story isn't too hard to imagine, since small stocks get little analyst coverage, are not held by many institutional investors, and generally fly under the radar of most investors. It seems like a prime place to find potentially neglected and underpriced securities.

What Number Do I Put in *eVal*?

Ultimately there is no good answer to the question "What is the cost of equity capital?" As a practical matter, we want to be able to compare the valuations of different firms on a risk-adjusted basis. If we evaluate 10 firms and then sort them based on the amount we think they are undervalued, we want this sort to reveal relative mispricing, not just differences in the riskiness across the 10 firms.

Rather than take the CAPM estimate as truth or the size model estimate as truth, we prefer that you use these models as guides, combining the resulting estimate with your own intuition and some common sense. You might want to ask yourself what rate of return you would personally require on an investment with a similar level of risk. How much extra return beyond the risk-free rate seems reasonable, given the riskiness of the firm's future payoffs, and evaluated in light of the diversification you have in your portfolio? The default value for the cost of equity capital in *eVal* is 10 percent, found on the Valuation Parameters sheet. You can think of it as 5 percent for the risk-free rate and 5 percent for the risk premium; at least it is easy to remember!

There is one constraint on your cost of equity capital input: it must be greater than your assumed terminal growth rate in sales. If this isn't the case, then you are assuming that the firm will grow faster than the discount rate forever. This makes the perpetuity formula in the valuation models invalid; effectively, the value of such a firm is infinite. If you mistakenly violate this condition, *eVal* will display the error message "Error! cost of equity capital <= growth rate" in red on the relevant valuation sheet. For more discussion, see the section on terminal value forecasts in Chapter 7.

9.3 COST OF NONEQUITY CAPITAL

The only reason you need to consider the cost of non-equity capital is if you are interested in computing the value of all investors' claims on the firm, commonly referred to as the *entity value,* rather than just the equity value. It is also a necessary computation if your approach to valuing equity is to first determine the entity value and then subtract the value of the non-equity claims to arrive at equity value. The Valuation Parameters sheet has an optional section for you to enter the cost of capital from debt holders, preferred stockholders, and minority interests (collectively called non-controlling interests). We strongly encourage you to ensure consistency between the cost of capital estimates here and the corresponding forecasting assumptions you input for the terminal period interest expense, preferred dividend, and minority interest income on the Forecasting Assumptions sheet. For example, if your terminal period estimate of the firm's interest rate is 6 percent, we highly recommend inputting 6 percent on the optional Valuation Parameters sheet for the cost of debt. In the short term, a firm may have debt outstanding that has a coupon interest rate different than its market interest rate. However, it would be quite odd to forecast that, forever into the future, the company will somehow manage to issue debt at a rate different than its market rate. Similarly, the cost of preferred stock and the cost of minority interests should probably match your terminal inputs for these items on the Forecasting Assumptions sheet. Note that the value of the equity is already determined by your financial statement forecasts and your assumption about the cost of equity capital. Consequently, as you change your assumptions about the cost of non-equity capital, you will change the entity value and the value of the non-equity capital, but equity value will remain constant.

Just as with the cost of equity capital, costs of non-equity capital should not be smaller than your forecasted terminal period sales growth rate. If they are, then the perpetuity formula we use to compute the present value of the free cash flows to these capital providers is invalid and an error flag will show up on the valuation sheet. Think about what it would mean for the cost of debt to be lower than the growth rate forever. In the terminal period, the growth rate drives the growth in debt, so debt would be growing faster than it was being discounted back and the present value would be infinite. If your forecasts violate this condition, you will see the message "Error! cost of capital <= growth rate" on the associated valuation sheet.

9.4 WEIGHTED AVERAGE COST OF CAPITAL

To compute the entity value (as opposed to the equity value), you need a discount rate that reflects the blended cost of capital for all providers: equity, preferred stock, minority interests, and debt. Another way to think about this problem is that we are trying to estimate the cost of equity capital for a hypothetical firm that has the same net operating assets of the actual firm but does not have any non-equity claims. Consequently, this rate is sometimes referred to as the cost of capital for the unlevered firm, or the expected return on net operating assets (not to be confused with the actual return on net operating assets, as computed in Chapter 5). To see this, examine the basic accounting equation:

Net Operating Assets − Debt − Preferred Stock − Minority Interests
= Common Equity,

which we can rearrange as

Net Operating Assets = Common Equity + Debt + Preferred Stock
+ Minority Interests,

or

Net Operating Assets = Unlevered Equity

To compute the cost of capital for this hypothetical firm, a logical approach is to take a weighted average of the cost of equity capital, the cost of preferred stock, the cost of minority interests, and the after-tax cost of debt. The *weighted-average cost of capital* (WACC), labeled r_w, does just this. It is computed as

$$r_w = \frac{r_e P_e + r_{ps} P_{ps} + r_{mi} P_{mi} + (1 - tx) r_d P_d}{P_e + P_{PS} + P_{mi} + P_d}$$

where

    tx is the estimated effective tax rate,

    r_e is the estimated cost of equity capital,

    r_d is the estimated cost of debt capital,

    r_{ps} is the estimated cost of preferred stock capital,

    r_{mi} is the estimated cost of minority interest capital,

    P_e is the estimated value of the equity,

    P_d is the estimated value of the debt,

    P_{ps} is the estimated value of the preferred stock, and

    P_{mi} is the estimated value of minority interest capital.

The value r_w is the cost of a dollar of additional capital, holding the firm's capital structure constant. Imagine the firm raising the dollar by issuing common equity, preferred stock, minority interest claims and debt in exact proportions to their estimated values. The weighted-average cost of capital is the natural benchmark for the firm's return on net operating assets.[1]

[1]The weighted-average cost of capital given here is "after-tax," meaning that the cost of debt has been adjusted down to account for the tax shield of interest (i.e., the $(1-tx)$ part in the formula). By accounting for the tax deductibility of interest in the discount rate, we do not adjust the free cash flow estimates for the tax benefits of interest. An alternative approach found in some texts is to define WACC on a pre-tax basis (i.e., without the $(1-tx)$ adjustment in the formula) and then add the tax deduction associated with interest to the free cash flows. This issue is discussed in greater detail in Chapter 10.

Note that the weights used to compute r_w are based on the estimated values of the equity, preferred stock, minority interests, and debt, not their book values, not their current market values, and not some estimate of their future values in some future capital structure. But this raises a problem. The formula makes reference to P_e, the value of the common equity, yet P_e is exactly what we are trying to figure out. How can we weight the different costs of capital based on their estimated values if we don't yet know the estimated value of equity? We sidestep this issue by using the estimate of P_e already found when we valued the equity directly. We do the same thing for P_d, P_{ps}, and P_{mi}. With P_e, P_d, P_{ps}, and P_{mi} determined, the value of the entity is then simply the sum of these four components. On the Valuation Parameters sheet *eVal* then approximates the WACC using the formula above (see the formula in cell J24).

Note that the thus-derived estimate of the WACC is only correct if the company's capital structure and effective tax rate are not forecast to change through time. For example, the approximation employed in cell J24 uses the forecast effective tax rate in the terminal year. But if the effective tax rate is different in the earlier years of the forecast horizon, the correct WACC will reflect a time-weighted average of these different effective tax rates. Fortunately, there is a simple shortcut to computing the correct WACC in such circumstances. Since we have already estimated the individual values of P_e, P_d, P_{ps}, and P_{mi}, the correct WACC is the one that gives an entity-level value that is equal to the sum of the values P_e, P_d, P_{ps}, and P_{mi}. So you simply need to adjust the starting WACC estimate until the equity value implied using the entity-level valuation is the same as that implied by the direct equity valuation method. The bottom of the Valuation Parameters sheet in *eVal* provides the necessary information to facilitate this process. The general rule is that a higher (lower) WACC will give a lower (higher) valuation, so if the implied entity-level valuation is too high (low), then simply bump the WACC estimate up (down) until the two equity valuations are equal. In this way, you can solve for the correct weighted-average cost of capital. This approach is completely valid, because the entity-level and equity-level valuations must ultimately yield the same equity value.

What Is Constant and What Is Changing?

In the previous sections, we estimated the cost of equity capital, the cost of preferred stock, the cost of minority interests, and the cost of debt as constants—a single rate for each that is used to discount all future flows to each of these capital providers. We then combined these constant costs of capital to compute the associated constant WACC. However, what if you forecast that the firm's capital structure will change in the future? For instance, suppose you think that the company will drastically increase its ratio of debt to equity in the future. Based on the formula above, if you were to re-compute the WACC in the future, it could be different than the WACC based on the current capital structure. Should you base your estimate of r_w on the current capital structure or on the forecasted future capital structure? Alternatively, should you use a different discount rate each period?

While the WACC formula suggests that r_w should change as the capital structure changes, this is not necessarily the case. Remember that r_w is essentially an estimate of the expected return on the company's net operating assets. As such, it is determined by the perceived riskiness of the company's future free cash flows and not by the particular capital structure employed.[2] To see how this all washes out in our WACC formula, note that the cost of debt is typically lower than the cost of equity, since debt is typically less risky. If a company cranks up its leverage ratio, then both debt and equity should become more risky. But at the same time, the value of debt will increase relative to the value of equity. Because the WACC computation now places relatively more weight on debt, which has a relatively lower cost of capital, the overall WACC should remain about the same. So unless you are anticipating some drastic change in the company's underlying business operations, there is no need to adjust the WACC for anticipated changes in the capital structure.

Finally, if you see the message "Error!, there is no internally consistent weighted average cost of capital," then *eVal* is telling you that your assumptions do not allow for a feasible solution to WACC. For example, if your assumptions imply an equity value of $10 and a debt value of negative $12, then you need an entity value of negative $2 to reconcile these two amounts. But if your forecasts imply positive future free cash flows, then the entity value cannot be negative, regardless of how high you set r_w. The cases that lead to this error message are rather bizarre, so, if you see the message, there is probably something very wrong with your forecasting assumptions.

[2] You may recall from your finance classes that the independence of the WACC from the capital structure employed is a direct implication of the well-known Miller-Modigliani theorem on capital structure.

9.5   CASES, LINKS, AND REFERENCES

Links

- Yahoo! Finance major U.S. indices, treasury: http://finance.yahoo.com/indices?e=treasury
- Yahoo! Finance: http://finance.yahoo.com/
- Morningstar: http://www.morningstar.com

References

- Dimson, E., P. Marsh, and M. Staunton. (2000). *The Millennium Book: A Century of Investment Returns*. London: ABN-AMRO and London Business School.
- Fama, E., and K. French. (1997). Industry costs of capital. *Journal of Financial Economics* 43: 153–93.
- Ibbotson and Associates. (2010). *Stocks, Bonds, Bills, and Inflation*. 2010 Yearbook. Chicago.

CHAPTER TEN

Valuation

10.1 INTRODUCTION

The hard work in valuation is already done. The forecasts you developed in Chapters 7 and 8 describe the future evolution of net distributions to equity holders. The cost of equity capital you chose in Chapter 9 determines how valuable future cash flows are today. All that remains is to combine the forecasts with the discount rate to compute the present value of the net distributions to equity holders. Why then are there so many pages in this chapter? It turns out that there are a number of different ways to compute the value of equity. While each of them leads to the same answer, each does so in a way that sheds a different light on the source of value creation. Further, different user groups have historically used different models: Accounting types like the residual income models and finance types like the discounted cash flow models. If all you care about is the final answer, any of the models will do. But if you want to see the answer presented in the particular way you learned in some other class or life experience, we have a smorgasbord of models for you to choose from.

There are two features that distinguish the different valuation models. First, the flow variable, the thing that is being discounted, can be either free cash flows or accounting residual income flows (we give precise definitions below). Second, we can compute the value of the flows to equity holders directly, or we can first compute the value of the flows to all investors and then back into the value of the equity claim by subtracting the value of the flows to nonequity capital providers. If we work carefully (and *eVal* is *very* careful), each model yields exactly the same result. Without boring you with algebraic proof, it should be obvious that each model will get the same answer if you feed each the same inputs. The forecasted financial statements and discount rate assumption *determine* the value; all we have to do is discover it.

All the models we describe allow for the possibility that the firm will live forever, so all models sum over time from the present, labeled time zero, to infinity. It takes a really long time to add up an infinite number of terms one at a time, so at some point in the future, known as the *terminal year,* we use a perpetuity formula to determine the present value of the flows in the remaining years. All the models solve this problem the same way, so we defer the discussion of the present value calculations until the end of the chapter and present each model as an infinite sum of terms. Don't worry about this; there is a nifty solution to this problem.

We present all the models in algebraic notation. If you want to work through some numerical examples, the case "Four Valuation Models—One Value" is a good place to start.

10.2   RESIDUAL INCOME VALUATION MODELS

Although actually quite old, the residual income model has recently come back into vogue on Wall Street. Its primary advantage is that it expresses value directly in terms of the financial statements that you worked so hard to forecast, rather than translating these amounts into free cash flows. Define *residual income* RI_t in period t as

$$RI_t = NI_t - r_e CE_{t-1}$$

where

NI_t is net income available to common equity for the period ending at date t,

r_e is the cost of equity capital, and

CE_{t-1} is common shareholders' equity at date $t-1$ (i.e., one year earlier than the NI_t date).

Residual income is the amount by which net income exceeds the capital charge on the book value of common equity invested in the firm. If the firm could deposit its book value in a bank account at the beginning of the year and earn interest at the rate r_e, it would earn $r_e CE_{t-1}$ for the year. Residual income is the amount by which NI_t exceeds or falls short of this benchmark. In this sense, it is *residual*.

The residual income model computes value as the sum of the initial book value plus the present value of future residual income flows. Both the book value and the net income component of residual income are accrual accounting constructs, which may make you incredulous about this model. How can the model work when we know that a firm's accounting book value is an imperfect measure of its market value and that earnings are an imperfect measure of value creation? How can these numbers be used to estimate a firm's market value? The key is to recognize that if book value is understated, then future residual income will be overstated, and by precisely enough to correct for the erroneous book value. For example, if a firm has a missing asset, one that the accounting rules don't recognize, then the asset isn't included in CE_{t-1}, but it produces future NI, making future RI positive. In a later section, we will illustrate how all this adds up perfectly.

The easiest version of this model is the one that values the common equity directly.

Residual Income to Common Equity

The algebraic statement of this model is

$$P_e = CE_0 + \sum_{t=1}^{\infty} \frac{RI_t}{(1 + r_e)^t},$$

where

P_e is the estimated market value of common equity as of the last financial statement date,

CE_0 is the common shareholders' equity as of the last financial statement date (i.e., time 0),

RI_t is residual income, equal to $NI_t - r_e CE_{t-1}$, as defined above, and

r_e is the cost of equity capital.

The model starts with the initial stock of accounting value CE_0 and adds to it the discounted sum of expected future residual income flows. The reason a firm's market value P_e will be different than its book value is because it is forecasted to earn positive or negative residual income in the future. To get a feel for this model, imagine a savings account with $100 in it and a 10 percent interest rate. The book value of this investment, by any reasonable accounting measurement, would be $100. Further, if 10 percent is the market rate of interest on savings accounts, then the return on a similar investment with equivalent risk is probably also 10 percent, so assume $r_e = 10$ percent. In this case, regardless of deposits or withdrawals (made at the beginning of each year), the earnings each period will be 10 percent of the beginning book value, which is exactly the capital charge $r_e CE_{t-1}$, so residual income in all future periods, is zero. Thus, the value of the savings account is $100. Seems pretty obvious. Now suppose that the savings account was going to pay 11 percent interest in some future years, yet the discount rate remained 10 percent. In this case the savings account would earn "residual income" in these years and its market value would exceed $100. It is as if every few years the bank manager threw some extra money into your account. If you knew this was going to happen, the account would be worth more than the $100 of book value.

Figure 10.1 shows the residual income valuation to common equity for Kohl's using a valuation date of January 31, 2010 and the default *eVal* forecasts. To see this valuation in *eVal*, first enter the valuation date on the Valuation Parameters sheet and then go to the Residual Income Valuations sheet. Each column shows the net income and beginning common equity for the fiscal year, taken directly from the Financial Statements sheet. Residual income is computed from these inputs and then discounted each period, using the default cost of equity capital of 10 percent. For instance, the first year has forecasted net income of $1,046,887 thousand and the beginning common equity is $7,853,000 thousand, resulting in $1,046,887 - .10(7,853,000) = $261,587 thousand of residual income. The present value of each period's residual income is added up for the first 10 years, and then the present value

FIGURE 10.1   **Residual Income to Common Equity for Kohl's**
Valuation based on *eVal* defaults as of January 31, 2010.

Residual Income Valuation	($000)			
Company Name	KOHL'S CORP			
Most Recent Fiscal Year End	10-01-31			
Date of Valuation	10-01-31			
Cost of Common Equity	10.00%			
Teriminal Growth Rate	3.00%			
Fiscal Year of Forecast	**11-01-31**	**12-01-31**	**13-01-31**	**14-01-31**
Valuation to Common Equity				
Net Income	1,046,887	1,093,460	1,140,301	1,187,266
Common Equity at Beginning of Year	7,853,000	8,218,108	8,586,636	8,957,529
Residual Income	261,587	271,649	281,637	291,513
Present Value of Residual Income	237,806	224,503	211,598	199,108
Present Value Beyond 10 Years	1,951,370			
Present Value of First 10 Years	1,830,093			
Common Equity **as of**				
10-01-31	7,853,000			
Forecast Equity Value Before Time Adj.	11,634,463		$= 271{,}649/(1+.10)^2$	
Forecasted Value as of Valuation Date	12,216,186			
Less Value of Contingent Equity Claims	0			
Value Attributable to Common Equity	12,216,186	$= 261{,}587/(1+.10)^1$		
Common Shares Outstanding at BS Date	307,000			
Equivalent Shares at Valuation Date	307,000			
Forecast Price/Share	**$39.79**			

of all the years beyond 10 is added on as one lump sum (this computation is discussed later). The result is added to the book value of common equity as of January 31, 2010, to arrive at $11,634,463 thousand, labeled as the "Forecast Equity Value Before Time Adj."

In the previous savings account example, the key comparison was between the discount rate and the rate of interest the account paid. For a real company, the key comparison is between the forecasted ROE and the cost of equity capital r_e. To see this, multiply and divide RI_t by CE_{t-1} so that

$$RI_t = (NI_t - r_e CE_{t-1}) = (ROE_t - r_e)CE_{t-1},$$

where ROE_t is computed on beginning equity.

The expression says that residual income equals the excess of ROE_t over the cost of equity capital times the beginning common equity book value for the period. If you forecast that the firm's ROE will exceed its cost of equity capital, then residual income will be positive; if ROE is forecast to be less than the cost of equity capital, residual income will be negative. Stated another way, a firm is worth more than its book value only if it is expected to earn an ROE in excess of its cost of equity capital. Remembering from previous chapters that ROE was our premier measure of profitability, this equation says that profitability creates value.

This expression also demonstrates that size by itself does *not* create value. If $ROE_t = r_e$, then residual income is zero regardless of the value of CE_{t-1}.

Similarly, growth in CE_t, by itself, does not create value. However, if ROE_t is forecast to exceed r_e in the future, then a firm wants to grow to be as big as possible. Think of it this way: If you forecast that a firm's ROE will always equal its cost of equity capital in the future, then you are really forecasting that the firm will always engage in zero net present value projects. If this is the case, then it doesn't matter how big or small those future projects are; none of them will create value. In contrast, if you forecast that ROE_t will exceed r_e in the future, then you are saying that the firm has positive net present value projects in the future. In this case, you want the projects to be as big as possible; in this case, growth is good. Wall Street analysts frequently confuse the value of growth with the value of profitability when assessing equity securities. Many research reports extol the huge growth potential of a company without explaining how the firm will ever turn the growth into profitability. If the company can't earn a return that is at least as great as its cost of capital, being a big firm just means that it will destroy more value than a small firm. We suspect that analysts like rapidly growing firms because such firms are likely to require investment-banking services, not because they think they are fundamentally good investment opportunities.

The residual income model has many desirable features. For one thing, it is written in terms of the accounting variables that you worked so hard to forecast. The net income and book value variables come straight from the forecasted financial statements in *eVal*. More fundamentally, the residual income model describes value in an economically appealing way. Value is driven by profitability and growth. Much of the previous chapters in this book have been aimed at building your intuition for how economic forces and accounting distortions will act on a firm's growth rate and especially on its ROE. By expressing value as a function of these two drivers, the residual income valuation model exploits this intuition.

Finally, because the residual income model is written in terms of accounting numbers, we will use it in the next chapter to describe some popular valuation ratios such as the market-to-book ratio, the price-to-earnings ratio, and the PEG ratio.

Bad Accounting and the Residual Income Valuation Model

Because the residual income model is stated in terms of accounting values, you may worry that distorted accounting measurements will make the model invalid or inaccurate. But, as the next example illustrates, the model is surprisingly resilient to accounting errors. Suppose that the sequence of forecasted common equity and net income, before any consideration of accounting errors, is CE_0, NI_1, CE_1, NI_2, CE_2, NI_3, CE_3 . . . , so that the residual income model yields

$$P_e = CE_0 + \frac{NI_1 - r_e CE_0}{(1 + r_e)} + \frac{NI_2 - r_e CE_1}{(1 + r_e)^2} + \frac{NI_3 - r_e CE_2}{(1 + r_e)^3} + \cdots$$

Now suppose that you are sure that K of value is missing from CE_0, possibly due to an R&D investment that cannot be capitalized but is forecasted to pay-off in NI_1. You could set out to correct for this error in the accounting model by adding K to CE_0 and subtracting it from your estimate of NI_1; that is, you could recognize the value creation in the current book value rather than waiting for it to materialize in future earnings. In this case the valuation would be

$$P_e = CE_0 + K + \frac{NI_1 - K - r_e(CE_0 + K)}{(1 + r_e)}$$

$$+ \frac{NI_2 - r_e CE_1}{(1 + r_e)^2} + \frac{NI_3 - r_e CE_2}{(1 + r_e)^3} + \cdots$$

noting that the addition of K to CE_0 increased book value at date 0 but that the book value at date 1 is back to normal because of the subtraction of K from NI_1. Simple algebra demonstrates that the two valuations are equal. At first blush, this may seem impossible. Shouldn't moving K to the present increase the value estimate, since money has time value? But look carefully at the second term in the second equation; not only has K been deducted from date 1 earnings, but the capital charge is also higher by $r_e K$, thus perfectly correcting for the time value of this manipulation. And you don't even have to forecast *when* the K of additional value will show up in future earnings. Suppose that you estimated that the additional value was going to materialize in year two rather than year one, such that your corrected forecasts yield the following value estimate:

$$P_e = CE_0 + K + \frac{NI_1 - r_e(CE_0 + K)}{(1 + r_e)}$$

$$+ \frac{NI_2 - K - r_e(CE_1 + K)}{(1 + r_e)^2} + \frac{NI_3 - r_e CE_2}{(1 + r_e)^3} + \cdots$$

With some hard work, you can show that this again equals the original amount (feeling like this is an algebra test?). By including a capital charge in the definition of residual income, the model perfectly corrects for accounting distortions. Consequently, you really don't need to get involved in correcting the historical financial statements for accounting distortions; if your forecasts anticipate the unraveling of the accounting distortion, the model will do the rest.

You *should not* conclude from this discussion that it isn't important that you understand accounting distortions. Your forecasts of the future are typically based on observations of the firm's past and, if that past is distorted by poor accounting, then you need to be aware of this. For instance, if the firm has generated unusually high income by capitalizing more expenses than is appropriate, and thus deferred the recognition of these expenses on the income statement, you need to be aware that future income will be lower when these capitalized expenses eventually flow through income (as they surely must in an accrual accounting system).

Residual Income to All Investors

This version of the model is less commonly used but reconciles nicely with the other valuation models. It computes the value of common equity by first computing the value to all capital providers combined, commonly labeled as the *entity value,* and then subtracting from this the value of the non-equity claims (debt, preferred stock and minority interests). It computes the value of each of these claims as the sum of the beginning book value and the present value of a flow of future residual amounts, just as we did for equity.[1]

To express this model algebraically, we need to remind you of some earlier notation. In Chapter 5, we defined NOA_t as the net operating assets of the firm, computed as the book value of operating assets less the operating liabilities. Next, define L_t as the accounting book value of the debt (current and non-current combined), PS_t as the accounting book value of the preferred stock, and MI_t as the accounting book value of the minority interest (in Chapter 5, we lumped debt, preferred stock, and minority interest together and labeled them as Net Financial Obligations, but here we will value each component separately). By the basic accounting equation, Net Operating Assets NOA_t is given as

$$NOA_t = CE_t + L_t + PS_t + MI_t$$

In Chapter 5, we also defined NOI_t as the net operating income, computed after tax. It is equal to net income available to common equity holders NI_t plus the after-tax interest flows to debtholders $(1 - tx_t)I_t$, plus the preferred dividend flows to preferred shareholders PD_t, plus the minority interest in earnings MIE_t. That is,

$$NOI_t = NI_t + (1 - tx_t)I_t + PD_t + MIE_t,$$

where tx_t is the firm's effective tax rate in year t (we typically do not adjust preferred dividends and minority interest in earnings for taxes because these outflows are not typically deductible for tax purposes). NOI_t is the amount the firm earned before expenses related to non-equity capital providers.

The idea behind the model is that all investors together own NOA_0 and the future stream of after-tax net operating income NOI_t. We can therefore compute the value of the entity as the initial balance of NOA_0 plus the present value of the future residual NOI_t stream. Denoting the weighted-average cost of capital as r_w, we define *residual net operating income* as:

$$RNOI_t = NOI_t - r_w NOA_{t-1}$$

Note the similarity with residual income defined in the previous section as $RI_t = NI_t - r_e CE_{t-1}$? To compute residual net *operating* income, NI_t is replaced

---

[1]In everything that follows, minority interest is treated exactly like preferred stock in all respects and so, if you find this source of non-equity capital a bit confusing (as at least one of the authors does), feel free to ignore it in all the formulas, remembering that it is accounted for exactly like preferred stock.

with NOI_t and CE_{t-1} is replaced with NOA_{t-1}. With this notation in place, the *entity value* P_f can be expressed as

$$P_f = NOA_0 + \sum_{t=1}^{\infty} \frac{RNOI_t}{(1+r_w)^t}$$

All investors together own P_f. To find the value of the common equity holders' claim, we need to subtract from P_f the value of the debt claim, the value of the preferred stock claim, and the value of the minority interest claim. And, in the spirit of residual income valuation, the value of the debt claim is computed as the initial book value of L_0 plus the present value of the future *residual interest expense* $I_t - r_d L_{t-1}$, where r_d is the cost of debt capital. Similarly, the value of the preferred stock claim is computed as the sum of the initial book value of PS_0 and the present value of the future *residual preferred dividends,* using the cost of preferred stock capital r_{ps} as the discount rate; and the value of the minority interest claim is computed as the sum of the initial book value of MI_0 and the present value of the *residual minority interest in earnings*. Denoting the debt value as P_d, the preferred stock value as P_{ps}, and the minority interests value as P_{mi}, we get

$$P_d = L_0 + \sum_{t=1}^{\infty} \frac{I_t - r_d L_{t-1}}{(1+r_d)^t},$$

$$P_{ps} = PS_0 + \sum_{t=1}^{\infty} \frac{PD_t - r_{ps} PS_{t-1}}{(1+r_{ps})^t},$$

and

$$P_{mi} = MI_0 + \sum_{t=1}^{\infty} \frac{MIE_t - r_{mi} MI_{t-1}}{(1+r_{mi})^t}$$

The entity value is the sum of the value of the common equity, the value of the debt, the value of the preferred stock, and the value of the minority interest:

$$P_f = P_e + P_d + P_{ps} + P_{mi}$$

and so we can solve for the value of common equity as

$$P_e = P_f - P_d - P_{ps} - P_{mi}$$

This may seem like the long way around to get to a common equity valuation. The advantage of this indirect approach to valuing the equity is that it focuses your attention on the value of the net operating assets and future net operating income of the firm. The idea is that we should first work hard on valuing the entity, since this is the fundamental source of value for the firm, and then worry about how the value gets divided between the capital providers.

To see the Residual Income to All Investors model in *eVal,* scroll down the Residual Income Valuations sheet. If you change the valuation date (on the Valuation Parameters sheet) to January 31, 2010, and set the weighted-average cost of capital to 9.372157 percent, you will get the same equity valuation as in the previous model. Notice how *eVal* computes the value of the debt, the value of the preferred stock, the value of the minority interests, and the entity value. In each case, the value is computed as a beginning book value plus the present value of a residual flow. Note that the flows to each capital provider are discounted at a different rate: Debt is discounted using the cost of debt capital (8 percent is the default rate in *eVal*), preferred stock is discounted using the cost of preferred stock (9 percent is the default in *eVal*), the minority interest claim is discounted using the cost of minority interests (10 percent is the default rate in *eVal*), and entity value is discounted using the weighted-average cost of capital (shown as 9.37 percent, but in reality is 9.372157 percent). By subtracting the value of the debt, the value of the preferred stock (which is zero) and the value of minority interest (which is zero) from the entity value, we arrive at $11,634,463 thousand for the Forecast Equity Value Before Time Adjustment. Note that this is exactly the same amount that we found using the residual income to common equity model in the previous section.

The Tax Shield on Interest

If you have been following all this very carefully, you may have noticed that some money went missing. By definition,

$$NOI_t = NI_t + I_t + PD_t + MIE_t - tx_t.I_t$$

NOI_t is in the income that flows to the entity. Similarly, NI_t is in the income claimed by the common equity holders, I_t is the income claimed by the debt holders, PD_t is the income claimed by the preferred stock holders, and MIE_t is the income claimed by the the minority interest holders. But what about the '$- tx_t.I_t$', the *tax shield on interest?* Where did it go? We could have simply left these tax savings in NOI rather than pretending that they don't exist by deducting them back out. While this might seem like the most logical approach, the most common "textbook" approach is to build the value of the tax shield into the entity value by lowering the cost of debt in the weighted-average cost of capital. In other words, instead of reflecting the cash savings from the tax deductibility of interest as a higher numerator, we instead use a smaller denominator.

Recall from Chapter 9 that the weighted-average cost of capital was a mix of the cost of equity capital r_e, the cost of preferred stock capital r_{ps}, the cost of minority interests r_{mi}, and the *after-tax* cost of debt capital $(1 - tx_t)r_d$. Using the after-tax cost of debt lowers the weighted-average cost of capital that is used to discount the flows to the entity and therefore raises the entity value. Figure 10.2 illustrates the accounting variables and discount rates that each model uses.

If it strikes you as a bit magical that making a simple tax adjustment to the cost of debt capital is all that it takes to get the value of the tax shield on interest built into the entity value, your skepticism is justified. To be theoretically valid, we would need to add two additional assumptions; namely, that the firm's effective tax rate and leverage ratio remain constant. But, as discussed in Chapter 9, we sidestep this whole issue by allowing you to pick the rate at

FIGURE 10.2 **The Variables in Each Residual Income Valuation Equation**

entity value		common equity value		preferred stock value		minority interest		debt value		tax shield
P_f	$=$	P_e	$+$	P_{ps}	$+$	P_{mi}	$+$	P_d		
uses		uses		uses		uses		uses		
NOA_t	$=$	CE_t	$+$	PS_t	$+$	MI_t	$+$	L_t		
and NOI_t	$=$	NI_t	$+$	PD_t	$+$	MIE_t	$+$	I_t	$-$	$tx_t I_t$

and discounts using

| r_w | | r_e | | r_{ps} | | r_{mi} | | r_d |

weighted average
of r_e, r_{ps}, r_{mi} and $(1-tx)r_d$ ←—— value of $tx_t I_t$ is incorporated into entity value by using $(1-tx)r_d$ in r_w computation.

the bottom of the Valuation Parameters sheet in *eVal* to find the internally consistent weighted-average cost of capital. You input the cost of equity capital, the cost of preferred equity, the cost of minority interests, and the pretax cost of debt capital on the Valuation Parameters sheet, and then with a little help from you, *eVal* figures out the weighted-average cost of capital that perfectly reflects the future tax savings.

The tax shield on interest is only an issue when valuing the common equity using this indirect approach. When valuing equity directly, interest payments and the associated tax deductions are just another type of expense that is tax-deductible, no different than utilities or marketing expenses. So if you didn't follow the discussion in this last section, you didn't really miss much.

10.3 DISCOUNTED CASH FLOW VALUATION

The discounted cash flow (DCF) model focuses on free cash flows rather than residual income flows. *eVal* computes the DCF model two ways: (1) Based on the free cash flows directly to common equity holders, and (2) Based on the free cash flows to all investors. With the "all investor" approach, the common equity is valued indirectly as the entity value less the value of the debt, the value of the preferred stock claims, and the value of the minority interest claims (just like the residual income to all investors model given in the previous section). The valuation attribute that drives the DCF model, in either form, is free cash flow. Chapter 6 describes in detail how this amount can be computed in several different, yet equivalent, ways. These derivations are shown in *eVal* on the Cash Flow Analysis sheet. We will give a few formulas for free cash flows here, but we refer you back to Chapter 6 for the details.

DCF to Common Equity

The *free cash flow to common equity* is the primary building block for all our valuation models. It is the net cash distributions to equity holders, labeled D_t. We can compute this amount directly as cash dividends plus stock repurchases less equity issuances. Alternatively, we can use the clean surplus relation and compute D_t based on net income and the change in common equity. That is, the clean surplus relation in accrual accounting requires that

$$CE_t = CE_{t-1} + NI_t - D_t.$$

Rearranging this expression gives

$$D_t = NI_t - (CE_t - CE_{t-1}).$$

This is the cash flow that ultimately determines the value of a common equity claim. Discounting these flows at the cost of equity capital gives us the mother of all valuation models, the *DCF to Common Equity Model,* shown formally as

$$P_e = \sum_{t=1}^{\infty} \frac{D_t}{(1 + r_e)^t},$$

where

P_e is the value of the common equity,

D_t is the net cash distributions to common equity holders, and

r_e is the cost of equity capital.

Your forecasted financial statements describe net income and common equity forever into the future. From these amounts, we compute D_t and discount these flows at rate r_e. Nothing could be simpler, really. The knock on this model is that it is hard to develop much intuition for future D_t flows. D_t is the distribution of wealth to equity holders, which typically happens much later than the actual creation of wealth. Further, past D_t is a poor predictor of future D_t, so you really need to rely on the financial statements to derive forecasts of future D_t. Extrapolation alone won't get you very far.

Since all four of the valuation models we discuss in this chapter are algebraically equivalent, it is hard to argue which of the models is the "original version." Nonetheless, this model is probably the first, most basic, expression of the value of an equity security. The formal derivations of the other models typically start here.[2] Figure 10.3 illustrates the DCF valuation to common equity for Kohl's as of January 31, 2010. To see this in *eVal*, go to the DCF Valuations sheet (after changing the valuation date to January 31, 2010 on the Valuation Parameters sheet). The figure illustrates the computation of net distributions to common equity holders, labeled as the Free Cash Flow to Common Equity,

---

[2]It takes little work to derive the residual income model from the DCF to common equity model. Start with the DCF model and write D_t as $NI_t - (CE_t - CE_{t-1})$. For each future date, substitute for NI_t the value $RI_t + r_e CE_{t-1}$. The first term in the summation (when $t = 1$) is $(1 + r_e)^{-1}[RI_1 + r_e CE_0 - CE_1 + CE_0] = CE_0 + (1 + r_e)^{-1}RI_1 - (1 + r_e)^{-1}CE_1$. The second term in the summation (when $t = 2$) is $(1 + r_e)^{-2}[RI_2 + r_e CE_1 - CE_2 + CE_1] = (1 + r_e)^{-2}RI_2 + (1 + r_e)^{-1}CE_1 - (1 + r_e)^{-2}CE_2$. Adding these two terms together gives $CE_0 + (1 + r_e)^{-1}RI_1 + (1 + r_e)^{-2}RI_2 - (1 + r_e)^{-2}CE_2$. As you can see, we are building the residual income model term by term. Every time we add another term in the summation we add in the appropriately discounted RI_t term and cancel the last term in the previous sum. Since the summation is infinite, the last term is pushed out infinitely far into the future, and hence has zero present value.

FIGURE 10.3   **Discounted Cash Flows to Common Equity for Kohl's**
Valuation based on *eVal* defaults as of January 31, 2010.

DCF Valuations	($000)			
Company Name	KOHL'S CORP			
Most Recent Fiscal Year End	10-01-31			
Date of Valuation	10-01-31			
Cost of Common Equity	10.00%			
Terminal Growth Rate	3.00%			
Fiscal Year of Forecast	11-01-31	12-01-31	13-01-31	14-01-31
Valuation to Common Equity				
Free Cash Flow to Common Equity	681,779	724,931	769,408	815,126
Present Value of FCF	619,799	599,117	578,067	556,742
Present Value Beyond 10 Years	6,392,730			
Present Value of First 10 Years	5,241,733			
Forecast Equity Value Before Time Adj.	11,634,463			
Forecasted Value as of Valuation Date	12,216,186			
Less Value of Contingent Equity Claims	0			
Value Attributable to Common Equity	12,216,186			
Common Shares Outstanding at BS Date	307,000			
Equivalent Shares at Valuation Date	307,000			
Forecast Price/Share	$39.79			

$$= NI_1 - (CE_1 - CE_0)$$
$$= 1,046,887$$
$$- (8,218,108 - 7,853,000)$$

$$= 724,931/(1+.10)^2$$

$$= 681,779/(1+.10)^1$$

and a few present value computations for individual years. For details on the computation of free cash flow to common equity, we refer you to Chapter 6, and to the Cash Flow Analysis sheet in *eVal*. The present value for the first 10 years is added to the present value for all years after year 10 to arrive at the Forecast Equity Value Before Time Adjustments. The details of the present value computations and the time adjustments are discussed in a later section. Note that the final result, before time adjustments, is $11,634,463 thousand, exactly the same result we reached using the residual income models.

DCF to All Investors

When someone in practice says "the DCF model," this is the model they typically have in mind. This model is the warhorse of MBA programs. Unfortunately, because the computation of the *free cash flow to all investors* is rather involved, and because "all investors" models require a weighted-average cost of capital that anticipates future tax rates and leverage ratios, it is the rare user who can successfully compute the DCF to all investors model without error. By automating the required computations, *eVal* makes sure you don't mess up along the way.

Because of the long history this model has enjoyed, a number of different ways to compute the free cash flow to all investors have emerged. We summarize two methods here; we refer you to Chapter 6 for more detailed explanations or to the Cash Flow Analysis sheet in *eVal* for an example using Kohl's for the year ended January 31, 2010. The free cash flow to all investors, denoted here as C_t, is computed most directly as

$$C_t = NOI_t - (NOA_t - NOA_{t-1}).$$

In words, the free cash flow to all investors equals the net operating income less the increase in net operating assets. This should feel right. All investors together claim the cash flows that emanate from the use of the net operating assets. Free cash flow differs from NOI_t because accrual accounting recognizes some NOI_t dollars that are not yet cash dollars, which necessarily means they are still in NOA_t. Subtracting the increase in NOA_t from NOI_t leaves us with the cash that the entity generated from its operations over the period.

You can also compute the free cash flows directly from data given on the statement of cash flows. Just ask yourself, what cash went to each investor group? The company sent equity holders the net distribution D_t (i.e., common dividends plus stock repurchases less equity issuances). The firm sent debt holders interest, and less any increase in principle, denoted ΔL_t. Similarly, the firm sent preferred stockholders preferred dividends PD_t less any new issuances, denoted ΔPS_t; and the firm sent the minority interests MIE_t less any increase in the minority interest balance, denoted ΔMI_t. Finally, recall that convention dictates that we exclude the cash taxes saved from the tax deductibility of interest from C_t (instead, reflecting these cash flows in the form of a lower after tax cost of debt). Putting it all together, we have:

$$C_t = D_t + I_t - \Delta L + PD_t - \Delta PS_t + MIE_t - \Delta MI_t - tx_t I_t.$$

If you suffer from insomnia and enjoy the finger exercises that only algebra can provide, you can show that this expression for C_t equals the previous one.[3]

Armed with the free cash flow to all investors C_t, we can now compute the *entity value*—the value of the operations to all investors before distinguishing between claimants. Denoting the weighted-average cost of capital as r_w and the entity value as P_f, we have

$$P_f = \sum_{t=1}^{\infty} \frac{C_t}{(1 + r_w)^t}$$

and, yes, this version of P_f is exactly equal to the P_f computed using the residual income to all investors model shown in the previous section. To compute the value of the common equity claim, we subtract from P_f the value of the debt P_d, the preferred stock claim P_{ps} and the minority interest claim P_{mi}. In the spirit of discounting cash flows, each of these non-common-equity claims is itself valued based on the cash flows it receives. Denoting the pre-tax cost of debt as r_d, the cost of preferred stock as r_{ps}, and the cost of minority interests as r_{mi}, we have

$$P_d = \sum_{t=1}^{\infty} \frac{(I_t - \Delta L_t)}{(1 + r_d)^t}$$

$$P_{ps} = \sum_{t=1}^{\infty} \frac{(PD_t - \Delta PS_t)}{(1 + r_{ps})^t}$$

[3]Here is the proof. By definition $NOI_t = NI_t + I_t(1 - tx_t) + PD_t + MIE_t$ and $\Delta NOA_t = \Delta CE_t + \Delta L_t + \Delta PS_t + \Delta MI_t$. Substitute these expressions for NOI_t and $(NOA_t - NOA_{t-1})$ in the first C_t expression. Next, note that by the clean surplus relation $NI_t = D_t + \Delta CE_t$. Substitute this in for NI_t, cancel the plus and minus ΔCE_t and you have the second expression for C_t.

and

$$P_{mi} = \sum_{t=1}^{\infty} \frac{(MIE_t - \Delta MI_t)}{(1 + r_{mi})^t}.$$

The values of P_d, P_{ps}, and P_{mi} computed based on their respective future cash flows are exactly the same as their values computed in the previous section based on residual income flows. Putting it all together, we compute the value of the common equity as:

$$P_e = P_f - P_d - P_{ps} - P_{mi},$$

just as in the previous section. Finally, we can mix and match between the residual income model and the discounted cash flow model. For instance, it is not uncommon to compute the value of the debt P_d or the value of the preferred stock using a residual income model, with the added assumption that all future residual flows to these claimants are zero. In other words, the value of the debt and the value of the preferred stock are simply assumed to equal their current book values, L_0 and PS_0, respectively.

Figure 10.4 illustrates the DCF valuation to all investors for Kohl's as of January 31, 2010 using the default *eVal* forecasts. To see this in *eVal*, go to the DCF Valuations sheet and scroll down (and set the valuation date to

FIGURE 10.4 Discounted Cash Flows to All Investors for Kohl's
Valuation based on *eVal* defaults as of January 31, 2010.

Fiscal Year of Forecast	11-01-31	12-01-31
Valuation All Investors		
Cost of Net Debt	8.00%	
Cost of Preferred Stock	9.00%	
Cost of Minority Interest	10.00%	= 40,902/(1+.08)¹
After Tax Weighted Average Cost of Capital	9.37%	
Free Cash Flow to Debt	40,902	46,257
Present Value of FCF to Debt	37,872	39,658
Value of Debt	1,438,346	
Free Cash Flow to Preferred Stock	0	0
Present Value of FCF to Preferred Stock	0	0
Value of Preferred Stock	0	= 46,257/(1+.08)²
Free Cash Flow to Minority Interest	0	0
Present Value of FCF to Minority Interest	0	0
Value of Minority Interest	0	= 717,314/(1+.0937)²
Free Cash Flows to Investors	671,158	717,314
Present Value of FCF to Investors	613,646	599,647
Entity Value	13,072,809	
Less Value of Net Debt	(1,438,346)	
Less Value of Preferred Stock	0	
Less Value of Minority Interest	0	
Forecast Equity Value Before Time Adj.	11,634,463	

Annotations: "= Int. Expense – increase in Debt = 137,049 – 96,147"; "= NOI – increase in NOA = 1,132,413 – 461,255 taken from Cash Flow Analysis sheet"; "sum of present values of FCF to Investors".

January 31, 2010 on the Valuation Parameters sheet). The figure shows the free cash flows each period to debt and then the free cash flows to all investors (preferred stock and minority interests are zero at Kohl's). Note that the value of debt, the value of preferred stock, and the entity value are each computed using a different discount rate. In particular, the entity value is computed using the weighted average cost of capital of 9.372157 percent. Recall that this rate was derived by *eVal* (with your help) by equating the directly-computed equity value with its indirectly computed counterpart. Note also that the result of $11,634,463 thousand, labeled as the Forecast Equity Value Before Time Adjustment, is exactly the same result as for the other three valuation models.

Tax Shield on Interest

Just as in the residual income to all investors model, the DCF to all investors reflects the cash tax savings from the tax deductibility of interest through a lower cost of debt. Free cash flow to all investors, C_t, is computed as:

$$C_t = D_t + I_t - \Delta L + PD_t - \Delta PS_t + MIE_t - \Delta MI_t - tx_t.I_t.$$

Notice that $tx_t.I_t$, *the tax shield on interest*, is explicitly backed out of C_t. Figure 10.5 shows the cash flows that are being discounted to estimate P_e, P_{ps}, P_{mi}, and P_d. How, then, can the sum of P_e, P_{ps}, P_{mi}, and P_d equal the entity value P_f, which excludes the tax shield? The answer is that the value of the tax shield is incorporated into the entity value through the lower discount rate r_w. Recall from Chapter 9 that the weighted-average cost of capital is a mix of the cost of equity r_e, the cost of preferred stock r_{ps}, the cost of minority interests r_{mi}, and the *after-tax* cost of debt $(1 - tx)r_d$. Using the after-tax cost of debt lowers the weighted-average cost of capital, which raises the present value of the C_t flows in the P_f formula. For more information, see the associated discussion on the tax shield on interest in section 10.2.

Figure 10.6 summarizes all four of the valuation models. To fit everything on one page, we have assumed there is no minority interest. As you may have noticed by now, minority interests get treated exactly like preferred stock in

FIGURE 10.5 **The Variables in Each DCF Valuation Equation**

entity value		common equity value		preferred stock value		minority interest		debt value	tax shield
P_f	$=$	P_e	$+$	P_{ps}	$+$	P_{mi}	$+$	P_d	
cash flows		cash flows		cash flows		cash flows		cash flows	cash flows
C_t	$=$	D_t	$+$	$PD_t - \Delta PS_t$	$+$	$MIE_t - \Delta MI_t$	$+$	$I_t - \Delta L_t$	$-$ $tx_t I_t$

discounted using

| r_w | | r_e | | r_{ps} | | r_{mi} | | r_d | |

weighted average of r_e, r_{ps}, r_{mi}, and $(1 - tx)r_d$ ⟵ value of $tx_t I_t$ is incorporated into entity value by using $(1 - tx)r_d$ in r_w computation.

FIGURE 10.6 **Summary of Valuation Equations (if minority interests present treat exactly like preferred stock)**

	Equity Valued Directly as P_e	Equity Valued Indirectly as $P_e = P_f - P_d - P_{ps}$		
	Value of Common Equity P_e	Value of Whole Entity P_f	Value of Debt P_d	Value of Preferred Stock P_{ps}
Residual Income Cash Flows	$\sum\limits_{t=1}^{T-1} \dfrac{D_t}{(1+r_e)^t} + \dfrac{D_T}{(r_e - g)(1 + r_e)^{T-1}}$	$\sum\limits_{t=1}^{T-1} \dfrac{C_t}{(1+r_w)^t} + \dfrac{C_T}{(r_w - g)(1 + r_w)^{T-1}}$	$\sum\limits_{t=1}^{T-1} \dfrac{I_t - \Delta L_t}{(1+r_d)^t} + \dfrac{I_T - \Delta L_T}{(r_d - g)(1 + r_d)^{T-1}}$	$\sum\limits_{t=1}^{T-1} \dfrac{PD_t - \Delta PS_t}{(1+r_{ps})^t} + \dfrac{PD_T - \Delta PS_T}{(r_{ps} - g)(1 + r_{ps})^{T-1}}$
Valuation Attribute	$CE_0 + \sum\limits_{t=1}^{T-1} \dfrac{RI_t}{(1+r_e)^t} + \dfrac{RI_T}{(r_e - g)(1 + r_e)^{T-1}}$ where $RI_t = NI_t - r_e CE_{t-1}$	$NOA_0 + \sum\limits_{t=1}^{T-1} \dfrac{RNOI_t}{(1+r_w)^t} + \dfrac{RNOI_T}{(r_w - g)(1 + r_w)^{T-1}}$ where $RNOI_t = NOI_t - r_w NOA_{t-1}$	$L_0 + \sum\limits_{t=1}^{T-1} \dfrac{RIT_t}{(1+r_d)^t} + \dfrac{RIT_T}{(r_d - g)(1 + r_d)^{T-1}}$ where $RIT_t = I_t - r_d L_{t-1}$	$PS_0 + \sum\limits_{t=1}^{T-1} \dfrac{RPD_t}{(1+r_{ps})^t} + \dfrac{RPD_T}{(r_{ps} - g)(1 + r_{ps})^{T-1}}$ where $RPD_t = PD_t - r_{ps} PS_{t-1}$

D_t is cash flow to common equity; $CE_t = CE_{t-1} + NI_t - D_t$
C_t is cash flow to all investors; $C_t = NOI_t - \Delta NOA_t$
L_t is the debt balance at time t
CE_t is the shareholders' equity at time t; $NOA_t - L_t - PS_t = CE_t$
NOI_t is the operating income for the period ending at time t, net of tax
I_t is the interest expense for the period ending at time t,
NI_t is the net income for the period ending at time t;
$\quad NI_t = NOI_t - (1 - tx)I_t - PD_t$
NOA_t is the net operating asset balance at time t

PD_t is preferred dividend at time t
PS_t is preferred stock balance at time t
r_e is the cost of equity capital
r_d is the cost of debt capital
r_{ps} is the cost of preferred stock capital
r_w is the average cost of capital:
$$r_w = \frac{r_e P_e + (1 - tx)r_d P_d + r_p P_{ps}}{P_e + P_d + P_{ps}}$$

all respects and so, at this point, you should be able to add them to the table yourself. The columns in Figure 10.6 describe what is being valued—the equity, the debt, or the preferred stock—and the rows describe which valuation attribute is being used—free cash flow or residual income. To compute the infinite sum of flows, each expression makes use of the perpetuity formula discussed in the next section.

10.4   PRESENT VALUE COMPUTATIONS

All four of the valuation models given above compute value as the present value of an infinite series of flows of the valuation attribute, either residual income or free cash flow. Since it is impossibly time consuming to compute the present value of an infinite series on a term by term basis, all valuation models compute the present value term by term up to the *terminal year* and then compute the present value beyond the terminal year using the formula for a growing perpetuity. In case you have forgotten, the present value of a growing perpetuity of payments, starting with K after one year and growing at rate g forever after, discounted at rate r, is given by the following formula

$$\frac{K}{(1+r)} + \frac{(1+g)K}{(1+r)^2} + \frac{(1+g)^2K}{(1+r)^3} + \frac{(1+g)^3K}{(1+r)^4} + \cdots\cdots = \frac{K}{r-g}.$$

The left-hand side of the formula shows the sequence of terms that continue in perpetuity in the present value computation and the right-hand side of the formula shows the simplified result.

Before the terminal year, your forecasts can be as erratic as you like. Each year's forecasts will imply a flow of valuation attributes, however unusual, and the model will compute the present value of each year's flow. However, starting with the terminal year, your forecasts are constrained to behave in a more predictable manner. Sales growth is fixed at the rate you input into *eVal* in the terminal year and this becomes the *g* in the perpetuity formula. Profit margins, asset turnovers, and leverage ratios also are assumed to remain constant after the terminal year. These forecasts project financial statements forever into the future, and they are financial statements that will generate residual income flows and free cash flows that will grow forever at rate *g*. Once everything is safely growing at this known rate, we can compute the present value of the subsequent flows using the formula given above.

In previous chapters, we noted that your terminal growth forecast should not exceed the discount rate; otherwise, the present value is infinite. In terms of the formula given above, if *g* is greater than *r*, then the result is negative. You shouldn't try to attach any meaning to this, as the formula is simply undefined when *g* exceeds *r*.

Let's use the growing perpetuity formula to rewrite the residual income to common equity model. The model given earlier is

$$P_e = CE_0 + \sum_{t=1}^{\infty}(1 + r_e)^{-t}RI_t.$$

Now suppose that, starting in year *T*, the financial statement forecasts imply that residual income will be RI_T and then grow at rate *g* forever after. We can now compute the present value as

$$P_e = CE_0 + \sum_{t=1}^{T-1}(1 + r_e)^{-t}RI_t + \frac{RI_T}{(r_e - g)(1 + r_e)^{T-1}}.$$

The first two terms are the present value for years 1 through *T* − 1 and the last term is the present value for year *T* and forever after. To apply the formula for a growing perpetuity in this setting, you need to think carefully about when the different residual income flows take place. The residual income in year *T* is RI_T; it is $RI_T(1 + g)$ in year *T* + 1, and so on, growing forever at rate *g*. If we were standing in year *T* − 1 and wanted to compute the present value of this growing perpetuity, we would apply the formula and get

$$\frac{RI_T}{(r_e - g)}.$$

But we want the present value at time 0, not time *T* − 1, so we need to discount back *T* − 1 more years. To do this we divide by $(1 + r_e)^{T-1}$, as shown in the denominator of the last term of our modified formula.

All of the other valuation models handle the present value computations exactly the same way. After the financial statement forecasts become sufficiently stable, insofar as they imply a constant growth rate in future free cash flows and residual income flows, the perpetuity formula kicks in to compute the remaining present value. As a summary, Figure 10.6 gives the precise definition of each model.

So what is the appropriate horizon for *T*, the terminal year? In *eVal*, it is always 11 years. This may not seem like the most obvious choice, so let us explain. On the Forecasting Assumptions sheet, you have 10 years of year-by-year forecasts followed by the terminal year in the next column. You can make your forecasts settle down to a stable growth rate before the terminal year but *eVal* assumes that after 10 years, all relationships stabilize and all balance sheet and income statement line items grow at the terminal sales growth rate. In general, you should try to make your forecasting assumptions converge to their steady state values as you approach the terminal year. Because the terminal value calculation is important, yet tedious, we let *eVal* handle the calculation.

Adjusting the Present Value to the Present

Figure 10.7 illustrates *eVal*'s present value computations for the DCF to common equity and the residual income to common equity models. The amounts are from Kohl's, valued as of January 31, 2010 using the default forecasting settings. Consider the DCF to common equity, shown in the top panel. *eVal* adds the present value of the first 10 years and present value beyond 10 years

FIGURE 10.7

Kohl's Present Value Computations
Valuation based on *eVal* defaults as of January 31, 2010.

Valuation to Common Equity	
Free Cash Flow to Common Equity	681,779
Present Value of FCF	619,799
Present Value Beyond 10 Years	6,392,730
Present Value of First 10 Years	5,241,733
Forecast Equity Value Before Time Adj.	11,634,463
Forecasted Value as of Valuation Date	12,216,186
Less Value of Contingent Equity Claims	0
Value Attributable to Common Equity	12,216,186
Common Shares Outstanding at BS Date	307,000
Equivalent Shares at Valuation Date	307,000
Forecast Price/Share	**$39.79**
Valuation to Common Equity	
Net Income	1,046,887
Common Equity at Beginning of Year	7,853,000
Residual Income	261,587
Present Value of Residual Income	237,806
Present Value Beyond 10 Years	1,951,370
Present Value of First 10 Years	1,830,093
Common Equity as of	
10-01-31	7,853,000
Forecast Equity Value Before Time Adj.	11,634,463
Forecasted Value as of Valuation Date	12,216,186
Less Value of Contingent Equity Claims	0
Value Attributable to Common Equity	12,216,186
Common Shares Outstanding at BS Date	307,000
Equivalent Shares at Valuation Date	307,000
Forecast Price/Share	**$39.79**

to arrive at the forecast equity value before time adjustment. Comparing the two amounts shows that a little less than half of the total value of the cash flows arrives in the first 10 years. But now compare this to the residual income model shown directly below. The residual income model also shows values for the first 10 years and beyond 10 years, but they aren't the same as for the DCF model. In particular, the value beyond 10 years is much smaller and, if we consider the value of common equity as of January 31, 2010 as part of the value during the first 10 years, then the residual income model shows a significantly greater portion of value arriving much earlier than the DCF model. Both models arrive at the same forecast equity value before time adjustment. So why do they allocate the value differently across time? The answer reveals a fundamental difference in the way the two models characterize value creation. The residual income model counts the balance of common equity as value already created and counts net income as value already earned, regardless of the actual cash flow. The DCF model, in contrast, waits for the actual cash to arrive. Another way to say this is that the DCF treats investment as a consumption of value (cash is leaving the firm) while the residual income model treats investment as a store of value (assets are put on the books). The two models ultimately get to the same total value because they are based on the same underlying financial statement forecasts, but they differ drastically on when they count value as being created.

Regardless of which model you are working with, it is useful to think about when the model says that value is being created. In most cases, you are probably more confident about your forecasts during the first 10 years than you are about your forecasts beyond 10 years, so if most of the value is concentrated more than 10 years away, then you might be less confident in your valuation. Are we more confident in the residual income model than in the DCF model because it records valuation creation sooner? The answer is absolutely not. One model can be derived algebraically from the other and so it would be silly to be more confident of the left-hand side of an equation than the right-hand side. Whatever uncertainty you have in your forecasts about book value and net income translate into exactly the same amount of uncertainty in future net distributions to common equity holders.[4]

So far we have discussed the present value calculations as of the end of the fiscal year for the most recent financial statements, which is January 31, 2010 in the Kohl's example, and have worked our way down Figure 10.7 to the line labeled Forecast Equity Value Before Time Adjustment. There are two more present value adjustments that take us to the next line, labeled Forecasted Value as of Valuation Date. First, the present value computation treats the cash flows and residual income flows as though they are realized on the last day of each fiscal year. In reality, wealth is created and distributed somewhat

---

[4]Lundholm and O'Keefe (2001) provide careful discussion of this issue, along with a list of common errors in the implementation of each model that generate apparent, but not real, differences between the residual income model and DCF models.

more evenly throughout the year. To correct for this, we multiply the value estimate by $(1 + r_e/2)$. This effectively moves the flows forward six months in time. Second, you will typically want to compute the value as of the day you are considering the stock, not the last day of the last fiscal year. You can enter whatever valuation date you like on *eVal*'s Valuation Parameters sheet; the default is your computer's current date. *eVal* then computes the fraction of the year (ρ) between the entered date and the fiscal year end, and accordingly adjusts the value estimate by $(1 + r_e \times \rho)$ to get the present value as of the inputted date. This adjusts your valuation estimate for the passage of time between the last set of financial statements and the date selected. As time passes, you get closer to the estimated future values, so the present value increases. In the Kohl's example shown in Figure 10.7 we set the valuation date to be the same as the fiscal year end. Consequently the only time value adjustment is to multiply 11,634,463 by $(1 + .10/2)$ to get 12,216,186 as the Forecasted Value as of Valuation Date. If you go to the Valuation Parameters Sheet and change the valuation date to a later date, say November 11, 2010, then this is 78.056 percent of the way through the next fiscal year, so the value increases further to

$$12,216,186 \times (1 + .10 \times (.78056)) = 13,169,728.$$

Solving for the Implied Cost of Equity Capital

So far we have input our estimate of the cost of equity capital and then solved for the value of the equity by discounting the cash flows or residual income flows using this estimate. But we can change the order of things. We could ask what discount rate equates the present value of our forecasts with the currently observed stock price. For example, if we start with the default forecasts for Kohl's and a valuation date of January 31, 2010, and discount at 10 percent, we get the $39.79/share value as shown in Figures 10.1 and 10.3. But Kohl's stock price at close on January 31, 2010 was $50.37. What discount rate would reconcile with this price? A bit of guesswork on the Valuation Parameter's sheet shows that setting the cost of equity capital to 8.548 percent would produce $50.37 in estimated value. (Go ahead, try it yourself!) This means that if investors' expectations at January 31, 2010 are the same as the default *eVal* forecasts, and the market is efficient (meaning that the price of $50.37 per share is "correct"), then investors should expect to earn an 8.548 percent return on their Kohl's investment. They may not earn this return every year—in fact, even if the future cash flows materialize exactly as the *eVal* forecasts predict, all the model says for sure is that the annualized return over the life of the firm will be 8.548 percent. If 8.548 percent strikes you as an unreasonably low return for an investment as risky as Kohl's, then effectively you are saying that investors' beliefs are more optimistic than the *eVal* defaults or the market price for Kohl's stock is too high.

There is one cautionary note we need to offer before turning you loose with the implied cost of capital. If your forecasts imply that the future net cash distributions to equity alternate between positive and negative, then it is possible for there to be more than one discount rate that equates the value of the future cash flows with the price. Without getting into the algebra behind this claim, the "correct" value is typically the one closest to whatever you believe the true cost of equity capital to be. As with all things in equity analysis and valuation, if the result looks unreasonable, then it probably is.

10.5 VALUING CONTINGENT CLAIMS AND OTHER ADJUSTMENTS

Valuing Contingent Claims

The value of *contingent claims* represents your estimate of the value of other potential claims on the future net cash distributions to equity holders that are not accounted for in the financial statements. These can include outstanding stock warrants, conversion options in debt issues, and outstanding employee stock options. They all give their holders the option to purchase new shares of stockholders' equity at a price that may be less than intrinsic value. These contingent claims therefore have value, and this value must be deducted from the value of common equity that we have already computed in order to figure out what is left for the existing common equity holders. Intuitively, these contingent claims give their holders the opportunity to get a share of the future net cash distributions to equity if the future works out well, but allows the holders to walk away if things turn out badly. Estimating the value of these contingent claims can be quite complicated. We will describe how to compute a lower bound for this value, how to approximate it more accurately using the Black-Scholes option pricing model, and then discuss limitations of each of these approaches.

At this point, we are trying to estimate the value of existing contingent claims; Chapter 12 confronts the related issue of estimating the value of contingent claims that we expect to be issued in the future. We will focus on estimating the value of existing employee stock options; the other types of contingent claims can be estimated in a similar fashion. Start by reading the firm's financial statement footnote on employee stock options. Here, they tell you the number of options outstanding in different ranges of option exercise prices. If any options' exercise prices are lower than the current market price of the stock, then these options are worth *at least* the difference between these two amounts. The holder could hypothetically buy shares at the exercise price, and then turn around and sell them at the current market price. In other words, the option is *in the money* by the difference between these two amounts. But this only represents a lower bound on the value of the option, because it doesn't account for the possibility that the stock price might increase even more before the option expires. How likely this is to occur depends on the remaining time before expiration of the option, the volatility in the stock price, and a few other details. There are a number of models for valuing options that take these things into account. The most popular is the Black-Scholes option pricing model, which requires the following inputs:

S is the current stock price,

K is the exercise or "strike" price,

y is the long-term forecasted annual dividend yield,

r is the annual risk-free interest rate,

t is the number of years before the option expires,

σ is the annual standard deviation of the log of the stock price, and

$N(\bullet)$ is the cumulative standard normal distribution function.

The Black-Scholes formula is then:

$$Option\ Value = Se^{-yt}\ N(d_1) - Ke^{-rt}\ N(d_2)$$

where

$$d_1 = \frac{\ln\left(\frac{S}{K}\right) + \left(r - y + \frac{\sigma^2}{2}\right)t}{\sigma\sqrt{t}} \text{ and } d_2 = d_1 - \sigma\sqrt{t}.$$

Without attempting to derive the specific form of this model, we offer some observations about it. First, note that the option's value increases with the gap between the current stock price S and the option's exercise price K. The deeper the option is in the money, the more valuable it is. Second, the option's value increases with t, the number of years remaining before the option expires, and with σ, the stock price volatility. Third, the option value decreases with the dividend yield y because future dividends decrease the future stock price, all else equal. Actually evaluating this formula by hand would be quite difficult because the function $N(\bullet)$ is itself quite complicated. Instead, we need a calculator. Fortunately, such calculators are readily available on the Internet; we recommend the ones available at http://www.money-zine.com/Calculators or http://www.maxi-pedia.com.

Most of the inputs to the contingent claims calculator are straightforward, but the one that you may not have a good feel for is the annual standard deviation of the log of the stock price. A good source for this data item is the employee stock option footnote. Companies provide an estimate of this amount because they are required to estimate the value of options issued to employees during the current fiscal year. A ballpark figure is 30 percent, but it can range from 20 percent for a large stable company to over 50 percent for a small growth company.

A problem with using the Black-Scholes option valuation model is that real world contingent claims may not conform to its restrictive assumptions. In particular, it has been shown that employees overwhelmingly exercise their options well before expiration. This doesn't make sense, from the model's point of view, because the option still has additional value right up to the expiration date. But an employee may exercise early to lock in existing gains and eliminate any risk. This means that the Black-Scholes estimates might be too high. This particular problem can be mitigated by reducing the time to expiration, t, to approximate the anticipated exercise date.

Adjusting for Stock Splits and Stock Dividends

In order to estimate intrinsic value per share and earnings per share, *eVal* uses the number of shares outstanding at the most recent balance sheet date. If the firm has undertaken a stock split or a *stock* dividend (as opposed to a *cash* dividend) between the date of the most recent balance sheet and your valuation date, then you need to adjust the number of shares outstanding by inputting a *dilution factor* on the *eVal* Valuation Parameters sheet. The adjustment factor is simply the ratio of the number of shares outstanding immediately after the split/dividend to the number of shares outstanding immediately before the split/dividend. For example, if your firm does a two-for-one stock split, then the number of shares outstanding doubles, resulting in a dilution factor of two. If we failed to account for the split, then our per-share valuation estimate and all of our EPS forecasts would be twice what they should be. Imagine the embarrassment from such a mistake! To see a list of recent splits for a company, go to Yahoo! Finance, type the company's ticker, and select the Chart option under More Info. You only have to adjust for splits/dividends between the date of the most recent balance sheet loaded into *eVal* and the valuation date that you input on the Valuation Parameters worksheet. Don't adjust for any splits made before the most recent balance sheet date or after your valuation date.

What if the firm issues new shares for cash, or as part of the acquisition of another company after the last balance sheet date? Interestingly, you do not need to adjust for these *if* you believe the shares were issued at their true intrinsic value. In a stock split or stock dividend, the number of shares increases but nothing of economic value is added to the firm, so adjusting the number of shares completely captures the effect of this event. However, if the firm receives something of economic value in exchange for the shares, then the value of the firm increases along with the number of shares. If the new shares are issued at a price equal to their intrinsic value, then the increase in firm value exactly offsets the dilution caused by the increase in the number of shares. To make this perfectly clear, imagine a firm that consists of $100 in a bank account and has one share outstanding, so its intrinsic value is $100 per share. If the firm issues another share for $100 and deposits it in the bank, the firm is now worth $200 and has two shares, so it is still worth $100 per share. Complications arise, however, if the firm issues the stock at $90 or $110. We address these complications in Chapter 12.

The last stock split for Kohl's was in April 2000, well before the last balance sheet date in our model (January 31, 2010), so we don't need to adjust the number of shares in our computations for a valuation after this date.

Putting It All Together

The valuation formulas given in the first part of the chapter compute the present value as of the most recent fiscal year end, assuming that all cash flows and residual income flows happen on the last day of each year. We then adjusted this value up by a half-year's worth of time value, because the flows typically happen evenly throughout the year, not on the last day. We also adjusted the value up to the date that we are actually doing the valuation (or whatever date we want), rather than the end of the most recent fiscal year. We then subtract the value of any contingent claims and adjust the number of shares for any stock splits or stock dividends that occurred between the fiscal year end and the valuation date. The final result is our forecast of the intrinsic price per share. This is what we think the stock is really worth.

For Kohl's as of a valuation date of January 31, 2010, the final result using the default *eVal* forecasts is $39.79/share. If we instead use the forecasts that we developed in Chapter 8, the estimated value is $52.63/share. The actual price of Kohl's on January 31, 2010 was $50.37/share. That is, our detailed forecasts imply that Kohl's is undervalued by $2.26/share, which isn't too far off the mark. Alternatively, the cost of capital implied by our detailed forecasts and the current market price is 10.302 percent. The Model Summary sheet in *eVal* gives a quick snapshot of the firm's historical performance, the profitability and growth implications of your detailed forecasts, and the resulting price-per-share estimate. It also shows the market-to-book and price-to-earnings ratios that are implied by your valuation; these ratios are discussed in the next chapter.

If the value estimate is ridiculously far from the current market price and you feel reasonably confident in your forecasts, here are a few things to check. First, are you sure you have the correct number of shares outstanding? If there was a stock split after the fiscal year end, then you may be way off in your estimate. In this respect, remember that firms sometimes do reverse splits, whereby each stockholder has to give back their shares, getting fewer in return. So make sure that what you first thought was a 10:1 stock split was not a 1:10 reverse split. Second, what if the estimated price is negative? Literally, a negative price means that you would pay this amount to *not* have to own the stock. We allow *eVal* to arrive at this conclusion if it is the logical implication of your forecasts related inputs, but we don't really expect you to get out your checkbook and send the firm money. If the estimated price is negative, it means that the present value of the cash flows that the equity holders are forecasted to send *to* the firm is greater than the present value of the cash flows that the equity holders are forecasted to receive *from* the firm. If this was literally true, then an equity holder might indeed be willing to pay to not have to own the stock. But since the firm can't force the equity holders to keep sending it money, and since equity holders are not liable to third parties for the firm's losses, the real lower bound on price is zero. If you really think the firm has positive value, you need to revise your forecasts accordingly. Negative stock prices are discussed in more detail in Chapter 12.

10.6   CASES, LINKS, AND REFERENCES

Cases

- Apple and the iFad (Questions 11–12)
- EnCom Corporation (Stage 3)
- Four Valuation Models—One Value
- Evaluating Intel's Earnings Torpedo
- Netflix, Inc. (Questions 13–15)
- Overstock.com (Questions 14–17)
- Can Salton Swing? (Questions 5 and 6)
- Sirius Satellite Radio, Inc. (Questions 19–21)
- Building *eVal* (Part E)
- The 80-Minute Valuation

Links

- Yahoo! Finance: http://yahoo.finance.com
- money-zine option calculator: http://www.money-zine.com/Calculators/ Investment-Calculators/Stock-Option-Calculator/
- maxi-pedia option calculator: http://www.maxi-pedia.com/Black+ Scholes+formula+option+value+calculator

References

- Lundholm, R., and T. O'Keefe. (2001). Reconciling value estimates from the discounted cash flow model and the residual income model. *Contemporary Accounting Research* 18: 311–35.

CHAPTER ELEVEN

Valuation Ratios

11.1 INTRODUCTION

In Chapter 5 we converted the financial statement data into ratios in order to reveal underlying economic properties and to make the data comparable across companies and over time. For the same reason, we can more easily compare the valuation of different companies by scaling our estimates of value by financial statement data. In this section we analyze the *market-to-book ratio*, the *price-to-earnings ratio* and the *price-to-earnings-to-growth (or PEG) ratio*, and we discuss what each ratio reveals about the market's expectations for the company's future. These ratios are commonly used summary statistics for a firm's valuation and each can be found on financial information portals, such as Morningstar or Yahoo! Finance. After we discuss each ratio we will give some historical and current benchmarks to get you grounded.

We offer a word of caution before proceeding. As we found in the last chapter, a valuation involves discounting many future years of forecast financial data. Only in very special cases is it possible to value a firm based on one or two numbers from its recent financial statements. Consequently, it is unlikely that you will be able to take a quick look at the price-to-earnings ratio or market-to-book ratio and know if a firm is mispriced. Do you really think that finding mispriced stocks is as easy as dividing one readily available number by another readily available number? Tempting as such shortcuts can be, there is no substitute for the hard work of building a detailed set of forecasts. Use these ratios as a way to make a quick assessment of the expectations built into a firm's current market price, but not as the sole basis for an investment strategy.

11.2 THE MARKET-TO-BOOK RATIO

This ratio divides the current market value of equity P_e by the book value of equity from the most recent financial statements CE_0. If we start with the residual income to common equity model and divide everything by CE_0 we get

$$\frac{P_e}{CE_0} = 1 + \sum_{t=1}^{\infty} \frac{(ROE_t - r_e)\frac{CE_{t-1}}{CE_0}}{(1 + r_e)^t}$$

where ROE_t is defined relative to beginning equity: $ROE_t = NI_t / CE_{t-1}$.

The first thing to note from this formula is that if you forecast that $ROE_t = r_e$ every period in the future then the market-to-book ratio is one. This is like a savings account; every period it earns interest at exactly its discount rate and so every period it is worth exactly the balance in the account. When firms have a market-to-book ratio greater than one, the market expects that, on average, they will earn a ROE_t higher than r_e in the future.

Note that the $\frac{CE_{t-1}}{CE_0}$ term in the numerator is the *cumulative* growth in common equity over the last $t-1$ periods. In other words, in year one it equals one, in year two it equals CE_1/CE_0, in year three it equals CE_2/CE_0 and so on. The numerator in our expression for the market-to-book ratio is therefore the firm's abnormal profitability $(ROE_t - r_e)$ times its cumulative growth in beginning book value (CE_{t-1}/CE_0). This simple observation speaks volumes about the source of value in a firm. A firm is worth more than its book value only if it is expected to have an ROE_t greater than r_e (as we keep repeating). Assuming the firm is expected to meet this profitability threshold, growth and profitability are multiplicative. This means that really high valuations come about when firms have both high profitability *and* high growth.

To give you a few reference points, suppose that ROE is forecasted to be constant forever, and equity is forecasted to grow at rate *g* forever. In this case the market-to-book ratio can be simplified to

$$\frac{P_e}{CE_0} = 1 + \frac{ROE - r_e}{r_e - g}.$$

Suppose the firm has a 10 percent cost of equity capital, a forecasted constant ROE of 20 percent and a perpetual growth rate of 5 percent. By historical standards, these would be very rosy forecasts. Using the preceding formula gives a P_e/CE_0 ratio of three. As a contrast, the market-to-book ratio for Kohl's was about eight in 2002—it has since come down to about two as of 2010. Kohl's ROE was about 20 percent in 2002, so why such a high valuation ratio back then? One reason is that their growth had been about 25 percent per year for a number of years prior to 2002, and the market must have (wrongly) expected similar growth far into the future. As we saw in Chapter 5, Kohl's did not sustain that rate of growth much past 2002; in fact, growth fell steadily each year all the way to zero in fiscal 2008. We will give lots of historical statistics later in the chapter, but as a final benchmark, the median market-to-book ratio between 1962 and 2009 for all publicly traded companies was 1.5; the bottom 25 percent were below .94 and the top 25 percent were above 2.7.

The market-to-book ratio is a very useful summary measure. It gives you a quick sense of what the market must think about the future growth and profitability of the firm. Of course, like everything else in valuation, our intuition can be thwarted by distortions in accounting. A good example of this is Kellogg, the maker of breakfast cereals (Tony the Tiger says "they're great!"). You may not think of Kellogg as a high flying, fast growing stock. And it isn't; annualized growth over the past 10 years was less than 5 percent. Nonetheless, its market-to-book ratio has been greater than nine for years! The story behind this is relatively simple. The great value of Kellogg is in its huge inventory of brands (think Rice Krispies, Cheez-Its, Pop-Tarts), yet none of this value is on Kellogg's balance sheet. Most of their brands have been developed internally over many years, and GAAP accounting doesn't capitalize internally developed intangible assets. Consequently, Kellogg's book value vastly understates its economic value, causing its ROE to bounce between 50 percent and 80 percent. If we plug a constant 60 percent ROE and a perpetual 5 percent growth rate into our simplified P_e/CE_0 model, assuming a 10 percent cost of equity capital, we get a market-to-book ratio of 13.

11.3   THE PRICE-TO-EARNINGS RATIO

This ratio divides the current market price per share by the past annual earnings-per-share, computed either as the most recent annual figure or as the sum of the past four quarters of earnings. It takes a fair bit of algebra, but you can derive the following expression from the residual income model:

$$\frac{P_e}{NI_0} = \frac{1 + r_e}{r_e}\left(1 + \sum_{t=1}^{\infty}\frac{\Delta RI_t}{(1 + r_e)^t NI_0}\right) - \frac{D_0}{NI_0}$$

where ΔRI_t is the *change in* residual income between date $t-1$ and date t, D_0 is the net distribution to common equity holders for period 0 and NI_0 is the net income for period *zero* (i.e., so that $CE_0 = CE_{-1} + NI_0 - D_0$).

To understand what this ratio measures, ignore the D_0/NI_0 term for the time being; this is the dividend payout ratio for the current year, and it is typically less than one. If $\Delta RI_t = 0$ forever (e.g., residual income is a constant) and $r_e = 10\%$ then the price-to-earnings expression reduces to $(1+r_e)/r_e = 11$. The reason the price-to-earnings ratio often differs from 11 is because of the summation term inside the brackets. Now look carefully at the summation term. It is the sum of the *changes* in residual income, scaled by the current period's net income (as opposed to the sum of the levels of residual income that you saw in the residual income model). So the price-to-earnings ratio will be greater than 11 if the market expects residual income to *grow* and it will be less than 11 if the market expects residual income to shrink (assuming a 10 percent cost of equity capital). It doesn't matter whether the *level* of residual income is positive or negative, only the direction and size of the expected change. This is very different from the market-to-book ratio, which is large only if the expected *level* of residual income is both positive and large relative to CE_0.

What will cause residual income to grow? Obviously, growth in net income will contribute to growth in residual income, but the relation is subtler than this. For *residual* income to grow, net income must grow *faster than* book value grows. This is much tougher than simply growing net income. We can better illustrate this point by stating the change in residual income in relative terms. Divide ΔRI_t by common equity at time $t-1$ to get

$$\frac{\Delta RI_t}{CE_{t-1}} = (ROE_t - ROE_{t-1}) + g_{t-1}(ROE_t - r_e)$$

where ROE_t is defined as NI_t/CE_{t-1} and g_{t-1} is the percentage growth in common equity from date t-2 to t-1. Suppose that $g_{t-1} = 0$, so that book value has not grown and the second term is zero. In this case, if the firm can deploy the existing book value more profitably, $(ROE_t - ROE_{t-1})$ will be positive and ΔRI_t will be positive. Alternatively, suppose that ROE_t is greater than r_e by a constant amount each period and that g_{t-1} is positive for all periods. In this case, the first term in brackets is zero, while the second term will be positive, reflecting the increasing scale of positive profitable investments. So the price-to-earnings ratio is increasing in the expected future change in ROE and, given that ROE_t is greater than r_e, it is also increasing in the expected growth rate in equity.

One logical benchmark for the price-to-earnings ratio that we have already discussed is to assume that residual income is a constant in perpetuity, and that the current dividend payout (D_0/NI_0) is zero, so that

$$\frac{P_e}{NI_0} = \frac{1 + r_e}{r_e}.$$

If $r_e = 10\%$ then this gives a price-to-earnings ratio of 11, as discussed above. Note that this is simply the capitalization factor for an up-front annuity. In other words, a regular cash payment of NI_0 received starting today and continuing at the end of every subsequent year would be worth 11 times NI_0.

A related benchmark is the "forward price-to-earnings ratio," defined as P_e divided by the forecasted net income for next year, NI_1. In this case, assuming subsequent residual income is a constant perpetuity (i.e., $\Delta RI_t = 0$ for $t > 1$), we get

$$P_e = CE_0 + \frac{RI_1}{r_e} = CE_0 + \frac{NI_1 - rCE_0}{r_e} = \frac{NI_1}{r_e},$$

or

$$\frac{P_e}{NI_1} = \frac{1}{r_e}.$$

If $r_e = 10\%$, then we get a price-to-forward-earnings ratio of 10.

For all companies between 1962 and 2009, the median price-to-earnings ratio was 19 and the bottom 25 percent were below 10. When NI_0 is negative, the price-to-earnings ratio isn't defined. However, we can say that these firms have "really high" price-to-earnings ratios. Imagine two firms, each with a price of $10, but one has earnings of one cent and the other has earnings of minus one cent. Which has more price per unit of earnings? While we can't quantify it, certainly the firm with the same price but less earnings has a higher relative value. On average, for all publicly traded firms between 1962 and 2009, approximately 25 percent of the firms had negative earnings, so we can loosely think of these firms as the top quartile of the price-to-earnings ratio. We will give more values for the distribution of price-to-earnings ratios in different industries in the next section.

11.4   THE PEG RATIO

We have one more valuation ratio to discuss, the PEG ratio, which stands for Price-Earnings-Growth. It is defined as follows:

$$PEG\ Ratio = \frac{price\text{--}to\text{--}earnings\ ratio}{earnings\ growth \times 100} = \frac{P_e/NI_1}{\left(\dfrac{NI_2 - NI_1}{NI_1}\right) \times 100}.$$

Note that the price-to-earnings ratio in the numerator is the forward ratio (i.e., the denominator is the forecast of next year's net income) and the forecast earnings growth rate is from one year ahead to two years ahead. The earnings growth rate may be defined over a longer period, say three to five years, but it still must be an annualized percentage. As we will explain shortly, the benchmark for the PEG ratio is one. Stocks with a PEG under one are considered undervalued and those with a PEG greater than one are considered overvalued (per the Yahoo! Education website).

This ratio is a rough heuristic. The idea is that the price-to-earnings ratio measures the amount of earnings growth that is reflected in the market price so, if we compare this ratio with forecasted earnings growth, we can see whether the market price correctly reflects the forecasted growth and thus determine whether a stock is underpriced or overpriced. This seems reasonable, but why is one the magic benchmark? Academics have searched for special cases of a more general valuation model that will make this formula true, but with only limited success. Here is one such case.

Define the forecasted *abnormal earnings* at time $t+1$ as

$$ae_{t+1} = NI_{t+1} - [NI_t + r_e (NI_t - D_t)].$$

This amount is "abnormal" in the following sense. At time $t+1$ you may reasonably expect to earn the same net income as you did at time t, plus a "normal" amount of earnings on any net income that you didn't distribute to equity holders, $r_e (NI_t - D_t)$. The amount that NI_{t+1} exceeds or falls short of this amount is therefore abnormal.

The PEG ratio follows from a valid valuation model when two conditions hold. First, net distributions to equity holders are forecasted to be zero one-year ahead (i.e., $D_1 = 0$). This implies that forecasted abnormal earnings in year two are

$$ae_2 = NI_2 - (1 + r_e)NI_1.$$

Second, forecasted net income and net dividends from year three forward are such that abnormal earnings is constant, and equal to the abnormal earnings in year two, computed assuming $D_1 = 0$. That is,

$$ae_t = ae_2 \text{ for } t \geq 2.$$

If these assumptions are met, then one can show that

$$P_e = \frac{NI_2 - NI_1}{r_e^2}.$$

Constructing the PEG ratio from this simple valuation model gives

$$\frac{P_e/NI_1}{\left(\dfrac{NI_2 - NI_1}{NI_1}\right) \times 100} = \frac{1}{r_e^2 \times 100}.$$

If r_e is 10 percent, then this gives a PEG ratio of one. And if all these assumptions hold then stocks with a PEG ratio less than one are undervalued and stocks with a PEG ratio greater than one are overvalued.

As you can see, with some work we can beat the PEG ratio back into our world of theoretically valid valuation models. But the real question is, how reasonable are the assumptions that were necessary to get the job done? We had to assume that abnormal earnings are constant forever in the future, and equal to the abnormal earnings computed based on the forecasted earnings for the next two years. We also had to assume that net distributions to equity holders are forecasted to be zero next year. Finally, for the ratio to be benchmarked at one, we needed to assume the cost of equity capital is 10 percent.

To put the underlying model that supports the PEG ratio into perspective, we can rewrite price in this special case as

$$P_e = \frac{NI_1}{r_e} + \frac{NI_2 - (1 + r_e)NI_1}{r_e^2}.$$

Note that the first term is the price we would get if we assumed that the forward price-to-earnings ratio is a constant (i.e., $P_e = NI_1/r_e$). In the previous section we showed that a constant forward price-to-earnings ratio occurs when residual income is a constant perpetuity (i.e., $NI_t - r_e CE_{t-1}$ is constant for all t). The model supporting the PEG ratio adds to this a bonus for abnormal earnings between year two and year one. In this sense the model behind the PEG ratio is more flexible at incorporating future growth than the forward price-to-earnings ratio, which is exactly what the PEG ratio was intended to do. If you were an analyst trying to "sell" investors on a stock with high forecasted growth in the near term, the PEG ratio is a good tool because it makes such stocks look more reasonably valued. However, such stocks are not necessarily undervalued, they may just look this way when evaluated using the PEG ratio.

11.5   PUTTING SOME VALUATION RATIOS TOGETHER

The market-to-book ratio is simply a scaled version of the residual income model and is therefore clearly related to the expected level of residual income. Because the price-to-earnings ratio scales by earnings in the most recent year, it is much more focused on expected growth in residual income. It is driven by how much residual income is expected to increase in the future relative to earnings today. And, to wrap all of this up into a neat package, note that

$$\frac{P_e}{CE_0} = \frac{NI_0}{CE_0} \times \frac{P_e}{NI_0}$$

or,

market-to-book ratio = ROE$_0$ × price-to-earnings ratio,

here defining ROE_0 as the return on *ending* equity.

Remember how we hammered away on the idea that value is created by a combination of profitability and growth? Here we see this once again. The market-to-book ratio is the product of profitability, measured as ROE_0, and growth, measured loosely by the price-to-earnings ratio.

The market-to-book and price-to-earnings ratios together give you a great snapshot of the market's expectations about the firm. To help you develop a feel for what a big or small ratio is, we have plotted the median market-to-book and median price-to-earnings ratios each year from 1974 to 2009 in Figure 11.1.

FIGURE 11.1
Valuation Ratios through Time

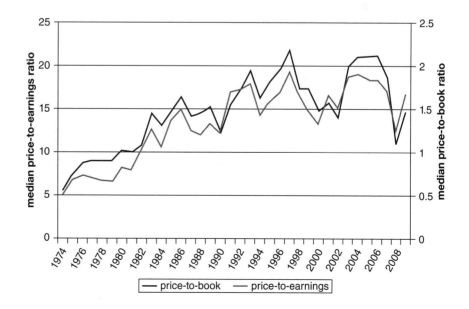

Two observations are immediately clear from the figure. First, valuations relative to fundamentals (i.e., net income and common equity) have been drifting steadily up over the past thirty years. This may be due to steadily declining interest rates over the same period, increasingly optimistic estimates about future growth and profitability, or a steady decline in the ability of accounting measures to capture true value. Which interpretation is correct is unclear; different scholars and practiners have championed each. The second observation is that the Internet boom and bust cycle, and the more recent financial crisis, are clearly present in the trend of valuation ratios. In both cases the median price-to-book ratio drifted above 2 and the median price-to-earnings ratio drifted to almost 20. That is, over half the firms in the economy were priced with very rosy expectations about the future. But even if you were sure that the market was overvalued in 2004, notice that it wasn't until 2008 that these ratios came back down. Bubbles are always easier to see in the rearview mirror.

The valuation ratios not only change over time, they also vary greatly across different sectors of the economy. Figure 11.2 plots the aggregate market-to-book and aggregate price-to-earnings ratios as of the end of 2009 for ten economic sectors.

Note the huge difference between the utility sector and the information technology sector. Not surprisingly, the market sees more growth potential and greater future profitability in information technology than it sees in utilities. This doesn't mean that utilities are a bad investment and information technology stocks are good investments. In fact, it may well mean that the

FIGURE 11.2
Aggregate Sector Valuation Ratios in 2009

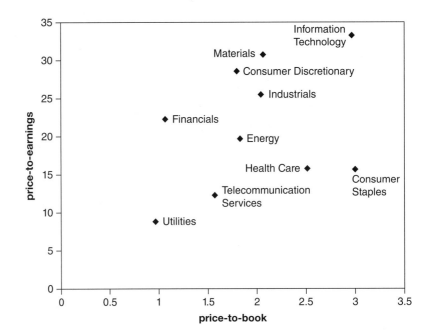

FIGURE 11.3
Valuation Ratio Examples

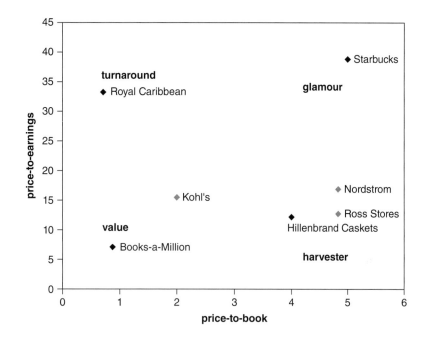

market is overpricing information technology stocks and underpricing utilities. We will return to the issue of picking stocks based on these simple valuation ratios in the next section.

We can use the market-to-book ratio and the price-to-earnings ratio together to see how the market views different firms in the consumer discretionary sector (where Kohl's and its competitors live). Figure 11.3 plots the valuation ratio for some representative firms.

The figure is divided loosely into four regions. Firms that are low on both dimensions are labeled as *Value* and firms that are high on both dimensions are labeled as *Glamour*. The off-diagonal categories identify more unusual firms. Firms that have very high price-to-earnings ratios, but relatively low market-to-book ratios are labeled *Turnarounds*. They currently have very little earnings but, based on a big restructuring, a new CEO, or blind faith, the market expects that they will have lots more earnings in the future. The future earnings growth may not coincide with a high ROE however, so while the price-to-earnings ratio is very high, the market-to-book ratio is still low. At the other extreme we have *Harvesters*. Imagine a firm that has lots of profitability but only moderate growth. Without much anticipated growth, the price-to-earnings ratio would be relatively low, while the high ROE would generate a high market-to-book ratio. Figure 11.3 plots the valuation ratios as of 2009 for four firms that illustrate the four quadrants. The Value firm is Books-a-Million, a book retailer with a price-to-book ratio of less than one and a price-to-earnings ratio of about seven. Clearly the stock market does not see much potential in selling books from retail outlets (and the recent bankruptcy of Borders Books would seem to validate this belief). At the other extreme, Figure 11.3 shows Starbucks as the representative Glamour stock, sporting a price-to-book ratio greater than 5 and a price-to-earnings ratio of about 39. Starbucks has managed to increase its gross margin at the same time it has grown sales, and the market seems to believe that it will continue to do so far into the future. The Turnaround stock in Figure 11.3 is Royal Caribbean Cruiselines, with a price-to-book ratio less than one but a price-to-earnings ratio of about 33. Vacationing is highly discretionary, and as the economy tanked in 2009, so did Royal's revenues. Unfortunately, all those ships continued to generate expenses with the net result that earnings plummeted in 2009. But the market expects that, as the economy improves, so too will Royal's earnings, hence the high price-to-earnings ratio. The Harvester company in Figure 11.3 is Hillenbrand Caskets. Unlike vacations, the rate at which people die is not generally discretionary and, consequently, casket sales are largely unaffected by the economy. Death is a profitable but low growth business (and let's hope it stays that way).

Turning our attention to Kohl's, Nordstrom, and Ross Stores, we see in Figure 11.3 that all three firms have a price-to-earnings ratio in the midteens, but the price-to-book ratio for Kohl's is considerably lower than for the other two companies. This reconciles nicely with the results in Chapter 5. Recall that Kohl's had a return on equity of about 14 percent while Ross Stores had a value of 32 percent and Nordstrom had a value of 40 percent. The price-to-book ratio is very sensitive to profitability and clearly the market expects the differential rate of profitability between Kohl's and the other two stores to continue into the future.

Can You Make Money with These Ratios?

The market-to-book and price-to-earnings ratios both compare the current market price to an accounting measure of fundamental value. It is natural to ask whether or not firms that are extreme on either of these measures tend to move back toward the average value. Do these statistics mean revert? And further, if they do mean revert, is it because the price corrects itself or is it because price predicts a future movement in the accounting fundamentals? If the correction is due to future price changes then it may be possible to form a profitable investment strategy based on these ratios.

Before giving you the answers to these titillating questions, we want to stress that the whole point of this book is to teach you how to develop a detailed forecast of the firm's future financial statements and then translate these forecasts into a value estimate. We expect you to arrive at a value estimate that is far superior to what you could get simply by looking at the company's earnings and book value and then comparing each to price. But with that thought in mind, the short answer is "yes," historically you would have generated unusually high investment returns by investing in stocks with low market-to-book and price-to-earnings ratios.

TABLE 11.1   Portfolio Returns to Different Price-to-Fundamental Investment Strategies

Next Year's Return	Market-to-Book Ratio	Price-to-Earnings Ratio	Book Value + 1.3 Residual Income
Return on Bottom 10% of Ratio	19.1%	20.7%	21.0%
Return on Top 10% of Ratio	11.8%	11.8%	11.1%
Hedge Return	7.3%	8.9%	9.9%

Returns are for investments in the top or bottom 10% of the indicated ratio for all publicly-traded firms between 1976–1995. The portfolio position is taken three months after the fiscal year end and held for 12 months. See Dechow, Hutton, and Sloan (1999) for details.

Table 11.1 gives the details of three different investment strategies based only on accounting book value, earnings and price.

Each strategy sorts the firms on their price-to-fundamental ratio, where the fundamental is either book value, earnings, or a combination of the two, and then buys firms with the lowest ratios and sells firms with the highest ratios. The portfolios are formed three months after the fiscal year end (to be sure that the book value and earnings data are publicly available) and are held for one year. The tests are conducted over a large sample of firms from 1976 to 1995. The first column of the table shows that the decile of firms with the lowest market-to-book ratio earned an average return of 19.1 percent while the decile of firms with the highest market-to-book earned an average return of only 11.8 percent. The hedge return is just the difference between these two portfolio returns. Our hedge portfolio has little exposure to marketwide risk, because it is equally long and short in the same dollar value of stocks, yet it would have returned 7.3 percent (i.e., it made 19.1 percent on the long position and lost 11.8 percent on the short position). The second column of the table shows a similar result for portfolios based on the price-to-earnings ratio. The hedge return to this strategy is 8.9 percent. The third column computes a crude "value" measure based on the current book value and residual income. It is defined as

$$V_e = CE_0 + 1.3RI_0$$

where the value 1.3 is based on an estimate of the rate at which residual income mean reverts in the entire economy. The strategy then computes the P_e/V_e ratio and forms portfolios. As shown in the table, the hedge return to this portfolio is 9.9 percent.

These hedge returns are quite large by Wall Street standards. A hedge return is equally long and short in the same dollar amounts, so it is zero net investment, at least in principle. Of course, you can't walk into a brokerage house and open an account with zero dollars. But imagine that you invested your wealth in a fund that tracked the entire market and, in addition, you took the zero net position in the hedge portfolio described above. This combined strategy would beat the market return by almost 10 percent. A money manager who consistently beat the market by 10 percent would be a god on Wall Street, so is it really this easy? Not really. First, the actual transaction costs of taking a long position in 10 percent of the market and a short position in a different 10 percent of the market could be prohibitively costly. An implementable strategy may have to limit itself to a much smaller set of more liquid firms, and this smaller set of firms may not have the same returns as those documented in Table 11.1. Further, while the hedge portfolio has no exposure to market-wide price movements, it still may have a significant exposure to other types of risk. What if all the short positions are in technology stocks and all the long positions are in utilities? If the techs were to invent a cheap and reliable source of green energy, so that their stocks rose and the traditional utility stocks fell, you would lose your shirt. The hedge portfolio is market-neutral but it certainly isn't without risk. In fact, the return to the market-to-book strategy is so thoroughly documented that many finance professors refer to it as a *risk factor*, although it isn't clear exactly what fundamental risk such a strategy exposes one to. This is always the debate—is it an exploitable return or is it compensation for bearing risk? Finally, even if this profitable strategy was available in the past, there is no guarantee that it will be available in the future. If enough investors notice this pattern in the data and invest to profit on it, they will push the price of low price-to-fundamental stocks up and push the price of high price-to-fundamental stocks down, eliminating the hedge returns in the process.

11.6 CASES, LINKS, AND REFERENCES

Cases

- The Restaurant Industry in 2011

Links

- *eVal* website: http://www.lundholmandsloan.com
- Morningstar: http://www.morningstar.com
- Yahoo! Finance: http://yahoo.finance.com
- Yahoo! Education: http://biz.yahoo.com/edu/

References

- Dechow, P., A. Hutton and R. Sloan (1999). An empirical assessment of the residual income valuation model. *Journal of Accounting and Economics* 26: 1-34.

CHAPTER TWELVE

Some Complications

12.1   INTRODUCTION

Up until this point, the valuation step has been quite straightforward. Given a series of forecast financial statements and the key valuation parameters, we just let *eVal* crank out the valuation. Unfortunately, life is not always this simple. In this chapter, we discuss some of the most common complications that arise in the valuation step. We stress that *eVal* does not provide any "quick fix" solutions to these complications. Instead, it is up to you, now as an informed user, to make sure that you anticipate these complications. Remember, as we have stated many times before, the maxim "garbage-in, garbage out" is the order of the day.

There are two primary categories of complications. The first category relates to negative values and the abandonment option. If you load a company that is losing money into *eVal*, you will typically find that the default valuation is negative. What does this mean? Stock prices are not negative in real life. This category of complications is the subject of section 12.2.

The second category of complications relates to value creation and destruction through financing transactions. *eVal* simply computes the intrinsic value of the company to the existing stockholders, assuming that they will be the only participants in all future net cash distributions. But what if the existing stockholders let some new stockholders invest in the company at a price that is different from intrinsic value? Whenever a company issues or repurchases shares of common stock at a price other than intrinsic value, it creates or destroys value for the existing stockholders. This category of complications is the subject of section 12.3.

12.2   NEGATIVE VALUES AND THE ABANDONMENT OPTION

Negative Values

In Chapter 10, we discussed what it means for *eVal* to return a negative stock price. In this section, we revisit this issue and offer some advice about how to deal with this unusual situation. A negative stock valuation is actually not an uncommon occurrence in *eVal* if you simply use *eVal*'s default forecasting assumptions on a company reporting a loss in its most recent year. Yet in

FIGURE 12.1
eVal **Model
Summary for Nektar
Therapeutics**

Model Summary

Historical Data For:
NEKTAR THERAPEUTICS
Most Recent Fiscal Year End:	12/31/10
Average ROE (last five years)	-35.30%
Sales Growth (last five years)	-6.09%

Forecast Data:
Forecast Horizon	10 years
This Year's ROE	-52.19%
Terminal Year's ROE	-42.23%
This Year's Sales Growth	110.36%
Terminal Year's Sales Growth	3.00%
This Year's Forecast EPS	-$0.79
Forecast 5 Year EPS Growth	81.78%

Valuation Data:
Cost of Equity Capital	10.00%
Valuation Date	8/15/11
Estimated Price/Share	-$427.10
Estimated Price/Earnings Ratio	541.44
Estimated Market/Book Ratio	-439.44

the real world, we never see negative stock prices. To understand why *eVal* generates negative stock prices, let's look at a specific example. Figure 12.1 provides the Valuation Summary sheet for a company called Nektar Therapeutics as of the end of fiscal 2010.

Nektar is a biopharmaceutical company that is incurring significant R&D expenses developing a variety of drug candidates that are in the clinical phase. At the end of 2010, Nektar had no products on the market and was only generating a small amount of royalty and licensing revenue. Consequently, Nektar had reported substantial losses for the last several years. The valuation in Figure 12.1 was obtained using the default forecasting assumptions in *eVal*. Note that the estimated price per share is –$427.10. The summary of the forecast data indicates a current ROE of −52 percent and a terminal ROE of −42 percent. If we were to look into the details of the forecasted financials, we would see that Nektar is forecast to have negative earnings, residual income, and cash flows for every future period—clearly a bleak future. We also see that sales grew at 121 percent in the immediate past year, and are forecast to trend to 110 percent this year and then gradually down to 3 percent by 2021. When we combine the recent negative earnings, cash flows, and residual income with the rapid sales growth, we get even larger forecasted negative earnings, cash flows, and residual income in the future. According to

FIGURE 12.2
eVal **DCF Valuation for Nektar Therapeutics**

DCF Valuations	($000)			
Company Name	NEKTAR THERAPEUTICS			
Most Recent Fiscal Year End	12/31/10			
Date of Valuation	8/15/11			
Cost of Common Equity	10.00%			
Terminal Growth Rate	3.00%			
Fiscal Year of Forecast	12/31/11	12/31/12	12/31/13	12/31/14
Valuation to Common Equity				
Free Cash Flow to Common Equity	(173,484)	(337,199)	(617,747)	(1,062,236)
Present Value of FCF	(157,713)	(278,677)	(464,123)	(725,521)
Present Value Beyond 10 Years	(23,715,943)			
Present Value of First 10 Years	(11,995,103)			
Forecast Equity Value Before Time Adj.	(35,711,045)			
Forecasted Value as of Valuation Date	(39,840,135)			
Less Value of Contingent Equity Claims	0			
Value Attributable to Common Equity	(39,840,135)			
Common Shares Outstanding at BS Date	93,281			
Equivalent Shares at Valuation Date	93,281			
Forecast Price/Share	-$427.10			

our forecasts, Nektar has a money-losing business model and plans to grow and operate the money losing business indefinitely, thereby losing even more money in the future. This all leads to a large negative valuation.

Now look at Nektar's forecasted future free cash flows on *eVal*'s DCF Valuation sheet, which is reproduced in Figure 12.2. In 2011, Nektar is forecast to have free cash flow to common equity of −$173 million. By 2014, the amount of negative free cash flow is forecast to grow to −$1,062 million. This means that, in order to keep operating the business consistent with our forecasts, enormous amounts of new common equity will have to be issued. If the existing stockholders act as forecast in our *eVal* model, then they will have to provide huge amounts of new equity injections into Nektar, even though they will never receive a positive cash distribution in return. Under this scenario, the value of the company to the existing stockholders is clearly negative because of the negative present value of the additional cash infusions that they plan to make.

Why then do we never observe negative stock prices in reality? The reason is that stockholders have limited liability. Management and creditors can never force the existing stockholders to pay more cash into the company, so the least that a stock can ever be worth is zero. This is where the *eVal* model doesn't jibe with reality. We have forecast that stockholders will be willing to pay in additional cash indefinitely, and *eVal* took the present value of those negative cash flows to common equity holders. But, in reality, either the company will develop successful products and generate profits, or stockholders will abandon the company and it will cease operations. The most obvious limitation of our forecasting model is that we have extrapolated Nektar's past losses into the indefinite future. But in reality, the stockholders of Nektar hope that the company will turn profitable as drugs that are currently under development start generating revenues.

Given that we never observe negative stock prices in the real world, why do we allow them to arise in *eVal*? The reason is that we want you to see just how bad an investment in such a company would really be. How much value are you forecasting that the company can destroy as investors send good money chasing after bad? We know that the quoted stock price will never actually be negative. Interpret the negative value estimate as how much worse off investors would be if they did continue to invest in the company as predicted by your forecasts. While real world stock prices are never negative, it is certainly true that real world investors have lost lots of money by financing businesses that never turned a profit. In the real world, a stage ultimately arrives when investors figure out that they should simply abandon the investment.

The present value computations in *eVal* assume that existing stockholders will finance any additional cash infusions implied by your forecasts. While we know that this is unrealistic, what if the existing management and stockholders are able to "hoodwink" new investors into providing the additional capital? While this would be a negative net present value proposition for the new investors, it is possible that the existing stockholders could make themselves better off at the expense of the new investors. This is one of the reasons why investment bankers who can "sell any deal" are able to charge such high fees. Figuring out the amount of wealth transfers between existing stockholders and new capital providers is complicated, and we will address this issue in more detail in section 12.3.

The Abandonment Option

We have now established that equity cannot have a negative value in practice because stockholders have limited liability. They are free to walk away from the company and cannot be forced to provide additional capital to fund money-losing operations or pay creditors. This stockholder right is sometimes referred to as the *abandonment option*. As with most options, the abandonment option has value. In this section, we will examine the abandonment option in more detail.

The forecasting assumptions we discussed in Chapter 8 are our "best guesses" as to what we think will happen in the future. They are each point estimates of the most likely outcome rather than ranges of the many possible outcomes. But, in reality, any number of possible outcomes could arise for most of our assumptions. Moreover, situations may arise where we know that our point estimates are imprecise and there is great uncertainty as to the ultimate outcome. As long as the range of possible outcomes is symmetric around our most likely estimate, and all the valuations are positive, then our best guess valuation is a reasonably unbiased estimate of expected value. Unfortunately, when some of the possible outcomes result in a negative valuation, the abandonment option will introduce significant asymmetries into the range of possible valuations. In particular, since equity holders can choose to abandon the firm in the case of poor outcomes, the left tail of the possible range of valuation outcomes is truncated at zero. The result is that the best guess valuation can seriously underestimate the expected valuation after taking the abandonment option into consideration. We illustrate the effect of the abandonment option in Figure 12.3.

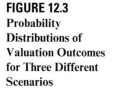

FIGURE 12.3
Probability
Distributions of
Valuation Outcomes
for Three Different
Scenarios

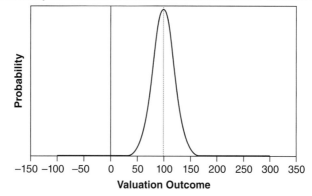

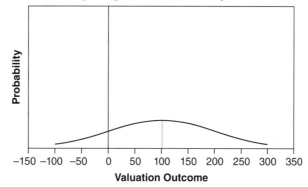

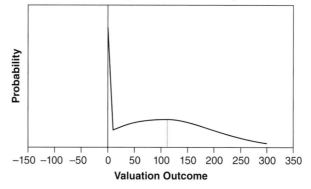

Figure 12.3 charts the probability distribution of possible valuation outcomes for three different scenarios. In each of the three scenarios, the most likely point estimate of value, represented by the peak of the valuation distribution, is $100. Sensitivity analysis reveals the range of other possible valuation outcomes. The first chart represents a low-variance scenario, where the range in possible valuation outcomes is quite closely clustered around the most likely estimate of $100. Note also that the range of possible outcomes is symmetric and all values are positive. This first scenario represents the typical case, where the range of possible valuation outcomes is symmetric around the most likely point estimate valuation, all reasonable valuations are positive, and so the most likely point estimate valuation is our best estimate of the expected valuation.

The second chart represents a high-variance scenario, where the range of possible valuation outcomes varies widely around the most likely point estimate of $100. As with the first chart, the range of possible outcomes continues to be symmetric around the most likely valuation estimate of $100, so the expected value is still $100, but a significant range of the possible valuation outcomes in the second chart falls below zero. As discussed above, all the negative valuations are unreasonable because the existing stockholders will not indefinitely continue to invest good money after bad; rather they will exercise their abandonment option and refuse to contribute additional capital.

The range of possible valuation outcomes, assuming that stockholders optimally exercise their abandonment option, is shown in the third chart of Figure 12.3. In this chart, the distribution of possible valuation outcomes is truncated at zero. All of the possible negative valuation outcomes in the second chart are now concentrated at zero. Note that stockholders still keep all of the upside in the case of very positive valuation outcomes, but they avoid the downside in the case of negative valuation outcomes. As a result, the expected valuation of the investment is now greater than the most likely point estimate of $100. In the particular case shown in the third chart, the expected value works out to be about $110. Thus, by using the most likely point estimate valuation, we would have undervalued the stock by about 10 percent.

What determines the value of the abandonment option? The third chart in Figure 12.3 should make it clear. The lower the most likely point estimate valuation and the greater the variance of possible valuation outcomes, the greater the probability of a negative outcome, and the greater the value of the abandonment option. Thus, the abandonment option tends to be the greatest in money-losing companies with great uncertainty in future outcomes. A company such as Nektar is a very good example. Owning a share in this company is like owning an option on the small chance that they will strike it big on some new drug.

To determine whether there is an abandonment option in play, you should always conduct sensitivity analysis for a plausible *worst-case* scenario. If this scenario yields a negative valuation, then the abandonment option has positive value. To make the analysis tractable, this worst-case valuation scenario

FIGURE 12.4   Value of the Abandonment Option

	Worst Case (25% prob.)	Most Likely Case (50% prob.)	Best Case (25% prob.)	Value Without Abandonment Option	Value With Abandonment Option
Healthy Low-Variance Firm	$50	$100	$150	$100	$100
Healthy High-Variance Firm	−$50	$100	$250	$100	$112.5
Distressed Low-Variance Firm	−$50	$0	$50	$0	$12.5
Distressed High-Variance Firm	−$150	$0	$150	$0	$37.5

should represent a plausible outcome—assumptions that you feel are in the bottom 25 percent tail of likely outcomes. You also should think about a representative *best-case* valuation scenario. By assigning probabilities to each of these scenarios and assigning a value of zero to the negative valuation outcomes, you can compute the expected value of the stock *after* incorporating the abandonment option. Figure 12.4 provides some representative computations assuming that the most likely outcome has a probability of 50 percent and the best- and worst-case scenarios each has a probability of 25 percent.

The table provides four representative cases. The first two cases represent a "healthy" firm, with a most likely valuation outcome of $100. The second two cases represent a "distressed" firm, with a most likely valuation outcome of $0. The first and third cases represent a "low-variance" firm, with the best and worst case scenarios deviating from the most likely case by $50. The second and fourth cases represent a "high-variance" firm, with the best and worst case scenarios deviating from the most likely case by $150. We compute the value without the abandonment option by summing the products of each of the valuation outcomes with their respective probabilities. We compute the value with the abandonment option using the same procedure, but after assigning a value of $0 to all negative valuation outcomes.

For the first case, of the healthy, low-variance firm, even the worst-case valuation outcome is positive, so the abandonment option has no value. In the second case, of the healthy, high-variance firm, the worst-case outcome has a negative value, giving value to the abandonment option. The value without the abandonment option is $100 and with the abandonment option is $112.5, so the value of the abandonment option is $12.5. Higher variance results in a greater value for the abandonment option. In the third case, that of the distressed, low-variance firm, the worst-case valuation outcome is again negative, giving a value of $12.5 to the abandonment option. In the fourth case, of the distressed, high-variance firm, the worst-case valuation outcome is very negative, resulting in an abandonment value of $37.5. Financial distress combines with high variance to give great value to the abandonment option. Note that in this fourth case, the value of the company with the abandonment option is $37.5, even though the most likely valuation outcome is zero. Ignoring the abandonment option can result in serious undervaluation.

12.3   CREATING AND DESTROYING VALUE THROUGH FINANCING TRANSACTIONS

Common Equity Transactions

The valuation computations in *eVal* assume that all future net cash distributions to common stockholders will accrue to the current common stockholders. This is equivalent to assuming that if the firm does sell additional shares to new investors, they do so at the share's intrinsic value. In reality, this is often not the case. Companies frequently issue new shares of stock to new stockholders and repurchase shares of stock from existing stockholders, and do so at values that are arguably wildly different from the stock's intrinsic value. An obvious question is whether these transactions can create or destroy value for existing stockholders. The answer is a resounding yes, and there have been numerous spectacular cases where companies have created or destroyed value for stockholders through transactions in their own common stock. This is exactly the stuff that keeps the fat checks coming to investment bankers.

To keep things simple, we will start by assuming that we have created a valuation model in *eVal* that correctly forecasts the future net cash distributions to common stockholders; that is, it captures equity's intrinsic value. By discounting these future cash distributions, *eVal* arrives at the value of common equity to the existing stockholders as a group. *eVal* then divides by the number of common shares outstanding to arrive at the estimate of intrinsic value per share. As long as all of the current stockholders continue to hold their stock and no new stock is sold, then the current stockholders will realize this intrinsic value.

But what if some existing stockholders sell their stock to new stockholders? Well, as long as these transactions take place at intrinsic value, no wealth is transferred between the selling stockholders and the buying stockholders. However, if these transactions take place at a price that differs from the intrinsic value, there is a wealth transfer between the old selling stockholders and the new buying stockholders. If trades take place above intrinsic value, the selling stockholders gain at the expense of the buying stockholders. Conversely, if trades take place below intrinsic value, the selling stockholders gain at the expense of the buying stockholders. These results should come as no surprise. After all, one of the key goals of *eVal* is to help you profit from buying underpriced securities and selling overpriced securities. The important point to emphasize at this juncture is that the value of the stock to ongoing

FIGURE 12.5
Wealth Transfers in
Stock Transactions

	Company repurchases stock from existing stockholders	Company sells stock to new stockholders
Transaction takes place at a price above intrinsic value	Wealth is transferred from ongoing stockholders to selling stockholders	Wealth is transferred from buying stockholders to ongoing stockholders
Transaction takes place at a price below intrinsic value	Wealth is transferred from selling stockholders to on-going stockholders	Wealth is transferred from ongoing stockholders to buying stockholders

stockholders continues to be the intrinsic value computed by *eVal*, regardless of the price at which trades take place between old and new stockholders.

But what if the company itself trades in its own stock? Well, as long as these trades take place at intrinsic value, again there are no wealth transfers. But if these trades take place at a price different from intrinsic value, then there are wealth transfers between the existing stockholders and the new stockholders transacting with the company. Figure 12.5 summarizes the direction of the wealth transfers.

The important issue here is that the ultimate value of a stock to an ongoing stockholder is determined not only by the intrinsic value of the stock, but also by the extent to which the company transacts in its own stock at a price differing from intrinsic value. This means that the market value of a stock is a potentially important determinant of the value of the stock even to a stockholder with no plans to trade the stock. A couple of examples help to clarify this fact. First, consider the case of a company with an intrinsic value of common equity of $1,000 and 10 shares outstanding. The intrinsic value per share is $100. Next assume that this company is able to issue an additional 10 shares at $300 per share. The company has a revised intrinsic value of $4,000 and 20 shares outstanding, giving an intrinsic value of $200 per share. By issuing new shares at a price that exceeds intrinsic value, the company has created additional intrinsic value for ongoing stockholders at the expense of the new stockholders.

As a second example, begin again with a company that has intrinsic value of common equity of $1,000 and 10 shares outstanding. But now assume that this company's stock is only trading at $50 per share. If this company repurchases six shares of its own stock, it will have a revised intrinsic value of $700 and four shares outstanding, giving an intrinsic value per share of $175. By repurchasing shares at a price below intrinsic value, the company has created additional intrinsic value for ongoing stockholders.

The above analysis has important implications for the valuation of an equity security. If the market value of the security differs from its intrinsic value, then we must consider the potential for the company to engage in transactions in its own stock to take advantage of this misvaluation. You can probably see that this argument has an element of circularity to it. If a company's market price is an important determinant of its intrinsic value, then how should we determine the appropriate market price? For this reason, stock prices can get caught up in speculative bubbles. But, at the end of the day, these speculative bubbles simply transfer wealth from one set of stockholders to another. The intrinsic value of a firm's total common equity is still determined only by the present value of its future net cash distributions.

It is difficult to identify airtight examples of firms issuing or repurchasing equity at prices different from the intrinsic value because we never really know for sure what a firm's intrinsic value is. Nonetheless, we offer AOL's acquisition of Time Warner as a likely illustration. In January 2000, AOL was trading at total market value of $164 billion, a value that was difficult to justify based on forecasts of AOL's future cash flows. AOL's management cashed in on its high stock price by issuing shares of AOL stock in exchange for all of Time Warner's stock. Whereas AOL had mostly Internet assets and a customer base with fading loyalty, Time Warner had hard assets, including magazines, cable networks, and recording studios. The acquisition converted AOL's overvalued stock into assets that had real value. In this way, they created value for the original AOL shareholders, but at the expense of the Time Warner shareholders. It didn't take long for the market to find its way back to intrinsic value. Prior to the merger announcement, Time Warner had a market value of about $84 billion, giving the combined entity a pre-merger valuation of $248 billion. By the time the deal closed a year later, the value of the combined entity had fallen to approximately $109 billion, not much more than the original value of Time Warner all by itself. Absent the acquisition, the original AOL shareholders may have had nothing in terms of future cash flows. As it stood, they owned over 50 percent of the new entity—and the original Time Warner shareholders, who used to own 100 percent of the valuable part of the new entity, now owned less than 50 percent. By February 3, 2003, the merged AOL Time Warner had a market value of only $52 billion, much to the chagrin of the original Time Warner owners.

From a practical perspective, how can we address the issue of potential wealth distributions resulting from a company trading in its own stock? Well, we should always be aware of significant deviations between the current market value of a stock and our estimate of its intrinsic value. If a company's market price exceeds its intrinsic value, we should consider whether the company is likely to issue new shares of stock. These issuances can take the form of seasoned equity offerings or stock-for-stock acquisitions of other companies. If such issuances are likely, then we should try to quantify their impact on stock values for ongoing stockholders. If a company's market price is below its intrinsic value, we should consider whether management is likely to undertake stock repurchases. If repurchases are likely, then we should try to quantify their impact on stock values for ongoing stockholders. You may have noticed that our guidance is somewhat vague on this issue. This is no coincidence. A company's ability to create and destroy value for ongoing stockholders by transacting in its own stock is one of the most difficult valuation issues to grapple with. Trying to forecast how much value will be created or destroyed is like trying to forecast when a Ponzi scheme will collapse.

The creation and destruction of value through financing activities is not restricted to transactions in a company's common stock. If companies are able to issue debt or preferred stock at inflated values, then they will likewise create value for existing stockholders. But there is one key difference for these non-common-equity forms of financing. We explicitly forecast these events in our *eVal* model. Hence, as long as we correctly forecast the favorable or unfavorable terms of issuance for non-equity capital, the resulting impact on the value of common equity will be incorporated by *eVal*.

Contingent Equity Claims

Issuing contingent equity claims is another way to create or destroy value through financing transactions. Contingent equity claims take many forms, including company warrants, employee stock options, and the conversion options embedded in convertible bonds. These contingent equity claims give their holders the right to purchase shares of common stock at prices that may differ from intrinsic value, and are in many cases well below intrinsic value. If such rights are exercised, then wealth is transferred between the ongoing stockholders and the new stockholders exercising their contingent equity claims. The accounting for contingent equity claims varies depending on the form the claim takes, but none of the existing accounting rules fully reflect the impact of contingent equity claims on the intrinsic value of a share of common stock.

We can give you a simple (but admittedly crude) procedure for dealing with contingent equity claims. To the extent that a company has *existing* outstanding contingent equity claims, you should value those claims and incorporate them into your *eVal* computation using the contingent claims calculator described in Chapter 10. To the extent that you forecast a company will issue contingent equity claims in the *future*, you can capture the economic effect of this by forecasting that the company will instead engage in a "plain vanilla" transaction of similar economic substance to the contingent claims. For instance, with warrants, you should simply assume that the company issues common stock of equivalent value. For employee stock options, simply assume that the company pays cash compensation of equivalent value. The accounting rules for stock compensation changed beginning in 2006, so financial statements now provide an estimate of the value of options issued to employees, which should help you forecast the future compensation value. For the issuance of convertible bonds, simply assume that the company issues plain bonds at the corresponding market interest rate. Note that these alternative transactions are not exactly economically equivalent to issuing contingent equity claims. But the key differences hinge on changes in the future stock price of the company. And if we knew how the future stock price was going to change, we wouldn't need to do a valuation in the first place. By replacing the contingent claim transactions with their plain vanilla counterparts, we obtain an estimate of intrinsic value that abstracts from the circularity of trying to determine a firm's current value as a function of its future market price.

12.4 CASES, LINKS, AND REFERENCES

Cases

- The AOL Time Warner Merger
- The Valuation of Amazon.com in June 2001

PART TWO

Cases

The AOL Time Warner Merger*

On January 10, 2000, AOL and Time Warner announced their intention to merge and create the world's first Internet-age media and communications company. The proposed deal represented the biggest corporate merger of all time, with the merged entity valued at approximately $350 billion. The deal was also unique in that it combined one of the leading names from the booming "new economy" with one of the largest "old economy" media companies. While the deal was billed by AOL and Time Warner as a "merger of equals," AOL was generally recognized as the "acquirer" and Time Warner as the "target." The objective of this case is to understand the structure and financial implications of the merger. Further details concerning the proposed merger are provided in the online exhibits included with the case, which can be found at www.lundholmandsloan.com.

Finally, you can load the case data for AOL into *eVal* (the AOL data are already adjusted for the November 1999 stock split) and examine the valuation. (*Note:* Case data can be imported by going to the Case Data sheet in *eVal* and selecting the yellow block of data for the company, and then pasting this block of data into the yellow cells at the bottom of the Financial Statements sheet using Paste Special—Values from the Edit menu.) Please use the number of shares on pages 13 and 16 of the proxy statement (2,255 for AOL and 1,301.5 for TW).

QUESTIONS

1. Describe the major synergies and other sources of value creation associated with the merger.
2. The terms of the merger represent a significant premium to Time Warner shareholders. Quantify this premium.
3. Do you think that the additional value created by the deal is sufficient to justify the premium being offered to Time Warner shareholders?

*This case was prepared by Richard Sloan as the basis for class discussion. Copyright © 2001 by Richard Sloan.

4. Estimate AOL's premerger intrinsic value by importing AOL's historical financial statements into *eVal*, setting the forecast horizon to 10 years and the valuation date to January 10, 2000, and leaving all other assumptions at their default values. What is the intrinsic stock price for AOL? Do you think that this is a reasonable pre-merger valuation?

5. Assume that the default assumptions in question 4 are appropriate for a pre-merger AOL and that the addition of Time Warner to AOL increases the value of AOL by exactly the $142 billion purchase price given in the online Exhibit 2 (i.e., the acquisition is a zero NPV investment). Compute AOL's post-merger intrinsic stock price. You do not need to use *eVal* for this question.

6. Reconcile the pre- and post-merger intrinsic valuations in questions 4 and 5. Why did a zero NPV investment change the value of AOL's intrinsic stock price?

7. Estimate whether the merger will be accretive (i.e., increase AOL's near-term EPS relative to what EPS would have been if the merger hadn't taken place) or dilutive (i.e., decrease AOL's near-term EPS relative to what EPS would have been if the merger hadn't taken place).

Apple and The iFad*

The fall of 2009 marked new highs in the runaway success of Apple, Inc. In the 12 years since his return to Apple, CEO and founder Steve Jobs had transformed Apple from an almost bankrupt also-ran into a consumer technology powerhouse that was the envy of Silicon Valley.

Jobs's turnaround strategy focused on Apple's most profitable products. He also revitalized the brand through a series of advertising campaigns and carefully choreographed product launches. This resulted in a slew of successful new product lines, including the iMac in 1998, the iPod in 2001 and the iPhone in 2007. Apple leveraged these product lines by integrating key services with its products, including retail stores in 2001, iTunes in 2003, and the App Store in 2008.

As Apple's sales and profits grew, its stock price skyrocketed. Sales grew from $6 billion in 2003 to $36 billion in 2009, while profits grew from just $68 million in 2003 to a staggering $6 billion by 2009. Adjusting for splits, Apple's stock price grew from $10 in late 2003 to $200 by late 2009.

Apple's stock was understandably popular on Wall Street, with over 30 sell-side analysts covering it. The consensus forecast for Apple's 2010 earnings was $8.37, representing 33 percent growth relative to 2009 EPS of $6.29. Most analysts were forecasting that Apple's stock price would rise substantially as well. Following Apple's fourth quarter 2009 earnings announcement, one enthusiastic analyst summarized his opinion as follows:[1]

> Fourth quarter revenues are up 25%Y/Y to $9.9B and EPS is up 45%Y/Y to $1.82. Apple crushed consensus $9.2B/$1.44 on strong Mac upside. iPhone supply constraints are no worse than feared, gross margin +30bps Q/Q to 36.6% (as higher mix and OS X Snow Leopard offset rising component costs) and 11c tax help. Moreover, we continue to see a BIG Dec-qtr driven by iPhone supply now catching up to demand and a MacBook/iMac refresh we think is imminent including lower entry prices. We are reiterating our buy rating and raising our FY10 EPS estimate to $8.40 and our price target to $260 from $235, valuing AAPL at ~16x EV/FCF on our CY10E FCF estimate of $11,241M.

*This case was prepared by Professor Richard Sloan as the basis for class discussion, rather than to illustrate either effective or ineffective handling of a business situation. Copyright 2010 by Richard Sloan.

[1] Apple's fiscal year ends in September and Apple's earnings for the fiscal year ended September 2009 were announced on October 19, 2009. The analyst quote is the case writer's synthesis of the views expressed by representative analysts.

Yet despite Apple's success, signs of a possible slowdown were appearing. Annual sales growth had slowed from 35 percent in 2008 to 12 percent in 2009. Aggressive competitors, such as Google and Microsoft, were introducing new products to challenge the iPhone and iPod. Apple's suppliers were also pushing for a bigger share of Apple's fat profit margins. Finally, Apple faced the relentless challenge of new product innovations in order to fuel sales growth and margins.

Detailed information on Apple's business strategy and financial situation is provided in Apple's 10-K for the year ended September 26, 2009. For comparative purposes, we will use an abridged version of International Business Machines Corporation (IBM) 10-K for the year ended December 31, 2009. These documents are available online at www.lundholmandsloan.com (*Note:* Case data can be imported by going to the Case Data sheet in *eVal* and selecting the yellow block of data for the company, and then pasting this block of data into the yellow cells at the bottom of the Financial Statements sheet using Paste Special—Values from the Edit menu.)

QUESTIONS

Business Strategy Analysis

1. Identify Apple's source(s) of competitive advantage in the technology sector.
2. Identify the key risks associated with Apple's strategy in the technology sector.
3. Briefly describe the key differences between Apple's and IBM's business strategies in the technology sector.

Accounting Analysis

4. Briefly explain Apple's revenue recognition policies for iPhone and Apple TV.
5. Assume that instead of using its then existing revenue recognition policies for iPhone and Apple TV, Apple instead recognized all revenues and associated costs at the time of sale. Estimate the Net Income that Apple would have reported for the fiscal year ended September 26, 2009.
6. Which of the above two methods of accounting for Apple TV and iPhone sales do you think better reflects the underlying economics of the business? Briefly explain your answer.

Ratio Analysis

7. Start the *eVal* software, load the data file for Apple and examine the Advanced Dupont Model on the Ratio Analysis worksheet. Next, repeat the same steps for IBM.

8. Using the analysis in question 7 above, identify the primary underlying reasons for differences in the 2009 return on equity (ROE) for the two companies.

9. Does your analysis identify any opportunities for Apple to potentially increase its return on equity?

Forecasting Analysis

10. Start the *eVal* software, load the data file for Apple and examine the default forecasting assumptions on the forecasting assumptions worksheet. Are these assumptions plausible? If not, which assumptions do you feel are the most implausible and how would you change them to make them more plausible?

Valuation Analysis

11. Start the *eVal* software, load the case data for Apple and set the valuation date to November 2, 2009. How does the estimated price per share in *eVal* differ from Apple's November 2, 2009 stock market price of around $190/share? Which do you think better approximates Apple's intrinsic valuation on that date?

12. The analyst quoted in the case write-up is forecasting a 12-month price target for Apple of $260. Provide a critical evaluation of the justification used by the analyst to arrive at this price target.

The Valuation of Amazon.com in June 2001*

BACKGROUND

Amazon.com was one of the darlings of the Internet stock boom of the late 1990s. Opening its virtual doors in 1995, Amazon's original mission was to use the Internet to transform book buying into the fastest, easiest, and most enjoyable shopping experience possible. Amazon went public in May of 1997, with an offer price of $18 per share, and opened at $29.25 per share. Over the next five years, Amazon's stock price went on a wild ride, peaking at over $100 per share in December 1999. During this period, Amazon split its shares by a factor of 12, implying a split-adjusted price of over $1,200 per share relative to its $18 offer price—a gain of over 6,000 percent in less than three years. Since December of 1999, however, Amazon's stock price, like many of its dot.com counterparts, has seen a steady decline. In June of 2001, Amazon's stock price had declined to $12 per share.

By June 2001, Amazon had grown into the leading inventory-carrying shopping destination on the Internet. Its new mission was "to be the place customers can go to find/discover anything they might want to buy online." The company had indeed expanded its product line to include items such as music and consumer electronics and had opened operations in the United Kingdom, Germany, France, and Japan. Sales had grown from just $16 million in 1996 to almost $3 billion in 2001. Despite this rapid growth, there were some problems. Perhaps most importantly, Amazon had yet to report a profit. Moreover, sales growth was declining and was forecast by management to drop to 20–30 percent for fiscal 2001.

*This case was prepared by Professor Richard Sloan as the basis for class discussion, rather than to illustrate either effective or ineffective handling of a business situation. Copyright © 2001 by Richard Sloan.

Wall Street analysts expressed widely divergent opinions concerning Amazon's future. At one extreme, some analysts argued that it was time to value Amazon like a "real-world" retailer. Pointing to its lack of a profitable business model combined with its high leverage and declining levels of working capital, these analysts forecast that Amazon could face a serious credit problem and possibly even bankruptcy before the end of fiscal 2001. For example, Ravi Suria, a convertible bond analyst with Lehman Brothers, argued that

> We believe that the low levels of working capital could trigger a creditor squeeze in the second half of the year, creating considerable downside risk to revenue and cash estimates for the second half.[1]

At the opposite extreme, some analysts saw Amazon as the dominant player in an important new industry. Armed with its valuable customer list and e-commerce brand name, these analysts saw Amazon as the future Walmart of "e-tailing." These analysts believed that margin improvement and scale economies would soon enable Amazon to turn profitable. For example, Mary Meeker and Mark Mahaney, equity analysts with Morgan Stanley Dean Witter, argued that

> Total worldwide online retail sales are expected to grow nicely over the next 3–5 years, and Amazon.com, with 32MM cumulative customers and one of the strongest e-commerce brands, should be well positioned to benefit from this growth.[2]

Accordingly, these analysts reiterated their "Long-Term Outperform" rating on Amazon.com. Amazon's management shared this optimistic view of their company's future with Chairman and CEO Jeff Bezos, promising pro forma operating profitability by the fourth quarter of 2001.

ASSIGNMENT

Your assignment is to use *eVal* to provide a comprehensive valuation analysis of Amazon as of June 30, 2001. To assist you with this task, three online exhibits are provided at www.lundholmandsloan.com.

The exhibits are (*a*) Amazon.com's fiscal 2000 annual report, (*b*) financial results for the first fiscal quarter of 2001, and (*c*) a valuation model for Amazon.com that is based on a leading sell-side research report on Amazon dated June 21, 2001. The valuation model includes both short-term income statement forecasts and a formal DCF valuation model (an uncommon event for sell-side research). Note that no balance sheet forecasts were provided in the report.

---

[1]Ravi Suria, Research Report on Amazon.com, *Lehman Brothers Convertible Bond Research,* February 6, 2001.

[2]Mary Meeker and Mark Mahaney, Research Report on Amazon.com, *Morgan Stanley Dean Witter Equity Research,* June 21, 2001.

TASKS

1. Load the Amazon.com data into *eVal*. (*Note:* case data can be imported by going to the Case Data sheet in *eVal* and selecting the yellow block of data for the company, and then pasting this block of data into the yellow cells at the bottom of the Financial Statements sheet using Paste Special—Values from the Edit menu.) Select a 10-year forecast horizon, set the valuation date to June 30, 2001, and examine the default valuation provided by *eVal*. You will note that the default estimate is a negative number. This seems odd, because limited liability prevents real-world stock prices from being negative. Explain why *eVal* provides a negative value.

2. Use *eVal* to *approximately* reconstruct the sell-side valuation model provided at the third online exhibit to this case. Your approximation should be close enough that the resulting *eVal* valuation is between $10 and $20 per share. You will have to make some additional assumptions in your *eVal* model because the valuation model provided is very terse. Provide a critical evaluation of this valuation model, paying special attention to the forecasted financial ratios implied by the model. [*Hints*: (*a*) As you change the forecasting assumptions, refer to the "Computation of Free Cash Flow to Investors" portion of the Cash Flow Analysis sheet to see the resulting free cash flows, and (*b*) to cleanly isolate depreciation in your forecasts, move 84460 out of SG&A and into Depreciation on the fiscal 2000 historical income statement.]

3. Use *eVal* to conduct a sensitivity analysis on the valuation model you constructed above with respect to the future EBITDA assumptions. First, construct a model in which EBITDA as a percent of revenue is higher by 0.20 than in the above model for every future forecast period. Second, construct a model in which EBITDA as a percent of revenue is lower by 0.20 than in the above model for every future forecast period. [To be clear, EBITDA is forecasted to be 5 percent of revenue in 2003; in your first model this will be 25 percent and in your second model it will be 15 percent, and you will make similar adjustments to all other years in the forecast horizon.]

4. Assume that there is a one-third probability of each of the three valuation scenarios you have computed above. What would this imply about the value of Amazon.com? How does this compare to the original valuation provided in the sell-side valuation model? Explain the sources of any differences. Based on the sum of all your analysis, what do you think Amazon.com was worth at June 30, 2001?

Turnaround at Bally Total Fitness?*

By 1999, the 1996 spin-off of Bally Total Fitness (ticker BFT) from Bally Entertainment had all the elements of a classic turnaround story. Under the leadership of President and CEO Lee Hillman, stagnant sales and losses had been converted to rapidly growing sales and profits. With over 4 million members and 350 facilities, BFT had firmly established itself as the dominant player in the growing health club business. However, despite its apparent success, BFT was experiencing mixed reactions from Wall Street. After reaching an all-time high of close to $40 in early 1998, BFT's stock price had dropped back into the $20s. The initial drop in its stock price was prompted by concerns about BFT's accounting procedures that appeared in *The Wall Street Journal*:

> The nation's largest health-club chain is getting worked over by skeptical investors, who quarrel with its accounting methods. The questions started at the end of July, when Bally Total Fitness Holdings reported an unexpectedly encouraging second-quarter profit of eight cents a share. The bulls credit new health programs and more than $100 million of revenue from a successful installment-membership plan devised by the two former accountants who run Bally, Chief Executive Officer Lee Hillman and John Dwyer, chief financial officer. But bears don't believe in the turnaround of the previously none-too-healthy fitness centers. They cite puzzling changes in depreciation and gaps between cash collection and anticipated revenue. And they don't think Chicago-based Bally is keeping enough reserves for membership fees that may not be paid. If Bally's accounting was more conservative, "it would have lost significant amounts of money, instead of making eight cents" in the quarter, says money manager Blair Baker of Precept Capital Management in Dallas[1]

Related concerns continued to plague BFT's stock price into 1999. Short sellers continually targeted the stock, with 4 million shares shorted by the

---

*This case was prepared by Professor Richard Sloan as the basis for class discussion, rather than to illustrate either effective or ineffective handling of a business situation. Copyright © 1999 by Richard Sloan.

[1]Extracted from "Bally Total Fitness' Accounting Procedures Are Getting Some Skeptical Investors Exercised," *The Wall Street Journal*, August 28, 1998. WALL STREET JOURNAL. CENTRAL EDITION [ONLY STAFF-PRODUCED MATERIALS MAY BE USED] by WALL STREET JOURNAL. Copyright 1998 by DOW JONES & COMPANY, INC. Reproduced with permission of DOW JONES & COMPANY, INC. in the format Textbook via Copyright Clearance Center.

middle of 1999, representing over one-third of BFT's float and 20 times BFT's average daily volume. As a result, BFT's stock price looked cheap compared to its expected future earnings performance, as indicated below:

BFT: Earnings Growth and Related Pricing Ratios, 1999

	Last Five Years	This Year (Dec. 1999)	Next Year (Dec. 2000)	Next Five Years	Price/Earn (Dec. 1999)	PEG Ratio (Next Five Years)
Bally Total Fitness Holding Corp	n/a	202.0%	49.6%	35.0%	14.2	0.4
Leisure and recreation services	2.1%	3.7	21.7	18.8	46.9	2.5
S&P 500	10.3	11.3	10.1	7.5	28.0	3.7

Source: Yahoo! Finance Website (1999).

Wall Street's sentiments about BFT also were reflected in its dwindling sell-side analyst coverage. From the beginning of 1998 through the middle of 1999, First Call indicated that sell-side analyst coverage declined from 6 to 3, while the consensus sell-side recommendation slid from 1.3 to 2.0. Merrill Lynch, who also happens to be BFT's primary investment banker, continued to be BFT's strongest sell-side supporter. Merrill analyst Seth Weber issued the following comments in response to continued criticism of BFT's accounting policies:

> Shares of Bally Total Fitness have been under pressure on another negative report. In our view, the report had no new information and basically rehashed the same issues we addressed last year. We recommend investors particularly use any weaknesses in the stock as a buying opportunity . . . With respect to the report, it discusses BFT's membership growth, deferral accounting and cash flow—all issues we feel comfortable with.[2]

Details concerning BFT's business strategy and financial performance are provided in BFT's Form 10-K for the year ended December 31, 1998. This document is available as an online exhibit at www.lundholmandsloan.com.

QUESTIONS

1. Evaluate BFT's business strategy, identifying the key success factors and risks.
2. Evaluate the appropriateness of BFT's revenue recognition policy with respect to financed memberships. Your evaluation should address:
   - Whether the policy is consistent with GAAP.
   - Whether the policy is consistent with the underlying economics of the business.

[2]Research comment on Bally Total Fitness Holding Corp., *Merrill Lynch*, September 29, 1999.

3. Recast BFT's 1998 income statement assuming that BFT recognized (and had always recognized) membership revenues when cash was received from members. List any assumptions or approximations that you make. (Financials are available in Excel format at www.lundholmandsloan.com)

4. Explain the major reasons for any differences between the original and recast financial statements. Do you think that the recast financial statements represent BFT's economic performance better or worse than the numbers reported by the company?

5. What actions would you advise BFT's management take in order to increase investor confidence in BFT's financial condition? What are the pros and cons of these actions?

Boston Chicken, Inc.*

At the end of 1996, Boston Chicken was one of the hottest names on Wall Street. Operating in the highly competitive restaurant industry, the chain had grown from 18 stores in 1991 to over 1,000 stores in 1996 and in its short history had raised over $1 billion in public offerings. EPS had grown from just $0.06 in 1993 to $1.01 in 1996, representing an annual growth rate of well over 100 percent. At the end of 1996, Boston Chicken traded around $40, representing a price-earnings multiple of 40 and a market-to-book ratio of 3. The company's spectacular success was attributed to the leadership of a group of investors headed by Scott Beck, former vice chairman of Block-buster Entertainment, who took control in 1992. Enthusiasm for the company in 1994 was summarized in *The Washington Post* as follows:

> Perhaps no company better captures the spirit of the new economy than Boston Chicken Inc., the hottest of last year's hot stock offerings, which aims to do for the rotisserie what Col. Sanders did for the deep fryer . . . But Boston Chicken is not really about poultry—it is about developing a market-winning formula for picking real estate, designing stores, organizing a franchise operation and analyzing data.[1]

However, enthusiasm for the company was not universal. Doug Kass, research chief of brokerage J. W. Charles of Boca Raton, Florida, commented:

> I wouldn't touch Boston Chicken with a 10-foot rotisserie spit. I'm concerned with some major accounting issues, excessive stock valuation, surging competition and heavy dependence on a single product.[2]

Boston Chicken's management staunchly defended the company against such criticism. CFO Mark Stephens responded:

> We've got great chicken, great side items, our accounting is fine, and we're growing like a weed. When you get a big profile, it's natural for people to shoot at you.

Boston Chicken also took two steps to reduce its reliance on rotisserie chicken in 1995. First, Boston Chicken extended its food offerings to include turkey, ham, and meatloaf, and concurrently changed the name of its stores

*This case was prepared by Professor Richard Sloan as the basis for class discussion, rather than to illustrate either effective or ineffective handling of a business situation. Copyright © 1998 by Richard Sloan.

[1]From Steven Pearlstein, "Boston Chicken: Hot Stuff," *The Washington Post,* July 4, 1994. © 1994, *The Washington Post.* Reprinted with permission.

[2]Dan Dorfman, "Pros Roast Chicken Stock," *USA Today,* August 12, 1994.

to Boston Market. Second, Boston Chicken diversified its food offerings further by investing in ENBC, which was created through the combination of a number of leading bagel retailers.

Against this backdrop, Boston Chicken entered 1997 with plans to open over 300 additional restaurants over the next 12 months. The continued expansion was to be financed through the issuance of over $400 million of convertible debt in the first half of 1997. Enthusiasm for Boston Chicken remained high on Wall Street, with many Wall Street analysts recommending the stock as a "strong buy."

Details concerning Boston Chicken's business strategy and financial performance and expansion plans are provided in the company's 10-K for the year ended December 29, 1996. This document is available as an online exhibit at www.lundholmandsloan.com.

QUESTIONS

1. Evaluate the structure of the restaurant industry and its ability to generate profits over the long run. As a starting point, consider the five forces of competition:
   - Competition from substitutes.
   - Rivalry between established competitors.
   - Threat of entry.
   - Bargaining power of customers.
   - Bargaining power of suppliers.

2. Some analysts argue that Boston Chicken is primarily in the business of operating restaurants. Other analysts argue that Boston Chicken is primarily a franchiser, as opposed to an operator of restaurants. Still others argue that Boston Chicken is primarily a financial institution that lends money to operators of restaurants. Based on the information provided in the case, what do you view as Boston Chicken's primary business and why?

3. Evaluate Boston Chicken's strategy for creating competitive advantage. What are the key success factors and risks associated with this strategy?

4. Evaluate the quality of Boston Chicken's earnings.

5. Restate Boston Chicken's earnings using a method that better reflects the underlying economics of the business. (Financials are available in Excel format at www.lundholmandsloan.com.)

6. Assuming that Boston Chicken continues to use its current accounting methods, what future event(s) are likely to cause its quality of earnings problems to surface (i.e., what future event(s) will cause Boston Chicken's future earnings to be lower because current earnings are potentially overstated)?

EnCom Corporation*

INTRODUCTION

EnCom is a fictitious corporation that is designed to illustrate (*i*) the impact of aggressive and conservative accounting on the quality of earnings and (*ii*) the correspondence between the discounted free cash flow model (DCF) and residual income model (RIM) approaches to equity valuation.

EnCom is a very simple corporation that operates a business for just five years. At the end of each year, all free cash flow generated by the business is paid out to the owners as a dividend. The case proceeds in three stages:

1. We value EnCom using the traditional DCF approach and we also compute EnCom's internal rate of return (IRR) and prepare accrual-based financial statements for EnCom. This first-stage analysis serves as a benchmark for the second two stages.
2. We introduce a marketing project representing an incremental investment opportunity for EnCom. By considering different methods of accounting for the marketing project, we illustrate the impact of aggressive and conservative accounting on the quality of earnings.
3. We use the RIM approach to valuing EnCom. This stage illustrates the correspondence between the DCF and RIM approaches to valuation and also illustrates the robustness of RIM valuations to accounting distortions.

INITIAL CASE FACTS

EnCom commences business and engages in operating activities for five periods, with data as follow:

- The initial required investment in property plant at the beginning of the first period is $1,000. The equipment has a five-year useful life and zero salvage value. For accounting purposes, the equipment is depreciated using the straight-line method and all depreciation is treated as a period expense (i.e., it is not part of cost of goods sold).

*This case was prepared by Professor Richard Sloan as the basis for class discussion, rather than to illustrate either effective or ineffective handling of a business situation. Copyright © 2003 by Richard Sloan.

- Sales per period are $1,200, with half of the sales revenue received in cash at the end of the period in which the sale is made and the other half received in cash at the end of the following period.
- The cost of goods sold is $720 per period, with all inventory acquired for cash at the end of the period prior to the period in which the sale is made.
- There are no other expenses or sources of income and no other required working capital or investment requirements.
- At end of each period, all free cash flow is paid out as a dividend.
- The discount rate is 10 percent.

STAGE ONE QUESTIONS

1. What is the total initial investment that is required at the beginning of the first period in order to start EnCom?
2. Compute the value of EnCom immediately after the initial investment at the beginning of period one using the discounted free cash flow method.
3. Compute EnCom's internal rate of return.
4. Prepare financial statements (income statements and balance sheets) for EnCom for each of the five periods that it is in business.
5. Compare EnCom's free cash flows and earnings for each of the five periods. Overall, which of the two measures do you think provides the best measure of EnCom's periodic performance? Why?
6. Compute EnCom's return on equity (ROE, computed as earnings for the period divided by book value of equity at the beginning of the period) for each of the five periods. Compare EnCom's ROE for each period to EnCom's IRR and provide a qualitative explanation for any major differences.

ADDITIONAL CASE FACTS FOR STAGE TWO

An incremental investment project is available to EnCom, with data as follow:

- EnCom can engage in a marketing campaign during period one, with total marketing costs of $300, payable in cash at the end of period one.
- The marketing project increases cash inflows at the end of periods one, two, and three by $150 per period.
- All other facts remain the same.

STAGE TWO QUESTIONS

1. Compute the value of EnCom with the incremental project immediately after the initial investment at the beginning of period one using the discounted free cash flow method. Should EnCom invest in the incremental project?

2. Compute EnCom's IRR with the incremental investment project.

3. Assume that EnCom accounts for the incremental marketing project by expensing all marketing costs in the period they are incurred. Prepare financial statements for each of the five periods under this accounting assumption. Do you think this accounting assumption is aggressive, conservative, or neutral?

4. Assume that EnCom accounts for the incremental marketing project by capitalizing marketing costs and then amortizing them in proportion to the benefits received. Prepare financial statements for each of the five periods under this accounting assumption. Do you think this accounting assumption is aggressive, conservative, or neutral?

5. Assume that EnCom accounts for the incremental marketing project by capitalizing marketing costs and then expensing all of these costs in the first period in which no benefits are received from the project. Prepare financial statements for each of the five periods under this accounting assumption. Do you think this accounting assumption is aggressive, conservative, or neutral?

6. Which of the above three accounting methods do you think provides the best measure of EnCom's periodic performance? Why?

7. Compute EnCom's ROE for each of the five periods using each of the above three accounting methods. Explain how each of the different accounting methods impacts EnCom's ROE.

8. Using the insights from the EnCom example, provide a qualitative explanation of the impact of aggressive and conservative accounting on a firm's ROE relative to its IRR.

STAGE THREE QUESTIONS

1. Provide a separate residual income valuation for EnCom immediately after the start of business using each of the three accounting methods from stage two.

2. In question 1 above, you should have arrived at the same valuation regardless of the accounting method employed. Provide a qualitative explanation as to why the different accounting methods have no impact on the valuation.

Four Valuation Models—One Value*

This case is designed to give you some practice computing the inputs to and final value estimate from some of the most standard valuation models. After you do the computations by hand, or if you give up in frustration, you can verify them using *eVal* (the details for using *eVal* are given in part B of the case). Part C of the case illustrates how accounting distortions flow through the different valuation models. We refer you to Chapter 10, "Valuation," for the precise definitions of the valuation models and their inputs.

The forecasted financial statements that extend into the infinite horizon are given in Figure 1. In addition, you should assume that the cost of equity capital is 10 percent, the pretax cost of debt is also 10 percent, and the effective tax rate is 40 percent. Also assume there are 1,000 shares outstanding and divide your valuation by 1,000 to get the price per share.

FINANCIAL STATEMENT FORECASTS

Figure 1 shows one historical year and four forecasted years of financial statements for our example company. Note that the sales growth is 20 percent in year one and 5 percent in years two and beyond. However, because depreciation expense and interest expense are based on average balances, net income doesn't start growing at 5 percent each year until year three (i.e., $NI_{2002}(1 + .05) = NI_{2003}$). Common shareholders' equity also starts growing at 5 percent in year three (i.e., $CE_{2002}(1 + .05) = CE_{2003}$).

QUESTIONS

Part A. The Four Valuation Models

Free Cash Flow to Common Equity Valuation Model

1. Find the forecasted free cash flow to common equity for 2001 and beyond.
2. Compute the value of common equity as of December 31, 2000, using the free cash flow to common equity model.

*This case was prepared by Russell Lundholm as the basis for class discussion. Copyright © 2002 by Russell Lundholm.

FIGURE 1   **Financial Statements for Part A**

7		Actual	Forecast	Forecast	Forecast	Forecast	
8	Fiscal Year End (MM/DD/YYYY)	12/31/2000	12/31/2001	12/31/2002	12/31/2003	12/31/2004	
10	**Income Statement**						
11							
12	Sales (Net)	20,000	24,000	25,200	26,460	27,783	
13	Cost of Goods Sold	(12,000)	(14,400)	(15,120)	(15,876)	(16,670)	
14	Gross Profit	8,000	9,600	10,080	10,584	11,113	
17	EBITDA	8,000	9,600	10,080	10,584	11,113	
18	Depreciation & Amortization	(2,000)	(2,200)	(2,460)	(2,583)	(2,712)	
19	EBIT	6,000	7,400	7,620	8,001	8,401	
20	Interest Expense	(1,000)	(1,100)	(1,230)	(1,292)	(1,356)	
22	EBT	5,000	6,300	6,390	6,710	7,045	
23	Income Taxes	(2,000)	(2,520)	(2,556)	(2,684)	(2,818)	
25	Other Income (Loss)	0	0	0	0	0	
26	Net Income Before Ext. Items	3,000	3,780	3,834	4,026	4,227	
29	Net Income (available to common	3,000	3,780	3,834	4,026	4,227	
30							
31	**Balance Sheet**						
32							
33	Operating Cash and Market. Sec.	1,000	1,000	0	0	0	
37	Total Current Assets	1,000	1,000	0	0	0	
38	PP&E (Net)	20,000	24,000	25,200	26,460	27,783	
41	Other Assets	0	0	0	0	0	
42	Total Assets	21,000	25,000	25,200	26,460	27,783	
43							
49	Long-Term Debt	10,000	12,000	12,600	13,230	13,892	
53	Total Liabilities	10,000	12,000	12,600	13,230	13,892	
55	Paid in Common Capital (Net)	10,000	8,220	3,986	590	(2,975)	
56	Retained Earnings	1,000	4,780	8,614	12,640	16,867	
57	Total Common Equity	11,000	13,000	12,600	13,230	13,892	
58	Total Liabilities and Equity	21,000	25,000	25,200	26,460	27,783	

Residual Income to Common Equity Valuation Model

3. Find the forecasted residual income for 2001 and beyond.

4. Compute the value of common equity as of December 31, 2000, using the residual income to common equity model.

Free Cash Flow to All Investors Valuation Model

5. Find the forecasted free cash flow to all investors for 2001 and beyond.

6. Compute the after-tax weighted-average cost of capital.

7. Compute the value of common equity by first computing the value of the free cash flows to all investors (i.e., the entity value) and then subtracting the value of the cash flows to debt holders. *Note*: At this point, the estimated value will only be approximately the same as in the other models.

8. Recompute the entity value using a discount rate of 9.3646 percent and then find the value of the equity. Why is there a discrepancy between the answers to questions 7 and 8?

9. Without doing any computations, contrast the residual income to all investors model with the free cash flow to all investors model.

Residual Income to All Investors Valuation Model

We will skip the computations for this model. You can see them in *eVal* under the Residual Income Valuations tab.

Practice on Haggar Inc. (the makers of the #2 brand in pants!)

In the appendix, you will find the income statement, balance sheets, and cash flow statement for Haggar Inc. for the fiscal year ending September 30, 2002.

10. Compute the free cash flow to common equity using only the income statement and balance sheet for Haggar in fiscal 2002 and then reconcile this amount with the free cash flow to common equity computed directly from the statement of cash flows.

11. Compute the free cash flow to all investors using only the income statement and balance sheet for Haggar in fiscal 2002 and then reconcile this amount with the free cash flow to all investors computed directly from the statement of cash flows. *Note*: Book overdrafts are included in accounts payable.

Part B. Verifying Your Computations with *eVal*

Load the data for the case into *eVal*. (*Note:* Case data can be imported by going to the Case Data sheet in *eVal* and selecting the yellow block of data for the company, and then pasting this block of data into the yellow cells at the bottom of the Financial Statements sheet using Paste Special—Values from the Edit menu.) To generate the financial statements shown in Figure 1, go to the Forecasting Assumptions sheet and set:

- The forecast horizon to five years.
- The first year sales growth to 20 percent and the sales growth for years 2002 and beyond to 5 percent.
- The operating cash/sales ratio forecast to 4.167 percent in year 2001 and 0 percent in years 2002 and beyond.
- The long-term debt/total asset ratio forecast to 48 percent in year 2001 and 50 percent in years 2002 and beyond.

These changes will yield the financial statements shown in Figure 1. Finally, go to the Valuation Parameters sheet and set:

- The cost of equity capital to 10 percent.
- The cost of debt capital to 10 percent.
- The valuation date to July 9, 2000.

By setting the valuation date halfway into the fiscal year, we remove the half-year time value adjustment in *eVal* and make the computations much easier to see. If you have followed all these instructions carefully, the price shown on the financial statements sheet (or anywhere else) should be $61.25. If this isn't the case, look carefully at the Financial Statements sheet in *eVal* and be sure that the forecasted net income and common shareholders' equity is exactly as shown in Figure 1. If these are okay and the price still isn't $61.25, then double-check your settings on the Valuation Parameters sheet. More importantly, if your answers to Part A of the case are not all $6,125,000/1,000 shares = $61.25 per share, then go to the Residual Income Valuations sheet or DCF Valuations sheet and see where your computations differ from *eVal*'s.

Part C. Accounting Distortions

This part of the case answers the question "how do accounting distortions, intentional or unintentional, affect the valuation models?" As an example, suppose that our company shifts $2,000 of noncash income from fiscal 2002 to fiscal 2001. There are many ways they could do this: accelerating the recognition of revenue or deferring the recognition of an expense. Because the shifted income is not a real cash flow, it must necessarily increase an asset account in 2001 by $2,000, and this account will reverse in 2002. To make the computations transparent, suppose the shifted income was in the line item Other Income and the associated asset account was Other Assets. Further, suppose that all other income statement items, assets, and liabilities remain the same (common shareholders' equity will obviously change).

1. Alter the financial statements in Figure 1 to show the income shifting just described. Based on these new financial statements (not *eVal*), compute the value of common equity as of December 31, 2000, using the residual income to common equity model.

2. The income shifting clearly moves the recognition of net income forward in time and money has time value, so why has this accounting distortion not changed the value of the equity? (*Hint*: Your answer to question 1 should match the value you computed in Part A: $61.25 per share.)

3. To completely clarify the answer to question 2, compute the free cash flows to common equity from the revised financial statements. Compare your answer to the cash flows you computed in Part A.

4. To illustrate the irrelevance of accounting distortions in *eVal*, make the following changes to the financial statement forecasts that you entered in Part B:
   - Hit the Enter Raw Forecast Data button on the financial statements sheet and enter $2,000 of Other Income in year 2001 and $2,000 in year 2002.
   - Enter $2,000 for Other Assets in year 2001. It is already entered as zero in 2002.
   - Reenter $12,000 for Long-Term Debt in 2001; otherwise the default forecasting algorithms in *eVal* will change debt slightly. *eVal* will automatically change Retained Earnings so that the balance sheet balances.

If you made all these changes correctly, you should once again have a $61.25 per share value. Now, to see how general this result really is, alter your forecasts so that the distortion doesn't reverse until 2004 (i.e., that Other Asset maintains its balance of $2,000 until 2004, when the $2,000 of Other Income is recorded). Note once again that the value is unchanged.

5. What about distortions in the existing financial statements? Suppose that you feel that there are $1,000 of unrecorded assets, such as an internally developed intangible asset. Suppose that you restate the year 2000 financial statements in Figure 1 by adding $1,000 to Other Assets and Retained Earnings. Further, suppose that your forecasted financial statements remain exactly as in Figure 1, with the exception that Retained Earnings is $1,000 larger and Paid in Common Capital is $1,000 smaller. In *eVal* be sure to set Other Assets back to zero in 2001 and beyond. What is your valuation now? Explain why the valuation changed in the amount that it did. (*Hint*: Follow the net dividends each period.)

APPENDIX   Haggar Inc. Financial Statements

Consolidated Statements of Operations and Comprehensive Income (In thousands, except per share amounts)

Year Ended September 30

	2002	2001	2000
Net sales	$ 481,831	$ 444,570	$ 432,855
Cost of goods sold	351,704	307,796	287,392
Reorganization costs	(3,812)	20,150	—
Gross profit	133,939	116,624	145,463
Selling, general and administrative expenses	(118,442)	(123,972)	(128,849)
Royalty income	1,326	1,856	2,436
Other income (expense), net	613	(107)	1,370
Interest expense	(3,600)	(5,140)	(4,084)
Income (loss) before provision (benefit) for income taxes and cumulative effect of accounting change	13,836	(10,739)	16,336
Provision (benefit) for income taxes	5,823	(2,069)	7,054
Income (loss) before cumulative effect of accounting change	$ 8,013	$ (8,670)	$ 9,282
Cumulative effect of accounting change	(15,578)	—	—
Net income (loss)	$ (7,565)	$ (8,670)	$ 9,282
Other comprehensive income (loss):			
Cumulative translation adjustment	16	15	(565)
Comprehensive income (loss)	$ (7,549)	$ (8,655)	$ 8,717
Net Income (Loss) Per Common Share:			
Basic			
Income (loss) before cumulative effect of accounting change	$ 1.25	$ (1.34)	$ 1.38
Cumulative effect of accounting change	(2.44)	—	—
Net income (loss)	$ (1.19)	$ (1.34)	$ 1.38

Net Income (Loss) Per Common Share:

	2002	2001	2000
Diluted			
Income (loss) before cumulative effect of accounting change	$ 1.25	$(1.34)	$ 1.37
Cumulative effect of accounting change	(2.42)	—	—
Net income (loss)	$(1.17)	$(1.34)	$ 1.37
Weighted average number of common shares outstanding-Basic	6,385	6,485	6,733
Weighted average number of common shares and common share-equivalents outstanding-Diluted	6,429	6,485	6,786

Haggar Corp. and Subsidiaries
Consolidated Balance Sheets (In thousands)

September 30

	2002	2001
Assets		
Current assets:		
Cash and cash equivalents	$ 4,124	$ 7,800
Accounts receivable, net	64,284	71,299
Inventories	100,996	97,726
Property held for sale	2,157	—
Deferred tax benefit	12,087	11,290
Other current assets	2,766	2,215
Total current assets	186,414	190,330
Property, plant and equipment, net	46,195	51,975
Goodwill, net	9,472	25,050
Other assets	7,896	7,870
Total assets	$ 249,977	$ 275,225
Liabilities and Stockholders' Equity		
Current liabilities:		
Accounts payable	$ 30,542	$ 35,645
Accrued liabilities	39,448	25,374
Accrued wages and other employee compensation	6,713	5,103
Accrued workers' compensation	4,468	3,645
Current portion of long-term debt	3,742	4,021
Total current liabilities	84,913	73,788
Long-term debt	21,343	49,338
Total liabilities	106,256	123,126

(*continued*)

Haggar Corp. and Subsidiaries

September 30

	2002	2001
Stockholders' equity:		
Common stock—par value $0.10 per share; 25,000,000 shares authorized and 8,660,609 and 8,591,000 shares issued at September 30, 2002 and 2001, respectively	866	859
Additional paid-in capital	42,911	42,014
Cumulative translation adjustment	(534)	(550)
Retained earnings	125,439	134,310
	168,682	176,633
Less-Treasury stock, 2,242,205 and 2,203,705 shares at cost at September 30, 2002 and 2001, respectively	(24,961)	(24,534)
Total stockholders' equity	143,721	152,099
Total liabilities and stockholders' equity	$ 249,977	$ 275,225

Haggar Corp. and Subsidiaries
Consolidated Statements of Cash Flows (In thousands)

Year Ended September 30

	2002	2001	2000
Cash Flows from Operating Activities:			
Net income (loss)	$ (7,565)	$ (8,670)	$ 9,282
Adjustments to reconcile net income (loss) to net cash provided by (used in) operating activities:			
Cumulative effect of accounting change	15,578	—	—
Depreciation and amortization	8,561	11,813	13,824
(Gain) loss on disposal of property, plant and equipment	(272)	2,458	(867)
Reversal of net realizable value on property held for sale	(2,157)	—	—
Deferred tax expense (benefit)	(129)	(666)	1,476
Changes in assets and liabilities			
Accounts receivable, net	7,015	(2,986)	(4,791)
Inventories	(3,270)	(5,145)	(6,596)
Other current assets	(551)	(478)	(98)
Accounts payable	(11,103)	10,469	(7,854)
Accrued liabilities	14,074	2,404	(4,984)
Accrued wages and other employee compensation	1,610	(1,003)	(908)
Accrued workers' compensation	823	(296)	(834)
Deferred long-term income tax liability	—	—	(867)
Net cash provided by (used in) operating activities	22,614	7,900	(3,217)

Year Ended September 30

	2002	2001	2000
Cash Flows from Investing Activities:			
Purchases of property, plant and equipment	(3,334)	(5,266)	(10,626)
Proceeds from sale of property, plant and equipment	135	38	1,563
Increase in other assets	(4)	(1,075)	(2,852)
Net cash used in investing activities	(3,203)	(6,303)	(11,915)
Cash Flows from Financing Activities:			
Purchases of treasury stock at cost	(427)	(1,807)	(8,191)
Proceeds from issuance of long-term debt	494,000	105,000	156,000
Proceeds from issuance of common stock	904	84	72
Payments on long-term debt	(522,274)	(102,020)	(131,064)
Increase in book overdrafts	6,000	—	—
Payments of cash dividends	(1,306)	(1,307)	(1,262)
Net cash (used in) provided by financing activities	(23,103)	(50)	15,555
Effects of exchange rates on cash and cash equivalents	16	15	(565)
Increase (decrease) in cash and cash equivalents	(3,676)	1,562	(142)
Cash and cash equivalents, beginning	7,800	6,238	6,380
Cash and cash equivalents, end	$ 4,124	$ 7,800	$ 6,238

The Gabelli Utility Trust*

"I personally think the premium is unsustainable. It's off the wall."

In early 2010, nobody was more puzzled about the price of The Gabelli Utility Trust (henceforth GUT) than its manager and namesake, Mario Gabelli. He made the quote above in a *Wall Street Journal* article published on February 20, 2010, when GUT traded at a premium of almost 70 percent to its net asset value. Yet despite Gabelli's quote, GUT continued to trade close to this premium over the following months.

Shares in investment funds like GUT that hold publicly traded securities are among the most straightforward securities to value. Recent prices of the securities that are held in these funds are usually readily observable and so shares in such a fund can be valued by summing the market values of the fund's investments and dividing by the fund's shares outstanding. The resulting amount is termed the "net asset value" of a share in the fund. So-called open-ended funds stand ready to redeem the shares of old investors or issue shares to new investors at net asset value. But so-called closed-end funds, such as GUT, do not. Instead, their existing shares are traded on securities exchanges at prices set by the investing public. In an efficient market, one would expect these prices to closely track the fund's net asset value. Yet GUT provided a glaring exception to this rule. GUT's premium to net asset value from January 1, 2005 to August 1, 2010 is shown in Figure 1.

GUT's investment objective is long-term growth of capital and income through common equity investments primarily in the utilities and energy sectors. The Fund's portfolio manager, Mario J. Gabelli, is a widely recognized manager and frequent commentator on CNBC and CNN. One unique feature of GUT is its generous managed distribution policy. Since 2003, GUT had maintained a regular monthly distribution of 6 cents/share. By early 2010, this represented an annual distribution rate of 14 percent on net asset

*This case was prepared by Assistant Professor Panos Patatoukas and Professor Richard Sloan as the basis for class discussion, rather than to illustrate either effective or ineffective handling of a business situation. Copyright © 2011 by Panos Patatoukas & Richard Sloan.

FIGURE 1

Closing Price and Net Asset Value for GUT

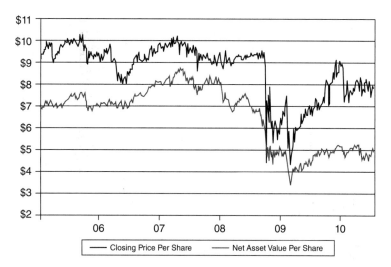

value and 9 percent on price. Further information concerning GUT's financial position at this time is provided in its 2009 annual report, available at www.lundholmandsloan.com.

QUESTIONS

1. It is well-established that the average closed-end fund sells at a small discount to its net asset value. Provide a potential explanation for this phenomenon.

2. Unlike most other closed-end funds, in early 2010, GUT was trading at a premium of almost 70 percent to its net asset value. Think of potential reasons why investors were willing to pay such a high premium for GUT's shares. As a starting point consider the following:

   a. Performance of GUT relative to a reasonable benchmark, and

   b. GUT's ability to create shareholder wealth through its managed distribution policy.

3. Based on your response(s) to the previous question, what type of events/outcomes would you expect to trigger a reduction in GUT's premium?

4. Describe an investment strategy that could be used to exploit the potential overpricing reflected in GUT's hefty premium. What might be the main obstacles to the practical implementation of this strategy?

The Home Depot, Inc.*

This is a real-time forecasting case. Your objective is to forecast The Home Depot's (NYSE: HD) income statement, balance sheet, and statement of cash flows for the current fiscal quarter. You will be evaluated on both the methodology underlying your forecasting model and the extent to which you accurately forecast The Home Depot's financial statements. You should place particular emphasis on trying to generate an accurate forecast of The Home Depot's EPS for the quarter.

The Home Depot makes a good pedagogical real-time forecasting case for several reasons:

- It is a large and important company (component of both the S&P 500 and the DJIA).
- A wealth of information about the company is readily available on the Web.
- Its basic business operation/strategy is well known and easy to understand.
- Its rapid growth illustrates forecasting techniques specific to growth companies.
- The seasonal nature of its business illustrates forecasting techniques specific to companies with seasonals.
- It is followed by a large number of sell-side analysts, who each publish their own forecasting models.

We recommend that you use the following framework and links in constructing your forecasting model:

1. Familiarize yourself with The Home Depot's business strategy and financial performance. You will find most of the information available from the Financial Info link on www.homedepot.com. Make sure that you study The Home Depot's recent Form 10-Ks and Form 10-Qs. You also may find it useful to compare The Home Depot's performance with industry

---

*This case was prepared by Richard Sloan as the basis for classroom discussion. Copyright © 2000 by Richard Sloan.

benchmarks and major competitors. Try http://money.msn.com/, enter HD for the ticker, and then go to Financial Results/Ratios. Also check out www.lowes.com.

2. Familiarize yourself with The Home Depot's expansion plans. Company press releases and the MD&A sections of the Form 10-Ks and Form 10-Qs are your best sources of information. This information is again available from the Financial Info link on www.homedepot.com.

3. Familiarize yourself with any information made available during the quarter that may have a bearing on The Home Depot's results. For example, did Home Depot's management issue any earnings forecasts or preannouncements? Was consumer spending relatively high during the quarter? Have any competitors already reported quarter's results? What was the weather like around the United States and how might this impact The Home Depot's sales?

4. Use the forecasting framework developed in the course, along with the insights generated by your analysis in steps one though four above, to prepare The Home Depot's pro forma financials for the current quarter. Your forecast should be based on more detailed analysis than simply repeating management's guidance.

5. Do a "reality check" on your forecasting model by comparing your model to the models published by leading Wall Street sell-side analysts and by comparing your EPS forecasts to the consensus sell-side forecast. You can often obtain full-text sell-side analyst reports from research libraries.

Evaluating Intel's Earnings Torpedo*

On September 21, 2000, Intel Corporation, the world's largest manufacturer of computer chips, issued an earnings warning indicating that third-quarter revenue was anticipated to be below previous expectations. This announcement prompted a huge sell-off in Intel's stock, which drove the price down from $61.48 to $47.94 over the course of the next 24 hours. This 22 percent stock price drop took place on daily volume of 300 million shares, a new record for the NASDAQ. In this case, you will build pro forma financial statements for Intel based on both Wall Street's expectations prior to Intel's earnings warning and Wall Street's revised expectations after the warning. You will then evaluate whether Intel's stock price decline was justified by the information in the earnings warning.

Intel's revenue growth was 11.9 percent in 1999 and had grown at an average annual rate of just over 12.5 percent for the five years ending in 1999. A surge in the worldwide demand for computer chips resulted in strong revenue growth in the first two quarters of 2000, with year-over-year revenue growth for the first and second quarter of 12.5 percent and 23.0 percent, respectively. In the press release accompanying the announcement of the financial results for the second quarter, Craig Barrett, president and CEO of Intel, stated: "Looking forward, we expect to see strong demand continue into the second half." Based on this guidance, most Wall Street analysts were expecting Intel's third-quarter revenue to be between $8.8 billion and $9.3 billion, representing year-over-year quarterly growth of between 20 and 27 percent, and sequential quarterly growth of between 6 and 12 percent.

Intel released its earnings warning after the close of regular trading hours on September 21, 2000. The full text of the press release is attached as Exhibit 1. In this press release, Intel indicated that it "now expects revenue growth for the third quarter to be approximately 3 to 5 percent higher than second quarter revenue of $8.3 billion."

*This case was prepared by Richard G. Sloan, Professor of Accounting at the University of Michigan Business School, for the purpose of class discussion, rather than to indicate the effective or ineffective handling of a business situation. Copyright © 2001 by Richard G. Sloan.

EXHIBIT 1
Intel Third-Quarter
Revenue to Be Below
Expectations
Demand in Europe
weaker than expected.

SANTA CLARA, Calif., Sept. 21, 2000—Intel's third quarter revenue is anticipated to be below the company's previous expectations, primarily due to weaker demand in Europe, the company said today. The company now expects revenue for the third quarter to be approximately 3 to 5 percent higher than second quarter revenue of $8.3 billion.

The company expects gross margin percentage for the third quarter to be 62 percent, plus or minus a point, lower than the company's previous expectations of approximately 63 to 64 percent. Interest and other is expected to be approximately $900 million for the third quarter, up from the company's previous expectations of $800 million.

Business Outlook

The following statements are based on current expectations. These statements are forward-looking, and actual results may differ materially. These statements do not reflect the potential impact of any mergers or acquisitions that may be completed after the date of this release.

- The company expects revenue for the third quarter of 2000 to be approximately 3 to 5 percent higher than second quarter revenue of $8.3 billion.
- The company expects gross margin percentage for the third quarter to be 62 percent, plus or minus a point. Gross margin percentage for 2000 is expected to be 63 percent, plus or minus a few points. In the short term, Intel's gross margin percentage varies primarily with revenue levels and product mix as well as changes in unit costs.
- Expenses (R&D, excluding in-process R&D, plus MG&A) in the third quarter of 2000 are expected to be up 7 to 9 percent from second quarter expenses of $2.2 billion, primarily due to higher spending on marketing programs and R&D initiatives in new business areas. Expenses are dependent in part on the level of revenue.
- R&D spending, excluding in-process R&D, is expected to be approximately $4.0 billion for 2000.
- The company expects interest and other income for the third quarter of 2000 to be approximately $900 million. Interest and other income is dependent in part on interest rates, cash balances, equity market levels and volatility, the realization of expected gains on investments, including gains on investments acquired by third parties, and assuming no unanticipated items.
- The tax rate for 2000 is expected to be approximately 31.8 percent, excluding the impact of the previously announced agreement with the Internal Revenue Service and acquisition-related costs.
- Capital spending for 2000 is expected to be approximately $6.0 billion.
- Depreciation is expected to be approximately $790 million in the third quarter and $3.4 billion for the full year 2000.
- Amortization of goodwill and other acquisition-related intangibles is expected to be approximately $400 million in the third quarter and $1.5 billion for the full year 2000.

(*continued*)

EXHIBIT 1
Intel Third-Quarter Revenue to Be Below Expectations
(continued)

Copies of this earnings release and Intel's annual report can be obtained via the Internet at http://www.intc.com/ or by calling Intel's transfer agent, Computershare Investor Services, L.L.C. (formerly named Harris Trust and Savings Bank), at (800) 298-0146.

Intel, the world's largest chip maker, is also a leading manufacturer of computer, networking and communications products.

The above statements contained in this outlook are forward-looking statements that involve a number of risks and uncertainties. In addition to factors discussed above, among other factors that could cause actual results to differ materially are the following: business and economic conditions and growth in the computing industry in various geographic regions; changes in customer order patterns; changes in the mixes of microprocessor types and speeds, purchased components and other products; competitive factors, such as rival chip architectures and manufacturing technologies, competing software-compatible microprocessors and acceptance of new products in specific market segments; pricing pressures; development and timing of introduction of compelling software applications; insufficient, excess or obsolete inventory and variations in inventory valuation; continued success in technological advances, including development and implementation of new processes and strategic products for specific market segments; execution of the manufacturing ramp, including the transition to the 0.18-micron process technology; shortage of manufacturing capacity; the ability to grow new networking, communications, wireless and other Internet-related businesses and successfully integrate and operate any acquired businesses; unanticipated costs or other adverse effects associated with processors and other products containing errata (deviations from published specifications); litigation involving antitrust, intellectual property, consumer and other issues; and other risk factors listed from time to time in the company's SEC reports, including but not limited to the report on Form 10-Q for the quarter ended July 1, 2000 (Part I, Item 2, Outlook section).

Based on the information provided above and using the *eVal* software to facilitate your analysis, perform the following tasks:

1. Import the data for this case into *eVal*. (*Note:* Case data can be imported by going to the Case Data sheet in *eVal* and selecting the yellow block of data for the company, and then pasting this block of data into the yellow cells at the bottom of the Financial Statements sheet using Paste Special—Values from the Edit menu.)
2. For the purpose of this case, you should set the valuation date to September 22, 2000, and the cost of equity capital to 12 percent on the Valuation Parameters worksheet.
3. Based on Wall Street's expectations immediately *before* Intel's earnings warning, provide a set of forecasting assumptions that (approximately) justify Intel's $61.48 pre-warning stock price.
4. Based on Wall Street's expectations immediately *after* Intel's earnings warning, provide a set of forecasting assumptions that (approximately) justify Intel's $47.94 post-warning stock price.
5. Based on your analysis in questions one through three, evaluate whether the 22 percent stock price drop was a reasonable response to the news about valuation fundamentals in Intel's earnings warning. To the extent that you do not think the stock price drop was justified, speculate as to why it occurred.

Interpreting Margin and Turnover Ratios*

INTRODUCTION

Return on investment is the product of profit margin and turnover, as illustrated by the Dupont model:

$$\frac{\text{Income}}{\text{Investment}} = \frac{\text{Income}}{\text{Sales}} \times \frac{\text{Sales}}{\text{Investment}}$$

In this exercise, you will get a better understanding of the determinants of profit margins and turnover ratios and the trade-offs that are made between them. The Ratio Analysis worksheet in *eVal* computes profit margins and turnover ratios for you. In particular, lines 30 and 31 of this worksheet compute profit margins and turnover ratios using net operating assets as the measure of investment. We will use these two ratios in our analysis.

DETERMINANT 1: INDUSTRY PRODUCTION TECHNOLOGY

One key determinant of margins and turnover ratios is the production technology of the industry in which a firm operates. Some industries require large investments in capital in order to produce relatively small amounts of sales, resulting in low turnover ratios. In order for investments in such industries to provide a competitive rate of return, profit margins must be high enough to compensate for the low turnover. A good example of such an industry is Telecom Services. The considerable investment in the wireline infrastructure that is required to operate a telecom services business results in very low turnover. To provide a competitive rate of return, net operating margin must be relatively high. Net operating profit margins have historically averaged over 10 percent in this industry.

A good example of an industry at the other end of the spectrum is Discount Variety Stores. Net operating asset turns in this industry exceed three times per year. This industry uses very basic stores that are designed to accommodate high volumes of sales. But competition is fierce, and profit margins are extremely low, resulting in competitive rates of return.

DETERMINANT 2: PRODUCT DIFFERENTIATION VERSUS COST LEADERSHIP

Another key determinant of margin and turnover ratios is the extent to which a firm follows a product differentiation versus a cost leadership strategy. A product differentiation strategy requires higher investment to generate a differentiated product, resulting in lower turnover. A successful strategy should generate higher margins. A cost leadership strategy, in contrast, generates the basic product more efficiently, resulting in higher turnover and lower margins.

DETERMINANT 3: CORPORATE STRATEGY—VERTICAL INTEGRATION VERSUS OUTSOURCING

Another key determinant of margins and turnover ratios is the extent to which a firm follows a strategy of vertical integration versus outsourcing. Outsourcing requires less investment in operating capacity, but also necessitates the sharing of margins with the outsourcing partner. Relative to vertical integration, outsourcing therefore results in higher turnover and lower margins. The franchising of retail outlets, the leasing of productive capacity, and the securitization and sale of customer receivables can all be considered as forms of outsourcing.

QUESTIONS

1. Identify another example of an industry that operates with low turnover ratios and high margins and another example of an industry that operates with high turnover ratios and low margins. In each case, illustrate your example using the ratios for a representative firm in the industry and explain the features of the industry's production technology that lead to these ratios.

2. Identify an example of a product differentiator and an example of a cost leader within a particular industry. In each case, try to select an example where the strategy is appropriately reflected in the turnover ratios and explain the source of the different ratios.

3. Identify an example of a vertical integrator and an example of an outsourcer within a particular industry. In each case, try to select an example where the strategy is appropriately reflected in the turnover ratios and explain the source of the different ratios.

Netflix, Inc.*

By early 2005, Netflix had revolutionized the movie rental industry, growing to 3 million subscribers in its eight short years of existence. Netflix's tremendous success was primarily attributable to its innovative business model, built on two disarmingly retro technologies: the DVD and the U.S. Postal Service. For a monthly subscription fee averaging $18, consumers gain access to an unlimited number of rentable DVDs, most delivered within a couple of days of being ordered online.

This was not the first business success for Netflix founder and CEO, 44-year-old Reed Hastings. Hastings had already sold his first company, Pure-Software, in the mid-1990s for $750 million. He then went back to school, getting a master's in education from Stanford, and subsequently became president of the California Board of Education. His career in education ended around the time he rented *Apollo 13* from a Blockbuster store. After getting socked for $40 in late fees, Hastings began wondering why video rentals don't work like health clubs, which give members unlimited access for a flat monthly fee. His original business plan relied on mailing VHS cassettes to customers, but in 1997 he realized that DVDs, still new at that time, would be a much easier and more durable format for mailing.

Hastings started Netflix in 1998 from a warehouse in the heart of Silicon Valley. By early 2005, Netflix had 35 warehouses around the country, mailing out over 1 million DVDs per day to customers. Netflix had increased its subscriber base to 9 percent of households in its local San Francisco Bay area market and just 2.3 percent of households in the rest of the country, leaving plenty of room for future growth. Netflix's success had caught the attention of industry giants, who struggled to imitate Netflix's business model. Both Blockbuster and Walmart introduced services similar to Netflix but couldn't match Netflix's combination of excellent customer servicing and shrewd marketing. Walmart subsequently exited this business in May 2005, outsourcing it to Netflix.

Yet competition and rapid expansion were taking their toll on Netflix's profitability. Quarterly EPS peeked at $0.29 in the third quarter of 2004 and had dropped to $0.08 by the fourth quarter of 2004, with a loss projected for the first quarter of 2005. The lower profitability stemmed primarily from squeezed margins due to greater competition and more aggressive use of the unlimited rental option by subscribers. Netflix's stock price followed its earnings, plunging from almost $40 in early 2004 to just $12 by early 2005. But even this seemed like a rich valuation given that losses were being projected for the first quarter of 2005.

Critics argued that Netflix was simply pricing its service too cheaply. The video rental market had long depended on hefty late fees to drive profitability. By eliminating late fees and allowing unlimited rentals, it seemed that Netflix was simply selling its service at too low a price to earn a respectable profit. Netflix countered that its low profitability was attributable to ongoing investments in growing its subscriber base. Once this subscriber base matured, economies of scale, strong subscriber retention, and reduced subscriber usage of the unlimited rental option were expected to deliver healthy profits.

While having appeal in the current marketplace, Netflix's argument had one fundamental flaw. Its business model was likely to become obsolete in a few short years. A similar fate had met America Online almost a decade earlier. America Online invested heavily in building the largest subscriber base in the online content provider business, only to see this business rendered largely obsolete by the ISP (Internet service provider) business a few years later. Few industry observers expected mail delivery of DVDs to be the long-run delivery format for movie rentals. Video on demand through cable and satellite TV companies and Internet downloading were widely expected to become the standard delivery channels within the next decade.

Despite these concerns, Netflix marched full steam ahead with its aggressive growth strategy. Numerous Wall Street analysts applauded this strategy and recommended the stock as a "buy" to their brokerage clients. For example, a representative analyst argued that.[1]

> **We are raising our EPS estimates and increasing our 12-month price target to $34.** We expect record levels of subscriber acquisitions during 2005 to bode well for future profitability and we are increasing our 2005 EPS estimate to $0.34 and our 2006 EPS estimate to $1.13. We are reiterating our Buy rating and increasing our price target to $34 (30 × 2006 EPS) based on increased 2006 estimates.

Detailed information on Netflix's business strategy, financial situation, and expansion plans are provided in its Form 10-K for the year ended December 31, 2004. For comparative purposes, similar information also is provided for Blockbuster in its Form 10-K for the corresponding period. These documents are available as online exhibits at www.lundholmandsloan.com.

---

[1] This analyst quote represents the case-writer's personal synthesis of the published views of the numerous analysts that were bullish on the stock in 2005.

QUESTIONS

Business Strategy Analysis

1. Identify Netflix's source(s) of competitive advantage in the movie rental business relative to (*i*) traditional bricks-and-mortar video rental outlets, such as Hollywood Entertainment, and (*ii*) Web-based services offering the downloading of movies over the Internet, such as Movielink.

2. Evaluate the sustainability of Netflix's current sources of competitive advantage in the movie rental business.

Accounting Analysis

3. Contrast and evaluate how Netflix and Blockbuster account for their movie rental libraries. Do you think that any differences are justified?

4. Assume that instead of using its current accounting practices for its DVD library, Netflix instead expensed all costs associated with its DVD library as they were incurred. Estimate the *operating income* Netflix would have reported for the year ended December 31, 2004.

5. Briefly explain why Netflix's provision for income taxes (i.e., tax expense) for its 2004 fiscal year is so small.

Ratio Analysis

6. Compute rental library turnover ratios for Netflix and Blockbuster for fiscal year 2004. Carefully justify your choice of numerator in each of these ratios.

7. Identify the major reason(s) for the difference between the two turnover ratios that you computed above. Be as specific as possible.

8. Compute the gross margin earned on *movie rentals* for Netflix and Blockbuster for fiscal year 2004.

9. Identify the major reason(s) for the difference between the two margins that you computed above. Be as specific as possible.

Forecasting Analysis

10. Load the Netflix case data into *eVal* and provide a set of forecasting assumptions that yield a $0.34 EPS estimate for FY2005 and a $1.13 EPS forecast for FY2006. (*Note:* Case data can be imported by going to the Case Data sheet in *eVal* and selecting the yellow block of data for the company, and then pasting this block of data into the yellow cells at the bottom of the Financial Statements sheet using Paste Special—Values from the Edit menu.)

11. Evaluate the plausibility of the forecasting scenario you provided in answer to the preceding question.

12. Define and evaluate the "churn" metric computed by Netflix and explain why low churn is crucial to Netflix's long-run profitability.

Valuation Analysis

13. Load the Netflix case data into *eVal*, set the valuation date to March 1, 2005, and critically evaluate the default valuation provided by *eVal*.

14. In early 2005, Netflix was trading at around $12 per share. Using *eVal*, provide a set of forecasting assumptions that approximates this price. Use a cost of equity capital of 10 percent and a valuation date of March 1, 2005. Do you think that these forecasting assumptions are plausible?

15. Evaluate the method used to establish the price target of $34 quoted in the introduction to the case.

Overstock.com*

At the beginning of 2004, Overstock.com, Inc., was one of the hottest growth stocks on Wall Street. Operating in the highly competitive "e-tail" industry, the company had grown revenue from less than $2 million in 1999 to over $200 million in 2003. By March of 2004, Overstock.com's stock price had risen to around $30, representing a price-sales multiple of 2 and a market-book multiple of 10. The company's spectacular rise was attributed in large part to its high-achieving chief executive, Dr. Patrick Byrne. Byrne, who holds a master's from Cambridge University and a doctorate from Stanford University, had previously run a subsidiary of Warren Buffett's Berkshire Hathaway. Enthusiasm for the company in early 2004 was summarized in *The Washington Post* as follows:

> Fifty-five venture capitalists turned down Patrick Byrne's discount-shopping Web site for funding at the peak of dot-com investing mania. So the graduate of Walt Whitman High, Stanford University and Warren Buffett's real-world school of business funded it himself. Five years later, Overstock Inc. is a publicly traded company, pulling in nearly 7 million shoppers a month to its Internet bargain bazaar and ranking right up there with Target.com and BestBuy.com as one of the Web's top 20 e-commerce sites. But Byrne, its maverick chief executive, won't be satisfied until Overstock.com becomes a household name on par with eBay and Amazon.com, the Internet's top shopping hangouts, each of which draws more than 30 million people a month.[1]

The news, however, was not all good. Overstock.com had yet to report a positive annual profit and had only logged one quarterly profit, with that being back in the fourth quarter of 2002. The last 12 months had seen the departure of the company's chief financial officer, chief operating officer, and president. Moreover, competition was heating up from the likes of industry giants Amazon.com and eBay as well as smaller start-ups, such as privately held SmartBargains.com.

Against this backdrop, Overstock.com entered 2004 with plans to raise an additional $50 million, primarily to fund the inventory acquisitions necessary to maintain the company's aggressive growth plans. Its capital-raising

---

[1]Leslie Walker, "Underestimated Overstock.com Aims Higher," *The Washington Post*, December 4, 2003.
© 2003, *The Washington Post*. Reprinted with permission.

plans called for the issuance of 1.5 million additional shares through an offering underwritten by W. R. Hambrecht and Co. and JMP Securities. Enthusiasm for Overstock.com remained high on Wall Street, with analysts at both W. R. Hambrecht and JMP Securities issuing "buy" recommendations on the stock. Analysts at W. R. Hambrecht summarized their investment opinion as follows:

> **Reiterating Buy rating and increasing price target to $40.** Our price target implies an enterprise value to CY04 revenue of 1.4x, vs. a 1.1x multiple for OSTK's discount retailing peers and vs. 8.7x for Internet bellwethers AMZN and eBay (EBAY: Buy Rated). We think OSTK shares deserve a premium to its discount retailing peers because of the company's superior top-line growth prospects.[2]

Detailed information on Overstock.com's business strategy, financial situation, and expansion plans are provided in its Form 10-K for the year ended December 31, 2003. This document is available as an online exhibit at www.lundholmandsloan.com.

QUESTIONS

Business Strategy Analysis

1. Evaluate the structure of the Internet retailing (e-tailing) industry and its ability to generate profits over the long run. As a starting point, consider the five forces of competition:
   - Competition from substitutes.
   - Rivalry between established competitors.
   - Threat of entry.
   - Bargaining power of customers.
   - Bargaining power of suppliers.

2. Evaluate Overstock.com's strategy for creating competitive advantage, identifying the key success factors and risks associated with this strategy. Make sure to evaluate Overstock.com's business strategy relative to established e-tailers such as Amazon.com, traditional liquidation retailers such as TJX Companies, and other liquidation e-tailers such as SmartBargains.com.

Accounting Analysis

3. Identify Overstock.com's critical accounting policies. Briefly comment on whether you think that these accounting policies fairly present Overstock's financial performance.

4. The growth rate in Overstock's total revenue from 2002 to 2003 exceeded 150 percent. Do you think that this growth rate is sustainable? Explain your answer.

---

[2]William J. Lennan and Andrew Mackay, "OSTK: Beating Amazon.com on NYT Bestsellers, but What Does It Mean for Margins?" *W. R. Hambrecht and Co. Research Report,* March 10, 2004.

5. The growth rate in Overstock's gross profit from 2002 to 2003 was less than 50 percent, despite the fact that total revenue grew by over 150 percent. Explain why the growth rate in gross profit was so much lower.

6. Overstock.com has reported substantial losses in each of the last three years. Do you think these accounting losses provide a good reflection of Overstock.com's underlying economic performance? If you answered no to the first part of this question, how might you go about restating Overstock.com's accounting results in order to better reflect Overstock.com's underlying economic performance?

Ratio Analysis

7. Maximizing return on equity involves a trade-off between operating profitability (margin on sales) and turnover (efficiency of asset utilization). Consider the different business models of:
   - A closeout e-tailer, such as Overstock.com (OSTK).
   - A regular e-tailer, such as Amazon.com (AMZN).
   - A traditional closeout retailer, such as Ross Stores (ROST).
   - A department store retailer, such as May Department Stores (MAY).

8. Discuss how the different business models involved in each of these categories will influence the trade-off between profitability and turnover.

9. Figures 1, 2, and 3 are *eVal* Ratio Analysis outputs for AMZN, ROST, and MAY through the end of fiscal 2003. Using *eVal*, load the Overstock.com case data and conduct a ratio analysis for OSTK. (*Note:* Case data can be imported by going to the Case Data sheet in *eVal* and selecting the yellow block of data for the company, and then pasting this block of data into the yellow cells at the bottom of the Financial Statements sheet using Paste Special—Values from the Edit menu.)

10. Provide both a time-series analysis of OSTK from 2001 through 2003 and a cross-sectional analysis using AMZN, ROST, and MAY as comparison companies. Summarize what you learn about the key strengths and weaknesses of OSTK's financial performance.

Forecasting

This is a real-time forecasting case. Your objective is to forecast Overstock.com's income statement, balance sheet, and statement of cash flows for its current fiscal quarter. You should place particular emphasis on trying to generate an accurate forecast of Overstock.com's current quarter EPS (both basic EPS and diluted EPS). Use the following framework and data sources in constructing your forecasting model:

11. Familiarize yourself with Overstock.com's business strategy and financial performance. You will find most of the information available from the Investor Relations link at the bottom of Overstock.com's homepage (www.overstock.com). Make sure that you review Overstock.com's recent SEC filings and press releases.

FIGURE 1   Ratio Analysis for Amazon.com

	Actual 12/31/1999	Actual 12/31/2000	Actual 12/31/2001	Actual 12/31/2002	Actual 12/31/2003
			Fiscal Year End Date		
Annual Growth Rates					
Sales		68.4%	13.1%	26.0%	33.8%
Assets		−13.6%	−23.3%	21.6%	8.6%
Common Equity		−463.2%	#N/A	#N/A	#N/A
Earnings		#N/A	#N/A	#N/A	#N/A
Free Cash Flow to Investors			#N/A	−1,308.2%	#N/A
Sustainable Growth Rate			47.1%	10.7%	−3.0%
Profitability					
Return on Equity		4.027	0.471	0.107	(0.030)
Return on Equity (b4 nonrecurring)		2.267	0.307	0.027	(0.118)
Return on Net Operating Assets		(0.876)	(0.449)	(0.007)	0.179
Basic Dupont Model					
Net Profit Margin	(0.439)	(0.511)	(0.182)	(0.038)	0.007
× Total Asset Turnover		1.199	1.655	2.168	2.535
× Total Leverage		(6.572)	(1.567)	(1.299)	(1.738)
= Return on Equity		4.027	0.471	0.107	(0.030)
Advanced Dupont Model					
Net Operating Margin	(0.387)	(0.464)	(0.137)	(0.002)	0.031
× Net Operating Asset Turnover		1.889	3.273	4.713	5.686
= Return on Net Operating Assets		(0.876)	(0.449)	(0.007)	0.179
Net Borrowing Cost (NBC)		0.072	0.065	0.064	0.061
Spread (RNOA − NBC)		(0.948)	(0.513)	(0.072)	0.117
Financial Leverage (LEV)		(5.171)	(1.793)	(1.598)	(1.775)
ROE = RNOA + LEV × Spread		4.027	0.471	0.107	(0.030)
Margin Analysis					
Gross Margin	0.218	0.238	0.239	0.273	0.253
EBITDA Margin	(0.192)	(0.123)	(0.032)	0.049	0.066
EBIT Margin	(0.364)	(0.240)	(0.074)	0.027	0.051
Net Operating Margin (b4 nonrec.)	(0.364)	(0.240)	(0.074)	0.027	0.051
Net Operating Margin	(0.387)	(0.464)	(0.137)	(0.002)	0.031
Turnover Analysis					
Net Operating Asset Turnover		1.889	3.273	4.713	5.686
Net Working Capital Turnover		8.002	8.867	9.098	9.272
Avge Days to Collect Receivables		0.000	0.000	5.210	8.472
Avge Inventory Holding Period		34.261	24.458	22.103	23.043
Avge Days to Pay Payables		80.458	70.558	69.293	68.349
PP&E Turnover		8.076	9.786	15.389	22.704

FIGURE 2   Ratio Analysis for Ross Stores

	Actual 12/31/1999	Actual 12/31/2000	Actual 12/31/2001	Actual 12/31/2002	Actual 12/31/2003
			Fiscal Year End Date		
Annual Growth Rates					
Sales		9.7%	10.2%	18.2%	11.0%
Assets		2.9%	11.0%	25.7%	21.7%
Common Equity		−1.2%	16.4%	18.1%	17.4%
Earnings		1.1%	2.2%	29.8%	13.4%
Free Cash Flow to Investors			#N/A	−336.3%	#N/A
Sustainable Growth Rate			28.0%	31.4%	30.1%
Profitability					
Return on Equity		0.323	0.306	0.339	0.326
Return on Equity (b4 nonrecurring)		0.323	0.306	0.339	0.326
Return on Net Operating Assets		0.306	0.292	0.332	0.310
Basic Dupont Model					
Net Profit Margin	0.061	0.056	0.052	0.057	0.058
× Total Asset Turnover		2.818	2.903	2.890	2.598
× Total Leverage		2.043	2.033	2.058	2.158
= Return on Equity		0.323	0.306	0.339	0.326
Advanced Dupont Model					
Net Operating Margin	0.061	0.057	0.053	0.057	0.058
× Net Operating Asset Turnover		5.391	5.551	5.824	5.321
= Return on Net Operating Assets		0.036	0.292	0.332	0.310
Net Borrowing Cost (NBC)		0.066	0.060	0.014	0.000
Spread (RNOA − NBC)		0.240	0.231	0.318	0.310
Financial Leverage (LEV)		0.068	0.063	0.021	0.054
ROE = RNOA + LEV × Spread		0.323	0.306	0.339	0.326
Margin Analysis					
Gross Margin	0.314	0.312	0.311	0.274	0.275
EBITDA Margin	0.123	0.114	0.107	0.112	0.115
EBIT Margin	0.103	0.093	0.086	0.094	0.095
Net Operating Margin (b4 nonrec.)	0.063	0.057	0.053	0.057	0.058
Net Operating Margin	0.061	0.057	0.053	0.057	0.058
Turnover Analysis					
Net Operating Asset Turnover		5.391	5.551	5.824	5.321
Net Working Capital Turnover		12.847	13.087	13.552	11.131
Avge Days to Collect Receivables		2.028	2.136	2.010	2.031
Avge Inventory Holding Period		103.866	104.916	95.437	100.076
Avge Days to Pay Payables		52.056	52.599	52.606	56.791
PP&E Turnover		9.426	9.433	9.619	8.841

FIGURE 3 Ratio Analysis for May Department Stores

	Fiscal Year End Date				
	Actual 12/31/1999	Actual 12/31/2000	Actual 12/31/2001	Actual 12/31/2002	Actual 12/31/2003
Annual Growth Rates					
Sales		4.7%	−2.3%	−4.8%	−1.1%
Assets		5.8%	3.0%	0.1%	1.3%
Common Equity		−5.4%	−0.4%	5.1%	3.9%
Earnings		−7.5%	−18.6%	−23.4%	−20.6%
Free Cash Flow to Investors			#N/A	162.5%	−26.3%
Sustainable Growth Rate			9.6%	5.5.%	2.6%
Profitability					
Return on Equity		0.212	0.178	0.133	0.11
Return on Equity (b4 nonrecurring)		0.210	0.177	0.147	0.154
Return on Net Operating Assets		0.131	0.107	0.091	0.078
Basic Dupont Model					
Net Profit Margin	0.065	0.058	0.048	0.039	0.031
× Total Asset Turnover		1.289	1.207	1.131	1.110
× Total Leverage		2.838	3.053	3.029	2.922
= Return on Equity		0.212	0.178	0.133	0.101
Advanced Dupont Model					
Net Operating Margin	0.080	0.074	0.065	0.058	0.049
× Net Operating Asset Turnover		1.764	1.650	1.585	1.609
= Return on Net Operating Assets		0.131	0.107	0.091	0.078
Net Borrowing Cost (NBC)		0.055	0.050	0.055	0.056
Spread (RNOA − NBC)		0.075	0.057	0.036	0.022
Financial Leverage (LEV)		1.074	1.233	1.161	1.016
ROE = RNOA + LEV × Spread		0.212	0.178	0.133	0.101
Margin Analysis					
Gross Margin	0.358	0.351	0.350	0.340	0.339
EBITDA Margin	0.164	0.156	0.145	0.134	0.138
EBIT Margin	0.131	0.120	0.105	0.093	0.096
Net Operating Margin (b4 nonrec.)	0.079	0.074	0.065	0.062	0.065
Net Operating Margin	0.080	0.074	0.065	0.058	0.049
Turnover Analysis					
Net Operating Asset Turnover		1.764	1.650	1.585	1.609
Net Working Capital Turnover		4.758	4.837	5.327	5.293
Avge Days to Collect Receivables		53.501	51.744	49.768	47.817
Avge Inventory Holding Period		111.519	115.175	117.459	115.828
Avge Days to Pay Payables		39.162	39.121	43.396	46.779
PP&E Turnover		3.002	2.790	2.515	2.514

12. Familiarize yourself with Overstock.com's expansion plans. Company press releases and the MD&A sections of the Form 10-Ks and Form 10-Qs are your best sources of information. This information is again available from the Investor Relations link at the bottom of Overstock.com's homepage.

13. Use the forecasting framework developed in the course, along with the insights generated by your analyses in questions 1 and 2 above to prepare forecasts of Overstock.com's income statement, balance sheet, and statement of cash flows for the current quarter.

14. Do a "reality check" on your forecasting model by comparing your EPS forecasts to sell-side analysts' forecasts (available at the following link: http://finance.yahoo.com/q/ae?s=OSTK).

Valuation Analysis

15. The case introduction summarizes an investment opinion issued by analysts at W. R. Hambrecht on March 10, 2004. Critically evaluate the valuation method(s) used to justify the $40 price target contained in this opinion.

16. Load the Overstock.com case data into *eVal* and critically evaluate the default valuation provided by *eVal*.

17. In early 2004, Overstock.com was trading at around $30 per share. Using *eVal*, provide a set of forecasting assumptions that approximate this price. Use a cost of equity capital of 10 percent and a valuation date of March 10, 2004. Do you think that these forecasting assumptions are plausible?

18. Using *eVal*, provide your own valuation of Overstock.com on March 10, 2004. Select what you consider to be the most plausible set of forecasting assumptions and justify these selections. Use a cost of equity capital of 10 percent and a valuation date of March 10, 2004.

Pre-Paid Legal Services*

The third week of October 1999 was a truly bizarre week in the history of Pre-Paid Legal Services (NYSE: PPD). It was marked by the following significant events.

Monday, October 18:	PPD's stock price opens at $36 on the NYSE, slightly above its Friday close of $35.50.
	Forbes magazine names PPD as number 13 on its annual list of the best 200 small companies in America.
Tuesday, October 19:	PPD announces record results for the third quarter of 1999. EPS increased 50 percent, meeting Wall Street's expectations and marking PPD's 25th consecutive quarter of increased revenues and earnings. The full text of PPD's earnings announcement is attached as Exhibit 1.
	Following the announcement, PPD's stock price plummets by over 20 percent in frenzied trading on the NYSE.
Wednesday, October 20:	After taking the night to digest PPD's earnings announcement, investors again pummel PPD's stock price, forcing it down another 10 percent. PPD steps into the market in an effort to shore up its stock price, repurchasing 140,000 shares over the remainder of the week.
Friday, October 22:	PPD's stock price closes at $25, a loss for the week of over 30 percent.

*This case was prepared by Professor Richard Sloan as the basis for class discussion, rather than to illustrate either effective or ineffective handling of a business situation. Copyright © 1999 by Richard Sloan.

EXHIBIT 1
Pre-Paid Announces
Record Third
Quarter Results

Earnings per share up 50 percent and recruiting up 42 percent
ADA, OK, October 19, 1999—Pre-Paid Legal Services, Inc. (NYSE:PPD), today reported record results for the third quarter and for the nine months ended September 30, 1999. As a result of the 1998 fourth quarter acquisition of TPN, Inc. ("TPN") that was accounted for as a pooling of interests, the 1998 periods have been restated to include the operating results of TPN.

Net income for the third quarter of 1999 rose 49 percent to $9,870,000 from $6,611,000 for the prior year's period, while total revenues rose 23 percent to $49,025,000 from $39,809,000 for the prior year's period despite planned decreases of $4.8 million in TPN product sales. The Company's membership revenues increased 41 percent to $39,748,000 from $28,105,000 for the same period last year. Earnings per share, diluted, increased 50 percent to 42 cents per share from 28 cents per diluted share for last year's comparable quarter.

Nine-month net income during 1999 increased 56 percent to $28,524,000 from $18,296,000 for the first three quarters of 1998. Earnings per share, diluted, for the 1999 nine-month period increased 59 percent to $1.21 per share from 76 cents per diluted share for last year's comparable period. Revenues for the nine months were up 20 percent to $141,567,000 from $117,500,000 for the initial nine months of the prior year despite planned decreases of $19 million in TPN product sales.

Even though commission advances increased $9.2 million as a result of increasing membership sales during the third quarter of 1999, cash flow from operations was $5,119,000, a decrease of $379,000, or 7 percent, from the cash flow of $5,498,000 for the comparable quarter of 1998. Cash flow from operations for the first nine months of 1999 was $12.9 million compared to $8.8 million for the comparable period of 1998, an increase of $4.1 million, or 46 percent. At September 30, 1999, the Company had cash and investment balances exceeding $42,500,000.

For the third quarter of 1999, the Company added 134,725 new members, 41 percent above the 95,619 new members added during the same period of 1998. New sales associates recruited during the third quarter of 1999 were 22,493 compared to 15,820 for the comparable period of 1998, an increase of 42 percent.

"We are obviously very pleased with our third quarter operating results, but more than ever, firmly believe the best is yet to come. As we celebrate our 28th year in business, we are in the best financial condition in our history with cash and investment balances of more than $42.5 million, no long term debt and significant positive cash flow while still continuing to grow our membership revenues at better than 40 percent. Our continued revenue growth, financial condition, enhanced Internet presence and increases in recruiting all contribute to our belief that the best is still ahead of us," Harland Stonecipher, Chairman, said.

Pre-Paid Legal Services, Inc., develops, underwrites and markets legal service plans nationally. The plans provide for legal service benefits, including unlimited attorney consultation, will preparation, traffic violation defense, automobile-related criminal charges, letter writing, document preparation and review and a general trial defense benefit. More information can be located at the Company's homepage on the worldwide web at prepaidlegal.com.

FIGURE 1
Pre-Paid Legal
Services, Inc.,
Fianancial Highlights
(Unaudited)
(Dollars and shares in
000s, except per share
amounts)

	Three Months Ended		Nine Months Ended	
	9/30/99	9/30/98	9/30/99	9/30/98
Revenues:				
Membership premiums	$39.748	$28,105	$112,017	$78.443
Product sales	1,256	6,102	4,426	23,437
Associate services	5,832	4,093	16,201	23,437
Interest income	897	819	2,665	1,881
Other	1,292	690	6,204	1,929
	49,025	39,809	141,567	117,500
Costs and expenses:				
Membership benefits	13,764	9,297	37,388	25,893
Product costs	790	3,711	2,899	14,321
Commissions	9,819	6,422	26,200	17,299
General and administrative	4,428	5,074	13,938	17,971
Associate services and direct marketing expenses	3,767	3,306	10,637	10,518
Depreciation and amortization	688	823	2,372	2,025
Premium taxes	389	277	1,090	908
Other	285	—	3,160	—
	33,839	28,910	97,684	88,935
Income before income taxes	15,186	10,899	43,883	28,565
Provision for income taxes	5,316	4,288	15,359	10,269
Net income	9,870	6,611	28,524	18,296
Less dividends on preferred shares	2	2	7	7
Net income applicable to common shares	$9,868	$6,609	$28,517	$18,289
Basic earnings per common share	$.43	$.28	$1.23	$.78
Diluted earnings per common share	$.42	$.28	$1.21	$.76
Weighted average number of common shares:				
Basic	22,927	23,496	23,246	23,446
Diluted	23,313	23,887	23,587	23,926
Net cash provided by operating activities	$5,119	$5,498	$12,852	$8,790
New membership sales	134,725	95,619	376,424	273,048
New sales associates recruited	22,493	15,820	68,035	46,530
Number of active memberships at end of period	759,341	546,358		

Statements in this press release other than purely historical information, including statements relating to the Company's future plans and objectives and expected operating results, constitute forward-looking statements within the meaning of Section 21E of the Securities Exchange Act of 1934. Forward-looking statements are based on certain assumptions which may not be correct and are subject to all of the risks and uncertainties incident to the Company's business which are described in the reports and statements filed by the Company with the Securities and Exchange Commission. As a result, actual results may vary materially from those described in the forward-looking statements.

Fred Russell, a Tulsa money manager who rates PPD as one of his favorite companies, explains the stock price drop as follows:

> The stock price drop is typical of Wall Street's reaction to significant news. Included in Tuesday's earnings statement was a somewhat complex accounting of increased commission payments. This caused short-term pain during the period for Pre-Paid, but the upswing in sales should benefit the company in the long run.[1]

PPD investor relations spokesperson Melanie Danielson notes that

> Another factor was the impact of comments made by a short-seller on CNBC on Tuesday. The seller pointed out that the company's cash flow for the third quarter, reported Tuesday, was $5.1 million, down $379,000 from the same period in 1998.[2]

Information concerning PPD's business strategy, accounting policies, and financial condition is provided in PPD's Form 10-K for 1998. Relevant portions of this document are available as an online exhibit at www.lundholmandsloan.com.

QUESTIONS

1. Identify and evaluate the key elements of PPD's business strategy. Make sure you understand the product they are selling and how they go about selling it.
2. Identify the problem revealed by the third-quarter earnings announcement that resulted in PPD's stock price drop. What was the cause of this problem?
3. Suggest an alternative method of accounting for the transactions that led to the problem identified in question 2 above and recompute PPD's earnings using this method.
4. Do you think that earnings computed using the method you identified in question 3 above provide a better or a worse indication of PPD's actual performance?
5. What actions would you advise PPD's management take in response to investors' reaction to the third-quarter earnings announcement?
6. What information would you seek from PPD's subsequent press releases and SEC filings in order to determine whether the price reaction to the third quarter announcement was warranted?

---

[1]Oklahoma-Based Legal Services Firm's Stock Price Plummets 22 Percent," *Tribune Business News*, October 20, 1999.

[2]Ibid.

Determinants of Valuation Ratios: The Restaurant Industry in 2011*

The restaurant industry has always represented a prime example of a competitive industry. New innovations are easily observed and imitated, start-up costs are generally quite low, and the entry and exit of new players is frequent. Despite the intense competition, a wide range of valuation ratios is typically observed in the industry. The year 2011 was no exception. It was characterized by the following industry medians:

Industry Median ROE = 15 percent

Industry Median Consensus Analyst Forecast of Five-Year EPS Growth = 15 percent

Industry Median Price-to-Earnings Ratio = 20

Industry Median Market-to-Book Ratio = 3.8

The brief sketches of four restaurant companies on the following pages illustrate the variety of experiences within the industry.

REQUIRED

Based on the information provided for each of the following four companies, rank the companies as to whether you expect them to have a higher or lower market-to-book ratio and a higher or lower price-to-earnings ratio relative to the median firm in the industry.

*This case was prepared by Richard Sloan as the basis for classroom discussion. Copyright © 2011 by Richard Sloan.

Brinker International, Inc.

Brinker International, Inc. owns, develops, operates, and franchises various restaurant brands primarily in the United States. It operates the restaurants under the Chili's Grill & Bar and Maggiano's Little Italy brand names. As of August 29, 2011, the company owned, operated, and franchised 1,534 Chili's Grill & Bar restaurants and 45 Maggiano's Little Italy restaurants in 50 states, and Washington, D.C.; and held a minority investment in Romano's Macaroni Grill.

Summary financial data are presented below:

Book Value of Equity/Share = $4.72
2010 EPS = $1.52
Consensus Analyst Forecast of 2011 EPS = $1.70
Consensus Analyst Forecast of Five-Year EPS Growth = 12 percent

Benihana Inc.

Benihana Inc. operates Benihana teppanyaki-style Japanese restaurants in the United States. It also operates other Asian restaurant concepts that include RA Sushi and Haru. The company's Benihana teppanyaki restaurant offers fresh steak, chicken, and seafood; RA Sushi concept provides sushi and Pacific Rim dishes; and Haru concept offers traditional Japanese and Japanese fusion dishes. It operates 63 Benihana restaurants, 25 RA Sushi restaurants, and 8 Haru restaurants, as well as 18 franchised Benihana restaurants in the United States, Latin America, and the Caribbean. The company was founded in 1964 and is based in Miami, Florida.

Summary financial data are presented below:

Book Value of Equity/Share = $9.59
2010 EPS = $0.02
Consensus Analyst Forecast of 2011 EPS = $0.37
Consensus Analyst Forecast of Five-Year EPS Growth = 20 percent

Chipotle Mexican Grill, Inc.

Chipotle Mexican Grill, Inc. develops and operates fast-casual, fresh Mexican food restaurants in the United States. It also operates restaurants in Toronto, Canada and in London, the United Kingdom. As of October 20, 2011, it operated 1,100 restaurants. Chipotle Mexican Grill, Inc. was founded in 1993 and is based in Denver, Colorado.

Summary financial data are presented below:

Book Value of Equity/Share = $31.92
2010 EPS = $5.64
Consensus Analyst Forecast of 2011 EPS = $6.82
Consensus Analyst Forecast of Five-Year EPS Growth = 22 percent

Ruby Tuesday, Inc.

Ruby Tuesday, Inc., together with its subsidiaries, develops, operates, and franchises casual dining restaurants in the United States, Puerto Rico, Guam, and internationally. The company operates its restaurants under the Ruby Tuesday brand, as well as owns and operates one Marlin & Ray's, one Truffles, and two Wok Hay casual dining restaurants. As of August 30, 2011, it owned and operated 746 Ruby Tuesday restaurants, and was a franchisor of 43 domestic and 52 international restaurants. The company was founded in 1920 and is based in Maryville, Tennessee.

Summary financial data are presented below:

Book Value of Equity/Share = $9.27
2010 EPS = $0.73
Consensus Analyst Forecast of 2011 EPS = $0.65
Consensus Analyst Forecast of Five-Year EPS Growth = 11 percent

Forecasting for the Love Boat: Royal Caribbean Cruises in 1998*

Much like Kate Winslet leaning over the bow of the *Titanic,* the North American cruise industry seems poised to either take flight or suffer a precipitous fall. The number of cruise passengers has grown from 500,000 in 1970 to 5,400,000 in 1998, a compounded average of 8.9 percent per year. Further, as the baby boomers mature, an increasing proportion of the population will fit the profile of a typical cruise customer—someone between 40 and 59 years old earning about $60,000. But all the news isn't bright. Based on the number of new ships that have already been ordered by major operators, the number of available berths in the North American market is expected to increase by over 40 percent in the next five years. Will the increase in demand for cruise vacations be sufficient to fill all the cabins on these new ships? Given the large fixed costs of operating a cruise vessel and the debt necessary to fund this capacity expansion, the cruise industry risks an encounter with an iceberg as it steams into the new millennium.

This case focuses on Royal Caribbean Cruises in 1998. The first part of the case asks you to conduct a detailed analysis of Royal Caribbean's past financial statements and to compare them with those of their rival, Carnival Cruises. The second part of the case asks you to forecast the financial performance of Royal Caribbean for the next three years. Note that the chilling effect of September 11, 2001, on the travel and vacation business occurs mostly after the three years that you will be forecasting, so you don't have to pretend that you don't know about this major event.

*Professor Russell Lundholm prepared this case at the University of Michigan Business School in 2002 as the basis for class discussion. Sources for this case include the Cruise Line International Association Market Overview, Cruise Industry News, the Tourism Industry Association of America, Royal Caribbean Cruises' 1998 10-K filing, and Carnival Cruises' 1998 10-K filing. I thank Cheryl Fenske at the Cruise Line International Association for her help in obtaining 1998 data.

The case material that follows will provide you with a comprehensive picture of the North American cruise industry as it stood in 1998 along with specific financial and operating details of Royal Caribbean Cruises and Carnival Cruises. There is a wealth of information available and no single correct way to put it all together in your financial analysis and forecasts. Please limit your analysis to the information available in the case and in the case's associated online exhibits at www.lundholmandsloan.com.

THE NORTH AMERICAN CRUISE INDUSTRY IN 1998

Cruise ships travel the world. Royal Caribbean Cruises, for instance, offers 175 destinations on six different continents. What defines the North American market is not the destination but the point of sale. Hence, North Americans purchase their trips in North America, but may fly to any part of the world to embark on a "North American" cruise. While all major cruise lines offer "Air and Sea" options, this is really just a convenience for their customers. The air portion is priced at cost, and this portion of the trip is handled completely by the airline. Virtually all cruise purchases take place through a local travel agent.

Demand for cruise vacations has grown rapidly over the past two decades as Figure 1 illustrates, with the only decrease in demand occurring in 1994–1995. Further, the average length of a cruise trip has grown to approximately 6.6 days, reaching levels not experienced since the early 1980s. Because of the fixed/variable cost structure in the cruise industry, longer trips are typically more profitable than short trips, so the industry has welcomed this trend.

FIGURE 1
North American Cruise Statistics

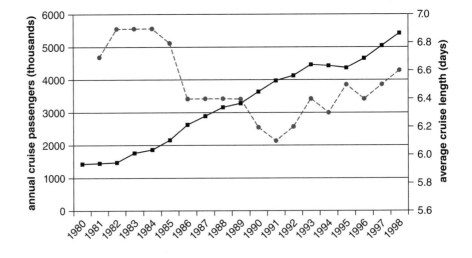

FIGURE 2
Market Shares

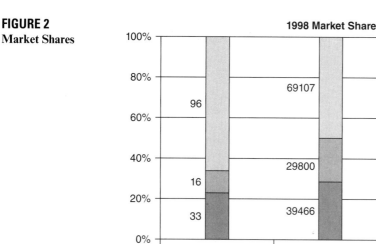

The North American cruise industry is composed of two very large companies and many small ones, as seen in Figure 2. Carnival Cruise Lines is the largest firm with 33 ships carrying 2,045,000 passengers in 1998, 38 percent of the North American cruise market. Royal Caribbean Cruises is the second largest company with 16 ships carrying 1,841,000 passengers in 1998, a total of 34 percent of the North American market. A host of smaller cruise lines make up the rest of the industry, dividing 1,542,000 passengers between 96 vessels. The relative market shares are illustrated in Figure 2.

THE CRUISE EXPERIENCE

The cruise industry offers a wide variety of ship sizes, luxury levels and itineraries. From small, quasi-research vessels that probe Artic passages to massive "mega-ships" that resemble floating Malls of America, the cruise industry offers something for everyone. The Caribbean is the most common destination for cruises sold in North America, with approximately 39 percent of all passenger-days devoted to this destination. However, the table also shows that there has been a significant increase in demand for trips to locations such as the Mediterranean, Alaska, and Europe. The latest trend is for huge ships that carry as many as 3,000 guests, and offer a wide variety of entertainment alternatives. Such vessels feature rock-climbing, ice-skating, miniature golf, cinemas, discos, spa facilities, libraries, casinos, extensive live entertainment, and entire shopping malls, all onboard the ship. The focus of these cruise alternatives is on the vessel, rather than the destination. Bob Dickinson, the president of Carnival Cruises, remarked "Now, the cruise itself is the destination—magnificent floating resorts. To me, the itinerary is a little Green Stamp, a little extra thing."

WHO'S ONBOARD

Obviously different types of cruises attract different types of customers. Nonetheless, certain demographic profiles are most likely to take a cruise. Figure 3 below compares the demographic profile of those who have taken a cruise with the entire U.S. population over the age of 24. Generally, the population of past cruisers is older, wealthier, and better educated than the overall population.

Examining those who have cruised most recently reveals a few different types of customers, as Figure 4 illustrates, but most seek the relaxation and pampering that a cruise can provide. Indeed, when the recent cruiser population was asked what cruising offered that was superior to other types of vacations, the top three responses were "being pamper," "fine dining" and "hassle free."

FIGURE 3
Demographics of Cruise Market

Demographic Profile		Ever Cruised	Past 5 Year Cruisers	Population over Age 24
Gender:	Male	49%	51%	50%
	Female	51%	48%	49%
Age:	25–under 40 years	27%	28%	43%
	40–59 years	42%	42%	44%
	60 years or older	32%	30%	13%
	Average	51 yrs.	50 yrs.	43 yrs.
	Median	51 yrs.	51 yrs.	42 yrs.
Marital Status:	Married	76%	78%	69%
	Not Married	24%	22%	31%
Household Composition:	Have children under 18	37%	35%	54%
	Adults only	63%	65%	46%
	Occupants	3	3	3
Education:	Some College or less	42%	36%	54%
	College Graduate or more	58%	64%	46%
Household Income:	$20,000–$29,999	8%	5%	13%
	$30,000–$39,999	12%	10%	17%
	$40,000–$59,999	32%	31%	31%
	$60,000–$99,999	28%	30%	29%
	$100,000 or more	20%	25%	9%
	Average	$72,600	$79,100	$60,400
	Median	$58,500	$64,500	$51,800

FIGURE 4

Types of People Taking Cruises

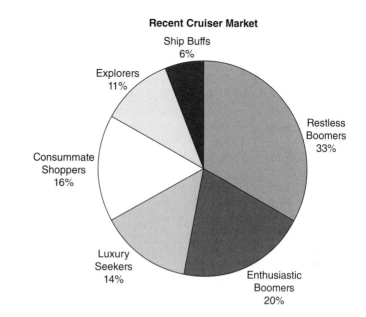

Recent Cruiser Market

Ship Buffs 6%

Explorers 11%

Consummate Shoppers 16%

Luxury Seekers 14%

Restless Boomers 33%

Enthusiastic Boomers 20%

Restless Baby Boomers are newest to cruising. They are at a point in time when they may be trying different vacation experiences.

Enthusiastic Baby Boomers are already convinced about cruising and its many activities. They live intense, stressful lives and look to vacations generally, and cruises in particular, for the escape and relaxation they offer.

Luxury Seekers can afford, and are willing to spend money for deluxe accommodations and pampering.

Consummate Shoppers are looking for the best value in a vacation and in a cruise.

Explorers are well-educated, well-traveled individuals with an intellectual interest and curiosity about different destinations.

Ship Buffs are the most senior segment: They have cruised extensively and expect to continue because they find the onboard experience of cruising so pleasurable and comfortable.

SUPPLY OF AVAILABLE BERTHS

The supply of available berths as of 1998 was shown in the market share figure given earlier. Further, because the lead-time necessary to design and build a cruise ship is approximately three years, a reasonably accurate forecast of future supply is available for the next three years, as seen in Figure 5 below (more detailed information about Royal Caribbean's new ships is available later in the case). It is more difficult to estimate the amount of capacity that will be retired in the future. Over the past five years, 48 ships with a total of 28,900 berths have been retired or moved out of the North American market. However, many of these retirements occurred because of a 1997 deadline to meet the heightened safety requirements imposed by the International Maritime Organization. From 1994 through 1996, retirements exceeded 7,000 berths per year but have slowed considerably since then.

FIGURE 5 Increases in Supply of Berths

| | New Capacity | | | | | | | |
| | 1999 | | 2000 | | 2001 | | Total New | |
	ships	berths	ships	berths	ships	berths	ships	berths
Carnival Cruises (includes Holland brand)	3	5480	2	6180	2	3900	7	15560
Royal Caribbean Cruises (includes Celebrity brand)	1	3100	2	5100	3	6100	6	14300
All Other Cruise Lines	7	7794	2	2800	4	6296	13	16890
Total New Ships/Berths	11	16374	6	14080	9	16296	26	46750

DEMAND FOR A CRUISE VACATION

To date only 11 percent of the U.S. population has ever taken a cruise. However, a recent cruise industry survey of people over the age of 24 found that 56 percent are interested in cruising sometime in the future and 31 percent responded that they will definitely take a cruise in the next five years. Demographic trends also favor the cruise industry. As the demographic profile showed, 42 percent of recent cruise passengers are between the ages of 40 and 59. As the baby boomers age, this segment of the U.S. population is estimated to grow at more than three times the national population growth rate over the next three years, as seen in Figure 6.

Along with growth in the U.S. population, it is possible that the amount of vacation time per individual will increase over time. Numerous studies have shown that the baby boomer generation values recreation more highly than previous generations. This is illustrated in the next figure that plots growth rates in the U.S. gross domestic product (GDP), personal consumption, and recreation expenditures. As Figure 7 shows, growth in personal consumption maps closely to growth in the gross domestic product (GDP). By comparison, recreation spending has grown faster than personal consumption in every year since 1980, with the gap between the two increasing dramatically after the 1991 recession. This increase is widely attributed to the consumption tastes of the baby boomer generation. Figure 7 also shows the 1998 Congressional Budget Office's forecasts for future GDP growth.

Finally, U.S. residents vacation far less than the citizens of all other developed countries, averaging just 13 days per year. As Figure 8 illustrates,

FIGURE 6
U.S. Population Growth

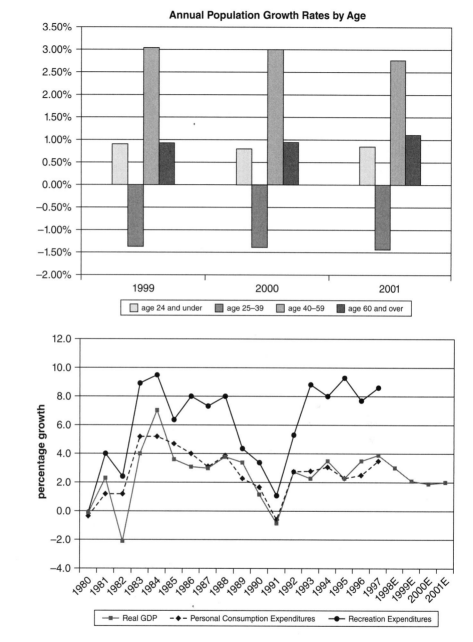

Annual Population Growth Rates by Age

Legend: age 24 and under | age 25–39 | age 40–59 | age 60 and over

FIGURE 7
Relation between GDP, Personal Consumption, and Recreation Expenditures

Legend: Real GDP | Personal Consumption Expenditures | Recreation Expenditures

even the hard-working Japanese and Koreans vacation almost twice as much as Americans. Italians, living the good life, vacation more than three times as much. It is certainly possible that Americans will increase their vacation expenditures even more in the future.

FIGURE 8

Average Vacation Days by Country

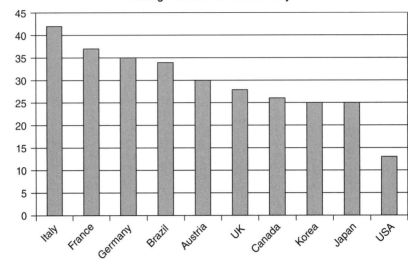

Average Number of Vacation Days

PART A. COMPREHENSIVE FINANCIAL ANALYSIS

Your task for this part of the case is to conduct a comprehensive financial analysis of Royal Caribbean Cruises and to compare their performance with Carnival Cruises. Excerpts from Royal Caribbean's 20-F filing and Carnival's 10-K filing are included as online exhibits at www.lundholmandsloan.com.

You will need to import the case data into *eVal*. (*Note:* Case data can be imported by going to the Case Data sheet in *eVal* and selecting the yellow block of data for the company, and then pasting this block of data into the yellow cells at the bottom of the Financial Statements sheet using Paste Special—Values from the Edit menu.) You should compare the financial statements in *eVal* with the ones in the 20-F and 10-K filings so that you can see exactly what data are used to compute each ratio and make any necessary adjustments. The definitions of each ratio are given in this textbook. Note that Royal Caribbean paid a preferred stock dividend of $12.5 million in 1998 but that this amount is not in the *eVal* data. You will have to correct the financial statements once they are loaded into *eVal*.

1. Compare the growth rates of Royal Caribbean and Carnival Cruises. What are the advantages to being large in this industry?

2. Compute the 1998 net operating income, net financing expense, average net operating assets, and average net financial obligations from the financial statements in Royal Caribbean's 20-F filing.

3. Using your answers to the previous question, compute return on equity (ROE) and then decompose ROE using the advanced Dupont decomposition:

$$ROE = RNOA + Leverage \times Spread$$

How does your decomposition compare to the one provided by *eVal?*

4. Using the financial ratios provided by *eVal*, evaluate any trends in Royal Caribbean's return on equity, compare it with Carnival Cruise's return on equity, and discuss the main causes of any differences.

5. Now consider each of the main drivers of return on equity: margins, turnovers, and leverage. Using *eVal*'s output as a starting point, evaluate any trends and compare Royal Caribbean with Carnival Cruises in each of these areas. Only note what is exceptional—do not discuss every possible ratio.

6. Does a dollar of revenue increase bring about a constant increase in expenses for Royal Caribbean, or do they enjoy economies of scale? Estimate any economies of scale that might be present.

7. Approximately 35 percent of Carnival Cruise's passengers also book their air travel through the cruise company (as an "air and sea" package) while only 25 percent of Royal Caribbean's passengers include the air portion in their booking. Conceptually, how will this affect your ratio comparison of the two companies and discuss how you might adjust the data to remove this distortion?

PART B. FINANCIAL FORECASTS

This part of the case asks you to forecast the financial performance of Royal Caribbean for the next three years. This is where you should bring together the industry facts given in the beginning of the case, the results of your financial analysis, and your understanding of Royal Caribbean's unique attributes gleaned from a careful reading of their SEC filings. Note that, while the events of September 11, 2001, had a dramatic effect on subsequent travel and tourism, this is largely after the periods you are forecasting. In their 2001 annual report, Royal Caribbean estimates a net cost of $47.7 million due to passenger's inability to fly to their departure locations, subsequent cancellations, and other costs incurred as a direct result of this event. Make your forecasts without regard to this event, but then subtract an extraordinary loss of $47.7 million from your final income estimate to control for this effect.

Your answers will not be graded on their accuracy but, rather, on the logic you give to support them. Use *eVal* to derive the forecasted financial data. Although your answers should be in the format given in *eVal*, your analysis should be *far more detailed* than a simple extrapolation from

Royal Caribbean's past performance (as the *eVal* defaults will do). Note that Royal Caribbean paid a preferred stock dividend of $12.5 million in 1998 but that this amount is not in the Global Access data. You will have to correct the financial statements once they are loaded into *eVal*. (*Note:* Case data can be imported by going to the Case Data sheet in *eVal* and selecting the yellow block of data for the company, and then pasting this block of data into the yellow cells at the bottom of the Financial Statements sheet using Paste Special—Values from the Edit menu.) Excerpts from Royal Caribbean's 20-F filing and Carnival's 10-K filing are included as online exhibits at www.lundholmandsloan.com.

1. Based on all the information provided in the case, forecast Royal Caribbean's gross revenue for 1999, 2000, and 2001. Please explain your reasoning.

2. Forecast the remaining portions of the income statement for 1999, 2000, and 2001. Comment only on the forecast components that differ significantly from past trends or ratios—do not discuss each line item if you don't have anything substantive to say.

3. Forecast complete balance sheets for the end of 1999, 2000, and 2001. Comment only on the forecast components that differ significantly from past trends or ratios—do not discuss each line item if you don't have anything substantive to say.

4. Can Royal Caribbean afford to purchase the ships that it has on order in the next three years? How do you anticipate that these acquisitions will be financed?

5. For this question, do not use *eVal* (because it is easier not to). Suppose your analysis indicated that Royal Caribbean would spend $810,261 thousand on additions to property and equipment in 1999. Given this, estimate the ending balance of property and equipment for 1999.

6. For this question, do not use *eVal* (because it is easier not to). Suppose your analysis indicated that Royal Caribbean's 1999 ending balance of customer deposits was $515,308 thousand. Estimate the amount of cash collected from customers in 1999.

Can Salton Swing?*

Sales growth and profitability are the two pillars of a high valuation. And, based on these two measures, Salton Inc.—the maker of the BreadMan bread machine, the Juiceman juice extractor, and the George Foreman electric grill—looks fabulous. As of fiscal 2000 (ending July 1, 2000), the average ROE for the past four years has been 50.5 percent, and the average annual sales growth has been 70.6 percent. Allowing *eVal* to extrapolate this past performance over the next ten years yields a valuation as of September 30, 2000 (approximately when the 10-K was filed), of over $1,400 per share. At the time, Salton's stock was trading at an all-time high, but this was still only $40 per share, and in the subsequent year it drifted back down to a $20 range. The purpose of this case is to figure out why the market expects so little out of Salton compared to its historical fundamentals, and to decide if this is an appropriate valuation or a severely undervalued stock.

To aid you in your analysis, there are online exhibits at www
.lundholmandsloan.com. These exhibits include excerpts from the fiscal 2000 10-K filing and an Excel file with ratio analysis for the four competitor firms and Salton. In its 10-K, Salton states that they have the leading domestic market share in toasters, juice extractors, indoor grills, bread makers, griddles, waffle makers, and buffet hotplates, and a strong presence in a number of other related products. They either own or license a number of major brand names, including Toastmaster, Maxim, Breadman, Juiceman, George Foreman Grills, White-Westinghouse, Farberware, Melitta, Timex, and Kenmore. Three principal product lines—George Foreman Grills, Juiceman, and Breadman—accounted for 55.2 percent of sales in fiscal 2000 and 55.4 percent of sales in fiscal 1999. All small appliances combined account for 89 percent of total sales in fiscal 2000.

Salton predominately sells its products to mass merchandisers and department stores, with only a small Internet business selling directly to consumers through infomercials and the company Web site. Its largest two customers in fiscal 2000 were Walmart and Kmart, representing 13 and 12 percent of its sales, respectively. The top five customers in fiscal 2000 represented 46 percent of total sales. With only minor exceptions, it has no long-term contracts with any of its customers.[1]

---

*Professor Russell Lundholm prepared this case as the basis for class discussion. Copyright © 2001 by Russell Lundholm.

[1]Salton has a contract with Kmart that technically runs through June 30, 2004, but Kmart can terminate the agreement without cause after June 30, 2002. Consequently, this contract by itself does not represent a sustainable competitive advantage.

BACKGROUND

Salton manufactures its products in the Far East using over 45 unaffiliated suppliers, although the largest producer accounted for 38 percent of purchases in fiscal 2000. Its purchases are typically denominated in U.S. dollars, limiting exposure to foreign currency risk. Finally, Salton must place a firm purchase commitment with its suppliers approximately 6–12 months prior to receiving a firm commitment from its customer.

THE DEAL WITH GEORGE

Salton's hottest product line is the George Foreman Grill, an electric grill that comes in various sizes and colors, and in both indoor and outdoor versions. The original agreement with George Foreman (former heavyweight boxing champion of the world) was that Mr. Foreman received in royalty fees 60 percent of the gross profit from this product line.[2] But midway through fiscal 2000, and effective as of the beginning of fiscal 2000, Salton negotiated a significant change in this agreement. Instead of annual royalty payments, Salton purchased the rights to the George Foreman trademark in perpetuity, paying with shares of Salton stock valued at $23.75 million and a note payable for $113.75 million, payable in five annual payments (one of which occurred in fiscal 2000). All together, the present value of consideration given for the trademark was $122 million, which is being amortized over 15 years.

QUESTIONS

1. Consider the competitive forces at work in the small-appliance industry. Do you think Salton can sustain its unusually high profits and return on equity in this industry?

2. For comparison purposes, the online exhibits for the case give a ratio analysis from *eVal* for four of Salton's competitors: Applica, Maytag, Sunbeam, and Whirlpool. Based on the Dupont analysis, how has Salton generated such a large return on equity relative to these other firms? Do you see any significant trends or changes in Salton's ratios over time?

3. For the past two years, Salton has stated in their Management Discussion and Analysis that a significant source of their sales growth has been from the George Foreman product line. Estimate what fraction of total sales is due to these products?

---

[2]December 9, 1999, company press release.

4. The deal with George Foreman has both real economic effects and cosmetic accounting effects that will bear upon your forecasts of Salton's future income. Discuss each. How will the deal with George Foreman change the relationship between sales and other income statement items?

5. Suppose you believe that the George Foreman trademark is grossly overvalued in Salton's books; in fact, rather than its book value of approximately $113.9 million ($122 million less $8.1 million in amortization), you believe it is worthless. Discuss the different ways you could express this belief in your forecast inputs to *eVal*.

6. Load the case data for Salton into *eVal*. (Case data can be imported by going to the Case Data sheet in *eVal* and selecting the yellow block of data for the company, and then pasting this block of data into the yellow cells at the bottom of the Financial Statements sheet using Paste Special—Values from the Edit menu.) Change the valuation date to be September 30, 2000, roughly the release date of the fiscal 2000 10-K. If you leave everything else at the default *eVal* levels, the resulting value estimate is over $1,000 per share. Modify the forecasting assumptions to represent a more realistic scenario. If you believe the Foreman trademark is overvalued, you may also want to modify the financial statements to correct for this distortion. Putting it all together, is Salton still an undervalued stock?

Sirius Satellite Radio, Inc.*

The nascent satellite radio industry got its start in 1997 when Sirius Satellite Radio and XM Radio were the winning bidders for two FCC licenses to operate a satellite radio service. It wasn't until the spring of 2001 that XM finally shot its two geostationary satellites (aptly named "rock" and "roll") into orbit. By fall of that year, XM subscribers could already tune in to 100 digital channels from coast to coast. Plagued by missteps, Sirius got off to a slower start. By the time that Sirius started nationwide service in the summer of 2002, XM already had well over 100,000 subscribers.

Building a large subscriber base is the crucial element of a successful business model in satellite broadcasting. Fixed costs, including FCC license, satellites, repeater network, content and marketing, run into the billions of dollars. Since consumers can tune into traditional AM/FM radio for free, pricing power is also limited in the satellite broadcasting business. In early 2006, both Sirius and XM were charging a $12.95 monthly subscription fee. Large numbers of subscribers are therefore the only way to get the economics to work.

By the end of 2005, Sirius had grown its subscriber base to over 3 million, while XM satellite radio had grown to over 6 million. Both companies were still reporting significant losses, but despite Sirius's lagging subscriber numbers, its market capitalization had overtaken that of XM, topping $7 billion. There were two key reasons for Wall Street's enthusiasm. First, well known "shock jock" Howard Stern had recently made a well-publicized move to Sirius. Stern was lured by a $500 million compensation package and the ability to peddle smut unimpeded by FCC decency rules governing the public airwaves. Second, Sirius had recently hired radio industry veteran Mel Karmazin to be its CEO. Karmazin's career included stints as CEO at Viacom, CBS and Infinity Broadcasting (which he built virtually from scratch). He was regarded as one of America's most aggressive and creative executives and Wall Street saw him as the perfect figure to accelerate subscriber growth and turn Sirius to profitability.

*This case was prepared by Professor Richard Sloan as the basis for class discussion, rather than to illustrate either effective or ineffective handling of a business situation. Copyright ©2007 by Richard Sloan.

A key factor in the growth strategies of both Sirius and XM were strategic partnerships with automakers. Sirius had partnered with Ford and DaimlerChrysler, while XM had partnered with GM and Honda. Under these partnerships, the automakers typically agreed to factory install satellite radios, with Sirius and XM subsidizing the cost of the radios and the initial subscription fees. The idea was that drivers would get hooked on their new radios and continue to pay subscription fees when the free trial ended. During 2005, over a quarter of Sirius's sales were derived from these partnerships.

By the middle of 2006, automaker production cuts were hampering Sirius's ability to meet its subscriber growth targets. With this background, Sirius's stock price dropped from $6 in early 2006 to $4 by mid-2006. Several Wall Street analysts saw this drop as a buying opportunity. A representative analyst made the case as follows:[1]

> We continue to be bullish on Sirius based on a strong secular growth outlook for satellite radio, attractive long-term economics and a favorable risk/reward ratio. Based on our scenario analysis we believe that Sirius has little downside risk from current levels (25% in the bear case) yet significant upside potential in the bull case (150%). Our expected value for Sirius is $6, with our base case forecast implying 70% upside.

Detailed information on Sirius's business strategy, financial situation and expansion plans are provided in its Form 10-K for the year ended December 31, 2005. For comparative purposes, similar information is also provided for Citadel Broadcasting Corporation in its Form 10-K for the corresponding period. Citadel is a traditional radio broadcasting company. Finally, we provide a representative example of a sell-side analyst model that was used to justify the analyst quote provided above. These documents are available as online exhibits at www.lundholmandsloan.com.

QUESTIONS

Business Strategy Analysis

1. Identify Sirius' source(s) of competitive advantage in the radio business relative to traditional AM/FM broadcast radio stations.
2. Identify two key risks associated with Sirius' business model relative to traditional broadcast radio stations.
3. Sirius uses automakers as a major distribution channel. Briefly evaluate Sirius' ability to generate and sustain competitive advantage through this distribution channel.

[1] This analyst quote represents the case-writer's personal synthesis of the published views of the numerous analysts that were bullish on the stock in 2006.

Accounting Analysis

4. Briefly describe how Sirius currently accounts for its subscriber acquisition costs.

5. Assume that instead of using its current accounting practices for its subscriber acquisition costs, Sirius instead capitalized all of its subscriber acquisition costs in the fiscal year that these costs are incurred and then amortizes them using the straight-line method over the subsequent two fiscal years. *Estimate* the *Loss from operations that* Sirius would have reported for the fiscal year ended December 31, 2005.

6. Which of the above two methods of accounting for subscriber acquisition costs do you think better reflects the underlying economics of the business?

7. Briefly explain how Sirius accounts for its subscriber revenue.

8. Assume that instead of using its current accounting practices for subscriber revenue, Sirius instead recognized subscriber revenue upon the receipt of subscriber payments. Estimate the *Loss from operations* that Sirius would have reported for the year ended December 31, 2005.

9. Briefly describe how Sirius accounts for its FCC license. Do you think that Sirius' current application of this accounting method is appropriate? Explain your answer.

Ratio and Cash Flow Analysis

10. Compute Property & Equipment turnover ratios for Sirius and Citadel Broadcasting Corp. for fiscal year 2005.

11. Briefly identify the major reason(s) for the difference between the turnover ratios that you computed above.

12. Compute operating margin ratios for Sirius and Citadel for fiscal year 2005.

13. Briefly identify the major reason(s) for the difference between the margins that you computed above.

14. Sirius' "Net loss" has been more negative than its free cash flow for fiscal years 2003, 2004 and 2005. Identify the major reason(s) why "Net loss" has been more negative than free cash flow during these years.

Forecasting Analysis

15. The sell-side analyst model provided with this case presents a "Base Case" model (see Exhibit 1 of the model) in which Sirius' total subscribers are forecast to grow to 17.3 million by the end of 2010. Briefly evaluate the plausibility of this forecasting assumption.

16. The sell-side analyst model provides a Revised Model (see Exhibit 2 of the model) in which Sirius' depreciation and amortization expense is forecast to grow at a much lower rate than its total revenues through 2010.

Do you think that this lower growth rate for depreciation and amortization expense is justified? Explain your answer.

17. Load Sirius into *eVal* and provide a set of forecasting assumptions that yield similar sales growth and EPS assumptions to those in the "Revised Model" (see Exhibit 2 of the model). (*Note:* Case data can be imported by going to the Case Data sheet in *eVal* and selecting the yellow block of data for the company, and then pasting this block of data into the yellow cells at the bottom of the Financial Statements sheet using Paste Special—Values from the Edit menu.) Evaluate the plausibility of the forecasting scenario you provided in answer to the preceding question.

18. The Revised Model (see Exhibit 2 of the model) assumes that the diluted weighted average number of common stock outstanding will remain constant at 1,628.3 million between 2006 and 2010. Compare these numbers to the number of shares outstanding in your own *eVal* forecasting model and explain any differences.

Valuation Analysis

19. Load the Sirius data into *eVal*, set the valuation date to June 1, 2006 and critically evaluate the default valuation provided by *eVal*.

20. In mid-2006, Sirius was trading at around $4.50/share. Using *eVal*, provide a set of forecasting assumptions that approximates this price. Use a cost of equity capital of 10 percent and a valuation date of June 1, 2006. Do you think that these forecasting assumptions are plausible?

21. Based on your analysis above, evaluate the plausibility of the $5.79 price target proposed in the sell-side analyst model (see Exhibit 1 of the model).

A Tale of Two Movie Theaters*

This case compares the financial statistics of two movie theater companies: one that defaulted on its debt and filed for bankruptcy in 2000 and the one that did not. Your task is to predict which company will ultimately be the one that declares bankruptcy. Until the solution of the case is presented, we will refer to the two companies as *Country Cinema* and *City Screens*.

THE MOVIE THEATER INDUSTRY

Attending a theatrical movie remains a thriving entertainment activity in North America, with ticket sales topping $7.6 billion in 2000. While the number of movie attendees has declined slightly in recent years, the decline has been more than off-set by increases in ticket prices, resulting in healthy year-to-year ticket revenue growth (see Figure 1). But despite the overall increase in sales, the movie theater industry has struggled in recent years. The number of screens has increased 34 percent since 1995, somewhat less than the total box office sales growth, but the cost of operating so many new screens has outstripped the increase in revenue. Multiplexes, theaters with eight or more screens, have become the industry standard, and megaplexes, theaters with at least 10 screens and stadium-style seating, have grown rapidly in popularity. While the multiscreen theater format offers many advantageous operating features—the ability to optimally match the theater size with the audience and a more evenly spaced demand for concession services—it also has required significant capital expenditures on stadium seating and state-of-the-art sound and projection equipment. The popularity of the new theater options has caused many older theaters to suffer, necessitating asset write-downs. Finally, the increased competition between screens has caused marketing costs to rise 54 percent since 1995 and shorter runs have raised the rental fees to distributors (which average about 50 percent of the total box office).[1]

*Professor Russell Lundholm prepared this case as the basis of class discussion.

[1]First-run motion picture rental fees are generally the greater of (*i*) 70 percent of box office admissions, gradually declining to as low as 30 percent over a period of four to seven weeks, and (*ii*) a specified percentage (i.e., 90 percent) of the excess of box office receipts over a negotiated allowance for theater expenses (commonly known as a "90/10" clause). Second-run motion picture rental fees typically begin at 35 percent of box office admissions and often decline to 30 percent after the first week. (Source: 10-K of City Screens.)

FIGURE 1
North American
Theater Statistics

	Box Office Gross Sales	Average Ticket Price	Attendance	Number of Screens	Number of Theaters	Average Screens/ Theater
1995	$5494 M	$4.35	1263 M	27805	7744	3.6
1996	$5912 M	$4.42	1339 M	29690	7798	3.8
1997	$6366 M	$4.59	1388 M	31640	7480	4.2
1998	$6949 M	$4.69	1481 M	34186	7418	4.6
1999	$7448 M	$5.08	1465 M	37185	7551	4.9
2000	$7661 M	$5.39	1421 M	37396	7421	5.0

TWO MOVIE THEATER COMPANIES

The two companies in this case are approximately the same size, each with approximately 2,800 screens as of fiscal 2000. For each company, ticket sales constitute approximately 65 percent of revenues, followed by concessions, which make up roughly 30 percent of revenues, with the remainder coming from video games and on-screen advertising. The two companies differ significantly in the size of town they operate in. *Country Cinema*, as we will call it, targets small to mid-sized communities. As of 2000, the management of Country Cinema believes it was the sole exhibitor in approximately 65 percent of its areas. In contrast, *City Screens* operates 69 percent of its domestic screens in the 20 largest "designated market areas" (as defined by Nielsen Media), as well as operating in certain large international cities.

WHO WILL DEFAULT: COUNTRY CINEMA OR CITY SCREENS?

From 1995–2000, both companies were expanding rapidly and changing over to multiplex and megaplex theater formats. And both were borrowing heavily to fund their growth and remodeling costs. But one company stumbles in the summer of 2000 and defaults on its loans. The summer season is traditionally the highest-volume period for movie theater attendance, but the summer of 2000 failed to deliver any blockbuster movies and attendance suffered. Consequently, one of the companies did not generate sufficient cash flow to stay within its loan covenants.

The detailed requirements of each company's loan covenants fill hundreds of pages, but the basic idea behind them is very simple. The covenants place limits on additional borrowing and on payments to equity holders. They also describe a number of financial health measures so that, if the company starts to get too sick, the bank can declare the loan in technical default. This makes the loan immediately due and payable in full, allowing the bank the opportunity to claim assets before they are all gone.

Two measures of financial health for Country Cinema and City Screens are the total leverage ratio, roughly defined as total debt/EBITDA before nonrecurring items, and the fixed charges coverage ratio, roughly defined as EBITDA plus rent/interest plus rent, where rent is the rent expense on operating leases and debt includes capital leases. At the time of the case, both companies were required to maintain the total leverage ratio below 6 and the fixed charges coverage ratio above 1.25. However, the precise definition of EBITDA differed between the two companies. The definition of EBITDA in the Country Cinema covenants was basically the traditional earnings before interest, taxes, depreciation, and amortization, and before any nonrecurring items such as gains/losses on asset sales or restructuring charges. For City Screens, the definition was more forward-looking, excluding the performance of theaters scheduled to close and extrapolating into the near future the performance of theaters that were recently opened.

REQUIREMENTS

Your task is simply to forecast which company you believe will default in the summer of 2000 and justify your prediction. It will aid your analysis greatly if you forecast the next year's financial statements for both firms. There are much data available to you. The case materials are as follows:

1. You can load the case data into *eVal* and examine the credit risk statistics at the bottom of the Ratio Analysis sheet. (*Note:* Case data can be imported by going to the Case Data sheet in *eVal* and selecting the yellow block of data for the company, and then pasting this block of data into the yellow cells at the bottom of the Financial Statements sheet using Paste Special—Values from the Edit menu.) Note that the 1998 fiscal year end for City Screens is actually April 1, 1999.

The fiscal 1998 financial statements and excerpts from the MD&A for both companies are available as online exhibits at www.lundholmandsloan.com.

Please note: The exact definitions of the financial health measures given in the loan covenants for each company are extremely detailed, and you do not have sufficient information to reconstruct them. The details about the covenants given above and a general investigation into the financial health, risk exposure, and, most importantly, a forecast of the future for each company will be sufficient to guide your analysis.

COUNTRY CINEMA FINANCIAL RATIOS

	Fiscal Year End Date			
	12/31/1995	**12/31/1996**	**12/31/1997**	**12/31/1998**
Analysis of Credit Risk				
Net Income to Total Assets	0.027	−0.015	0.033	−0.044
Implied default probability	3.0%	5.5%	3.0%	5.5%
Total Liabilities to Total Assets	0.613	0.636	0.673	0.676
Implied default probability	4.5%	5.5%	5.5%	5.5%
Quick Ratio	0.553	0.337	0.323	0.226
Implied default probability	5.0%	9.0%	9.0%	9.0%
EBIT to Interest Expense	2.36	2.66	2.41	1.89
Implied default probability	3.0%	3.0%	3.0%	5.0%
Inventory Holding Period	7.12	5.51	5.98	7.11
Implied default probability	3.9%	3.9%	3.9%	3.9%
Annual Sales Growth	11.3%	17.0%	7.5%	5.0%
Implied default probability	3.0%	3.2%	3.0%	3.0%
Average Implied Default Probability	3.7%	5.0%	4.6%	5.3%
Other Ratios				
Rent expense (from footnotes)	45,600	54,800	57,600	66,800
Fixed Charge Coverage	1.79	1.83	1.82	1.66
Total Debt/EBITDA	3.5	3.21	4.05	3.96
(b/f non-recurring charges)				

CITY SCREENS FINANCIAL RATIOS

	Fiscal Year End Date			
	3/28/1996	**4/3/1997**	**4/2/1998**	**4/1/1999**
Analysis of Credit Risk				
Net Income to Total Assets	0.057	0.026	−0.031	−0.016
Implied default probability	2.0%	3.0%	5.5%	5.5%
Total Liabilities to Total Assets	0.671	0.764	0.825	0.882
Implied default probability	5.5%	7.0%	9.0%	9.0%
Quick Ratio	0.296	0.256	0.132	0.167
Implied default probability	9.0%	9.0%	9.0%	9.0%
EBIT to Interest Expense	2.38	2.74	1.03	0.34
Implied default probability	3.0%	3.0%	7.0%	7.0%
Inventory Holding Period	0.00	0.00	0.00	0.00
Implied default probability	3.0%	3.0%	3.0%	3.0%
Annual Sales Growth	16.5%	14.4%	13.3%	20.4%
Implied default probability	3.2%	3.0%	3.0%	3.2%
Average Implied Default Probability	4.3%	4.7%	6.1%	6.1%
Other Ratios				
Rent expense (from footnotes)	64,813	80,061	106,383	165,370
Fixed Charge Coverage	1.89	1.89	1.5	1.31
Total Debt/EBITDA	1.67	3.31	3.78	5.95
(b/f non-recurring charges)				

Building *eVal**

INTRODUCTION

This case starts with raw financial statements and then (*a*) develops standardized financial statements, (*b*) constructs a statement of cash flows, (*c*) builds all the key ratios, (*d*) links forecast inputs to future financial statements, and (*e*) builds discounted cash flow and residual income valuation models based on the forecasts. The result is *eVal*, the spreadsheet model that is provided with "Equity Valuation and Analysis" by Russell Lundholm and Richard Sloan, but one that you should completely understand (because you built it yourself!). To save you some time, many of the cells are completed; you only need to finish the blue-shaded ones.

There are five parts to this case, corresponding to the five tasks listed above. The case requires two files: "Building eVal.xls" and "General Mills 10-K.pdf". Both can be found at www.lundholmandsloan.com.

PART A: STANDARDIZED FINANCIAL STATEMENTS

The financial statements filed with the SEC are not standardized, meaning that the company is free to report and label line items however they please (within obvious limits). For this reason, there is an intermediary business that takes the filed financial statements and sorts the line items into a predetermined set of accounts. We will explore this important part of the reporting process in this part of the case.

1. Find the "as reported" financial statements in General Mills's 10-K filing (in the pdf file). Compare the results with the Financial Statements sheet in Building eVal4.xls. Now compare the "as reported" financial statements with the version found at finance.yahoo.com shown in Exhibit 1. How do the different versions of the financial statements compare? What has been lumped together with what?

---

*This case was prepared by Professor Russell Lundholm as the basis for class discussion, rather than to illustrate either effective or ineffective handling of a business situation. Copyright ©2010 by Russell Lundholm.

EXHIBIT 1

| Income Statement | | | Get Income Statement for: [_____] (GO) |

View: **Annual Data** | Quarterly Data   All numbers in thousands

Period Ending	2010-05-30	2009-05-31	2008-05-25
Total Revenue	14,796,500	14,691,300	13,652,100
Cost of Revenue	8,922,900	9,457,800	8,778,300
Gross Profit	**5,873,600**	**5,233,500**	**4,873,800**
Operating Expenses			
Research Development	-	-	-
Selling General and Administrative	3,236,100	2,951,800	2,625,000
Non Recurring	31,400	41,600	21,000
Others	-	-	-
Total Operating Expenses	-	-	-
Operating Income or Loss	**2,606,100**	**2,325,000**	**2,227,800**
Income from Continuing Operations			
Total Other Income/Expenses Net	-	84,900	5,300
Earnings Before Interest And Taxes	2,204,500	2,027,100	2,233,100
Interest Expense	-	390,000	427,000
Income Before Tax	2,204,500	2,027,100	1,806,100
Income Tax Expense	771,200	720,400	622,200
Minority Interest	(4,500)	(9,300)	-
Net Income From Continuing Ops	1,530,500	1,389,300	1,294,700
Non-recurring Events			
Discontinued Operations	-	-	-
Extraordinary Items	-	-	-
Effect Of Accounting Changes	-	-	-
Other Items	-	-	-
Net Income	**1,530,500**	**1,304,400**	**1,294,700**
Preferred Stock And Other Adjustments	-	-	-
Net Income Applicable To Common Shares	**1,530,500**	**1,304,400**	**1,294,700**

Currency in USD.

2. The financial statement line items are themselves summary measures. See how much extra detail you can find about 2008 total revenue and other assets by reading the Management Discussion and Analysis on page 14 and the footnotes that follow the financial statements, especially notes 16 and 17 on pages 73–74.

PART B: CREATE A STATEMENT OF CASH FLOWS

1. Build the links between the Financial Statements sheet and the Cash Flow Analysis sheet. As an organizing formula, recall that

$$\Delta Cash = -\Delta nonCashAssets + \Delta Liabilities + \Delta Shareholders' \ Equity.$$

As you go down the balance sheet line by line, sort each change into operating, investing or financing and be sure you account for the entire change in each line item. Finally, recall that net income, the top line on the statement, is a major source of change in Shareholders' Equity.

2. Compare the finished Statement of Cash Flows in *eVal* with General Mill's "as reported" Statement of Cash Flows. Why is it different? (*Hint:* Don't attempt to reconcile every item—it isn't possible.)

EXHIBIT 1
(continued)

Balance Sheet

Get Balance Sheet for: [ ] (GO)

View: **Annual Data** | Quarterly Data

All numbers in thousands

Period Ending	2010-05-30	2009-05-31	2008-05-25
Assets			
Current Assets			
Cash And Cash Equivalents	673,200	749,800	661,000
Short Term Investments	-	23,400	-
Net Receivables	1,084,300	969,000	1,081,600
Inventory	1,344,000	1,346,800	1,366,800
Other Current Assets	378,500	469,300	510,600
Total Current Assets	**3,480,000**	**3,534,900**	**3,620,000**
Long Term Investments	-	473,100	404,800
Property Plant and Equipment	3,127,700	3,034,900	3,108,100
Goodwill	6,592,800	6,663,000	6,786,100
Intangible Assets	3,715,000	3,747,000	3,777,200
Accumulated Amortization	-	-	-
Other Assets	763,400	895,000	1,345,400
Deferred Long Term Asset Charges	-	-	-
Total Assets	**17,678,900**	**17,874,800**	**19,041,600**
Liabilities			
Current Liabilities			
Accounts Payable	849,500	803,400	4,215,600
Short/Current Long Term Debt	1,157,400	1,320,700	450,100
Other Current Liabilities	1,762,200	1,481,900	190,600
Total Current Liabilities	**3,769,100**	**3,606,000**	**4,856,300**
Long Term Debt	5,268,500	5,754,800	4,348,700
Other Liabilities	2,118,700	1,932,200	1,923,900
Deferred Long Term Liability Charges	874,600	1,165,300	1,454,600
Minority Interest	245,100	244,200	242,300
Negative Goodwill	-	-	-
Total Liabilities	**12,276,000**	**12,702,500**	**12,825,800**
Stockholders' Equity			
Misc Stocks Options Warrants	-	-	-
Redeemable Preferred Stock	-	-	-
Preferred Stock	-	-	-
Common Stock	75,500	75,500	37,700
Retained Earnings	8,122,400	7,235,600	6,510,700
Treasury Stock	(2,615,200)	(2,473,100)	(1,658,400)
Capital Surplus	1,307,100	1,212,100	1,149,100
Other Stockholder Equity	(1,486,900)	(877,800)	176,700
Total Stockholder Equity	**5,402,900**	**5,172,300**	**6,215,800**

PART C: RATIO ANALYSIS AND CREDIT ANALYSIS

Armed with standardized financial statements, you can now create a sheet that computes all the usual ratios of financial statement analysis. To help with the computation of the Advanced Dupont Ratios, below the standardized financial statements on the Financial Statements sheet there are computations of the following: net operating income, net financial expense, net operating assets and net financial obligations. Be sure that net operating income less net financial expense equals net income and that net operating assets less net financial obligations equals common equity.

1. Open Building eVal.xls and derive all the ratios on the Ratio Analysis sheet by linking back to the Std Financial Statements sheet. You only have enough data for General Mills to do the most recent year.

PART D: LINKING FORECASTS TO FUTURE FINANCIAL STATEMENTS

1. Enter the following forecasts in the yellow cells on the Forecasting sheet. For Sales, enter 5 percent for all years. For all other yellow cells, enter the same value as the most recent historical year (you can simply cut-and-paste the value).

2. On the Forecasting sheet the yellow cells you just filled in are ratios that imply future financial statement values. Your task is to figure out these future financial statement values and create links from the Forecasting sheet to the Financial Statements sheet.

3. You will note that the ratios on the Forecasting sheet are defined in terms of ending balance sheet amounts, whereas the ratios on the Ratio Analysis sheet are defined in terms of average balance sheet amounts. To see why this is, construct a temporary line on the Forecasting sheet to input the ratio of Average Receivables/Sales and then compute the resulting ending Receivables balance each year. Set this ratio to 15 percent. Now compare the ending balance from this method of forecasting with the ending balance from *eVal* (again assuming a 15 percent ratio), preferably by plotting the two resulting series. Notice anything funny about the implied balance when the average receivables are used as the basis for forecasting?

PART E: VALUATION

1. Compute the value of General Mills as of July 1, 2008 using the discounted cash flow model. Do so by linking to the statement of cash flow data, or directly to the financial statement data. Set the cost of equity capital, debt capital and the weighted average cost of capital at 10%, 8% and 8.96%, respectively, as given on the spreadsheet.

2. Compute the value of General Mills as of July 1, 2008 using the residual income model. Do so by linking to the financial statement data. Set the cost of equity capital, debt capital, and the weighted average cost of capital at 10 percent, 8 percent, and 8.95 percent, respectively, as given on the spreadsheet.

3. Make sure your answers to the two questions above are both $58.34 per share (or within a few cents of this amount).

Hogs and Chestnuts: Who Profits When the Chinese Eat?*

INTRODUCTION

Selling food to the growing Chinese middle class would seem like a no-brainer. This case focuses on two mid-sized Chinese companies, Zhongpin Inc. (ticker HOGS), who sells pork products, and American Lorain Inc. (ticker ALN), who sells chestnuts. Both companies looked like very attractive investments based on their valuation ratios at the end of 2009. This case proceeds in three steps. In part I we will develop detailed forecasts and a valuation for Zhongpin. In part II we will evaluate the forecasts and valuation models from an analyst report on American Lorain, and in part III we will consider the particular risks of investing in a Chinese company that came to be traded in the United States through an unusual transaction known as a "reverse merger."

Case materials found at www.lundholmandsloan.com include Zhongpin 10-K excerpts, an *eVal* file for Zhongpin, American Lorain 10-K excerpts American Lorain and an excerpt from an analyst report. (*Note:* We recommend NOT printing out the 10-K excerpts as they are each quite long. Read electronically!)

PART 1: ALL THE PORK IN CHINA

An agricultural rule-of-thumb known as Bennett's Law states that as income increases consumers shift their calorie source towards animal proteins and away from carbohydrates. As Figure 1 illustrates, between 1980 and 2006 China's per capita income increased 759 percent, and during this period the per capita consumption of cereals and grains fell 16 percent while the per

*This case was prepared by Professor Russell Lundholm as the basis for class discussion, rather than to illustrate either effective or ineffective handling of a business situation. Copyright © 2010 by Russell Lundholm.

FIGURE 1

Chinese Diet and Income (per capita)

Source: Food and Agricultural Organization of the United Nations. Rome 2008.

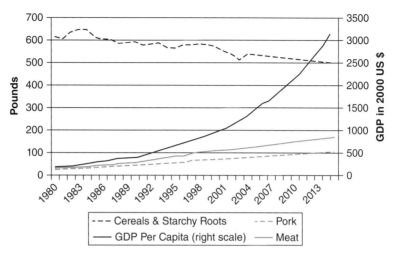

capita consumption of meat increased 274 percent. As of 2006, China consumed 30 percent of the world's meat and 50 percent of the world's pork. And with forecasted GDP growth of 7–8 percent, the number of consumers who can afford to consume pork is reliably increasing.

Zhongpin Inc. would appear to be optimally situated to capitalize on these trends. In 2009 they were the fourth largest pork producer in China. They were also a leader in using western-style pork production methods, an initiative that the Chinese government was promoting heavily. But demand for pork does not necessarily mean profit for Zhongpin. We will have to investigate their profitability. But their valuation ratios are undeniably attractive for a firm with such growth potential. The price-to-earnings ratio at the end of 2009 was 11.4, compared to the S&P 500 ratio of 18.6. And the price-to-book ratio was 1.8, compared to the S&P 500 ratio of 2.2. These facts, plus a detailed set of forecasts, caused the investment bank Morgan Joseph to set a target price of $21 per share at a time when the stock was trading at $15.

The case materials include excerpts from Zhongpin's 2009 10-K filing (found online). To keep this case from becoming an exercise in forecasting sales growth, we will take the sales growth forecasts from the analyst report as given. This will allow us to focus our attention on forecasting Zhongpin's profitability and investment. Also, for this part of the case ignore all the various predecessor company names and the reverse merger transaction; we will return to it in Part III.

To save some time, the *eVal* file included with the case has input the financial statements so they roughly match the "as reported" financial statements. In addition, based on the analyst report at the time, the sales forecasts are already given: 29 percent sales growth in 2010 and 24 percent sales growth in 2011, and then trending down to 3 percent over 10 years.

Assume these forecasts are correct (with hindsight we know that they are slightly conservative).

Other relevant facts from the analyst report are as follows:

> . . . processing capacity should increase 41% from now to the end of 2012. Besides capacity expansion efforts, Zhongpin should be able to increase capacity utilization over time. Over the last three years, capacity utilization has been 74%, 57%, and 65%, respectively. While we would expect utilization to fall in 2010 given the high level of capacity expansion, these plants should be able to reach utilization rates of 90% or better, similar to Western processors, as the business matures.

PART 1 CASE QUESTIONS

1. Based on your reading of the 10-K (particularly item 1 and item 7) what are the most relevant factors to consider when forecasting Zhongpin's net operating margin? Where on the income statement will these factors materialize?

2. Based on your investigation in question 1, complete the income statement assumptions in *eVal* for the next three years, remembering to leave the Sales Growth line at 29 percent, 24 percent and then trending to 3 percent.

3. What are the most relevant factors to consider when forecasting Zhongpin's net operating assets? Where on the balance sheet will these factors materialize?

4. Based on your investigation in question 3, complete the balance sheet assumptions in *eVal* for the next three years. Bear in mind the capacity utilization estimates from the analyst report shown earlier.

5. If you do nothing else, *eVal* will extrapolate your third year forecasts into the future. If you find any of these extrapolations unreasonable, input more reasonable values in the terminal year. What would be evidence of an "unreasonable" terminal value forecast?

6. Using a 10 percent cost of equity capital and setting the valuation date to March 31, 2010, what is your estimated value of Zhongpin?

PART II: THE CHINESE LOVE CHESTNUTS!

China currently produces and consumes over half the world's chestnuts, as shown in Figure 2. Roasted, peeled, and then mixed with honey, salt, and sugar, chestnuts are a fragrant treat traditionally served warm in the winter months. And of the 600 thousand tons of chestnuts consumed in China in 2009, American Lorain produced roughly 10 percent of them. The next closest competitor in terms of production capacity is only a tenth as big. Besides the traditional honey-roasted chestnut, the company produces a variety of more heavily processed chestnuts that sell for higher margins.

FIGURE 2 World Chestnut Production and Consumption in 2009

Source: Food and Agriculture Organization of the United Nations.

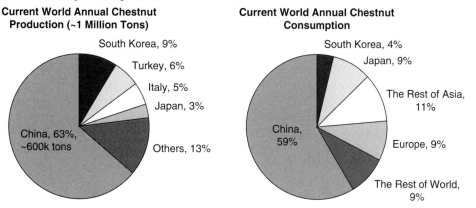

Current World Annual Chestnut Production (~1 Million Tons)

South Korea, 9%
Turkey, 6%
Italy, 5%
Japan, 3%
China, 63%, ~600k tons
Others, 13%

Current World Annual Chestnut Consumption

South Korea, 4%
Japan, 9%
The Rest of Asia, 11%
China, 59%
Europe, 9%
The Rest of World, 9%

In addition, the chestnut business puts American Lorain in all the major retail chains in China, including Walmart, Carrefour, and 7-Eleven. This foothold has allowed them to expand into convenience foods, which accounted for 24 percent of their revenue in 2009. Featuring ready-to-eat rice dishes and other packaged foods, the company hopes to capitalize on the growing demand for convenience food as China's urbanization continues. And if China follows the path of western countries, this could represent a sizeable growth opportunity, as seen in Figure 3.

FIGURE 3 Chinese Consumption of Packaged Food

Source: Euromonitor International.

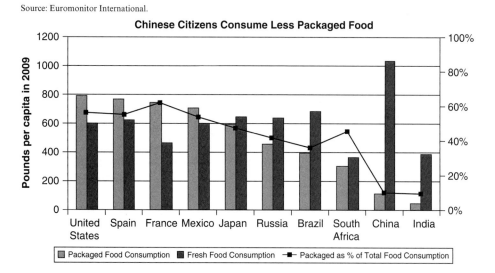

Chinese Citizens Consume Less Packaged Food

(y-axis left: Pounds per capita in 2009; y-axis right: 0%–100%)

United States, Spain, France, Mexico, Japan, Russia, Brazil, South Africa, China, India

Legend: ■ Packaged Food Consumption ■ Fresh Food Consumption —■— Packaged as % of Total Food Consumption

At the end of 2009 American Lorain was very successfully turning these opportunities into profits. As the case materials show, they earned $0.55 per share in 2009 and $0.58 per share in 2008. And yet on June 1, 2010 (approximately the time the analyst report was issued), they only traded for $3 per share. The stable margins, growth potential, and appealing valuation of American Lorain attracted the attention of a number of analysts in 2010. For example, one analyst set a target price of $5.50 per share based on nine times the 2010 EPS estimate of $0.62 per share, and backed this up with a discounted cash flow model that placed the value at $9 per share. This part of the case asks you to assess the reasonableness of these valuation methods and estimates. The case materials include excerpts from American Lorain's 2009 10-K filing, the financial statement forecasts from the analyst report, and an *eVal* file with the financial statements entered (but not the analyst forecasts). All materials can be found at www.lundholmandsloan.com. Assume a valuation date of June 1, 2010.

Note: The complete analyst report from the Maxim Group LLC is available through Investext, which you can access through any business school library. However, the only material you will need from the report is in the excerpt provided in this case.

PART II QUESTIONS

1. Assess the reasonableness of the value estimate for American Lorain based on nine times next year's forecasted EPS of $0.62, assuming the EPS forecast is accurate. Under what circumstances is such an approach reasonable?

2. Now reverse engineer the analyst forecasts for American Lorian found in the excerpt by inputting the income statement assumptions into *eVal*. Note that you are only interested in the analyst's annual forecasts for 2010, 2011 and 2012. Set the terminal growth rate to 4 percent and leave all the other balance sheet estimates at *eVal*'s default values. Setting the valuation date to June 1, 2010 and the cost of equity to 10 percent, what value estimate does this yield?

3. The analyst report does not give all the specific computations for the DCF model that yields an estimate of $9 per share. However, it does state that the model horizon is 10 years, the assumed terminal growth rate is 4 percent, and the weighted average cost of capital is 14 percent (with a cost of equity capital of 16 percent). Estimate the cost of debt and cost of minority interest based on the financial statement ratios estimated in 2012 and then input all these rates into the valuation parameters sheet in *eVal*. What is the value estimate now?

4. If all went well in questions 2 and 3, the DCF estimate should be around $5/share, far short of the $9 estimate given in the analyst report. Is it because the *eVal* default balance sheet estimates are far from the balance

sheet forecasts given in the analyst report? (*Note:* Do not attempt to reverse engineer the entire balance sheet forecasts, unless you can't resist the temptation. But be warned, this exercise is not for the weak of heart).

5. Without changing your income statement forecasts, give a set of *eVal* balance sheet forecasts that raise the value estimate to $9 per share. Are these assumptions reasonable? Was it even possible?

PART III: CHINESE REVERSE MERGERS

Both Zhongpin and American Lorain are publicly traded companies in the United States, yet both have all their operations in China. They both came to have this structure in the same way: a reverse merger. A reverse merger occurs when the primary company—in this case the Chinese company—purchases a shell company that is listed and traded in another country—in this case the United States. For example, the shell company that preceded Zhongpin was Strong Technical, a former personnel outsourcing service, but Strong Technical had ceased all operations in 2005, a year before the reverse merger. And the predecessor to American Lorain was named Millennium Quest, but had no operations or business activity since 1986 other than to seek an acquiree as part of a reverse merger.

Why engage in such a transaction? Proponents say that merging with an existing publicly listed company is quicker and easier than the traditional initial public offering process, and it gives the Chinese company access to western capital markets (new capital is often raised as part of these transactions by issuing new shares to institutional investors when the merger occurs). This is a particularly important source of capital for Chinese companies because going public in China is very difficult. And for their part, western investors get access to investments in fast-growing Chinese markets. Critics maintain that by sidestepping the traditional offering process, reverse mergers avoid the scrutiny of the securities regulators and stock exchanges, and consequently also avoid the heightened legal liability imposed on auditors and underwriters in a public offering.

A few high profile frauds among Chinese reverse merger firms caught the attention of the financial press in 2010. For example, in an article titled "Beware this Chinese Export" (August 26, 2010), Barron's writes that:

> The group has been a minefield of revenue disappointments and earnings restatements. Financial filings the companies make with the Securities and Exchange Commission often diverge from those filed with the Chinese government—by drastic amounts. Investor and analyst visits to corporate facilities in China reveal operations smaller and less impressive than shown in U.S. presentations. The companies too often select auditors who have previously signed off on the financials of companies that turned out to be busts.

The Chinese reverse merger firms have proven difficult for regulators to monitor. The SEC cannot subpoena documents from China, and the Chinese government will not allow the Public Accounting Company Oversight Board (i.e., the auditors of auditors) to investigate auditors in China. Still, according to Thomas Kloet, the CEO of the Toronto stock exchange, reverse mergers are not inherently bad, stating in the *Wall Street Journal* that "I don't think it is in any way an indictment of the reverse-merger program" (June 10, 2011).

So what is an investor to do? The valuations for many of the Chinese reverse merger companies look very compelling. But what if the financial statements are fraudulent?

PART III QUESTIONS

1. If the financial statements are completely fraudulent—if every number is fabricatedthen this would represent a complete failure of the audit function and the company could easily be worthless. But stepping back from this extreme view, what numbers in the financial statements are easiest to audit, and hence most likely to be true? Can you build a valuation around these numbers alone?

2. What other evidence did you see in the case materials about Zhongpin Inc. or American Lorain that might increase your confidence in these investments? What other evidence could you collect? Be sure to see the last few pages of the American Lorain 10-K excerpt.

Create Your Own Standardized Financials*

INTRODUCTION

To use *eVal* you need standardized financial data. That is, you need someone to take the "as reported" financial statements and sort the different line items into predefined line items, preferably the ones used in *eVal*. For this case, you are the person doing the standardizing. Follow the instructions below to create standardized data for General Mills (ticker = GIS).

The spreadsheet "datamaker.xls" found at www.lundholmandsloan.com is designed to translate from any Excel-based set of financials to the standardized yellow block of data that *eVal* accepts as input. If you don't already have it, get a copy of "datamaker.xls" and proceed as follows:

1. Go to www.morningstar.com, enter GIS as the ticker, and then hit the "financials" link in the middle of the page.

2. Select the statement type to be Annual, the period to be five years, and the show report dates to be in Descending order, then hit the "export" button on the right. Do this for the income statement, the balance sheet, and the cash flow statements.

3. Stack all three Excel outputs from step 2 on top of one another in a single Excel spreadsheet. The order and format doesn't matter, as long as the most recent period is in the column closest to the line item name.

If you want to skip steps 1 to 3 the case files (found at www.lundholmandsloan.com) includes a file named "GIS financials raw from Morningstar.xls." This is the General Mills data for the year ended in May 2009.

4. Open datamaker.xls and go to the "Create Standardized Data" tab. In the red box, paste your raw financials created in step 3. It doesn't matter exactly where you paste them.

*This case was prepared by Professor Russell Lundholm as the basis for class discussion, rather than to illustrate either effective or ineffective handling of a business situation. Copyright © 2010 by Russell Lundholm.

5. Here is the main task. For each line item that contains unique data, go to the yellow column and select the appropriate standardized data label from the drop-down menu. For instance, for a line titled "revenue" select "Sales." For all other line items (such as labels of sums), make sure the value in the yellow column is blank. Note that you can use the same line item label more than once—the spreadsheet will add them together. For instance, there will be three different lines labeled "Non-operating income (loss)." Continue with this process until you have captured all the unique data from the income statement and the balance sheet.

6. As you completed step 5, a set of financial statements is created in the middle of the spreadsheet. Use this to check that all the subtotals are correct. Is the Net Income correct? Is the Total Common Equity correct? In the case of GIS, they won't be. This is because each data service has different line items and sign conventions. In the case of GIS, the signs on two of the three "Non-operating income (loss)" items are wrong. Correct these by changing the formula in the financial statements in the middle of the page.

7. GIS does not list depreciation and amortization as a separate line item on their income statement; instead, it is probably included as part of SG&A expense. However, you can find the depreciation and amortization amount on the statement of cash flows. Using the yellow column, label the depreciation and amortization found on the cash flow statement. Because this amount was already included in SG&A expense, this will result in double counting. You will therefore need to subtract an equivalent amount out of SG&A. Do this correction on the financial statements in the middle of the page.

8. If you have done all the steps correctly, the subtotals and totals shown in the middle of the sheet should match the "as reported" values from your raw Morningstar data. If not, work backwards from net income, or total common equity, to find your error.

9. That's it! The solid yellow block of data at the far right can be copied and pasted onto the bottom of the financial statements sheet in *eVal*. If you used the data from the case (for the year ended in May 2009), the data block will look like this:

Company Name and Ticker	General Mills	GIS			
Common Shares Outstanding	663,700				
Fiscal Year End (YYYY-MM-DD)	1904-01-01	1904-01-01	2007-05-01	2008-05-01	2009-05-01
Sales (Net)	0	0	12,441,500	13,652,100	14,691,300
Cost of Goods Sold	0	0	(7,955,100)	(8,778,300)	(9,457,800)
R&D Expense	0	0	0	0	0
SG&A Expense	0	0	(1,971,500)	(2,165,800)	(2,498,200)
Depreciation & Amortization	0	0	(417,800)	(459,200)	(453,600)
Interest Expense	0	0	(426,500)	(421,700)	0
Non-Operating Income (Loss)	0	0	(39,300)	(21,000)	(339,500)
Income Taxes	0	0	(560,100)	(622,200)	(720,400)
Minority Interest in Earnings	0	0	0	0	0
Other Income (Loss)	0	0	72,700	110,800	82,600
Ext. Items & Disc. Ops.	0	0	0	0	0
Preferred Dividends	0	0	0	0	0
Operating Cash and Market. Sec.	0	0	423,600	661,000	749,800
Receivables	0	0	952,900	1,081,600	953,400
Inventories	0	0	1,173,400	1,366,800	1,346,800
Other Current Assets	0	0	503,800	510,600	484,900
PP&E (Net)	0	0	3,013,900	3,108,100	3,034,900
Investments	0	0	0	0	0
Intangibles	0	0	10,529,400	10,563,300	10,410,000
Other Assets	0	0	1,586,700	1,750,200	895,000
Current Debt	0	0	2,988,400	2,650,800	1,320,700
Accounts Payable	0	0	777,900	937,300	803,400
Income Taxes Payable	0	0	0	0	0
Other Current Liabilities	0	0	2,078,800	1,268,200	1,481,900
Long-Term Debt	0	0	3,217,700	4,348,700	5,754,800
Other Liabilities	0	0	2,663,000	3,378,500	3,097,500
Deferred Taxes	0	0	0	0	0
Minority Interest	0	0	1,138,800	242,300	244,200
Preferred Stock	0	0	0	0	0
Paid in Common Capital (Net)	0	0	(426,200)	(294,900)	(2,063,300)
Retained Earnings	0	0	5,745,300	6,510,700	7,235,600
Common Dividends	0	0	0	0	0

The Eighty Minute Forecast*

INTRODUCTION

There is a wealth of information available on the Internet about any publicly traded company. Government statistics about the industry, articles in the financial press, and the company's own disclosures are just a few of the sources you can access to learn more about the company. The purpose of this case is to access as many sources as you can in one class session and then weave the discovered facts into a coherent forecast of the upcoming quarter's earnings per share. Refer to the end of chapter two for a list of websites to get you started.

To get the most amount of information collected in the least amount of time, we will divide the class into groups and make each group responsible for one part of the forecast (as described below). On the 75th minute, the instructor will ask for the inputs, type them into the simplified *eVal* model included with the case, and just like that, we will have a forecast!

Before we can get started, we need to pick a company. The steps below can apply to any company, but you might want to pick one that everyone has heard of, has relatively homogeneous goods or services, and is easy to understand. Retail firms often work well. For the purpose of this case, make sure the company didn't recently undergo some crazy transaction—you want a "business as usual" year. It is also a good idea to pick a company where their basic earnings per share is the same as their diluted earnings per share, so that the share computations in the denominator do not get unduly complex (unless, or course, you like this kind of thing).

CASE MATERIALS

Most of the materials for this case are generated in class. However, all groups will need some basic financial statements from the most recent historical quarter, and preferably from many past quarters. If you selected the company prior to class, the instructor may start you off with a basic Excel file with this data. How rich your initial data is depends on what source you have. You can export five quarters of data into Excel from www.morningstar.com (enter your ticker, hit the "Financials" link, change the settings to be quarterly, and hit the "export" button). For more history, you will need a subscription service, such as CapitalIQ, Bloomberg, or Thomson Analytics. Any business school library will have one of these sources.

The case materials at www.lundholmandsloan.com are data from Lululemon Athletica (ticker LULU on the NASDAQ or LLL.TO on the TSX). They sell clothes for women who love yoga, and for the men who love them. But this is just an example—pick any company you like. The case materials also include the simplified version of *eVal* that handles quarterly data and is tailored to this case. It is currently loaded with Lululemon data, but you can copy over that with your company.

NOTE TO INSTRUCTORS: You will need to provide the students with the simplified *eVal* file loaded with the relevant data before class, or be really fast at typing in the data while class is in session, because at the end, you need to be ready to receive their inputs. You can cut-and-paste a yellow block of data into the simplified *eVal* file provided with the case, just be sure it is the past five *quarters* of data, not the past five years. Access whatever source of standardized data you use and then use datamaker.xls to get *eVal*-ready data (datamaker.xls is available at our website). Alternatively, cut and paste from any financial website.

SEASONALITY

Every group will have to consider the seasonal pattern in the input they are trying to forecast. Consider, for example, the graph of quarterly revenue for Lululemon between 2007:Q3 and 2011:Q1, as shown below:

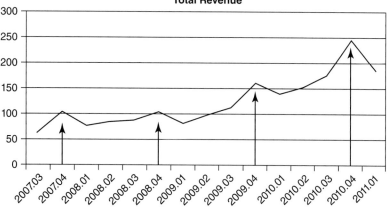

No big surprise—retail firms do the biggest share of their business during the holiday season in the fourth quarter. In general, the two most relevant quarters from the past are the same quarter a year ago and the most recent quarter.

And costs can also be seasonal. Maybe there is a big advertising promotion that coincides with holiday sales. Or maybe the cost of air conditioning in the summer is a major expense for your firm. Turning again to Lululemon, the graph below shows their selling, general and administrative expenses as a percent of revenue between 2007:Q3 and 2011:Q1. It would appear that SG&A expenses fall in the fourth quarter. Or, could it be that they remain constant in dollar terms, and the pattern is simply induced by the pattern of revenue in the denominator? You will need to think about this for your particular company.

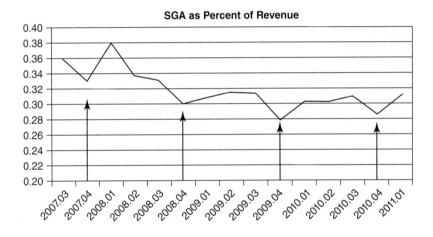

THE GROUP TASKS

Divide the class into four groups. Each group is responsible for the input in some of the yellow cells on the simplified *eVal* file. Here are their specific tasks.

Sales Forecasting Team

Your task is easy to say but hard to do: Figure out what total revenue will be in the next quarter. Prepare your answer as a percentage of growth from the previous quarter (for easy *eVal* input). Besides the seasonal pattern we just discussed, what other factors drive revenue for your company? What guidance has the company given on this issue? Have other firms in their industry already reported their results? There is a wealth of information to consider, but only 80 minutes to arrive at an answer.

Major Cost Forecasting Team

Your task is to forecast Cost of Good Sold, SG&A expense, and R&D expense. Express your forecasts as a percent of revenue. Note that you are going to take the sales forecasting team's work as given; don't duplicate their work. If you are forecasting some fixed costs then you will need to do some quick calculations after the Sales Forecasting Team reports, but be ready with your formula and calculator. Besides the seasonal component of expense that we have discussed, you should think about what else drives these expenses at your firm. Did they disclose a budget for their R&D? Have they initiated cost cutting measures? Will they pay themselves fat bonuses? Inquiring minds want to know, and the clock is ticking.

Miscellaneous Forecasting Team

Not the most glamorous team title, but your task is vitally important. Often the company will give guidance on the big-ticket items listed above, so everybody gets these right, and what separates the clever analysts from the dullards is their ability to nail all the other little details. Your task is to forecast all the rest of the income statement inputs on the simplified *eVal* spreadsheet. Many of these items are driven by the balance sheet, not revenue. The default forecasts in the *eVal* spreadsheet maintain the asset turnover ratios and leverage ratios; only change these if you have a specific reason to do so. Listed below are your specific line items from the Forecasting Assumptions sheet. Hopefully your firm has zeros for some of these items; otherwise, manage your time wisely because on the 79th minute, the instructor will demand your answers.

Income Statement Item	Input as
Depreciation and Amortization	percent of average PP&E plus Intangibles
Interest Expense	percent of average Debt
Non-Operating Income	percent of Sales
Tax Expense	percent of pretax income
Minority Interest Expense	percent of after-tax income
Other after-tax Income	percent of Sales
Preferred Dividends	percent of average preferred stock

Market Surveillance Team

You have one small, specific task, and one large ill-defined task. The large task is to search the web for analyst reports, company announcements, and other juicy facts that you think the other groups should be aware of. When you find something good, shout it out! Or write it on the board at the front of the room. The other groups have to figure out how to use the facts you find, your task is to find as many facts as possible. At a minimum, you should find other analyst forecasts of the earnings per share that the class is trying to forecast.

Your smaller, but still important, task is to forecast the number of shares to be used in the denominator of the earnings per share forecast. To be precise, we are looking for the weighted average number of shares outstanding. So, for instance, if the firm had 100 million shares outstanding at the start of the quarter, and at the beginning of the third month issued 20 million more, then the weighted average would be $(2/3) \times 100 + (1/3) \times 120 = 106.67$. The *really big mistake* your group could make would be to miss a stock split during the quarter. The earnings per share forecast would be twice as big as it should be, and *it would be entirely your fault*. So go to finance.yahoo.com, enter the ticker, hit "key statistics," and make sure the number of shares outstanding isn't twice the amount you were expecting.

The Complete GICS System

Industry Group Code	Industry Group	Industry Code	Industry	Sub-Industry Code	Sub-Industry
Code: 10	**Economic Sector: Energy**				
1010	Energy	101010	Energy Equipment & Services	10101010	Oil & Gas Drilling
				10101020	Oil & Gas Equipment & Services
		101020	Oil, Gas & Consumable Fuels	10102010	Integrated Oil & Gas
				10102020	Oil & Gas Exploration & Production
				10102030	Oil & Gas Refining & Marketing
				10102040	Oil & Gas Storage & Transportation
				10102050	Coal & Consumable Fuels
Code: 15	**Economic Sector: Materials**				
1510	Materials	151010	Chemicals	15101010	Commodity Chemicals
				15101020	Diversified Chemicals
				15101030	Fertilizers & Agricultural Chemicals
				15101040	Industrial Gases
				15101050	Specialty Chemicals
		151020	Construction Materials	15102010	Construction Materials
		151030	Containers & Packaging	15103010	Metal & Glass Containers
				15103020	Paper Packaging
		151040	Metals & Mining	15104010	Aluminum
				15104020	Diversified Metals & Mining
				15104030	Gold
				15104040	Precious Metals & Minerals
				15104050	Steel

(continued)

Industry Group Code	Industry Group	Industry Code	Industry	Sub-Industry Code	Sub-Industry
		151050	Paper & Forest Products	15105010	Forest Products
				15105020	Paper Products
Code: 20	**Economic Sector: Industrials**				
2010	Capital Goods	201010	Aerospace & Defense	20101010	Aerospace & Defense
		201020	Building Products	20102010	Building Products
		201030	Construction & Engineering	20103010	Construction & Engineering
		201040	Electrical Equipment	20104010	Electrical Components & Equipment
				20104020	Heavy Electrical Equipment
		201050	Industrial Conglomerates	20105010	Industrial Conglomerates
		201060	Machinery	20106010	Construction & Farm Machinery & Heavy Trucks
				20106020	Industrial Machinery
		201070	Trading Companies & Distributors	20107010	Trading Companies & Distributors
2020	Commercial & Professional Services	202010	Commercial Services & Supplies	20201010	Commercial Printing
				20201020	*Data Processing Services (Discontinued effective April 30, 2003)*
				20201030	*Diversified Commercial & Professional Services (Discontinued effective August 31, 2008)*
				20201040	*Human Resource & Employment Services (Discontinued effective August 31, 2008)*
				20201050	Environmental & Facilities Services
				20201060	Office Services & Supplies
				20201070	Diversified Support Services
				20201080	Security & Alarm Services
		202020	Professional Services	20202010	Human Resource & Employment Services
				20202020	Research & Consulting Service

Industry Group Code	Industry Group	Industry Code	Industry	Sub-Industry Code	Sub-Industry
2030	Transportation	203010	Air Freight & Logistics	20301010	Air Freight & Logistics
		203020	Airlines	20302010	Airlines
		203030	Marine	20303010	Marine
		203040	Road & Rail	20304010	Railroads
				20304020	Trucking
		203050	Transportation Infrastructure	20305010	Airport Services
				20305020	Highways & Railtracks
				20305030	Marine Ports & Services
Code: 25	**Economic Sector: Consumer Discretionary**				
2510	Automobiles & Components	251010	Auto Components	25101010	Auto Parts & Equipment
				25101020	Tires & Rubber
		251020	Automobiles	25102010	Automobile Manufacturers
				25102020	Motorcycle Manufacturers
2520	Consumer Durables & Apparel	252010	Household Durables	25201010	Consumer Electronics
				25201020	Home Furnishings
				25201030	Homebuilding
				25201040	Household Appliances
				25201050	Housewares & Specialties
		252020	Leisure Equipment & Products	25202010	Leisure Products
				25202020	Photographic Products
		252030	Textiles, Apparel & Luxury Goods	25203010	Apparel, Accessories & Luxury Goods
				25203020	Footwear
				25203030	Textiles
2530	Consumer Services	253010	Hotels, Restaurant & Leisure	25301010	Casinos & Gaming
				25301020	Hotels, Resorts & Cruise Lines
				25301030	Leisure Facilities
				25301040	Restaurants
		253020	Diversified Consumer Services	25302010	Education Services
				25302020	Specialized Consumer Services

(*continued*)

Industry Group Code	Industry Group	Industry Code	Industry	Sub-Industry Code	Sub-Industry
2540	Media	254010	Media	25401010	Advertising
				25401020	Broadcasting
				25401025	Cable & Satellite
				25401030	Movies & Entertainment
				25401040	Publishing
2550	Retailing	255010	Distributors	25501010	Distributors
		255020	Internet & Catalog Retail	25502010	Catalog Retail
				25502020	Internet Retail
		255030	Multiline Retail	25503010	Department Stores
				25503020	General Merchandise Stores
		255040	Specialty Retail	25504010	Apparel Retail
				25504020	Computer & Electronic Retail
				25504030	Home Improvement Retail
				25504040	Specialty Stores
				25504050	Automotive Retail
				25504060	Home Furnishing Retail
Code: 30	**Economic Sector: Consumer Staples**				
3010	Food & Staples Retailing	301010	Food & Staples Retailing	30101010	Drug Retail
				30101020	Food Distributors
				30101030	Food Retail
				30101040	Hypermarkets & Super Centers
3020	Food, Beverage & Tobacco	302010	Beverages	30201010	Brewers
				30201020	Distillers & Vintners
				30201030	Soft Drinks
		302020	Food Products	30202010	Agricultural Products
				30202020	*Meat, Poultry & Fish (Discontinued effective March 28, 2002)*
				30202030	Packaged Foods & Meats
		302030	Tobacco	30203010	Tobacco
3030	Household & Personal Products	303010	Household Products	30301010	Household Products
		303020	Personal Products	30302010	Personal Products

Industry Group Code	Industry Group	Industry Code	Industry	Sub-Industry Code	Sub-Industry
Code: 35	**Economic Sector: Health Care**				
3510	Health Care Equipment & Services	351010	Health Care Equipment & Supplies	35101010	Health Care Equipment
				35101020	Health Care Supplies
		351020	Health Care Providers & Services	35102010	Health Care Distributors
				35102015	Health Care Services
				35102020	Health Care Facilities
				35102030	Managed Health Care
		351030	Health Care Technology	35103010	Health Care Technology
3520	Pharmaceuticals, Biotechnology & Life Sciences	352010	Biotechnology	35201010	Biotechnology
		352020	Pharmaceuticals	35202010	Pharmaceuticals
		352030	Life Sciences Tools & Services	35203010	Life Sciences Tools & Services
Code: 40	**Economic Sector: Financials**				
4010	Banks	401010	Commercial Banks	40101010	Diversified Banks
				40101015	Regional Banks
		401020	Thrifts & Mortgage Finance	40102010	Thrifts & Mortgage Finance
4020	Diversified Financials	402010	Diversified Financial Services	*40201010*	*Consumer Finance (Discontinued effective 5/1/03)*
				40201020	Other Diversified Financial Services
				40201030	Multi-Sector Holdings
				40201040	Specialized Finance
		402020	Consumer Finance	40202010	Consumer Finance
		402030	Capital Markets	40203010	Asset Management & Custody Banks
				40203020	Investment Banking & Brokerage
				40203030	Diversified Capital Markets
4030	Insurance	403010	Insurance	40301010	Insurance Brokers
				40301020	Life & Health Insurance
				40301030	Multi-line Insurance

(*continued*)

Industry Group Code	Industry Group	Industry Code	Industry	Sub-Industry Code	Sub-Industry
				40301040	Property & Casualty Insurance
				40301050	Reinsurance
4040	Real Estate	404010	Real Estate *(Discontinued effective C.O.B. 4/28/06)*	40401010	Real Estate Investment Trusts *(Discontinued effective C.O.B. 4/28/06)*
				40401020	Real Estate Management & Development *(Discontinued effective C.O.B. 4/28/06)*
		404020	Real Estate Investment Trusts (REITs)	40402010	Diversified REITs
				40402020	Industrial REITs
				40402030	Mortgage REITs
				40402040	Office REITs
				40402050	Residential REITs
				40402060	Retail REITs
				40402070	Specialized REITs
		404030	Real Estate Management & Development	40403010	Diversified Real Estate Activities
				40403020	Real Estate Operating Companies
				40403030	Real Estate Development
				40403040	Real Estate Services

Code: 45   Economic Sector: Information Technology

Industry Group Code	Industry Group	Industry Code	Industry	Sub-Industry Code	Sub-Industry
4510	Software & Services	451010	Internet Software & Services	45101010	Internet Software & Services
		451020	IT Services	45102010	IT Consulting & Other Services
				45102020	Data Processing and Outsourced Services
		451030	Software	45102010	Application Software
				45103020	Systems Software
				45103030	Home Entertainment Software
4520	Technology Hardware & Equipment	452010	Communications Equipment	*45201010*	*Networking Equipment (Discontinued effective 4/30/03)*
				45201020	Communications Equipment
				45201020	*Telecommunications Equipment (Discontinued effective 4/30/03)*

Industry Group Code	Industry Group	Industry Code	Industry	Sub-Industry Code	Sub-Industry
		452020	Computers & Peripherals	45202010	Computer Hardware
				45202020	Computer Storage & Peripherals
		452030	Electronic Equipment, Instruments & Components	45203010	Electronic Equipment & Instruments
				45203015	Electronic Components
				45203020	Electronic Manufacturing Services
				45203030	Technology Distributors
		452040	Office Electronics	45204010	Office Electronics
		452050	*Semiconductor Equipment & Prods (Discontinued effective 4/30/03)*	*45205010*	*Semiconductor Equipment (Discontinued effective 4/30/03)*
				45205020	*Semiconductors (Discontinued effective 4/30/03)*
4530	Semiconductor Equipment	453010	Semiconductors & Semiconductor Equipment	45301010	Semiconductor Equipment
				45301020	Semiconductors
Code: 50	**Economic Sector: Telecommunication Services**				
5010	Telecommunication Srvs	501010	Diversified Telecommunication Srv	50101010	Alternative Carriers
				50101020	Integrated Telecommunication Services
		501020	Wireless Telecommunication Srvs	50102010	Wireless Telecommunication Services
Code: 55	**Economic Sector: Utilities**				
5510	Utilities	551010	Electric Utilities	55101010	Electric Utilities
		551020	Gas Utilities	55102010	Gas Utilities
		551030	Multi-Utilities	55103010	Multi-Utilities
		551040	Water Utilities	55104010	Water Utilities
		551050	Independent Power Producers & Energy Traders	55105010	Independent Power Producers & Energy Traders

Index